Halakhic Realities
Collected Essays on Brain Death

I
R
F

מגיד
MAGGID

HALAKHIC REALITIES

COLLECTED ESSAYS ON BRAIN DEATH

Edited by
Zev Farber

Maggid Books

Halakhic Realities
Collected Essays on Brain Death

First Edition, 2015

Maggid Books
An imprint of Koren Publishers Jerusalem Ltd.

POB 8531, New Milford, CT 06776-8531, USA
& POB 4044, Jerusalem 9104001, Israel
www.korenpub.com

The publication of this book was made possible
through the generous support of *Torah Education in Israel*.

ISBN 978-1-59264-406-3, *hardcover*

A CIP catalogue record for this title is
available from the British Library

Printed and bound in the United States

This book has been dedicated by the following institutions

Additional benefactors who have made this book possible:

Institutions

Bais Abraham Congregation, St. Louis
Beit Chaverim Synagogue, Westport, CT
Beth Tfiloh Congregation, Baltimore
Congregation Beth Israel, Berkeley
Congregation Beth Israel, Metairie, LA
Congregation Shearith Israel, New York
Congregation Sherith Israel, Nashville
Hebrew Institute of Riverdale, New York
Institute for Jewish Ideas and Ideals
United Orthodox Synagogues, Houston
Young Israel of Toco Hills, Atlanta

Individuals

Sari Abrams and Rabbi Yosef Kanefsky
Lisa and Rabbi David Almog
Shalom Bronstein
Gwen and Brett Cohen
Dr. Marvin Den
Cindy and Noam Drazin
Jennifer and Yaron Elad
Alan Hoffman – in memory of Dr. Alexander and Sandy Hoffman
Steven Levine
Meryl and Joseph Mark
Rena Schlussel
Sharona and Marc Schlussel
Dr. Irena Veksler-Offengenden
Zev and Cara Wainberg

Contents

Foreword

I t is with great satisfaction that the first book published under the auspices of the International Rabbinic Fellowship is this work of major significance for all of us. This extraordinary collection of essays by such an esteemed group of scholars presents an important contribution to the public on the topic of halakhic perspectives on brain death and organ donation. I am sure that this book will help shape the discussion and policy decisions reached on this issue for years to come.

We are all indebted to Rabbi Dr. Zev Farber, who has tirelessly edited this book, and without whose efforts it would never have been completed. We owe him a great debt of thanks. We are also indebted to Rabbi Jason Herman, who put more time and energy into this project than we could have reasonably asked of our executive director.

I would like to thank Maggid Books, its publisher, Matthew Miller, and its editor-in-chief, Gila Fine, for leading us through the publication process with such professionalism. I'd also like to express my *hakarat ha-tov* to Tomi Mager and Nechama Unterman, who worked so hard editing this volume.

It is a privilege to serve as president of the International Rabbinic Fellowship. The rich talent of our members in both scholarship and leadership throughout North America and Israel offers our people great hope as we tackle the many challenges going forward. May Hashem grant us the wisdom to bring His holiness into this world through our words and actions.

Rabbi Joel Tessler
President (2011-2013), International Rabbinic Fellowship
Senior rabbi, Beth Sholom Congregation, Potomac, MD

List of Abbreviations

EH: *Even ha-Ezer*
ḤM: *Ḥoshen Mishpat*
OḤ: *Oraḥ Ḥaim*
YD: *Yoreh De'ah*
IM: *Iggerot Moshe* by Rabbi Moshe Feinstein
MT: *Mishneh Torah*
b.:   Babylonian Talmud
j.:   Jerusalem Talmud
m.:   Mishna
t.:   Tosefta

BMJ: *British Medical Journal*
JAMA: *Journal of the American Medical Association*
NEJM: *New England Journal of Medicine*

Introduction

The State of the Question

Life is over when brain waves cease.
DR. WILLIAM BRICKLEY, *TIME*, JUNE 2, 1941

Mostly dead is slightly alive.
MIRACLE MAX, *THE PRINCESS BRIDE*

I t is with some trepidation that I undertake to introduce a topic as serious and fraught as organ donation. Most halakhic issues are not matters of life and death, but the stakes surrounding whether to donate organs are quite literally just that. The mantra of the Halachic Organ Donor Society is "Sign one card, save eight lives." Exploring the question from only this angle makes the choice to sign an organ donor card seem obvious. Nevertheless, the issue becomes more complicated when one looks at the process from the perspective of the donor.

Since organs that experience a period of time without being perfused with oxygen become unusable in transplantation, most organs can be harvested only from "live" bodies. For this reason, organs are harvested from the deceased only in cases of brain death, with the body being kept alive through mechanical ventilation.

Mechanical ventilation is a modern miracle that can buy doctors time to properly diagnose a patient and administer treatment, allowing the patient to convalesce and begin breathing again on his or her own. This is the main use of a ventilator. However, due to the heart's unique ability to control its own beating without regulation by the brain, the body of a brain dead patient connected to a ventilator can continue to "live." As long as the lungs keep pumping – and the ventilator ensures that they do – the blood will continue to be oxygenated. The oxygenated blood will keep the heart alive, and the heart will keep beating, causing the blood to circulate and preserving the remaining organs of the body. A brain dead patient cannot be preserved this way indefinitely, but it is not unusual for the body to remain alive for days and sometimes longer.

The status of a person whose brain is dead but whose body is alive is a complex question and the subject of major debate among halakhists and ethicists. The question revolves around the definition of human life. Is a live human body without a functioning brain considered a human life? How does one define human life? Are there halakhic sources or *hashqafic* (Jewish-philosophical) axiomata that can help answer these questions? Can scientific arguments conclusively demonstrate the presence or absence of life? This book – a collection of essays on brain death – does not profess to answer these questions unequivocally. The purpose of the collection is to continue the vibrant conversation on this topic, and offer insights and perspectives from multiple vantage points.

PREVIOUS ESSAY COLLECTIONS

The controversy over brain death and organ donation in halakha has been raging from as early as the procedures became scientifically possible, and the matter was debated in Jewish communities around the world, especially in the two largest, Israel and the United States.[1] In the

---

1. An important monograph on the Israeli debate was penned by Naftali Moses: *Really Dead? The Israeli Brain-Death Controversy 1967–1986* (2011). For an overview of some of the issues and a survey of some of the main positions, see Rabbi Yitzchak Breitowitz, "The Brain Death Controversy in Jewish Law," http://www.jlaw.com/Articles/brain.html. For a longer, more thorough treatment, see Eytan Shtull-Leber,

United States, several responsa, articles, and even monographs have been written on brain death and halakha. Most important, two seminal journals focused on the debate in the Orthodox community.[2]

The first was the *Journal of Halacha and Contemporary Society*, volume 17, published in 1989. In this publication, a section called "Determining the Time of Death" included five articles. The first article, by Dr. Marshal Kielson, explored medical aspects, and the final article, by Chaim Dovid Zweibel, Esq., examined legal ones. The middle three articles offered three halakhic perspectives on the nature of brain death. The first – and I am oversimplifying all three articles – by Dr. Fred Rosner and Rabbi Dr. Moshe Tendler, argues that brain death should be considered death according to halakha.[3] The second, by Rabbi Hershel Schachter, questions that. The third, by Rabbi Ahron Soloveichik, argues that brain death should *not* be considered death.[4]

The second journal to address the issue was *Tradition*, whose winter 2004 issue featured an exchange between two Orthodox Jewish doctors, Joshua Kunin and Edward Reichman. In "Brain Death: Revisiting the Rabbinic Opinions in Light of Current Medical Knowledge," Dr. Kunin argues that shifts in the medical understanding of brain death call into question the possibility of using this definition in halakhic discourse. In "Don't Pull the Plug on Brain Death Just Yet," Dr. Reichman responds that the use of brain death in halakhic discourse remains sound.

"Rethinking the Brain Death Controversy: A History of Scientific Advancement and the Redefinition of Death in Jewish Law" (BA honors thesis, University of Michigan, 2010), http://deepblue.lib.umich.edu/bitstream/2027.42/77671/1/eytansht.pdf.

2. I am merely offering highlights. A full bibliography of the massive amount of writing on this topic is well beyond the scope of this introductory essay.

3. One classic article that paved the way for this perspective by pushing for the importance of organ donation was that of Rabbi Nachum L. Rabinovitch, "What Is the Halakha for Organ Transplants?" *Tradition* 9, no. 4 (spring 1968): 20–27. And in the 1970s, Rabbi Shlomo Goren, Israel's Ashkenazic chief rabbi (1973–83), campaigned for organ donation in Israeli hospitals. One of the first major *posqim* to embrace the brain death definition of death, Rabbi Goren remained a firm advocate of organ donation throughout his life.

4. Another well-known and vociferous opponent of brain death as halakhic death is Rabbi J. David Bleich; see his *Time of Death in Jewish Law* (New York: Z. Berman Publishing, 1991).

I call these two publications "seminal" because each updated the debate, crisply presenting where the issues lie. The former focused on the halakhic debate and traditional sources, and the latter focused on advances in medicine.[5]

THE TWO RCA PRECEDENTS

One stimulus for the current publication has been the work of the Rabbinical Council of America (RCA). In 1991, the RCA took an important stand on organ donation by publishing its health care proxy.[6] Knowing the importance of clarifying one's wishes beforehand so as not to burden loved ones with tough decisions and great doubt, the RCA – under the leadership of Rabbis Marc Angel and Binyamin Walfish – published a health care proxy that allowed for organ donation.

With the many changes in the medical understanding of the mechanics of brain death, most poignantly clarified in the 2008 Presidential White Paper on brain death, the RCA – under the leadership of Rabbi Asher Bush – conducted a new study of the subject, publishing its conclusions in 2010.[7] Although it wasn't presented as a new *pesaq*, the study questioned many premises of the 1991 proxy.[8] This challenge led numerous rabbis to wonder whether a new position on brain death and halakha was in order and spawned critical responses from a host of perspectives.[9] One group issued a "Rabbinic

---

5. Since medicine changes and develops continuously, there is a persistent need for this type of updating.

6. For details, see Marc Angel, "The RCA Health Care Proxy: Providing Responsible Halachic Leadership to Our Community," *Jewish Action* 52, no. 2 (spring 1992): 60, 62, https://hods.org/pdf/Angel%20RCA%20Health%20Care%20Proxy.pdf

7. For the white paper: http://bioethics.georgetown.edu/pcbe/reports/death/pellegrino_statement.html; for the RCA study: http://www.rabbis.org/pdfs/Halachi_%20Issues_the_Determination.pdf.

8. That the study was not intended to "override" the RCA's position was clarified in a letter posted on the RCA website: http://www.rabbis.org/news/article.cfm?id=105607.

9. For a critique of the RCA document from a medical standpoint, see Noam Stadlan, "Death by Neurological Criteria: A Critique of the RCA Paper and the Circulation Criteria," http://torahmusings.com/2010/12/death-by-neurological-criteria/. For a critique from a medical ethics perspective, see Drs. Kenneth Prager and Neil Schluger, "RCA and Brain Death," *The Jewish Week*, http://www.thejewishweek.com/editorial_opinion/letters/rca_and_brain_death. For critiques from a halakhic

Statement Regarding Organ Donation and Brain Death,"[10] informing the observant public that many Orthodox rabbis still believed in the halakhic relevance of the brain death definition and the importance of donating organs.

Although I signed the petition, I felt that what was really needed was neither a univocal study (such as that of the RCA) nor a petition reaffirming the 1991 health care proxy, but a comprehensive update of the conversation, attacking the problem from more angles than merely the halakhic.[11] Several members of the International Rabbinic Fellowship (IRF) shared this sentiment, and it was decided that I would put together this comprehensive update under the auspices of the IRF. As an IRF publication, this book includes contributions by many important *posqim* and Jewish thinkers from the Modern Orthodox world.[12] Hopefully,

---

perspective, see Baruch A. Brody and Shlomo M. Brody, "Case for Organ Donation Remains Solid," *Jewish Daily Forward*, http://forward.com/articles/135146/case-for-organ-donation-remains-solid/; and the three-part series by Rabbi Daniel Reifman, "The Brain Death Debate: A Methodological Analysis," on the RCA's *Text and Texture* blog; for part 1: http://text.rcarabbis.org/the-brain-death-debate-a-methodological-analysis-part-1-yoma-passage-by-daniel-reifman/.

10. "Rabbinic Statement Regarding Organ Donation and Brain Death," http://organdonationstatement.blogspot.com/.

11. Two important such updates have recently been penned. For a defense of brain death as halakhic death, see Avraham Steinberg, *Respiratory-Brain Death* (ed. Yigal Shafran; trans. Fred Rosner; Science, Halacha and Education Series; Jerusalem: Merhavim, 2012). The book includes a translation of primary sources as well as appendices with detailed explanations of medical procedures. For a more critical approach to the halakhic status of brain death, which deals with the medical information and includes an up-to-date survey of the relevant *posqim*, see David Shabtai, *Defining the Moment: Understanding Brain Death in Halakhah* (New York: Shoresh Press, 2012). Both authors are rabbinic scholars as well as medical professionals. For a review of both books, see Noam Stadlan, "New Books and Points of Discussion in the Halakhic Definition of Death: *Respiratory-Brain Death* by Avraham Steinberg, and *Defining the Moment – Understanding Brain Death in Halakhah* by David Shabtai," *Me'orot* 10 (5773/2013), http://www.yctorah.org/images/stories/about_us/%235%20-%20stadlan.pdf. See as well http://www.hakirah.org/Vol18Stadlan.pdf.

12. A similar approach was taken by Rabbi Gil Student, who ran a nine-part online symposium on the ethics of brain death and organ donation in 2011. The contributions there are op-ed-style, not article-style, so the pieces are much shorter than most of those in this book. For an introduction and links to the pieces, see http://torahmusings.com/2011/02/symposium-on-the-ethics-of-brain-death-and-organ-donation-introduction/.

the collection will facilitate important debate and discussion within our ranks and in the Jewish community at large.

THE STRUCTURE OF THE BOOK

This book is the first in a two-part series on brain death and organ donation. This volume focuses on brain death itself and is divided into four sections. Section I discusses the medical and legal reality surrounding brain death. The essays describe how a person is declared dead, outline the legal history of the brain death diagnosis, and debate the medical reality behind the concept. Sections II and III contain responsa focusing on the halakhic approaches to brain death. Section IV tackles the problem historically, philosophically, and ethically. Finally, the Afterword expresses some of my own views on the subject – it is in no way meant as a summary of the book or a consensus position – as well as some thoughts about the direction of future studies.[13]

This book has not been edited for content, and each author expresses his own opinion. On a personal note, compiling this volume was daunting, as I tried to avoid repetition without overlooking important issues. Although I agree with some essays more than others, I have learned from each one and each author. I hope the work will serve as a catalyst for discussions as well as a resource for rabbis and laypeople trying to navigate the exceedingly complex issues surrounding the definition of death and the donation of organs.

Rabbi Zev Farber, Ph.D., Editor
Rosh Ḥodesh Kislev 5775

---

13. Three further notes on the book. First, throughout the essays, I've added notes referencing where one can read similar or alternative discussions of the same point elsewhere in both volumes. Second, dividing the essays into brain-death-themed and organ-donation-themed was exceedingly difficult, since many touch on both topics. I apologize if I overlooked a better way to divide the volumes. Third, I originally planned on an appendix of translations of key primary sources. However, since the book turned out to be rather long, and other published works (such as Steinberg's recent book) include these translations, I decided that this addition didn't justify the added size and expense. Instead, the IRF will be including a link to my translations on its website (http://internationalrabbinicfellowship.org/).

Section I

The Medico-Legal Issues:
An Overview

Chapter 1

How a Person Is Declared Dead

Zelik Frischer

INTRODUCTION

It was 1975, and I was sitting outside the office of Israeli chief rabbi Shlomo Goren. It had taken me quite a while to get this appointment, and I was unsure how the consultation would unfold. I wasn't there to ask him for a personal favor or even a halakhic ruling. I was there to request his participation in an urgent project.

I originally trained as a urologist at Mechnikov University Hospital in Leningrad (today St. Petersburg).[1] Since then, I had immigrated to Israel and was practicing in Beilinson Medical Center in Petaḥ Tiqva.[2] I was being called on more and more to do kidney transplants. The problem was (and remains) that there were many more patients who required a new kidney than there were kidneys looking for new owners.

---

1. The university is named after the Russian scientist Ilya Mechnikov, known as the father of immunology, who won the Nobel Prize in medicine in 1908.
2. Now known as the Rabin Medical Center.

Although kidneys can be harvested from live donors, the main way of procuring a kidney is by harvesting the organ from a brain dead patient. To do so, one needs the family's permission – a very touchy matter. In some countries, hospitals facilitate this process by assigning a social worker or chaplain to sit with brain dead patients' families, answer their questions, and help them decide how to handle the situation.

In Israel, no such service was provided. Facing the natural fear, confusion, and suspicion of family members charged with making the most painful of decisions, Israeli hospitals were encountering an overwhelming refusal to participate in the harvesting of organs from what many of us consider to be a ventilated cadaver. This is why I came to Rabbi Goren.

My idea was simple if somewhat avant-garde. I was going to ask the chief rabbi to set up a system whereby the rabbis employed by the Chief Rabbinate could counsel the families. Of course, Rabbi Goren would agree only if he believed that donation of organs from brain dead patients was halakhically valid.

Although somewhat reticent at first, Rabbi Goren quickly warmed to the idea, and with his characteristic energy, he organized a highly successful network of rabbis who took charge of ministering to patients' families and helping them through the decision-making process. In a sense, the Israeli system was one of the most active and competent of its kind. Donation rates rose, and Israel became a model state when it came to kidney transplants.[3]

Sadly, this is no longer true. I say so as a distant observer, since I've been practicing in Stony Brook University Hospital on Long Island for twenty-five years. Nevertheless, the same problems that now plague the hospitals in the State of Israel plague the United States as well.

Procurement of organs and tissues from heart-beating cadavers is a daily necessity. In 1999, UNOS (United Network for Organ Sharing) published a national transplant waiting list of 65,000 organs. Since then, the number has almost doubled. Unfortunately, organ donation has not kept pace with the ever-increasing recipient waiting lists. The critical

---

3. My role in effecting this change was minimal; many doctors and rabbis participated in the effort.

shortage of organs has resulted in increased use of live donation and expanded criteria for determining what cadaveric organs may be donated, but this response is hardly sufficient. The crisis is real.

Organ donation occurs only through the education and good will of the general public. Participation of professionals in the fields of ethics, law, and religion, as well as in the behavioral and social sciences, is a *sine qua non*. This is the reason I sat in Rabbi Goren's office that day, and it's why I participate in publications like this one. I hope to use my experience and knowledge to narrow the gap between the supply and demand for transplantable organs. If I can contribute to narrowing this gap even a little, it's all worthwhile.

BRAIN DEATH: DEFINITION AND HISTORY

A patient may be declared dead by either neurological or cardio-pulmonary criteria. Currently, 98% of organ donors are declared dead by brain death. Brain death is declared when complete and irreversible loss of brain and brainstem function occurs. This phenomenon presents clinically as complete apnea, brainstem areflexia, and cerebral unresponsiveness.

The definition of brain death was first suggested in a report by an ad hoc committee associated with Harvard Medical School in 1968. In 1981, with the Uniform Determination of Death Act (UDDA), irreversible loss of brain function was officially put forward as one of two ways to determine death.[4]

PREREQUISITES FOR A BRAIN DEATH DECLARATION

There are several prerequisites for a brain death determination. First, the patient must be in a grade 4 coma. Second, all appropriate diagnostic and therapeutic procedures (the cephalic reflex tests) must be performed. Third, the patient must be on a ventilator and unable to breathe independently. Fourth, the patient's condition must be irreversible. These prerequisites will be detailed below.

---

4. The other being irreversible loss of circulation; the UDDA has been adopted by law or precedent by essentially every state in the US.

(1) Coma

As stated, to be diagnosed as brain dead, a patient must be in a grade 4 coma.[5] The level of coma is demonstrated by the response to stimulation, usually presented in the form of pain. The most common response to pain is grimacing, which can be tested by applying deep pressure to the nail beds, supraorbital ridge, or temporomandibular joint (TMJ), or by placing a cotton swab in the nose.

(2) Cephalic Reflex Tests

Additionally, diagnostic tests must demonstrate the absence of cephalic reflexes.[6] Evaluation can begin six hours after the onset of coma and apnea.[7] Furthermore, in some states and/or countries this evaluation must be repeated.[8]

The tests are relatively straightforward. The following is a standard battery:[9]

a. Pupillary testing: Light is shined into the patient's eyes. The pupils' lack of response to the light is consistent with brainstem injury.[10]

---

5. There are four levels of coma:
    Grade 1 – reactivity to vocal stimuli;
    Grade 2 – absence of reactivity to vocal stimuli, but with a coordinated response to painful stimuli;
    Grade 3 – absence of reactivity to vocal stimuli with an uncoordinated response to painful stimuli;
    Grade 4 – absence of response to painful stimuli.
    In truth, this scale is somewhat outdated and no longer in use, but it remains suitable as a heuristic device.
6. For a chart summarizing this section, see Jeffrey A. Norton et al., *Essential Practice of Surgery: Basic Science and Clinical Evidence* (New York: Springer-Verlag, 2003), 610.
7. These regulations are intended to prevent hasty diagnoses.
8. Such was the law in New York State until recently.
9. I say "a standard" and not "the standard," since one difficulty of brain death determination is that there is no uniform legal standard. The most commonly used criteria are based on the American Academy of Neurology (AAN) guidelines published in 1995 and reviewed in 2010.
10. Since no single test proves brainstem death, the more cautious term "consistent with" is preferred in the medical community. Brainstem death is proven by the combination of tests and the overall medical picture.

As a rule, the pupils of brainstem-dead patients remain dilated at around 4–9 mm.

b. Corneal reflex testing: The eye is daubed with a cotton swab or a gloved finger. Failure to blink is consistent with brainstem injury.

c. Oculovestibular or oculo-auditory testing, also known as cold caloric testing: Ten to twenty ml of iced saline is sprayed into the auditory canal of each ear, irrigating the tympanic membranes.[11] Lack of eye movement is consistent with brainstem injury.

d. Oculocephalic testing, also known as the doll's eye test: The patient's head is turned from side to side. Normally, the eyes turn away from the direction of movement. If the patient's eyes remain fixed in position and don't rotate with the head, it is consistent with brainstem injury, and is referred to as "negative doll's eyes."

e. The cough or bulbar-function test: A suction catheter suctions all the way down the ETT (endotracheal tube). As the catheter is withdrawn, it is moved from side to side. No cough (as well as no head movement or facial twitch) is consistent with brainstem injury.

f. Absence of the jaw jerk reflex, or masseter reflex: When the chin is tapped with a reflex hammer, the mandible should jerk slightly upward. Failure to do so is consistent with brainstem injury.

g. The gag, swallowing, or pharyngeal reflex test: The oropharynx is stimulated with a tongue depressor or a Yankauer (long-tipped) suction tip. Failure to gag is consistent with brainstem injury.

No single reflex test proves brainstem death. It is the failure on *all* of them that confirms the likelihood of brainstem injury.

(3) Ventilation and the Apnea Test

Although the patient has already proven unable to sustain breathing – hence the need for ventilation – this inability is insufficient to demonstrate brainstem death.[12] What must be demonstrated is the

---

11. The ears must be tested five minutes apart.
12. Many patients, for one reason or another, require ventilation.

absence of any spontaneous *effort* on the patient's part to initiate a breath. Therefore, the apnea test is administered.

To be eligible for the test, the patient must have a core temperature greater than or equal to 36.5°C (97°F) and a systolic blood pressure of greater than or equal to 90 mmHg (millimeters of mercury). Additionally, the patient's fluid volume must be normal (euvolemic).

Assuming the patient meets these criteria, his blood is preoxygenated for ten minutes. Next, the concentration of carbon dioxide in the arterial blood ($PaCO_2$) is tested; it should be at 35–45 mmHg. This can be determined by an arterial blood gas (ABG) test or by testing the end-tidal carbon dioxide ($ETCO_2$) concentration.[13]

At this point, the ventilator is disconnected, and physicians watch the patient for any sign of breathing.[14] At around the eight-minute mark, another ABG test is administered. If the patient has shown no signs of attempting to breathe, and the $PaCO_2$ has risen to 60 mmHg, this is conclusive demonstration of total and irreversible apnea.

(4) Irreversibility

The cause of the underlying brain damage (trauma, brain hemorrhage, cerebral tumor, cerebral infection, or various types of cerebral hypoxia)[15] must be known. Reversible causes of brainstem depression (hypothermia, drug or alcohol intoxication) must also be excluded.

Summary

With the patient in a grade 4 coma, demonstrating no signs of breathing with the apnea test and no cephalic reflexes (usually in two separate examinations), if all confounding factors have been excluded, he is declared brain dead.

Critically, brain death is declared by a team of specialists; such teams never include interested parties or those making procurement.

---

13. This is the maximal concentration of carbon dioxide in an exhaled breath.
14. If any such sign occurs, the patient is immediately reconnected to the ventilator.
15. Hypoxia occurs when the brain is deprived of adequate oxygen.

CONFIRMATORY TESTS

Confirmatory studies, although not always necessary, are performed where there may be confounding factors.[16] Furthermore, they can be performed at the request of the patient's health care proxy.[17]

There are many kinds of confirmatory tests,[18] falling into two basic categories. The first type tests electrical activity in the brain. The second tracks blood flow to the brain. I will discuss some of the most common or well-known tests in both categories.[19] Since 2008, confirmatory testing has been legally required in Israel, although not in the United States.

Type 1 – Electrical Activity

a. *Electroencephalography* (EEG) – This was the first confirmatory test, suggested in the original Harvard criteria. In this procedure, eight or more electrodes are placed on the patient's scalp. If the patient is, in fact, brain dead, the test should show no brain waves and no reactivity to intense somatosensory or audiovisual stimuli.[20]

b. *Evoked Potentials* (EP) or *Sensory Evoked Potentials* (SEP) – Similar to the EEG but more accurate, these tests measure electrical potentials generated by the nervous system in response to sensory stimuli. The tests are performed by placing electrodes on the patient's skin. Three main types of EP tests are relevant to brain death evaluation:

• *Brainstem Auditory Evoked Potentials* (BAEP), also known as *Brainstem Auditory Evoked Response* (BAER) or *Auditory Brainstem Response* (ABR) – This is the EP test most commonly used

---

16. Confirmatory tests are also administered when the apnea test cannot be performed for physiological reasons, although whether it is appropriate to declare someone brain dead without an apnea test is a matter of some controversy.

17. For details, see Rabbi Prof. Daniel Sinclair's essay in this volume.

18. For a more technical discussion, see W. Mel. Flowers Jr. and Bharti R. Patel, "Persistence of Cerebral Blood Flow After Brain Death," *Southern Medical Journal* 93, no. 4 (2000): 364–70.

19. Some tests are not conducted because they're either too expensive or hard to access, such as PET (Positron Emission Tomography) or xeCT (Stable Xenon Computed Tomography).

20. Although the EEG remains useful, it is the least effective test of its kind. Among other shortcomings, it is subject to electrical artifacts in the intensive care environment, and has failed to recognize coma reversibility in drug-intoxicated patients.

to check for brain death. When sound enters the ear and stimulates the cochlea in the inner ear, the cochlea produces an electrical response along the nerve pathways. Lack of electrical response is consistent with brainstem injury.[21]

- *Somatosensory Evoked Potentials* (SSEP) – Stimulation occurs at the extremities, and recordings are made on the scalp, near the sensory cortex. In brain dead patients, potentials generated by structures above the lower medulla are absent. Bilateral absence of response to median nerve stimulation is consistent with brain death.

- *Visual Evoked Potentials* (VEP) – Although this test is not commonly used for determining brain death, it can be. The examiner uses a photoelectric, checkerboard-pattern flash to stimulate the optic nerve. This pattern is then recorded on the cortex, arriving at the back of the head, near the visual centers. In the visual pathways of brain dead patients, electrical activity is confined to the retina.

Type 2 – Blood Flow

a. *Cerebral Angiography* – Angiography uses x-rays and a contrast material to produce pictures of blood vessels. Cerebral angiography tests blood flow in the brain. Although the various types of cerebral angiography use different imaging technologies, all (except the MRA) require the injection of contrast. In patients with normal kidney function, and in the absence of a known allergy to the contrast, the risks are minimal.

- *Four-Vessel Cerebral Angiography* – Iodinated contrast media are injected into the aortic arch or the cerebral vessels. If the test shows no intracerebral filling from either the carotid or vertebral arteries, the brain is receiving negligible blood flow if any.[22]

---

21. To explain, a reaction from the auditory nerve without an electrical response from the brainstem demonstrates that the patient's ears are functioning but the brain isn't processing the sound. If the patient's ears weren't functioning, or if the patient were deaf, this test would be meaningless.

22. The problem with this test is that it's expensive and invasive and carries a risk (albeit low) of significant side effects.

- *Radionuclide Angiography* – A bolus[23] of radioactive material is administered intravenously. If the patient is brain dead, no venous sinuses will be observable due to lack of blood flow.[24] The test is consistent with brain death when the tracer doesn't show up in the territories supplied by the intracranial arteries (internal carotid arteries and vertebro-basilar arteries). While the intracranial venous sinuses usually don't appear either, the venous sinuses may show up after a while, because they can receive blood from tissue supplied by arteries that don't enter the brain, such as the external carotid artery.
- *Computed Tomography Angiography* (CTA) – This technique combines computerized analysis with x-rays to visualize blood vessels.[25] There should be no evidence of blood flow in the brain for brain dead patients.
- *Magnetic Resonance Angiography* (MRA) – This method utilizes magnetic resonance imaging to generate images of blood vessels.[26] As in the CTA, there should be no evidence of blood flow in the brain for brain dead patients.[27]

b. *Cerebral Perfusion Scintigraphy* (CPS) – Scintigraphy is the production of two-dimensional images using a scintillation or gamma camera. A radiopharmaceutical agent is injected,[28] and the distribution of the radioactivity in tissues is determined. Cerebral perfusion scintigraphy tests brain function by tracking the amount of blood taken up by the brain. As a type of

---

23. A *bolus* (Latin for "ball") is the medical term for a dose of a drug or some other compound that is administered to raise its concentration in the blood to a specific quantity.
24. The major disadvantage of this procedure is that it doesn't evaluate circulation in the posterior fossa, i.e., the area of the brainstem and cerebellum.
25. Among its numerous advantages over standard angiography, this method is less invasive, more available, less operator-dependent, and faster, plus it can evaluate patients in the presence of CNS depressants. See E. Frampas et al., "CT Angiography for Brain Death Diagnosis," *American Journal of Neuroradiology* 30 (2009): 1566–70.
26. Aside from sparing the patient exposure to ionizing radiation, this method tends to be less toxic than certain others.
27. This test requires no injection, although some versions – such as the Contrast Enhanced MRA – use one.
28. No bolus is necessary.

radionuclide testing,[29] it is similar to radionuclide angiography. Yet angiography looks for blood flow in the arteries, while this test looks for whether the labeled chemical is absorbed by the tissue.[30] There are two basic types of CPS:

- *Planar CPS* – The patient is given an intravenous injection of a radiopharmaceutical agent, and a static planar imaging of the brain is performed with the scintillation camera. In brain dead patients, there is no uptake of the isotope in the brain parenchyma,[31] demonstrating an absence of cerebral filling. The use of new tracers that normally enter the brain has made the test more accurate in visualizing all parts of the brain.

- *Tomographic CPS* or *Single-Photon Emission Computed Tomography* (SPECT) – This test works essentially the same way as the planar CPS, but a single-photon emission computed tomographic (SPECT) scintillation camera is used instead of the standard scintillation camera, allowing for three-dimensional images.[32]

c. *Transcranial Doppler* (TCD) – This is an ultrasound test of the brain, with the probe placed on the temporal bone. If the TCD shows total absence of blood flow, to-and-fro flow (blood moves forward with the pumping of the heart, but backward when the heart relaxes), or small systolic spikes, this is sufficient to demonstrate that the brain is not receiving oxygen and is consistent with a determination of brainstem death.[33]

---

29. The favored agent for these tests is technetium-99m HM-PAO (hexamethylpropyleneamineoxime), and the process is sometimes referred to as a technetium scan.
30. Frequently the same tracer is used, and the early images correspond to the angiography, while the later ones (giving the chemicals time to be absorbed) correspond to the perfusion.
31. I.e., the brain itself, not the blood vessels.
32. Although it adds great detail to the images, this method is extremely expensive and may not be significantly more accurate than the planar CPS.
33. This test requires a highly competent ultrasonagrapher experienced in TCD techniques. One benefit of the test is that it's totally non-invasive.

CARDIOPULMONARY DEATH

Death may be declared by cardiopulmonary criteria (CPC), and in certain instances – particularly when patients are being withdrawn from support – organ donation is possible. The donors are referred to as non-heart-beating organ donors (NHBD). Prior to the Harvard criteria, all organ donors were NHBD. Currently they constitute 2% of the total, and the percentage will likely increase. However, the majority of their organs are no longer viable for implantation.[34]

CONCLUSION

The debate raging in Jewish and general society about brain death is a serious one. One of the principal qualities of a free mind, and its essential right, is the right of doubt, and it is no surprise that doubts plague the enterprise of organ harvesting. Some doubt whether a brain dead patient is really dead. Some doubt the integrity of the process of determining death, or the competence of the doctors involved.

I myself have doubts on occasion. Whenever I'm called in for a diagnosis of brain death, I perform a barrage of cephalic reflex tests on my own, regardless of who performed them before I was called in and what the findings were. In a matter this serious, it seems only proper to double-check one's colleagues, no matter how much one trusts them. Nevertheless, I don't doubt the vital importance of maintaining the brain death standard and encouraging the harvesting of organs from heart-beating cadavers wherever and whenever possible. The life-giving potential of both is simply too great to do otherwise.

I don't know whether I can offer conclusive medical proof that brain death should be equated with death. Certainly, I can offer none in the realm of halakha. However, I can say this: I have never seen a patient whose brainstem was determined to be dead return to the land of the living or even show any sort of improvement *at all*. The same cannot be said for the recipients of their organs, whose lives are saved by this miraculous process.

---

34. For details, see Dr. Kenneth Prager's essay in this volume.

I recently met a rabbi whose son underwent a successful liver transplant. This son is a rabbi himself, and the father of seven children. In this case, neither the donor nor the transplant surgeon knew about the recent halakhic debates on this subject in Israel and the United States. Whether this is good or bad I cannot say, but it was certainly fortunate for the patient, who is now alive and well and with his family.

Chapter 2

The Legal History
of Brain Death

Daniel Sinclair

I. THREE STAGES IN THE DEVELOPMENT OF THE
CONCEPT OF BRAIN DEATH

Stage 1

Brain death was first described clinically in 1959 when two French physicians, Pierre Mollaret and Maurice Goulon, investigated the effects of artificial respiration techniques on twenty-three patients suffering from serious brain damage. The two were highly impressed by the potential of resuscitative techniques, referring to their findings as *"une revelation."* The term they coined to describe the newly discovered condition in which their brain-damaged patients found themselves as a result of being connected to a respirator was *coma dépassé* – literally, a state beyond coma.

In a paper, Mollaret and Goulon reported their clinical and electro-encephalographic findings in these twenty-three cases, including the blocking of cerebral blood circulation as a result of raised intracranial pressure.[1]

---

1. Pierre Mollaret and Maurice Goulon, "Le coma dépassé (Mémoire préliminaire)," *Revue Neurologique* 101 (1959): 3–15.

Mollaret and Goulon didn't assert that such patients were dead, but their paper – and others in the decade that followed – led to a discussion of that issue, and to the eventual adoption of brain death as a medical definition of death.[2]

Stage 2

In 1968, an ad hoc committee at Harvard Medical School published a report entitled "A Definition of Irreversible Coma."[3] This title reflected the influence of the French paper; in retrospect, however, it is some-what confusing, since the term "irreversible coma" came to be identified with the condition known as persistent vegetative state (PVS), in which the brainstem is still functioning, and the patient is certainly not dead.

The Harvard committee report explicitly stated in its first sentence that its primary purpose was to define irreversible coma as "a new criterion for death," and it outlined the clinical tests necessary for the establishment of death. The Harvard tests required that the patient be "unreceptive and unresponsive, the most intensely painful stimuli evoking no vocal or other response, not even a groan, withdrawal of a limb, or quickening of respiration." No movements were to occur during observation for one hour.

Apnea was to be confirmed by disconnecting the patient from the respirator for three minutes. The Harvard criteria also required that there be "no reflexes," the emphasis being on no brainstem reflexes. A flat or isoelectric electroencephalogram (EEG) was of "great confirmatory value." And all tests were to be repeated twenty-four hours later with no change in the results.

A year later, Dr. Henry K. Beecher, chairman of the Harvard committee, stated that the committee was unanimous in its belief that an EEG was not essential to a diagnosis of irreversible coma, although it could provide valuable supporting data.

---

2. See Daniel Silverman et al., "Cerebral Death and the Electroencephalogram," *JAMA* 209, no. 10 (1969): 1505.
3. "A Definition of Irreversible Coma: Report of the Ad Hoc Committee of the Harvard Medical School to Examine the Definition of Brain Death," *JAMA* 205, no. 6 (1968): 337–40.

According to Martin Pernick, a leading American medical historian, Dr. Beecher had three concerns in mind when drawing up the report. The first concern was organ transplantation. Kidney transplants from cadavers had become possible in 1954, and were relatively common by the late 1960s. Beecher hoped the Harvard criteria would not only increase the supply of organs but, more broadly, defend the medical establishment against the public perception that transplant surgeons were organ-stealing killers.

Another concern was the wasteful use of respirators, which Beecher sought to avoid by changing the definition of death. Finally, Pernick points out that Beecher was famous in the late 1960s not simply as a founder of academic anesthesiology, but also as the author of a powerful exposé of medical abuses in human experimentation. Beecher apparently hoped that experimenting on brain dead bodies would reduce the need for live human guinea pigs, thereby avoiding the ethical complications of using such subjects.[4]

Stage 3

Three years after the Harvard report, two neurosurgeons from Minnesota made the challenging suggestion that "in patients with known but irreparable intracranial lesions," irreversible damage to the brainstem was the "point of no return" and should be defined as death.

In their view, the etiology of the patient's condition was of prime importance, and death could be diagnosed mainly on the basis of "clinical judgments."[5] In addition, the "Minnesota criteria" included the establishment of apnea by disconnecting the respirator for four minutes. Also, no movements were to occur during one hour of constant observation, and there should be no brainstem reflexes. All tests were to be repeated twelve hours later, and death would be declared only if there was no

---

4. Martin S. Pernick, "Brain Death in a Cultural Context: The Reconstruction of Death, 1967–1981," in *The Definition of Death: Contemporary Controversies* (ed. Stuart J. Youngner, Robert M. Arnold, and Renie Schapiro; Baltimore: Johns Hopkins University Press, 1999).
5. Anavankot Mohandas and Shelley N. Chou, "Brain Death: A Clinical and Pathological Study," *Journal of Neurosurgery* 35, no. 2 (1971): 211.

change in the results. It was emphasized that a flat EEG was not mandatory for the diagnosis.

These three papers constitute the basis for the modern medical definition of brain death.

II. LEGISLATION AND CASE LAW ON BRAIN DEATH IN COMMON LAW JURISDICTIONS

In the wake of these developments, the notion of brainstem death gained widespread acceptance in legal circles in the common law world, and in a 1980 American case, it was noted that at least twenty-five states in the US had enacted brain death statutes. In other states, brain death had been approved by judicial ruling.[6]

In the same year, the United States passed the Uniform Determination of Death Act, which provides two criteria for the establishment of death: "irreversible cessation of circulatory and respiratory functions" or "irreversible cessation of all functions of the entire brain, including the brainstem." The actual clinical determination of death "must be made in accordance with accepted medical standards."[7]

State statutes in the US can be divided into three categories: those that provide for brain death as an express alternative to heart-/lung-oriented death, those that admit the use of brain-based criteria when a cardiorespiratory diagnosis is obviated by artificial maintenance, and those that recognize brain death as an independent and sufficient means of determining death. All states have now adopted the concept of brain death either by statute or by court recognition.[8]

Australian states also adopted the dual criteria model. The Victorian Human Tissue Act (1983), section 41, provides that "a person has died when there has occurred: (a) irreversible cessation of the circulation of the blood in the body of the person, or (b) irreversible cessation of all functions of the brain of the person." There are similar provisions in the New South Wales Human Tissue Act (1983), section 33.

---

6. See *Re Welfare of Bowman* 617 P2d 731 (Wash 1980).
7. Twelve Uniform Laws Annotated (ULA) 589 (West 1993 and West Supp. 1997).
8. See Alexander M. Capron, "Brain Death – Well Settled Yet Still Unsettled," *NEJM* 344, no. 16 (2001): 1244.

As far as Britain is concerned, the *Medico-Legal Journal* observed in 1975 that the concept of brain death was still "regarded warily in the United Kingdom."[9] By 1979, however, the situation had changed quite dramatically, and two developments in the British medical community indicated that the predominant medical view was that a patient was dead once brain death had occurred.

The first was the 1979 publication by the Conference of Medical Royal Colleges of a report entitled "Diagnosis of Death." Paragraph 7 of this report stated in no uncertain terms that "brain death represents the stage at which a patient becomes truly dead." The final paragraph likewise confirmed that "the identification of brain death means that the patient is dead, whether or not the function of some organs, such as a heartbeat, is still maintained by artificial means."[10]

The second development was the Code of Practice published by the Department of Health and Social Security to regulate the removal of cadaver organs for transplantation.[11] According to the code, death could be diagnosed "by the irreversible cessation of brainstem function – 'brain death'" (paragraph 27). The code also approved of the practice of maintaining artificial respiration and heartbeat until the completion of the removal of organs for transplantation (paragraph 33).

In addition, the code advised that brainstem death be diagnosed by two doctors, one of whom should be the consultant in charge of the case and the other suitably experienced and clinically independent of the first. While most medical practitioners abide by these guidelines, the United Kingdom lacks a legal definition of death.

The issue of the definition of death does figure in United Kingdom case law, however, and in the 1963 case of *R. v. Potter*,[12] the English courts were challenged by the new medical procedure of establishing brain death, then harvesting organs for transplantation. In this case, the kidney donor had fought with the defendant and suffered severe injuries to his head as a result. Upon arrival in the hospital, he stopped breathing

9. Editorial, "The Beating-Heart Cadaver," *Medico-Legal Journal* 43 (1975): 37.
10. *BMJ* 1 (February 3, 1979): 332.
11. *The Removal of Cadaveric Organs for Transplantation: A Code of Practice* (HMSO, 1979).
12. *Times*, July 26, 1963; D. Meyers, *The Human Body and the Law* (Stanford, CA: Stanford University Press, 1990), 196.

and was connected to an artificial respirator for twenty-four hours. During this period, one of his kidneys was removed for transplantation purposes. Following the nephrectomy, the respirator was shut off, and there was no spontaneous respiration or circulation.

The defendant argued that the physician's shutting off the respirator and allowing the patient-victim to die broke the chain of causation between the original wrongful act – the assault – and the death. This argument would, if accepted by the court, release the defendant from any legal liability for the homicide. In 1963 the judge agreed with this argument, and the defendant was convicted only of common assault.

In another assault case, in 1981, an estranged husband stabbed his wife nine times with a kitchen knife. She was connected to a respirator for three days, after which her consultant – following the protocol for the establishment of brain death laid down by the Conference of Medical Royal Colleges – disconnected her, and she was certified dead. In this instance, however, the defense's argument that the termination of artificial respiration broke the chain of causation between the assault and the victim's death was rejected by the Court of Appeal:

> Where a medical practitioner, using generally acceptable methods, came to the conclusion that the patient was, for all practical purposes, dead, and that such vital functions as remained were being maintained solely by mechanical means, and accordingly disconnected treatment, that did not break the chain of causation between the initial injury and the death.[13]

Yet the court did not go as far as to declare that under English law, brain death is a legal definition of death.

By 1992, there was no longer any doubt that brain death constituted a legal definition of death in the United Kingdom. In Re A. 3 Med. LR 303 (1992), the parents of a child who had been certified brainstem-dead sought to retain him on an artificial respirator. The judge held that A. was dead for all legal as well as medical purposes, and that any doctor who disconnected the apparatus was not acting unlawfully.[14]

---

13. *R. v. Malcharek; R. v. Steel* (1981) 2 All ER 422.
14. *Medical Law Review* 3 (1992): 303.

This case is often taken as establishing that brainstem death constitutes a definition of death in English law.

III. BRAIN DEATH IN ISRAELI CRIMINAL LAW

Belker v. State of Israel

In *Belker v. State of Israel* (1982),[15] the appellant's wife was brought into the hospital in critical condition. She had either fallen or been thrown from the window of the fourth-floor apartment she shared with her husband. She was suffering from severe head injuries and total absence of blood pressure, and was in a deep coma. The doctors concluded that she was brain dead.

A decision was then made to connect her to a respirator and transplant her kidneys. Some five days later, the respirator was disconnected, she was officially declared dead, and the transplant was performed.

The circumstances surrounding the woman's fall were in dispute. According to the appellant, his wife's fall was an act of suicide, which he had done his best to prevent. The neighbors testified that the appellant had deliberately thrown his wife out the window in the course of a domestic brawl. The District Court accepted the testimony of the neighbors, and the appellant was found guilty of premeditated murder under section 300 of the Penal Law (1977).

The appeal turned on the question of whether causing brain death constitutes murder under Israeli law. According to the appellant, the fact that his wife had ceased to breathe only upon being disconnected from the respirator meant that his throwing her out the window (as he'd been convicted of doing) was not the direct cause of death. His wife's death was caused by the doctors who had removed her respirator five days after her admission to the hospital. The respondent argued that brain death was a well-established criterion for the determination of death, and that causing brain death was therefore an act of murder.

Justice Moshe Beiski (= Beiski J.), writing for the majority, reviewed a wide range of Israeli and foreign medical, legislative, and judicial material on the topic of brain death, and concluded that brain death constitutes valid proof of the victim's death for the purposes of the law of murder. He ruled that the clinical details of death, for the purpose of its

---

15. Cr. A. 341/82, PD 41 (1) 1.

establishment in legal terms, have always been a matter for the medical profession, and that its determination in any particular case fell within the competence of the physicians concerned. In the present case, there was ample evidence that the physicians treating the appellant's wife had acted in accordance with standard medical procedure in coming to their conclusion that she was legally dead. The appeal was dismissed.

Survey of Halakha

In the course of his survey of the relevant material, Beiski J. also dealt with the issue of brain death in Jewish law.[16] The principal source is the talmudic discussion concerning a person or persons upon whom a building collapsed on the Sabbath. The Mishna (*Yoma* 8:7) rules that the pile of debris is to be excavated, notwithstanding the breach of the Sabbath laws entailed by such a step, and that this is the case even if there is a doubt as to whether there are, in fact, people buried there, and if so, if they are still alive. In the course of the excavation, any dead bodies found by the rescuers must be left *in situ* until the end of the Sabbath. Any living people, however, are to be rescued from the rubble, and anything required for the restoration of their health may be done on the Sabbath. In relation to the establishment of death, the Talmud (b. *Yoma* 85a) mentions the following criteria:

תנו רבנן: עד היכן הוא בודק? עד חוטמו, ויש אומרים: עד לבו [ס״א: טיבורו].	Our rabbis taught: Up to where do we check [for signs of life]? Up to his nose. Some say: Up to his heart. (Some texts read: his navel.)
אמר רב פפא: מחלוקת ממטה למעלה, אבל ממעלה למטה, כיון דבדק ליה עד חוטמו שוב אינו צריך, דכתיב: ״כל אשר נשמת רוח חיים באפיו״.	Rav Pappa said: The dispute is when [uncovering the person] from bottom to top, but from top to bottom, once one checks the person's nose [for signs of breath], one need check no further, as it says: "All in whose nostrils was the breath of life" (Gen. 7:22).

---

16. For a detailed analysis of the halakhic approaches to brain death, see the essays in the halakha sections of this collection.

According to Rav Pappa, cessation of breathing in the nose is definitive evidence of death. The absence of any sign of life in the heart is not a sure sign that the person is dead. Hence, if the individual buried under the debris is discovered lying head down, his nose must also be checked, even in the absence of any identifiable life in his heart. Once his nose has been checked, it is unnecessary to check the heart; death is determined by the nostrils alone. The halakha is decided in accordance with the view of Rav Pappa.[17]

The talmudic position is based upon the biblical notion that the seat of the breath of life is in the nostrils. In the Middle Ages, however, the dominant view was that of Galen,[18] according to whom the seat of breathing was in the heart; hence, Rashi explains that one may establish if someone is alive by detecting signs of life in the heart, "which is where the soul pulsates (נשמתו דופקת שם)." The reason for examining the nose, Rashi claims, is that the presence of the breath in the heart is sometimes difficult to detect.[19]

The true relationship between the respiratory and circulatory systems was discovered only in the early seventeenth century by William Harvey, and even then, halakhic authorities continued to attribute breathing to the heart. Rabbi Tzvi Ashkenazi (*Ḥakham Tzvi*) states quite categorically:

ודבר ברור מאוד שאין	It is very clear that breathing can take place
נשימה אלא כשיש חיות	only when the heart is undamaged, since
בלב שממנו ולצורכו היא	it is the source and site of the respiratory
הנשימה.	process.[20]

Following Rashi, Rabbi Ashkenazi explains that signs of breath in the heart might go undetected as a result of disease or weakness, so the conclusive test for establishment of death is the absence of breath in the nose.

17. Rambam, MT Laws of Shabbat 2:19; *Shulḥan Arukh* OḤ 329:4.
18. See Charles Singer, *A Short History of Medicine* (Oxford, 1928), 56–58.
19. B. *Yoma* 85a, s.v. *hakhi garsinan.*
20. *Ḥakham Tzvi* 77.

In the early nineteenth century, Rabbi Moshe Sofer (*Hatam Sofer*), basing himself upon both the Talmud and the later authorities, established three criteria for the determination of death: no breath, no heart activity, and absolutely no movement.[21] In Beiski J.'s view, Rabbi Sofer was responding to his time by adding medically approved tests – namely, lack of cardiac activity and movement – to the biblical criterion of the cessation of breathing as recorded in the Talmud.

According to Beiski J., the interesting feature emerging from this survey of Jewish law is the tendency to alter the definition of death in accordance with the state of scientific knowledge in any particular era. Originally, cessation of breathing was conclusive evidence of death. Later, the idea of the heartbeat was introduced, and even later, the threefold criterion of the *Hatam Sofer* became standard halakha. Jewish law therefore adapts to changing scientific perceptions.

Beiski J. cited another example of halakha accommodating changing scientific views in relation to the establishment of death. According to the Talmud (b. *Arakhin* 7a–b), it is permitted to profane the Sabbath by cutting open the stomach of a woman who died in childbirth in order to save the fetus in her womb. This ruling is codified in the *Shulhan Arukh* (OH 330:5); nevertheless, in his glosses, Rabbi Moshe Isserles writes:

ומה שאין נוהגין עכשיו כן אפילו בחול, משום דאין בקיאין במיתת האם בקרוב כל כך שאפשר לולד לחיות.	We don't carry out this practice even on weekdays, since we are not expert enough to establish the [moment of the] mother's demise with sufficient precision to justify this operation.[22]

Once again, halakhic rulings vary with contemporary medical knowledge.

---

21. *Hatam Sofer* YD 338.
22. In other words, by the time we're sure the mother has died, the child will have died anyway. On this topic, see also Rabbi Eliezer Waldenburg, *Tzitz Eliezer* 10:25.

It follows from all this that there is little precedential value in past halakhic pronouncements on fundamentally scientific issues such as the definition of death. Indeed, Rambam makes this point quite unequivocally in the following comment on past halakhic rulings in the area of astronomy:

> You must, however, not expect that everything our sages say respecting astronomical matters should agree with observation, for mathematics was not fully developed in those days; and their statements were based not on the authority of the prophets but on the knowledge they themselves possessed or derived from contemporary men of science.[23]

Contemporary Halakha

Beiski J. then turned his attention to the contemporary halakhic attitude toward brain death. Noting that several current halakhic authorities insisted upon the fulfillment of all three criteria mentioned by the *Ḥatam Sofer*, he pointed out that Dr. Jacob Levi did as well. As a physician, Levi was undoubtedly well aware of the scientific developments regarding brain death. He nevertheless rejected brain death on two grounds. First, he worried that physicians interested in organ transplantation would play fast and loose with the medical criteria for establishing brain death in order to secure the necessary organs. Second, he doubted that the proposed means of testing for brain death, i.e., an electroencephalogram, were sufficiently reliable.[24]

According to Beiski J., both problems raised by Dr. Levi were readily solvable. That of overenthusiastic transplant surgeons could easily be solved by the strict enforcement of the existing practice that only an independent and disinterested medical team is qualified to test for brain death. As for the efficacy of the EEG, other tests could be used to determine actual brain death. These tests, e.g., the apnea test as well as the Brainstem Auditory Evoked Response (BAER) Test, are required

---

23. Moses Maimonides, *The Guide for the Perplexed* (trans. M. Friedländer), III:14.
24. Jacob Levi, "At What Point in Time May an Organ be Removed for Transplanting?" *Ha-Ma'ayan* 10 (1970): 3 [Hebrew].

under medical regulations and international conventions for the establishment of brain death in many jurisdictions; the EEG is used solely as a monitoring device when carrying out the mandatory tests.

Moreover, a number of contemporary halakhic authorities don't feel bound by the opinion of Rabbi Moshe Sofer and are prepared to determine death on the basis of cessation of brain activity alone. According to Rabbi Shlomo Goren, once the brain is clearly and irreversibly dysfunctional, there is no need to continue any form of life-prolonging treatment, including respiration.[25] Clear support for the brain death criterion in the context of cardiac transplants is expressed by Rabbi Chaim David Regensberg of Chicago, who rules that a negative EEG *is* sufficient evidence of the donor's death, and the heart may then be extracted without hesitation.[26] His only reservations are purely practical, such as concerns about the trustworthiness of the medical staff and the accuracy with which it tests for irreversible cessation of brainstem function. Beiski J. pointed out that all these objections were dealt with in his rebuttal of Dr. Levi's arguments.

Beiski J. concluded his lengthy and detailed survey of Jewish law with the decision of the Israeli Chief Rabbinate, published in November 1986, to accept brain death for the purpose of determining death in relation to cardiac transplants.[27] This decision is based upon classical halakhic sources and relies heavily upon a responsum by Rabbi Moshe Feinstein (IM YD 3:132). According to this responsum, cessation of breathing is definitive evidence of death, and brain death constitutes valid evidence that independent breathing has indeed ceased. The medical examinations that must be conducted before brain death is declared are enumerated in the body of the Israeli Chief Rabbinate's decision, and they correspond to those required by the medical profession.

In light of this recent development, and the generally flexible relationship between halakha and scientific progress, Beiski J. concluded

---

25. Shlomo Goren, "Defining Death in Jewish Law," *Shana be-Shana* 125 (1974): 130 [Hebrew].

26. Chaim David Regensberg, "Heart Transplants," *Halakha u-Refu'a* 2 (1981): 8 [Hebrew].

27. Chief Rabbinate of Israel, "Heart Transplants in Israel," *Assia* 42–43 (5747/1986–87): 70–81 [Hebrew]; Yoel Jakobovits, "Brain Death and Heart Transplants: The Israeli Chief Rabbinate's Directives," *Tradition* 24, no. 4 (summer 1989): 1–14.

that brain death is also recognized by Jewish law as a valid criterion for the establishment of death.

IV. ISRAEL'S BRAIN-RESPIRATORY DEATH LAW, 2008

In 2008, the Knesset passed the Brain-Respiratory Death Law, which provides a legal framework for the determination of brain death. Under section 4 of this law, the irreversible cessation of brainstem function constitutes a legal definition of death, and it may be established on the basis of any one of the following tests: Brainstem Auditory Evoked Response (BAER), Transcranial Doppler (TCD), Sensory Evoked Potentials (SEP), Computed Tomography Angiography (CTA), and Magnetic Resonance Imaging (MRI) Angiography.[28] Neither the terminal patient's attending physician nor any doctor involved in organ transplantation is permitted to certify brain death.

Section 3 of the law provides that brain death is to be determined only by licensed physicians, who are to be drawn from specified medical areas such as neurology and cardiology. The syllabus for physicians wishing to gain certification for purposes of determining brain death includes medicine, law, ethics, and halakha (section 6). The certification course is to be designed and overseen by a ten-member committee consisting of a chair appointed by the Israel Medical Association, three physicians appointed at the discretion of the chair, three rabbis appointed by the Chief Rabbinate (one of whom must also be a physician), an ethicist, a jurist, and a philosopher. The last three are to be appointed by the Supreme Court; one of them must also be a physician, and one must be a member of a recognized non-Jewish faith (section 5).

Clearly, this legislation seeks to ensure that any doctor who establishes brain death is fully sensitive to all the ramifications of such a step, including those of a halakhic nature. In this respect, it is significant that halakha is required reading for physicians qualifying for brain death accreditation, and three members of the ten-person committee responsible for the qualifying course are rabbis.

---

28. For more details on these and other confirmatory tests, see Dr. Zelik Frischer's essay in this volume.

The law also protects the rights of those who believe death is to be established only on the basis of cardiorespiratory failure. According to section 8(4):

> Notwithstanding anything said in this law, life support may not be removed, even after the establishment of brain death, if the patient's family informs the physicians that he opposed brain death on religious or other grounds. In such a case, death is to be declared only when the heart ceases to beat.

Section 8(3) of the law requires a hospital to provide the full medical record of any determination of brain death to the family of the deceased upon request.

V. LEGAL, HALAKHIC, AND PHILOSOPHICAL CONCLUSIONS

The medical origins of the concept of brain death in the latter half of the twentieth century are to be found at the confluence of the developing science of the brain, the technology of artificial respiration, and the technique of organ transplantation. Once accepted by the medical community, the idea of brain death gradually took hold in general society[29] and was eventually incorporated into most Western legal systems, including Israel's.

Law, however, tends to be cautious in adapting to change, especially in relation to fundamentally scientific matters, and, as noted in part 2 of this essay, many legal systems are careful to provide two alternative definitions of death. The first is the classical cardiac-respiratory criterion, and the second is based upon cessation of all brain activity.

---

29. An illustration of the role played by the media in the popularization of the brain death idea is the public debate that ensued in the wake of a TV program broadcast by the BBC on this subject, "Transplants: Are the Donors Really Dead?" *Panorama*, October 13, 1980. See Christopher Pallis, "Medicine and the Media," *BMJ* 280 (April 12, 1980): 1064; Bryan Silcock, "Facts Behind the Transplant Row," *Sunday Times*, November 9, 1980, 14. The debate continued for months in both the general and medico-legal presses, resulting in an overwhelming victory for the concept of brain death in the United Kingdom.

In several jurisdictions, the means of testing for brain death are left entirely to the medical profession, and in the United Kingdom, as stated, there is still no law on brain death; the entire issue is in the hands of the medical community. Also as mentioned, Israel passed a brain death law in 2008. The law, however, is fairly demanding in terms of the qualifications required of physicians seeking a license to determine brain death, and it permits the families of patients opposed to brain death on religious or other grounds to prevent the termination of life support, even if brain death has been determined.

One important issue in the legal history of brain death is its role in criminal law. As observed above, the legal systems of both the United Kingdom and Israel effectively recognized brain death for the first time in cases in which the accused sought to absolve himself of liability for murder by claiming that the death in question was caused not by his assault on the victim but by the removal of life support by physicians.

To dismiss this argument, courts in the United Kingdom, Israel, and the US[30] have held that brain death constitutes death for purposes of defining murder. Any other conclusion would allow the perpetrators of extremely violent attacks to escape liability for murder because of the existence of sophisticated resuscitative technology. Also, it would effectively turn any heart transplant surgeon into a murderer. Once the courts adopted brain death in criminal law, the path was clear to use it to establish death in all contexts.

In this respect, it is interesting to speculate on how contemporary halakha would view brain death if Jewish law still possessed criminal jurisdiction and a rabbinic court was required to rule on the criminal liability of an individual who had caused brain death. In fact, this is precisely what Beiski J. attempted to do in the Belker case, albeit from the perspective of a secular jurist marshaling halakhic sources in order to arrive at a legally sound conclusion. He concluded that brain death was a valid way of establishing death under Jewish law, and that Belker was guilty of murder.

Now it is certainly arguable that Beiski J.'s survey of Jewish law on the topic of brain death falls short of the comprehensive and richly

---

30. *People v. Lyons*, Sup Ct No 56072, Alameda Co (Cal, 1974).

textured halakhic analysis one would expect from an expert in Jewish law. Indeed, as the 2010 study of the Vaad Halacha of the Rabbinical Council of America indicates, there is a halakhic case to be made against relying upon brain death as a valid basis for terminating life support. At the same time, even if a *beit din* rejected brain death as a satisfactory halakhic definition of death for purposes of terminating life support, such a court would be highly unlikely to rule that an accused similar to Belker was innocent of murder. Such an outcome would surely be both legally and morally counterintuitive.

Accordingly, this *beit din* would undoubtedly find a way to recognize brain death as halakhic death for the purpose of establishing the guilt of a person who deliberately brought about the brain death of his or her victim. It is not inconceivable that such a finding would be established along the lines of Beiski J.'s decision, albeit in a much more detailed and nuanced form. In the wake of such a development, there would be more than one definition of death in Jewish law, i.e., brainstem dysfunction in the criminal sphere, and respiratory failure in relation to the termination of life support and for purposes of organ transplantation.[31]

Once brain death obtained widespread halakhic recognition in the criminal sphere, it would be difficult to reject it regarding life-support termination and heart transplants. The logical course of action would then be for halakhists to recognize individual choice as the prime factor in deciding whether to rely on brain-respiratory death in relation to cardiac transplants. This is indeed the policy adopted under Israel's Brain-Respiratory Death Law, outlined above. The law accepts brain death as an appropriate definition of death with regard to termination of life support and for cardiac transplantation, but recognizes the concerns of those who reject this definition by giving the families of patients diagnosed as suffering from irreversible brainstem dysfunction the right to register their opposition with the medical team, which is then obliged to continue life support until the establishment of death under

---

31. In effect, this is the situation that exists under the American and Australian legal systems, as cited above – namely, two definitions of death. Although the American and Australian statutes laying down these definitions don't divide them along the lines of criminal law and termination of life support, as would the above-mentioned contemporary *beit din*, such a division is by no means inconceivable.

the cardiac-respiratory test. The individual-choice option would seem to be the wisest in an era in which there is still halakhic opposition to brain death in the context of determining death for heart transplantation and related medical purposes.

The notion that in Jewish law there may very well be more than one definition of death, and that it may vary according to context, is neither novel nor surprising. For example, the evidence required to establish death in relation to the obligation to commence mourning rites[32] differs from that which is required to permit a man's wife to remarry.[33] Rabbi Eliezer Waldenburg points out that nowhere does the Talmud itself actually offer a biological definition of the dying state (*goses*). In his view, this omission is intended to maintain flexibility, enabling the halakha to adopt various definitions in accordance with current medical science.[34]

The determination of fetal status in Jewish law affords another example of the use of contextual definitions in what is often thought of as a purely biological matter.[35] Rabbi J. David Bleich has suggested that as a result of the equally trenchant claims of genetics and birth on the definition of motherhood in a surrogacy situation, the best halakhic solution is to recognize two mothers, endowing each with requisite halakhic significance.[36]

Hopefully, the recognition of more than one halakhic definition of death would result in a more fine-tuned approach across the board to practical decision-making in this area, including, for example, sensitivity to those who regard the practice of receiving donated hearts but refusing to donate their own as morally and ethically unacceptable.

Finally, the definition of death is not only a medical and legal question; it is also a philosophical one. There is nothing biologically or legally sacrosanct about any one definition of death. As already observed, the concept of brain death came about as a result of the developing

---

32. *Shulḥan Arukh* YD 339:2.
33. Ibid. EH 17:31; also see *Otzar ha-Posqim* EH 17:57.
34. Rabbi Eliezer Waldenburg, *Tzitz Eliezer* 13:89; Daniel Sinclair, *Jewish Biomedical Law: Legal and Extra-legal Dimensions* (Oxford University Press, 2003), 187–88.
35. Sinclair, *Jewish Biomedical Law*, 15.
36. J. David Bleich, *Contemporary Halakhic Problems* 4 (New York: KTAV and Yeshiva University Press, 1995), 251–258; Sinclair, *Jewish Biomedical Law*, 105–8.

science of the brain and the technology of artificial respiration and organ transplantation. In the absence of any one of these factors, the concept may very well never have taken root. A good illustration of the philosophically laden nature of brain death is that its critics almost inevitably complain that society values organ transplantation more than the terminal patient's life. Clearly, this is a fundamentally philosophical issue rather than a biological one.

The application of brain death in practice has always been accompanied by attempts to rebut this criticism by placing the determination of death in the hands of independent physicians. Indeed, the 2008 Israeli law takes great pains to ensure that only physicians trained broadly in the philosophy of brain death are to be entrusted with its clinical determination. Philosophically, as well legally and halakhically, therefore, the wisest course is to avoid setting any one definition in stone, and to allow the halakhic and legal definitions of death to remain inherently open-textured.

Chapter 3

Neurological Death: A Twenty-First-Century Definition

Noam Stadlan

INTRODUCTION

A patient contracts a viral infection that attacks the heart muscle and weakens it to the point that the heart cannot adequately pump blood through the body. He requires a heart transplant but none is available. In an attempt to preserve his life, doctors remove his heart and implant a mechanical heart. While the heart itself is inside the chest, the power source is outside the body.[1]

Unfortunately, the patient falls and suffers a high cervical spinal cord injury, which results in paralysis of the entire body, making it impossible for him to breathe. A ventilator outside the body must now pump air in and out of the lungs. Above the neck, however, he's neurologically

---

1. For example, a Jarvik-7 heart or one of its descendants; I took care of several such patients as a surgical intern.

intact; he's awake and can think, feel, hear, see, taste, and talk (with a specially modified breathing tube), or at the least mouth words.

If this paralyzed body were replaced by a machine that pumped blood directly into the head, and the brain continued to function as described, would the patient still be seen as a live human being? If the body that had been separated from the head continued to be supplied with circulation, and air continued to be pumped into the lungs, would the body by itself constitute a human being, with all the attendant rights and privileges?

Consider the following situation: You come across this patient (with the body attached), and someone has just unplugged both the heart pump and the ventilator. He lacks both circulation and respiration. For at least the first fifteen seconds or so, he would retain normal neurological function; he would be able to think, talk, etc. After that he would gradually lose neurological function. Unless the machines were plugged back in, more bodily and neurological functions would be lost, and eventually permanent damage would set in, and the loss of functions would become irreversible. Even if the machines were reconnected, no tissue-based function would return, because every cell has been damaged irreversibly. The only "function" would be supplied by the machines pumping blood through the arteries and air in and out of the lungs.

How would one determine that the patient was dead, and how would one pinpoint when death occurred? What tests or examinations should one perform? What information is needed to make the determination? If the machines are turned back on prior to death, then life obviously continues unimpeded. If the machines are turned on after death, the result is a corpse with air flow in the lungs and circulation. Since it is obviously possible for a corpse to have circulation and air flow in the lungs – and a corpse is a dead body – defining death solely by the cessation of circulation and air flow in the lungs is absurd.

The above example illustrates that while circulation and respiration may be necessary for human life,[2] they don't actually determine

---

2. There is an extraordinary difference between a situation in which air is moved in and out of a person's lungs and a situation in which the human brain can signal the diaphragm to make the air move in and out of the lungs. Air moving in and out of the

whether human life is present.[3] This essay will review the medical data relevant to determining death based on neurological criteria, address common concerns voiced about the criteria, discuss the philosophical basis for using neurological criteria to determine death, and show how the medical data can address the demands of halakha.

I. PRELIMINARY ANATOMY REVIEW

The Brain

The brain can be divided into two parts, the brainstem and the cerebrum (which here will also include the cerebellum). The brainstem is sometimes referred to as the lower brain, the cerebrum as the higher brain, and the combination is the "whole brain."

The brainstem is relatively small but contains the respiratory centers as well as the ascending reticular activating system (ARAS), which can be thought of as an on/off switch for the cerebrum. The brainstem is filled with closely packed areas that control the cranial nerves. These nerves control and allow for – among other functions – sight, eye movement, facial movement and sensation, hearing, swallowing, tongue movement, and the gag reflex. In addition, the cerebrum and the body exchange signals via neuronal pathways running through the brainstem.

Clinical Tests

The clinical examinations that determine if a person is brain dead test for functions mediated by the brainstem. Since the brainstem contains many closely packed areas whose function can be directly tested, if even a small area of the brainstem is intact, some function will likely be found. Absence of any function appears to be a reliable indicator of severe damage.[4]

---

lungs is a mechanical process that can be produced by a machine. The brain's ability to signal the diaphragm to function is a fundamental example of brain function. The reference above is solely to the mechanical process.

3. It also shows how the distinction between "permanent" and "irreversible" loss of circulation as used in the discussion of donation after cardiac death (DCD) is totally artifactual and has no actual utility in addressing whether one is alive or dead.

4. For details on the testing of brainstem function, see Dr. Zelik Frischer's essay in this volume.

The cerebrum, on the other hand, is much larger, and many areas lack directly testable function. In addition, if the brainstem isn't functioning, it's impossible to test directly for cerebral function, because the input and output of the cerebrum are destroyed. Destruction of the brainstem includes destruction of the ARAS, so without a working brainstem the cerebrum will demonstrate very low levels of activity as measured by electroencephalography (EEG), and these levels are thought to be inadequate for consciousness.[5] However, the hormone secretion functions of the hypothalamus (which will be discussed later) can still be intact despite brainstem destruction.

Terminology

The importance of these distinctions lies in the terminology used in describing brain death. Some criteria define brain death as occurring when the brainstem has irreversibly ceased to function. Others refer to cessation of function of the entire brain. A more controversial definition of death by neurological criteria uses cessation of function of just the cerebrum, higher-brain death. This last usage has not been generally accepted, as it would categorize anencephalic children and those with permanent loss of consciousness[6] (but some intact brainstem function, including possibly respiration) as dead.

II. HISTORY: WHAT ARE WE TESTING?

Technology

In the 1950s, mechanical ventilators came into common usage. Even if the brain didn't signal the lung muscles (diaphragm) to move, these machines blew air in and out of the lungs, and the body could get oxygen to the tissues. For the first time, the brain could cease to function while the rest of the body could continue.

The heart has its own pacemaker, so even without the brain or any other outside influence, it will continue to beat and pump blood

---

5. Neural correlates of consciousness will be discussed later.
6. In these patients it is assumed, based on the examination and degree of brain damage, that consciousness is not present and the situation is permanent. In the presence of some intact brainstem function, neither of those assumptions can be made with total certainty.

as long as the heart muscle receives a supply of blood and oxygen. Shortly after ventilators, however, bypass pumps and heart transplants became a reality, and a few decades later, artificial hearts. With these developments, a person's own heart was no longer necessary for circulation in the body.

Origins of the Concept

The first reports of what was to become "brain death" were in the late 1950s. Doctors observed that some patients attached to ventilators had no observable brain function and didn't breathe on their own (they were totally dependent on the ventilator). The studies available at that time were EEG and angiography.

EEG consists of placing electrodes on the skull and measuring the electrical function of the brain. This method doesn't pick up the function of each cell, just when enough are working together for their activity to be measurable through the skull. Angiography consists of injecting dye into an artery (in the groin or neck), then x-raying the skull to see which arteries fill with the dye.

Many patients without observable neurological function also showed no electrical activity on the EEG, and the arteries inside the skull didn't fill with dye. On autopsy the brains showed a typical pattern of damage, which at first was attributed to the ventilator, so it was called "respirator brain." Only later was it realized that the damage was wrought by a lack of blood flow to the brain.

The Harvard Criteria

In 1968, a group of physicians met in Boston and produced a list of steps known as the Harvard criteria. The question the criteria were designed to answer was this: Under what circumstances can we be certain that a person has irreversibly lost clinically observable brain function?[7] The list included the following:

---

7. Brain function comes in two types. Usually, function refers to things that are clinically observable: brainstem reflexes, movement, etc. However, if there is even one working brain cell (i.e., one with an intact cell membrane, so an electrical potential can be measured across it), that can also be considered function, but on a cellular

1. There must be evidence of major damage to the brain.
2. It is necessary to rule out any other factors that can cause a temporary loss of brain function, such as certain medications, low temperature, and low blood pressure.
3. The reflexes present in a functioning brain must be totally absent.
4. There can be no brain-mediated response to stimulation.[8]
5. If possible, an EEG should be done, and it should show an absence of activity.

If, after twenty-four hours, retesting showed no sign of function, the patient was considered dead.

The stated basis for declaring death based on these criteria was "An organ, brain or other, that no longer functions and has no possibility of functioning again is for all practical purposes dead. Our first problem is to determine the characteristics of a permanently nonfunctioning brain."[9]

The goal of the criteria was to gauge whether any clinical function would return. The goal was not to predict who would lack blood flow or EEG function. Similar criteria were published by various groups, and gradually the idea of brain death – or more accurately, death based on the cessation of neurological function – was accepted.

The Uniform Determination of Death Act

In 1981 the Uniform Determination of Death Act (UDDA), which became the basis for most state laws defining death, codified that death could be determined either by the cessation of circulation and respiration, or by

---

level. The Harvard group wasn't concerned with this type of function. In truth, we simply don't know how much cellular function must be linked together until we get something we would label brain function.

8. A response to stimulation, or a reflex, means there is an intact loop of neurons. Consider the knee reflex. When the reflex hammer hits the tendon in the knee, a sensory nerve travels to the spinal cord, sends a message to another nerve, and then the message goes out to the muscle that makes the leg kick out. This particular reflex doesn't need a brain; it goes through the spinal cord. Other reflexes travel through the brain (primarily the brainstem) and must therefore be absent in someone who is a candidate to be declared brain dead. Spine-related reflexes can be present in those who are brain dead.

9. "A Definition of Irreversible Coma: Report of the Ad Hoc Committee of the Medical School to Examine the Definition of Brain Death," *JAMA* 205, no. 6 (1968): 337–40.

the irreversible cessation of all functions of the entire brain. The wording clearly states, "the entire brain, including the brainstem," following the recommendation of the President's Commission for the Study of Ethical Problems in Medicine.

The accompanying commentary states that "the 'functions of the entire brain' that are relevant to the diagnosis are those that are clinically ascertainable."[10] The authors also reduced the recommended waiting time to six hours if an EEG confirmed absence of activity, but recommended waiting twenty-four hours under certain circumstances. While the UDDA seems to take a whole-brain approach, the commentary, by using the term "clinically ascertainable," appears to limit testing to brainstem reflexes, ignoring untested cerebral function.

Formulations of the American Academy of Neurology and Others

The most recent somewhat official guidelines are those of the Quality Standards Subcommittee of the American Academy of Neurology.[11] The guidelines again focus on clinically observable function (brainstem function) and call for confirmatory tests only if "clinical examination cannot be fully performed due to patient factors." Furthermore, "there is insufficient evidence to determine the minimally acceptable observation period to ensure that neurologic functions have ceased irreversibly."

According to other recent opinions, death should be determined based only upon one examination,[12] and confirmatory tests are not routinely necessary: "A comprehensive clinical examination, when performed by skilled examiners, should have perfect diagnostic accuracy."[13]

---

10. "Guidelines for the Determination of Death: Report of the Medical Consultants on the Diagnosis of Death to the President's Commission for the Study of Ethical Problems in Medicine and Biomedical and Behavioral Research," *JAMA* 246, no. 19 (1981): 2184–86.

11. Eelco F. M. Wijdicks et al., "Evidence-Based Guideline Update: Determining Brain Death in Adults: Report of the Quality Standards Subcommittee of the American Academy of Neurology," *Neurology* 74, no. 23 (2010): 1911–18.

12. Dana Lustbader et al., "Second Brain Death Examination May Negatively Affect Organ Donation," *Neurology* 76, no. 2 (2011): 119–24.

13. Eelco F. M. Wijdicks, "The Case Against Confirmatory Tests for Determining Brain Death in Adults," *Neurology* 75, no. 1 (2010): 77–83.

Consensus

The current medical consensus is that a person is considered dead by neurological criteria (i.e., brain dead) when the observable functions of the brain have irreversibly ceased.[14]

While the legal criteria refer to cessation of function of the entire brain, the clinical determination has focused on observable function and therefore on the brainstem. The practical difference between the two approaches involves functions of the cerebrum that are not directly clinically observable, namely electrical function (EEG) and hypothalamic hormone secretion. These will be discussed in detail.

III. THE SCIENCE OF BRAIN DEATH

Anatomy and Pathophysiology

Brain cells require blood flow to survive. Blood brings fuel-glucose and oxygen to these cells. Blood also carries away waste products, particularly carbon dioxide. When blood flow decreases, the cells malfunction. If blood flow reaches a low enough level, or stops for a period of time, the cells die.

The brain sits inside the cranium, which is essentially a bony box with rigid sides. The volume of this box is constant and cannot expand (except in young children, when the skull bones have not yet fused together). Under normal conditions, the cranium contains the brain, blood vessels bringing blood to the brain arteries, blood vessels taking blood away from the brain veins, and cerebrospinal fluid (CSF). CSF is formed within fluid spaces in the brain (ventricles) and flows out and around it to be absorbed into the venous sinuses in the dura, which covers the brain. CSF occupies approximately 125 cc of space, and the body produces approximately four times that volume a day, or about 500 cc.

Under abnormal conditions, space inside the skull can be occupied by tumors, abscesses, or blood clots (hematomas). The brain reacts to damage by swelling (edema). The brain tissue takes up water, increasing the volume occupied by the tissue. Since the total volume of the skull must remain constant because of its rigid walls of bone, any swelling of

---

14. A vocal minority disagrees. For example, see "Correspondence," *Neurology* 76, no. 3 (2011): 307–9.

one intracranial component has to result in a concomitant decrease in volume of another part. If the swelling increases, or the space-occupying lesion enlarges, eventually the rest of the intracranial contents will no longer be able to compensate. Then the intracranial pressure (ICP), the pressure inside the skull, will begins to rise.

The heart pumps blood into the skull. The systemic pressure pushing the blood has a high (systolic), a low (diastolic), and an average (mean arterial pressure – MAP). The amount of force available to push blood into the skull (cerebral perfusion pressure – CPP) is the difference between the MAP and the ICP. As the ICP rises, blood flow will decrease unless the systemic blood pressure (MAP) also increases. Indeed, cerebral autoregulation will raise blood pressure as the ICP increases.

However, at some point, the ICP can rise and the MAP cannot, and blood flow to the brain diminishes. The brain requires a significant amount of blood flow to function, about 20% of the output of the heart. As this intracranial blood flow drops below a certain level, nerve cells stop functioning. With further diminution of flow, cells die, causing more edema. The increase in edema increases the ICP, which further reduces blood flow (CPP). As the brain swells, the path of the cerebrospinal fluid (CSF) is frequently blocked, leading to buildup of fluid in the ventricles (hydrocephalus), which adds to the increased pressure in the skull.[15]

This feedback mechanism continues until eventually, the intracranial pressure becomes equal to the mean arterial pressure, and blood flow to the brain essentially halts. The heart may keep pumping blood to the rest of the body, but no blood enters the cranium. Bereft of blood flow, brain cells die.

Cerebral Circulatory Arrest and Its Implications
The absence of blood flow to the brain (also termed cerebral circulatory arrest – CCA) has been documented by different studies.[16] The first

---

15. It is similar to a flowing river being blocked by a dam.
16. The finding of absent blood flow is dependent on the sensitivity of the test. Flow below its level of sensitivity won't be detected. Because flow depends on pressure, when the CPP reaches zero or below, flow is absent or extraordinarily minimal. Since persistent absent flow on these tests results in a cessation of function, it is clear that even if flow exists below the level of sensitivity, it is inadequate in amount and/or

study used arteriograms. In certain patients, the arteriograms showed non-filling of the brain arteries, with the dye in the arteries halting outside the cranium.

Another early study was a nuclear medicine scan. Here a radioactive tracer is injected into a vein, and the skull is monitored to visualize if the tracer appears in the brain. One drawback of this method was the lack of visualization of the entire brain. However, the tracer has been modified to solve this problem.[17]

Other studies that confirm CCA include CT angiograms, Transcranial Doppler (TCD) studies, and MRI angiograms.[18] Comparisons between tests have shown remarkable consistency.[19] The Transcranial Doppler studies have been validated in laboratory animals, where the absence of flow correlated with absent electrical activity.[20] A meta-analysis of TCD studies revealed that all but two patients with findings of CCA on a single exam were clinically brain dead (showing no sign of neurological function on exam). The two who did display some function quickly lost any measurable level thereof and became brain dead.[21]

---

quality (inadequate oxygen or glucose) and therefore is the functional equivalent of absent flow. Very sensitive laser Doppler studies have been performed and an attempt made to correlate capillary flow with TCD findings. These indicate that when the TCD shows absent blood flow, there may be minimal flow in the capillaries, but not enough to prevent the loss of brain function and electrical function in the brain cells. This will be discussed further in the context of defining circulation.

17. Lionel Zuckier and Johanna Kolano, "Radionuclide Studies in the Determination of Brain Death: Criteria, Concepts, and Controversies," *Seminars in Nuclear Medicine* 38, no. 4 (2008): 262–73 [268].

18. Akira Matsumura et al., "Magnetic Resonance Imaging of Brain Death," *Neurol Med Chir* (Tokyo) 36 (1996): 166–71.

19. John Poularas et al., "Comparison Between Transcranial Doppler Ultrasonography and Angiography in the Confirmation of Brain Death," *Transplant Proc.* 38, no. 5 (2006): 1213–17. See also Marina Munari et al., "Confirmatory Tests in the Diagnosis of Brain Death: Comparison Between SPECT and Contrast Angiography," *Critical Care Medicine* 33, no. 9 (2005): 2068–73.

20. Hidemasa Nagai, Kouzo Moritake, and Mikio Takaya, "Correlation Between Transcranial Doppler Ultrasonography and Regional Cerebral Blood Flow in Experimental Intracranial Hypertension," *Stroke* 28, no. 3 (1997): 603–607.

21. Louisa Monteiro et al., "Transcranial Doppler Ultrasonography to Confirm Brain Death: A Meta-analysis," *Intensive Care Medicine* 32, no. 12 (2006): 1937–44; the patients had persistent CCA in further studies. The situation is analogous to the

Without blood supply, the brain is metabolically dead; it won't receive or use oxygen, nor will it generate carbon dioxide, and its glucose supply will be depleted. Indeed, no oxygen was found in the brain tissue of brain dead patients.[22] Conversely, every patient whose brain-tissue oxygen level stayed at zero for more than half an hour became brain dead. The glucose level in this brain tissue also approached zero, far below that of patients who maintain function.[23]

A brain dead patient can be identified by measurements of the oxygen and carbon dioxide levels in the blood going to and from the brain. These measurements reveal that the brain is not using oxygen or producing carbon dioxide.[24] The cells of the body, including the brain, need to manufacture phosphorus in a particular form (ATP) in the utilization of energy. A small study using MRI scanning revealed that brain dead patients had no phosphorus in this form in their brains.[25]

---

determination of death by cardiac criteria. At the very moment the heart stops, the brain can still function, if only briefly. Indeed, in some situations (with or without CPR) the heart can restart. However, if time passes and circulation is not reestablished, brain non-function becomes permanent. Therefore, the brain may function minimally very early after CCA, before the full effects of the lack of blood flow become manifest. However, if CCA is not reversed, any lingering brain function is quickly and irrevocably lost.

22. Sylvain Palmer and Mary Kay Bader, "Brain Tissue Oxygenation in Brain Death," *Neurocritical Care* 2, no. 1 (2005): 17–22. None of the patients with oxygen levels above zero became brain dead. Jack Rose et al., "Continuous Monitoring of the Microcirculation in Neurocritical Care: An Update on Brain Tissue Oxygenation," *Current Opinion in Critical Care* 12 (2006): 97–102.
23. Alex B. Valadka et al., "Comparison of Brain Disuse Oxygen Tension to Microdialysis-Based Measures of Cerebral Ischemia in Fatally Head-Injured Humans," *Journal of Neurotrauma* 15, no. 7 (1998): 509–19. See also Mette K. Schulz et al., "Cerebral Microdialysis Monitoring: Determination of Normal and Ischemic Cerebral Metabolisms in Patients with Aneurismal Subarachnoid Hemorrhage," *Journal of Neurosurgery* 93, no. 5 (2000): 808–14; Nils Ståhl et al., "Intracerebral Microdialysis and Bedside Biochemical Analysis in Patients with Fatal Traumatic Brain Lesions," *Acta Anaesthesiologica Scandinavica* 45 (2001): 977–85.
24. Nino Stocchetti et al., "Oxygen and Carbon Dioxide in the Cerebral Circulation During Progression to Brain Death," *Anesthesiology* 103 (2005): 957–61.
25. Franz Aichner et al., "Magnetic Resonance: A Non-Invasive Approach to Metabolism, Circulation, and Morphology in Human Brain Death," *Annals of Neurology* 32, no. 4 (1992): 507–11.

Cells that are alive use energy and produce heat. Normally the brain is warmer than the rest of the body, partly because of blood flow and partly because the brain is very metabolically active. As stated, the brain receives approximately 20% of the blood flow from the heart. The brain of a brain-dead patient is significantly colder than a normal brain, indicating a lack of metabolic activity and blood flow.[26] Patients who are brain dead also use approximately 25% less energy (resting energy expenditure – REE) than would be predicted, again corresponding to the total cessation of metabolic activity in the brain.[27] In fact, the REE decrease correlates with worsening blood flow. As the blood flow (measured by TCD) decreases, the REE decreases, reaching a nadir when blood flow ceases.

In summary, victims of cerebral circulatory arrest can be clearly identified by their lack of oxygen, very low to no glucose, absence of oxygen uptake by the brain, absent carbon dioxide production by the brain, absent organic phosphorus compounds that are vital for energy production and utilization, significantly lower brain temperature, and a decrease in energy utilization by the body that is consistent with the total lack of energy utilization by the brain.

The brain is dead by every metabolic parameter measured. In fact, a search of the medical literature failed to identify a single paper supporting the presence of normal biochemical activity in the brain of a patient who fulfilled the criteria for brain death and/or whose study confirmed CCA.[28]

The Historical Role of Blood Flow Studies

The contemporary definition of brain death is composed of two conditions: cessation of brain function, and irreversibility. This definition emphasizes function. The lack of blood flow to the brain therefore

---

26. Christopher Rumana et al., "Brain Temperature Exceeds Systemic Temperature in Head-Injured Patients," *Neurologic Critical Care* 26, no. 3 (1998): 562–67.
27. Militsa Bitzani et al., "Resting Energy Expenditure in Brain Death," *Intensive Care Medicine* 25, no. 9 (1999): 970–76.
28. Other brain chemicals have been studied. In brain dead patients, pyruvate (a chemical critical for energy utilization) has been measured at 0 – compared to 151 – mmol/L in patients with no sign of ischemia. Lactate (a waste product) levels in brain dead patients are twice the norm. Similar abnormalities have been measured with glycerol and glutamate (see note 23 earlier in this essay).

contributes proof that the situation is irreversible, and provides a sound basis for finding a total and irreversible loss of brain function.

Some patients lose brain function but still have blood flow. The determination of brain death is based on the clinical exam; consequently, many patients have been declared brain dead either without a determination of cerebral blood flow or even with some blood flow present. Patients who fulfill the clinical criteria for brain death, even if blood flow persists, have never been shown to regain any function.[29] (Three exceptions were published in 2011 and will be discussed later.) The absence of blood flow is thus a supporting but perhaps not always necessary finding in the determination of brain death. While the vast majority of brain dead patients have CCA, sometimes massive brain damage occurs without total CCA.[30] Even in these cases, assuming the clinical criteria of absent function have been fulfilled, there has been no return of function.

---

29. "Change in neurologic examination has not occurred in adults when conducted properly." Eelco Wijdicks, "Clinical Diagnosis and Confirmatory Testing of Brain Death in Adults," in *Brain Death* (ed. Eelco F. M. Wijdicks; Philadelphia: Lippincott Williams and Wilkins, 2001), 86. Also: "To the best of my knowledge, there is no clinical or technological evidence contradicting the conclusion that a nondrugged, nonfunctioning brainstem represents an absolute – not a probable – indication that the entire brain shortly will die, usually within a day or so, but in rare cases, after a few weeks." Fred Plum, "Clinical Standards and Confirmatory Tests," in *The Definition of Death: Contemporary Controversies* (ed. Stuart J. Youngner, Robert M. Arnold, and Renie Schapiro; Baltimore: Johns Hopkins University Press, 1999), 38. Plum's statement restates the case for total and irreversible death of the brainstem. To clarify: The claim being made is, first, that someone whose brainstem is not functioning will never regain any function. Second, even *if* some neurons have *cellular* function (not something clinically measurable) in parts of the brain *outside the brainstem*, that function will inevitably soon cease. (It is important to distinguish between brainstem and whole brain, though many authors have confused the two.) After searching the literature on brain death, I haven't found any refutation of Wijdick's and Plum's statements.

30. Several reasons have been advanced to explain this finding. The common denominator is that there appears to be a range where blood flow is low enough to permanently and irrevocably end brain function but not low enough to be seen as absent in studies. For further discussion, see W. Mel. Flowers Jr. and Bharti R. Patel, "Persistence of Cerebral Blood Flow After Brain Death," *Southern Medical Journal* 93, no. 4 (2000): 364–70; and W. Mel. Flowers Jr. and Bharti R. Patel, "Radionuclide Angiography as a Confirmatory Test for Brain Death: A Review of 229 Studies in 219 Patients," *Southern Medical Journal* 90, no. 11 (1997): 1091–96.

Establishing the Absence of Neurological Function

The function of the brain can be defined by its output to nerves, either to the cranial nerves or to the spinal cord.[31] Therefore, to document the cessation of brain function, a complete examination of the cranial nerves is necessary. This examination includes documenting the absence of reflexes from the cranial nerves,[32] and the absence of movement (except for reflex movement) or response to stimulation below the neck. The control center for breathing lies in the brainstem, and an absence of breathing (apnea) is crucial.[33]

As stated, certain drugs and conditions can cause a temporary loss of function, and these need to be ruled out.[34] To ensure that the clinical findings are due to brain damage and not some other condition, brain imaging studies such as MRI or CT must reveal the presence of an intracranial disaster. These studies are necessary since one must determine that there has been brain damage that can cause irreversible loss of function; this determination serves as a sort of prerequisite of brain death evaluation. One cannot consider a patient dead based on neurological criteria without solid evidence that something serious enough has happened to his brain that death could be a reasonable possibility. If the scans look normal (or at least not too bad), one must look very hard for other reasons for the loss of function.

---

31. Cranial nerves exit directly from parts of the brain rather than from the spinal cord. They essentially relate to function above the neck, including olfaction, vision, eye and facial movement, facial sensation, hearing, balance, tongue and palate movements, and parasympathetic autonomic function in the face and body but *not* sympathetic function in the body. Sympathetic autonomic function below the neck is mediated by the thoracic spinal cord. The nerves entering and exiting the spinal cord control movement and sensation below the neck, including reflex movements, and sympathetic autonomic function in the body.
32. These reflexes require no volition on the patient's part. A reflex by definition is something beyond conscious control. Patients who are asleep or have only fainted still have these reflexes.
33. A number of protocols are available to confirm apnea. Most require a CO_2 greater than 60 mmHg.
34. The standard list includes hypothermia, hypotension, paralytic or sedative medications, metabolic derangements, as well as a few unusual neurological conditions.

IV. POTENTIAL DISCREPANCIES AND CONTRADICTIONS

The major flaw in many papers purporting to study brain death is inadequate clinical testing. If the detailed clinical tests are not done properly, especially the breathing (apnea) test, the results are meaningless, because the patient may have had some undetected function and should not have been labeled brain dead in the first place.

Because of this flaw, the medical literature is replete with studies showing "survival" from "brain death." However, when the literature is examined with an eye toward identifying patients who actually fulfill valid criteria, not a single patient has regained any function, and not a single adult patient has regained any sign of respiration.[35]

Regaining Function: Three Case Studies

In 2012, two papers documented a total of three patients who apparently regained function after adequate testing for cessation of neurological function.[36]

Case 1

The patient suffered from an abscess in the brain, which not only occupied space but caused swelling. The result of these two processes created so much pressure inside the head that the brain ceased to function. The patient was declared dead based on one examination. However, since there

---

35. I say adult patients since the criteria for children are a bit different. Children have pliable skulls and a higher capacity for regeneration, among other differences. The criteria for declaring brain death in children involve longer waiting periods, more testing, etc. See, for example, "Guidelines for the Determination of Brain Death in Infants and Children: An Update of the 1987 Task Force Recommendations," *Pediatrics* 128 (2011): 720, http://pediatrics.aappublications.org/content/128/3/e720.full.html. There are reports of infants who regained function after determinations of brain death, but the criteria varied and in many cases could have been inadequate. For a case report and review of incidents, see Ari R. Joffe et al., "A 10-Month-Old Infant with Reversible Findings of Brain Death," *Pediatric Neurology* 41, no. 5 (2009): 378–82.

36. Derek J. Roberts et al., "Should Ancillary Brain Blood Flow Analyses Play a Larger Role in the Neurological Determination of Death?" *Canadian Journal of Anesthesia* 57, no. 10 (2010): 927–35; Adam C. Webb, "Reversible Brain Death After Cardiopulmonary Arrest and Induced Hypothermia," *Critical Care Medicine* 39, no. 6 (2011): 1538–42.

was the possibility of his donating organs, the infection was treated with antibiotics, and he was given steroids (which decrease swelling) and kept on a ventilator. In fact, an MRI study two hours after the declaration showed blood flow in the brain, and twenty-six hours after that, he was found to have some breathing or at least triggering of the ventilator.[37] He had no other neurological function. A repeat MRI showed loss of blood flow, and five days later he was declared dead after cessation of cardiac function.

The infection and swelling were treatable causes of increased pressure in the head (treated with antibiotics and steroids), so it shouldn't be surprising that some function returned (if indeed it did) when the problem was treated. This case highlights the need to be sure there is no *treatable* and *potentially reversible* cause of the patient's poor neurological status. It is a case of erroneous determination of death, not of "recovery from death." The determination should not have been made in the presence of a treatable and potentially reversible cause of neurological dysfunction.

Case 2

The patient fell down stairs and when found by emergency personnel had no pulse (and therefore very low to absent blood pressure). After five minutes of CPR, heartbeat and blood pressure returned. An exam six hours later showed a lack of neurological function. A subsequent test showed blood flow, and five hours after that the patient began breathing.[38] Exams showed no other return of function.

If indeed respiration returned, this case highlights the problem with rushing to make a determination of death. One potential cause of the loss of function was lack of blood pressure and oxygen (hypotension and hypoxia), and, as noted in the 1981 guidelines, these pathologies require longer waiting periods than other causes, such as trauma.

Case 3

The patient suffered a cardiac arrest and had an extended resuscitation period (twenty minutes) combined with a deliberate lowering of body

---

37. Some question whether this was actual breathing triggered by the brainstem. See Eelco F. M. Wijdicks, "Correspondence," *Neurology* 76, no. 3 (2011): 309.
38. As in the previous note, some question whether actual breathing was triggered by brain function in this case as well.

temperature (hypothermia) in an attempt to preserve brain function. After his temperature was back to normal, and seventy-two hours after the arrest, he showed no neurological function on exam, and the same was true six hours later. Twenty-six hours after that, the patient exhibited a cough reflex, a corneal reflex, and some breathing. An EEG showed no activity, and approximately two days later neurological function was again lost. MRI and blood flow studies showed no sign of blood flow, and eventually support for the patient was terminated (the ventilator was removed), and death was declared based on cardiopulmonary criteria.

This report demonstrates the complexity of determining the irreversibility of loss of neurological function, and the hazards of ignoring possible confounding factors. A number of factors indicated the tenuousness of the determination of irreversibility, including mechanism of injury (hypoxia/hypotension) and the use of hypothermia, which can protect brain function. While straightforward cases may not require confirmation of irreversibility, cases such as these do.

Analysis
The criteria for brain death started with two exams, then the period between the exams gradually lessened, and now some advocate only one exam. This is not unexpected, as it's useful and desirable to identify the onset of death as early as possible. A similar process occurred regarding the determination of death by absence of circulation. In 1772, the duke of Mecklenburg mandated that after a determination of death, a body must be observed for three days prior to burial.[39] In fact, even now there is no standard waiting period for determining death by loss of circulation.

Several pathways lead to loss of observable neurological function. Some, such as trauma, result in increased ICP and frequently cause the cessation of cerebral blood flow discussed above. This cessation, coupled with the loss of observable function, provides at least a theoretical basis for the certainty that said loss is irreversible. Other causes of loss

---

39. For how this decree affected Jews and Jewish practice, see Samuel S. Kottek, "The Controversy Concerning Early Burial: A Historic Chapter in Halacha," *ASSIA – Jewish Medical Ethics* 1, no. 1 (May 1988): 31–33, http://www.medethics.org.il/articles/JME/JMEB2/JMEB2.36.asp.

of function, such as anoxia (lack of oxygen) or hypotension, can result in damage primarily to neurons, not to the glial cells (support cells).

Most swelling in the brain (and the resulting increased pressure) stems from damage to the glia. A process that selectively damages neurons can result in loss of function without a concomitant devastating rise in ICP. If enough neurons are damaged, the patient will exhibit no clinically observable function. However, if some neural damage is reversible, and circulation is preserved, function may return.

Until recently, this unusual set of circumstances hadn't been reported. While it doesn't refute the concept of death by neurological criteria, it does point toward the need for certainty with regard to irreversibility. Indicators of irreversibility include lack of cerebral blood flow (as measured by a variety of means), ICP greater than MAP, biochemical signs of no metabolic function, and signs of massive damage and high ICP on imaging studies. In cases where there is a treatable cause of brain damage (abscess), and where selective neuronal damage is likely (anoxia and hypotension), it is especially important to establish a basis for the irreversible nature of clinical findings.

In the cases reported here, there was the potential for selective damage to the neurons without significant damage to the glia, resulting in a potential preservation of cerebral circulation. Indeed, one patient had flow present on a nuclear flow study. In the case of the abscess, treating the infection with antibiotics could have reduced the pressure it was causing and decreased swelling, again creating a potentially reversible situation.

Although these cases could potentially impugn the concept and not just the practice of determining death by neurological criteria, an analysis of the facts reveals that under these circumstances death *should not* have been declared. However, *meticulous application* of proper criteria leads to an appropriate determination. Furthermore, determinations of death by circulation criteria are themselves not foolproof. In fact, thirty-eight cases of reported recovery after such determination have been documented.[40]

---

40. See Vedamurthy Adhiyaman, Sonja Adhiyaman, and Radha Sundaram, "The Lazarus Phenomenon," *Journal of the Royal Society of Medicine* 100 (2007): 552–55.

Other Reports of "Recovery"

The popular media occasionally report on patients who've "survived brain death." Unfortunately the medical records of these patients haven't been made public, so it's impossible to know if adequate testing/examination was done. While it's difficult to assign much persuasive power to an argument based on an absence of data, none of these cases has been reported in peer-reviewed scientific journals, suggesting that adequate testing was *not* done. One recent such case, that of Zach Dunlap, is described in Wikipedia as "clearly a case of negligent misdiagnosis."

Response to "Pain"

Some patients, after fulfilling the criteria for brain death, have responded to stimulation – such as neck bending or a skin incision – with increased pulse or blood pressure. If these responses were signs of brain function, they would negate the idea that the patient was brain dead. However, they are not pain-related or mediated by brain function. They are either spinal reflexes or responses of the sympathetic nervous system, and have nothing to do with brain function.[41]

Another concern is that the sympathetic nervous system can remain active in a brain dead patient.[42] Control over this sympathetic function is contained in the spinal cord, and this activity is independent of any brain control or input. Therefore, none of these responses signifies brain activity. As far as I know, there has been no documented case of response to pain in a patient who fulfilled adequate criteria for brain death.

---

41. Responses to pain should disappear with adequate pain medication (narcotics). However, the blood pressure response didn't change even when patients were given large amounts of fentanyl. The responses to neck movement did disappear when patients were given medications that block the responses of the sympathetic nervous system, which, as noted above, can remain active in the spinal cord. See R. D. Fitzgerald et al., "Intraoperative Catecholamine Release in Brain-Dead Organ Donors Is Not Suppressed by Administration of Fentanyl," *European Journal of Anesthesiology* 20, no. 12 (2003): 952–56. See also Yasuyuki Kuwagata et al., "Hemodynamic Response with Passive Neck Flexion in Brain Death," *Neurosurgery* 29, no. 2 (1991): 239–41.

42. The sympathetic nervous system is part of the autonomic nervous system. The latter controls functions that aren't consciously regulated, such as digestion, sweating, and blood pressure (to some extent).

Hypothalamic Function

Several reports discuss hormonal function in brain dead patients. The pituitary gland is partially an offshoot of the brain; it is partly regulated by the hypothalamus (a part of the brain). In some "brain dead" patients, the pituitary gland secretes hormones. This is not unexpected, as a portion of the gland is not part of the brain, and the gland receives blood supply from arteries that don't enter the cranium.

Some data imply that the hypothalamus continues to regulate certain hormonal activity in brain dead patients. Although quite plausible alternative explanations have been advanced,[43] it does appear that in some patients the hormonal control of the hypothalamus continues to at least some extent.

Partially preserved hypothalamic function in a brain dead patient doesn't impugn the concept of brain death. The anatomic explanation is quite simple. The internal carotid artery supplies blood flow to the brain.[44] When the perfusion pressure hits zero, the blood flow in the internal carotid stops at the edge of the cranium. The hypothalamus is the brain structure closest to the arrested flow.[45] Therefore, if a minimal

---

43. Tsuyoshi Sugimoto et al., "Morphological and Functional Alterations of the Hypothalamic-Pituitary System in Brain Death with Long-Term Bodily Living," *Acta Neurochirurgica* 115, nos. 1–2 (1992): 31–36. The paper proposes that hormones originate from extracranial tissues such as the pancreas. The authors conclude that the detection of hypothalamic hormones after a diagnosis of brain death doesn't contradict the concept of total brain death.

44. The internal carotid arteries are paired (one on each side). The vertebrobasilar system supplies blood to the posterior part of the brain and the brainstem. The carotid arteries travel through the skull and then enter the cranial vault through a foramen, or hole, in the bone. The pressure exerted on the artery by the swollen brain would therefore compress it against the wall of the cranium. The vertebral arteries, on the other hand, enter the cranial vault by crossing an edge of bone at the foramen magnum. This is the only opening of any size in the cranium, and with high ICP the swollen brain frequently herniates out. Therefore, the vertebral arteries would be compressed on either side of a bony ridge, making the cessation of flow in these arteries much more definitive than in the internal carotid artery. (The issue of unequal distribution of ICP in the different cranial compartments has no practical significance and is beyond the scope of this review.)

45. The first major branch of the carotid artery in the skull is the meningo-hypophyseal trunk, and blood flow from this artery can reach the pituitary and hypothalamus.

amount of flow enters, or if oscillating flow is present, a small amount of the hypothalamus theoretically could be perfused.[46] In addition, the hypothalamus/pituitary could receive flow from the external carotid artery via branches in the dura, which theoretically are more protected from pressure-induced compression. However, any structure farther away would receive no blood flow. In other words, minimal hypothalamic function or flow would absolutely not imply that other areas of the brain might receive blood flow.

The brain is usually thought to function by means of synaptic transmission. Nerves communicate with each other by releasing a neurotransmitter that crosses the synaptic junction.[47] The neurotransmitter causes the next nerve to change electrically, thus starting a new transmission in the new nerve. This is how the brain processes information and sends output through the cranial nerves and spinal cord.

However, the hypothalamic function discussed here operates not via synaptic transmission but via secretion of chemicals into the bloodstream. This secretion in response to a stimulus is not unique to the brain; it occurs in every endocrine organ, including the thyroid and adrenal glands. If such secretion is categorized as brain function, then the thyroid or adrenal glands could also be classified as such![48]

The brain functions controlled by the cranial nerves and spinal cord are easily identifiable by physical examination. The hormonal

---

46. Picture trying to inflate a balloon using air pressure that on average is the same as inside the balloon but is sometimes greater and sometimes less. When the pressure pushing air into the balloon is greater than the pressure inside it, some air will be forced in. However, when the forward pressure of air falls below the pressure inside the balloon, an equal amount of air will escape it. With each cycle, air moves in and out of the balloon, but there's no net increase in the amount of air inside. This appears as "to and fro" flow on Transcranial Doppler (TCD) studies. The blood moves forward in the arteries, then backward (whereas in normal circulation, blood flows through the arteries, through the tissue, and exits via the veins). A small amount of blood may reach the tissue closest to the entrance, but it flows backward again, and only the tissue near the entrance may benefit from this blood flow.

47. The synaptic junction is the very short distance between the end of one nerve and the beginning of another.

48. Similarly, the heart secretes atrial natruretic hormone, yet this is not usually considered when evaluating heart function.

activity of the hypothalamus is not. The presence or absence of hormonal function can be identified only by testing the urine for specific gravity or the blood for the presence or absence of hormones.[49]

Finally, the hypothalamus has no role whatsoever in controlling respiration, and the areas involved in hormone secretion play no significant part in establishing consciousness. While it has been claimed that stable body temperature signifies intact hypothalamic function, alternate explanations are available. This claim appears to be based solely on observations of body temperatures, without considering how even a normally functioning hypothalamus cut off from any neural output can influence body temperature.[50]

The initial report of the ad hoc committee in 1968 didn't mention hypothalamic activity, nor did the President's Commission in 1981. However, the 1995 report by the American Academy of Neurology specifically stated that the absence of diabetes insipidus[51] – which would imply a functioning pituitary gland – "should not be misinterpreted as evidence for brainstem function."[52]

---

49. Vasopressin is a hormone secreted by the posterior part of the pituitary gland under control from the hypothalamus. Lack of this hormone causes the kidneys to retain sodium in the blood, and therefore little to no sodium passes into the urine. As a result, the urine becomes dilute, approaching the chemical composition of water. The specific gravity (amount of ions) in this urine approaches 1.000, which is that of water. Over time, a lack of hormones affects urine quantity or metabolism. However, since these changes can have various etiologies, blood or urine testing is necessary to confirm the cause.

50. The topic of whether a person whose sole identifiable function is the endocrine output of the hypothalamus should be considered alive or dead is discussed later. The only theoretically possible output for the hypothalamic control of temperature outside of direct neural control would be via secretion of thyrotropin-releasing hormone to stimulate thyroid activity. In fact, most patients who've been identified as dead by neurological criteria have normal or low thyroid hormone levels, leading some transplant protocols to call for replacement of this hormone.

51. Diabetes insipidus occurs when the pituitary gland fails to secrete antidiuretic hormone, which controls the secretion of sodium into the urine.

52. See "Practice Parameters: Determining Brain Death in Adults (summary statement); Report of the Quality Standards Subcommittee of the American Academy of Neurology," *Neurology* 45, no. 5 (1995): 1012–14.

Living Cells

The first reports on the pathology of brain dead patients detailed findings labeled "respirator brain," because they were thought to be the result of being maintained by respirator. Later it was realized that the pathology stemmed from cessation of blood flow to the brain. The findings included diffuse swelling and cell damage in many areas of the brain. However, even these early reports didn't reveal – nor did they claim to – that every cell was damaged. More recent studies of patients who were removed from the respirator soon after the declaration of brain death show significant brain damage, but again, not every cell is abnormal on examination.[53]

Nonetheless, being classified as "not dead" by pathological staining methods doesn't necessarily imply that a cell is capable of functioning. In other words, although the neuropathology of brain dead patients doesn't conclusively reveal the death of every brain cell, or even the majority in some cases, these pathological findings don't imply the possibility of *return of function*. No patient declared brain dead by valid criteria has ever regained any neurological function, regardless of the final pathology.

Long-Term Survival and Somatic Function

The 1981 President's Commission stated that the reason a brain dead person was indeed dead was that the "integrative" function of the brain had ceased. Therefore, the ability to support the body of a brain dead patient over a long period was inconsistent with this definition.

This idea was challenged when an analysis of reports of "brain-dead" patients found that 175 had "survived" more than a week after being declared brain dead, including one who hung on for years.[54] However, a closer evaluation showed that in many of these accounts, the criteria for the declaration were either flawed or absent.[55] Furthermore, no

53. The staining may not adequately classify the cells as dead or alive. See Gustavo Saposnik and David Munoz, "Dissecting Brain Death: Time for a New Look," *Neurology* 70, no. 15 (2008): 1230–31.

54. D. Alan Shewmon, "Chronic 'Brain Death': Meta-Analysis and Conceptual Consequences," *Neurology* 51, vol. 6 (1998): 1538–45.

55. Eelco F. M. Wijdicks and James L. Bernat, "Chronic 'Brain Death': Meta-Analysis and Conceptual Consequences – Correspondence," *Neurology* 53, no. 6 (1999): 1369–70.

patients regained any neurological function. Recently, a study of over one thousand brain dead patients revealed that most couldn't be supported more than a week, though some were maintained for up to sixty days.[56]

The long-term survival of the body after brain death should not be surprising. The ventilator can supply lung function indefinitely. The heart, as long as it's supplied with sufficient oxygen, fuel, and nutrients, will beat on its own with its internal pacemaker, even if removed from the body. Hormones can be replaced. In most brain dead patients, blood pressure drops and cannot be normalized over the long term, even with medication. However, advances in blood pressure support, hormone replacement, and other measures allow for longer-term somatic support. In other words, long-term somatic function should not be considered a sign of a live brain, since one can theoretically keep a body going without a brain, as long as oxygenated blood is consistently pumped through it.

Variability in Criteria

A number of papers have demonstrated that the criteria used to determine brain death vary from institution to institution.[57] This is a valid issue in implementation but has no bearing on the legitimacy of determining death via neurological criteria. Additionally, much of the variability is insignificant.

For example, eleven temperature standards were utilized to determine if the patient's low temperature contributed to the lack of observable brain function. The threshold for what is considered a low temperature would be a concern if the standard did not rule out the contribution of hypothermia to lack of brain function. As long as all these standards mandate that the patient's temperature was close enough to normal (i.e., high enough) that low temperature (hypothermia) was not a factor, it doesn't matter if the threshold is set above that or not. For example, the lowest acceptable temperature according to any criteria is 90°F.

56. Besher At-Attar et al., "Implications of ICU Stay After Brain Death: The Saudi Experience," *Experimental and Clinical Transplantation* 4, no. 2 (2006): 498–502. The study contains some of the data, and the authors sent me the rest via e-mail.

57. David M. Greer et al., "Variability of Brain Death Determination Guidelines in Leading US Neurologic Institutions," *Neurology* 70, no. 4 (2008): 284–89.

The fact that others set the bar higher is a problem only if it is demonstrated that a body temperature of 90°F can mimic the clinical picture of brain death.

I would also note that criteria for declaration of death based on circulation are similarly vague or nonexistent. How long does one wait after the heart has stopped beating to declare a person dead?

Medications and Toxins
Another area of concern has been the possible confounding effects of medications or toxins. Certainly some medications, especially at high doses, can reduce neurological function. However, most can be tested for, and recommendations have been made to make sure medications and/or toxins do not confound the clinical pictures.[58]

Where it's unclear if medications or toxins are confounding the picture, a determination of death by neurological criteria may not be feasible, at least until further time has elapsed. This situation does not intrinsically refute the idea of using neurological criteria to determine death. Rather, these factors need to be taken into account when formulating and applying criteria.

Measuring Electrical Responses
Brain function can be divided into two types: clinically observable and electrically measurable. Observable function is exactly that, something that can be seen (movement, responses to pain, reflexes) or heard (speech).

Since neurons function by sending electrical impulses to each other, electrical activity can also be measured. This activity can be either spontaneous, such as measured by the EEG, or in response to a stimulus, such as measured by the Brainstem Auditory Evoked Response (BAER) test.

EEG
The initial criteria for brain death published in 1968 labeled EEG as a confirmatory test, but it should be clear that it confirms a state where

---

58. David M. Greer et al., "Pitfalls in the Diagnosis of Brain Death," *Neurocritical Care* 11, no. 2 (2009): 276–87.

not enough neurons are working together for the signal to be measured outside the skull. Unlike CCA, there are no concomitant biochemical changes or inherent implications for irreversibility. However, loss of EEG signals does indicate massive loss of electrical function.

In addition, in situations where imaging (CT or MRI) shows primary brainstem damage and is equivocal regarding the degree of cerebral hemisphere damage, the EEG is useful to show if a significant amount of activity is present. The damage to the brainstem will block any output of the hemispheres, and the EEG (or similar testing, such as functional MRI) may be the only test that shows possible cerebral hemisphere function. However, if the ARAS is destroyed, the EEG will be very slow and, as far as is known, any capacity for consciousness will be lost. Therefore, a flat EEG should be seen as a sign of very significant brain dysfunction, and EEG activity a sign of some cells functioning together enough that the signal is seen.

As noted, the criteria for brain death were designed to predict which patients would never regain clinically observable function. Consequently, a patient can fulfill brain death criteria and still show some activity on the EEG. However, as observed over twenty years ago, the vast majority of patients who fulfill criteria but retain EEG activity soon lose it.[59] Ultimately it is a philosophical question as to whether such activity is enough to classify one as a living human being. At this point, it seems to me that minimal EEG activity is not enough if the criteria for brain death have otherwise been fulfilled.

BAER

In the BAER[60] test, an audio signal is presented to the patient (basically, a tone in the ear), and the resulting responses are measured from the auditory nerve and then through the brainstem. In an intact brain, characteristic waves are seen, starting with the nerve, then in the brainstem, and then higher in the brain, ultimately reaching the cortex. In

---

59. Christopher Pallis, "The ABC of Brain Stem Death: The Arguments About the EEG," *BMJ* 286 (January 22, 1983): 284–87.
60. BAER, Brainstem Auditory Evoked Potentials (BAEP), and Auditory Brainstem Responses (ABR) all refer to the same type of testing.

patients with a destroyed brainstem, no propagation of waves is seen in the brain.[61] This test can confirm massive dysfunction of the brainstem.

Summary

As a matter of policy, the law in the United States identifies death as the irreversible cessation of neurological function.[62] The above discussion has demonstrated that the guidelines used in determining cessation of neurological function produce the necessary results, and that concerns regarding recovery of function are misplaced.

Documenting loss of cerebral blood flow not only adds to the certainty of irreversibility, but also provides a biological basis for the determination that the loss of function is permanent. However, the determination of death is predicated on loss of function, not of blood flow. Hence, if irreversible loss of function is determined through means other than lack of blood flow, these patients are still considered dead.

A permanently damaged non-functioning brain, even if it receives blood flow, fulfills the criteria for the determination of death. However, the presence of blood flow, or the absence of a study, means that the examiner needs to be quite convinced (based on other information) of the irreversibility of the situation. The lack of a specific biological basis

---

61. William D. Goldie et al., "Brainstem Auditory and Short-Latency Somatosensory Evoked Responses in Brain Death," *Neurology* 31, no. 3 (1981): 248–56. This study compared patients who fulfilled brain death criteria and patients with significant brainstem damage but still some observable function. Most of those who fulfilled the criteria for brain death exhibited either no response or just a localized one from the nerve. Two, however, showed some responses farther into the brainstem, but none farther up in the brain. None had normal responses. Of the patients who still had some neurological function (not brain dead), some also didn't respond, but most responded more than the brain dead patients. In other words, there was some overlap between the results in the brain dead and non-brain dead patients. Therefore, even absent responses don't predict brain death with complete accuracy, and someone brain dead can still respond slightly. Consequently, an absent response merely confirms significant brainstem damage. A significant response would be inconsistent with the fulfillment of brain death criteria.

62. For an interesting and relevant discussion of terminology, see Dan Egonsson, "Death and Irreversibility," *Reviews in the Neurosciences* 20 (2009): 275–81.

for the presumption of irreversibility also leaves the determination open to critique from a statistical point of view.[63]

The criteria established in 1968 have been shown to reliably identify patients who've irreversibly lost neurological function. In addition, patients who lack blood flow on testing will also exhibit

1. lack of energy utilization by the brain on a global basis;[64]
2. brain biochemical changes consistent with absent function.

The criteria do not require a flat EEG or absent hypothalamic function. Many patients who fulfill the criteria will also lack EEG activity or hypothalamic functions, but some will not. Nevertheless, these tests can be done, and in the majority of patients these functions can also be documented as absent. Similarly, as noted, the criteria do not require an absence of blood flow to the brain, but this too can be demonstrated in a large majority of patients. Whether the presence of EEG function or signs of hypothalamic function constitute life depends on exactly how life is defined.[65]

---

63. See D. Alan Shewmon, "The Probability of Inevitability: The Inherent Impossibility of Validating Criteria for Brain Death or 'Irreversibility' Through Clinical Studies," *Statistical Medicine* 6, no. 5 (1987): 535–53. Shewmon asks: "Faced with a specific situation, if a certain outcome is observed a certain number of times, what is the probability that the next time this situation occurs, that certain outcome will occur as well?" He answers that if the observations of previous outcomes are the only basis of a prediction, a huge number of observations are necessary to be certain regarding the outcome. The implication here is that the many reports of patients who have irreversibly lost neurological function don't provide adequate predictive value for irreversibility unless there is an underlying basis for thinking they have irreversibly lost function. Put another way, we know an apple will fall down from a tree and not up because we know the laws of gravity. If we were depending only on multiple observations of apples falling from trees, we'd have to observe a huge number to achieve certainty that the next apple would fall down.

64. It is impossible at this point to measure the energy usage of each and every cell and therefore impossible to state that no cell is using energy.

65. These are functions of the whole brain, and death definitions requiring cessation of function of the entire brain would therefore require cessation of these functions. While the UDDA as written requires the cessation of function of the entire brain, the notes accompanying this legislation specify *observable* function, which is usually taken

V. ESTABLISHING A DEFINITION OF LIFE AND DEATH

Several authors have quite cogently criticized the determination of death by neurological criteria on the basis that it lacks a conceptual foundation.[66] In other words, there has been a failure to address the question of why someone who has lost neurological function should be considered dead.

The Three-Tiered Model

Stuart Youngner has suggested a three-tiered approach to defining death:

> A concept or definition of what it means to die, operational criteria for determining that death has occurred, and specific medical tests showing whether or not the criteria have been fulfilled.[67]

In addition, he notes that proposed definitions of death lack a conceptual framework for determining what quality is so essential to a living entity that its loss constitutes death.

Combining these points (and concentrating on defining the death of a human being, rather than death in general), the approach to death needs to include three interrelated levels:

- Tier 1: Since human death is the irreversible loss of human life, it is necessary to identify as accurately as possible what quality is so essential to a living human being that its loss constitutes death.

---

to mean clinically observable function. Ultimately, the UDDA leaves the determination to practitioners, and the consensus of those in the United States has been that testing for hypothalamic function is unnecessary, and death can be declared even in the presence of evidence of some hypothalamic/pituitary endocrine function. I think that most in the United States would not declare a patient dead if the EEG showed significant activity, but low-level activity would not be considered inconsistent with a determination of death. See Madeleine M. Grigg et al., "Encephalographic Activity After Brain Death," *Archives of Neurology* 44 (1987): 948–54. The emphasis since 1968 has been on clinically observable function.

66. A prime example: Ari Joffe, "Are Recent Defenses of the Brain Death Concept Adequate?" *Bioethics* 24, no. 2 (2010): 47–53.

67. Stuart J. Youngner, "Defining Death: A Superficial and Fragile Consensus," *Archives of Neurology* 49 (1992): 570–72.

- Tier 2: Criteria to establish not only that whatever was identified in tier 1 has been lost, but that the loss is irreversible.
- Tier 3: Diagnostic tests to show that what has been identified in tier 2 has actually been fulfilled.

Circulation or Cardiac Criteria

Before examining critiques of defining death by neurological criteria (NC), it would be useful to apply Youngner's system to definitions of death based on circulation and/or cardiac criteria (CC). CC could possibly be identified as a tier 1 definition. In other words, circulation is the essential feature of human life, so anything that exhibits circulation, without restriction, is human life. Taken to its logical endpoint, this definition means that an isolated kidney attached to a pump – or even a transplanted kidney – retains the rights and privileges of a human being. One could potentially divide a human body, attach each part to a pumping machine, and wind up with multiple independent entities, each fulfilling the criteria for human life.

Keep in mind that "a determination of death is a legal determination that a collection of living cells is no longer entitled to the rights granted to human beings, rather than a scientific or medical determination that all biologic life has ended."[68] If all body parts with circulation are considered human life, they need to be treated as such, with all the absurd consequences.

Alternatively, CC could be considered a tier 2 definition. In other words, the essence of human life is not identified, but loss of circulation is enough to establish that this quality has been irreversibly lost.

In premodern medicine, two related assumptions could be made:

1. All bodily functions and tissues would cease to function very soon after circulation was lost.
2. Circulation could not be restored once the heart had irreversibly ceased to function.

With these assumptions, the CC was a reasonable tier 2 criterion. However, in modern medicine these assumptions are no longer accurate,

---

68. Michael J. Broyde, "Correspondence," *NEJM* 345, no. 8 (2001): 616–18.

so defining death based on circulation or heartbeat is no longer reasonable.

Establishing a tier 1 definition was unnecessary in the premodern world, because the entire body ceased to function essentially simultaneously. No matter which part of the body or which function was the essence of human life, they all ceased to exist at approximately the same time. In the modern era, organs fail at different times, they can be preserved with circulation or transplanted, and the assumption of total body interdependence is false. Today, advocates of CC must identify a tier 1 definition, just as advocates of NC must do so.

Since, as demonstrated, circulation alone cannot be a tier 1 definition, one option for CC advocates is to combine the circulatory and neurological definitions. The definition of human life would then be the presence of circulation supplying the human brain.

However, even this definition fails in the modern world, because circulation is not irreversible when the heart stops. Even if the heart cannot be restarted, chest compressions (CPR) provide circulation, as can artificial pumps, transplants, and artificial hearts. Circulation is irreversibly lost only when the arteries and veins have deteriorated to the point where fluid can no longer flow in them.

Advocates of CC need to revise the practical guidelines (tier 3) used in determining death by cessation of circulation. It is no longer enough to wait ten, twenty, or even thirty minutes after circulation has stopped to declare death. Death, as determined by loss of circulation, can be declared only days to weeks after the heart stopped beating, because circulation can be restarted at any time prior to decomposition of the arteries.

Another problem for CC is posed by patients whose hearts are deliberately stopped during surgery. For some complex brain and heart surgeries, respiration and circulation can be halted for up to seventy-two minutes.[69] When the surgery is complete, the heart is restarted. If cessation of circulation and respiration are the tier 2 criteria for death,

---

69. Francisco A. Ponce, "Cardiac Standstill for Cerebral Aneurysms in 103 Patients: An Update on the Experience at the Barrow Neurological Institute," *Journal of Neurosurgery* 114, no. 3 (2011): 877–84.

CC advocates must explain why some are declared dead after ten or thirty minutes without circulation, but others are not so declared even after more than seventy minutes without it.

This discussion should make it totally clear that cessation of circulation has always substituted for a less identifiable concept of death. One option has been to claim that life cannot be identified by just one characteristic.[70] For example, Potts and Byrne have stated:

> A person should not be declared dead unless the circulatory, respiratory, and nervous systems (the three most important vital systems in the body) have been destroyed.[71]

This approach, while recognizing the importance of neurological function, would still recognize a perfused kidney as human life. Compound definitions like this serve to enlarge the pool of what is considered human life. Not only is anything with neurological function considered life, but so is anything with cardiac or respiratory function. However, because any tissue exhibiting cardiac or respiratory function is still considered life, the problems listed above persist.

Another option is to identify human life with "integrated function." This approach is probably best expressed by Dr. D. Alan Shewmon:

> A probably valid criterion close to the moment of death might be something like "cessation of circulation of blood for a sufficient time (depending on body temperature) to produce irreversible damage to a critical number of organs and tissues throughout the body, so that an irrevocable process of disintegration has begun".... I do not believe that the critical number of organs and

---

70. In philosophical parlance, the idea that life can be reduced to one characteristic is "essentialist," and those who feel otherwise are "non-essentialists." For a discussion of this second approach, see Winston Chiong, "Brain Death Without Definitions," *Hastings Center Report* 35, no. 6 (2005): 20–30.
71. Michael Potts, Paul A. Byrne, and Richard G. Nilges, *Beyond Brain Death: The Case Against Brain-Based Criteria for Human Death* (Dordrecht, the Netherlands: Kluwer, 2001), 2–3.

tissues can be universally specified, as it will no doubt vary from case to case; surely the brain is included, but not *only* the brain.[72]

One obvious problem with this formulation is its failure to specify which organs are included. Another problem, as Dr. Shewmon himself acknowledges, is that this formulation allows for the creation of two people from one. Regarding the thought experiment presented at the beginning of this paper, Dr. Shewmon would classify both the functioning head and the body as human beings (he is unsure about the status of the soul in the headless body, and discusses this at some length). A third problem, which Dr. Shewmon doesn't address, is that of multiple organ transplants. If someone receives a heart, lung, kidney, and liver transplant from a single donor, these organs are all producing "integrated function." Why would the donor not be considered alive, since his organs are fulfilling the criteria for life-integrated function?

The linkage of human life solely with neurological function is the only definition that avoids these logical pitfalls. I would suggest that all along there has been an unrecognized entry criterion in the determination of death. In the past, no one with identifiable neurological function was even a candidate to be considered dead. In other words, someone with neurological function was not tested for circulation or respiration, because there was an assumption that this function was the equivalent of life. Similarly, cardiac or respiratory functions were also observable functions and therefore signs of life. The irreversible loss of neurological, cardiac, and respiratory function therefore signified death.

In the modern era, there is recognition of a human being's primary function as opposed to supporting functions. Kidneys perform a supporting function. Replacing a kidney with a machine doesn't mean the person has died. Similarly, the liver, lungs, heart, digestive system, and other organs all perform supporting functions. The primary function of the human being, his essence, is based on neurological function.

---

72. D. Alan Shewmon, "Mental Disconnect: 'Physiological Decapitation' as a Heuristic for Understanding 'Brain Death,'" *Working Group on the Signs of Death 11–12 September 2006* (ed. H. E. Msgr. Marcelo Sanchez Sorondo; Vatican City: Pontifica Academia Scientiarum, 2007), 292–333.

Neurological Criteria

Establishing a Tier 1 Definition

The 1968 Harvard criteria included this statement:

> An organ, brain or other, that no longer functions and has no possibility of functioning again is for all practical purposes dead.

In other words, while it may not be possible to know exactly what about the brain contains the essence of human life, they maintained that when the brain irreversibly ceased to function, it could be assumed that that essence was gone and that the person could be considered dead.

In 1981 the President's Commission established that the essence of life was "body integration," and that loss of integration was the reason someone who fulfilled NC was dead. More recently, the President's Council on Bioethics declared that the work of the organism, expressed in its commerce with the surrounding world, depends on three fundamental capacities:

1. openness to the world, that is, receptivity to stimuli and signals from the surrounding environment;
2. the ability to act upon the world to obtain selectively what it needs;
3. the basic felt need that drives the organism to act as it must, to obtain what it needs and what its openness reveals to be available.[73]

Unfortunately, these definitions fail to resolve the critiques mentioned previously, and to provide a solid basis for distinguishing between life and death. Indeed, NC advocates have generally failed to adequately answer the question of why one who irreversibly lost neurological function should be considered dead. I will try to offer my own responses here.

First of all, both the NC and CC approaches lack a tier 1 definition, only this lack isn't commonly appreciated regarding CC, because the obsolete medical assumptions discussed above are still being made.

---

73. The full report is available here: http://bioethics.georgetown.edu/pcbe/reports/death/index.html.

My second response requires some nuance. It is important to differentiate between "life" and "human life." While "life" can be defined as biological, electrical, or cellular activity, "human life" is more complex, since most people don't equate it with isolated function in a part of the body (for example, an isolated kidney).

Those who follow Jewish, Muslim, or Christian tradition might invoke the concept of the soul as the presence that defines life. Others would invoke an idea of self-awareness, or consciousness.[74] However, none of these ideas can be measured objectively. Indeed, there still is a significant mystery underlying how a human being can be a sentient, self-aware creature, and a consensus position on this question is unlikely to be formed in the near future. Even if there were agreement on the fundamental concept of human life, there is no way to specifically measure it. Therefore, ambiguity is unavoidable in both the concept of life and its translation into criteria for determining if life is present or not. Consequently, the time of death is the moment when there is certainty that death has occurred.

Despite the disagreement on the fundamental concept of life, and the current impossibility of measuring the presence or absence of that fundamental essence, it is possible to limit what needs to be present for a person to be considered alive. Under certain circumstances, society has accepted a determination of whether a person is alive or dead, and a casuistic approach can be used to identify the underlying principles applied in each situation, consciously or not.

---

74. See Calixto Machado, "Describing Life to Define Death: A Cuban Perspective," MEDICC *Review* 12, no. 4 (2010): 40; for another justification of defining life neurologically, see Patrick Lee and German Grisez, "Total Brain Death: A Reply to Alan Shewmon," *Bioethics* 26, no. 5 (2012): 275–84. Drs. Lee and Grisez state:

[T]he loss of the radical capacity for sentience (the capacity to sense or to develop the capacity to sense) involves a substantial change, the passing away of the human organism. In human beings total brain death involves the complete loss of the radical capacity for sentience, and so in human beings total brain death is death.

While this is a rationale for equating life with neurological function, the authors note that it is not an endorsement of current criteria for brain death. In a similar vein, the article lacks specific criteria for the determination of the presence or absence of "the radical capacity for sentience."

Case 1 – Conjoined Twins

When a child is born, one life is considered to have come into existence. Under specific circumstances, the child is considered two lives, or twins. If circulation and/or respiration are indeed the determining factor in distinguishing between life and death, then a child with an extra heart, lung, or perhaps even tissue should be considered twins.

Nevertheless, as should be obvious to all, only when the child has an extra head do we claim twins have been born. Furthermore, independent neurological function in each brain is presumably necessary for the possibility of two legal lives. One extreme case is dicephalus, where two heads are attached to one body.[75] Even if no other duplications are present, the existence of two functioning brains suffices for two lives to be present. In this circumstance, a functioning brain is the difference between one life and two.[76]

Case 2 – Tissue Removal and Transfer

A similar conclusion can be drawn from the accepted results of tissue removal or transfer. An anatomically intact, normally functioning human being is obviously considered alive. Essentially, every organ and limb except the brain can be removed, and the person will still be deemed alive. In other words, a person is not considered dead if he has lost a limb. In addition, vital organs such as kidneys, livers, and hearts have been removed from a person and replaced with machines or donor organs without the person being considered dead. Therefore, the brain alone is the critical factor in determining life and death.

While circulation is necessary for survival, it is not the determining factor in the identity of a person. A pump can be disconnected from one person and attached to another with no transfer of identity. In fact,

---

75. Frequently, there is some duplication in the body as well, but that duplication by itself is not enough to warrant the label of twins.

76. A prime example of dicephalus is the case of Brittany and Ashley Hensel. While there have been reports of dicephalus twins whose parents gave them only one name, this decision was based on Eastern culture/religion and highlights the subjective nature of defining life/death. There has been one reported case in the literature of a person born with two hearts, and the person obviously was considered only one person.

when hearts are transplanted, the recipient maintains his own identity, rather than assuming that of the donor. In recent years, hearts have been transplanted into patients without removing the native heart. Nonetheless, to my knowledge there has been no call to identify a person with two hearts as two people.

Analysis
Clearly, the brain somehow constitutes the quality that is so essential to a living entity that its loss constitutes death. However, this doesn't mean that the presence of a single neuron (brain cell) implies human life.

When a brain biopsy is done, neurons are removed and can continue to function, at least for a time, in a culture medium. If the definition of human life were the presence of an intact human neuron, those neurons in the Petri dish would need to be protected and given "human rights." Furthermore, research has shown that human neurons can be cultured from brains even more than eight hours after a declaration of death.[77] To my knowledge, there has been no consequent outcry to identify the time of death as no less than eight hours after the irreversible cessation of circulation. It would appear that isolated neurons cannot be labeled human life.

Establishing the Minimum Brain Function That Qualifies as Life

Beyond the Casuistic Approach
From the above analysis, the usefulness of the casuistic approach should be clear. It allows for the determination that human life is present when clinically identifiable function is present, but not when only isolated cellular neuronal activity is present.

Nevertheless, this approach has its limits, and it's difficult to move further with only the casuistic model. A conceptual approach, combined with what's known regarding neural functions, as well as keeping in mind the limited testing options, may provide an adequate conclusion.

---

77. Ronald W. H. Verwer et al., "Cells in Human Postmortem Brain Tissue Slices Remain Alive for Several Weeks in Culture," *The FASEB Journal* 16 (2002): 54–60.

Determining Consciousness

Science cannot test for the presence of a soul. However, there are some theoretical neural bases for consciousness.[78] Consciousness requires an intact ARAS and a functioning thalamus, and may be related to EEG activity at low amplitude in the gamma band at 40 Hz. The ARAS can be considered the on/off switch. It may be possible to directly stimulate the thalamus to initiate consciousness,[79] but loss of thalamus function implies loss of any hope of consciousness. Therefore, a patient with irreversible loss of brainstem and thalamic function coupled with an absence of 40 Hz EEG activity, as best as can be determined, has lost the capacity for consciousness.

From a practical point of view, the demarcation line between life and death has to be drawn somewhere. Science is limited by the tests that are available. There is no way to scientifically disprove the claim that secretion of hormones by the pituitary under hypothalamic control is the essence of human life. However, the hypothalamus is not considered part of the essential neuroanatomy for consciousness, and, as noted, other areas of the body secrete chemicals under a variety of controls. Similarly, for any test it is necessary to view the results, positive and negative, and decide if they in any way assist in determining whether the essential aspect of human life is present or not.

Ultimately the tier 1 definition cannot be isolated with great precision, and in fact a consensus on what exactly it constitutes may be impossible to achieve. Yet there is a consensus that the essence of human life depends on the brain,[80] and that it constitutes more than just isolated cellular function.

78. See, for example, Bianca Lee Negrao, "Neural Correlates of Consciousness," *African Journal of Psychiatry* (2009): 265–69; Adam Z. J. Zeman, "What Do We Mean by 'Conscious' and 'Aware'?" *Neuropsychological Rehabilitation* 16, no. 4 (2006): 356–76; Gerald Leisman et al., "Networks of Conscious Experience: Computational Neuroscience in Understanding Life, Death, and Consciousness," *Reviews in the Neurosciences* 20 (2009): 151–76; and Steven Laureys et al., "Self-Consciousness in Non-Communicative Patients," *Consciousness and Cognition* 16 (2007): 722–41.
79. Calixto Machado, "Consciousness as a Definition of Death: Its Appeal and Complexity," *Clinical Electroencephalography* 30, no. 4 (1999): 156–64.
80. I have avoided the philosophical discussion regarding the nature of the person's relationship to the brain, and focused on the determination of a practical definition of life and death.

A reasonable – but not automatic – tier 2 criterion is therefore that when all clinically observable neurological functions are irreversibly absent, coupled with imaging findings of a massive intracranial disaster, whatever constitutes the tier 2 definition is absent as well. Those who want to use consciousness as tier 1 may want to add absence of specific EEG activity and imaging signs of thalamic damage. This approach is somewhere between the brainstem and whole-brain definitions. The presence of some cerebral functions (secretion of hormones by the hypothalamus) would not be inconsistent with the determination of death, but a normal EEG would be.

The tier 3 criteria essentially comprise the criteria that have been used in some form since 1968.

Conclusion
The only definition of death that's consistent with current medical achievements is based on the irreversible cessation of neurological function. It's impossible to identify exactly what about neurological function enables a collection of tissue to be considered a human being. The current criteria (with possible modifications) are a reasonable approach and avoid the logical problems inherent in defining death by cardiac or respiratory parameters. To paraphrase Winston Churchill: The definition of death based on neurological criteria is the worst definition of death, except for all those others that have been tried from time to time.

VI. HALAKHIC DEFINITIONS

What is the definition of death according to halakha? For the Jew who follows Torah and mitzvot, this question is of overarching importance. Applying Youngner's approach, halakha can supply its own version of the three-tiered model:

1. a philosophical/metaphysical conception of death (which has no practical application, since it cannot be measured);
2. a more practical description of death, based on an analysis of halakhic material;
3. practical criteria, designed so that whoever fulfills them matches the description of death in tier 2.

Many would identify the departure of the soul as the conception of death.[81]

Death by Neurological Criteria

Several descriptions of death appear in the halakhic literature. Three in particular accord with the neurological determination of death.[82]

A. The Criteria of the Chief Rabbinate of Israel
The criteria for the determination of death published by the Chief Rabbinate of Israel in 1986 state:

> The halakha holds that death occurs with cessation of respiration. (See also IM YD 3:132.) Therefore one must confirm that respiration has ceased completely and irreversibly. This can be established by confirmation of destruction of the entire brain, including the brainstem, which is the pivotal activator of independent respiration in humans.[83]

It appears that the tier 2 definition is cessation of respiration. However, the Chief Rabbinate adds an intermediate criterion – the destruction of the entire brain, including the brainstem – and then describes tier 3 criteria, which include five components:

---

81. The first to address this issue in modern times and establish the brain as the seat of the soul may have been Rabbi Azriel Rosenfeld. See Azriel Rosenfeld, "The Heart, the Head, and the Halakhah," *New York State Journal of Medicine* (1970): 2615–19.

82. The category of "neurological determination of death" includes those halakhic approaches that define death as the irreversible cessation of respiration. Someone who is considered dead based on irreversible absence of neurological function will also be dead based on irreversible cessation of respiration. Furthermore, the criteria of irreversible cessation of respiration are usually understood in the context of brainstem dysfunction and loss of consciousness. Opponents of brain death frequently cite opinions that define death as the cessation of respiration. While this perhaps makes sense philosophically, on a practical level it is an admission that those classified as brain dead are in fact halakhically dead – they have suffered irreversible cessation of respiration.

83. See http://www.hods.org/pdf/Chief%20Rabbinate%20English%20and%20 Hebrew%20Side%20by%20Side.pdf

1. knowledge of the cause of the injury;
2. complete cessation of natural breathing;
3. detailed clinical proof that the brainstem is destroyed;
4. objective proof of brainstem destruction through scientific tests such as the BAER;
5. proof that complete cessation of breathing and brainstem inactivity have continued for twelve hours while the patient is cared for properly.

Patients who fulfill these criteria essentially fulfill the Harvard criteria (with the addition of the BAER) and provide the same certainty that function will not return. However, this set of criteria focuses on the cessation of brainstem function, ignoring the possibility of hypothalamic activity or minimal activity on EEG. These criteria are scientifically valid and, in fact, when applied will result in identifying patients who have irreversibly lost respiratory function (tier 2).

However, without an EEG and testing for hypothalamic function, the intermediate criterion – destruction of the whole brain – may not be fulfilled. The statement regarding this destruction would seem incongruent with the objective of establishing irreversible cessation of respiration. Moreover, it certainly is clear now, if not then, that irreversible cessation of respiration can and does occur despite minimal EEG activity and some hypothalamic hormone secretion.

B. Physiological Decapitation
The concept that the cessation of neurological function can be equated with physiological decapitation is mentioned by, among others, Rabbi Dr. Moshe Tendler and Dr. Fred Rosner.[84] They describe death as "the absence of spontaneous respiration in a patient with no bodily function." However, they also state:

> If one can medically establish that there is total cessation of all brain function, including the brainstem, the patient is as if

---

84. Fred Rosner and Moshe David Tendler, "Definition of Death in Judaism," *Journal of Halacha and Contemporary Society* 17 (1989): 14–31.

"physiologically decapitated." There are a number of objective tests that can evaluate the viability of the brainstem. Brainstem death may be the preferable definition of death in Judaism since it is irreversible.

Several possible tier 2 definitions are implicit here:

1. irreversible cessation of respiration;
2. total cessation of all brain function including the brainstem;
3. brainstem death;
4. physiological decapitation.

In the above description, there appears to be some conflation of the concepts of whole-brain death and brainstem death.[85] As noted

---

85. Although Rabbi Tendler bases much of his work on his father-in-law's position, opponents of brain death frequently claim that Rabbi Moshe Feinstein in fact opposed it, or that his opinion is unclear. This argument is beyond the scope of this paper; however, Rabbi Feinstein may not have defined life and death based on respiration. For a superb analysis of Rabbi Feinstein's responsa on this topic, see an article by Daniel Reifman on the RCA's *Text and Texture* blog, http://text.rcarabbis.org/the-brain-death-debate-a-methodological-analysis-part-3b%E2%80%94rabbi-moshe-feinstein-by-daniel-reifman, a version of which appears in this volume. Reifman concludes:

> The position articulated in Rabbi Feinstein's two main *teshuvot* on this issue is that we determine death at [the] point where the body as a composite organism is permanently incapable of supporting spontaneous respiration.

Even Rabbi J. David Bleich, an outspoken and vigorous critic of brain death, wrote:

> Rabbi Feinstein is firm in his opinion that the irreversible cessation of spontaneous respiration is halakhically both a necessary and a sufficient condition of death. (J. David Bleich, "Survey of Recent Halakhic Periodical Literature: Time of Death Legislation," *Tradition* 16, no. 4 [summer 1977]: 133)

While Rabbi Bleich argues that Rabbi Feinstein didn't support brain death, there is no question that, according to Rabbi Feinstein (as reported by Bleich himself during Rabbi Feinstein's own lifetime), one who has fulfilled neurological criteria for death is also considered dead. Rabbi Feinstein may have considered the person dead due to irreversible cessation of respiration, not irreversible brain damage, but the practical result is the same.

in discussing the first halakhic model, the major practical differences between brainstem death and whole-brain death are the presence of EEG function and the secretion function of the hypothalamus. If the tier 2 definition is the absence of spontaneous respiration, then patients who fulfill the Harvard criteria and the Chief Rabbinate's criteria will also fulfill these criteria. In fact, the authors specifically state a tier 3 definition: that a patient who meets the Harvard criteria is dead.

Another option is to derive tier 3 criteria from the concept of physiological decapitation and determine in what way the patient needs to resemble someone who has been decapitated. One obvious indicator is blood flow.[86] In truth, even if testing reveals no flow, there can be

---

On a similar note, many opponents of brain death cite responsa of Rabbi Feinstein describing both heart donors and recipients of heart transplants as victims of murder. Yet these responses were written when the survival of transplant patients was dismal. Rabbi Feinstein's views were clarified by Dr. Fred Rosner:

> Rabbi Moses Feinstein…considers this [i.e., heart transplantation] to involve a double murder. However, a personal interview with Rabbi Feinstein by this writer as well as careful reading of his lengthy unpublished responsum on this subject discloses the following clarification of his position. If the donor is absolutely and positively dead by all medical and Jewish legal criteria, then no murder of the donor would be involved and the removal of his heart or other organ to save another human life would be permitted…. [W]hen medical science will have progressed to the point where cardiac transplantation becomes an accepted therapeutic procedure with reasonably good chances for success, then the recipient would no longer be considered murdered. (Fred Rosner, "Organ Transplantation and Jewish Law," in *Jewish Youth Monthly: A Science and Torah Reader* [ed. Yaakov Kornreich; Union of Orthodox Jewish Congregations of America, June 1970])

Clearly, Rabbi Feinstein intended to deter transplantation attempts, not to define death.

86. The question becomes: What exactly is the halakhic meaning of circulation? In other words, when a CC advocate states that a person is alive because there is circulation in the body, what exactly is meant? Does bodily circulation of water constitute the presence of life? If blood flow is infinitesimal (perhaps a pump is being used rather than a heart made of tissue), is the person still alive? Is there a minimum pressure, an amount of oxygen or glucose, that must be present in the circulation in order for it to be considered present according to halakha? See the extensive discussion of this topic here: http://text.rcarabbis.org/problems-with-defining-death-as-the-irreversible-cessation-of-circulation-what-would-we-measure-and-why-by-noam-stadlan-md/.

some minimal flow that's below the sensitivity of the study. However, this minimum, if present, cannot sustain brain function.[87] This blood flow can be termed inadequate flow, i.e., incapable of sustaining the function of the tissue to which it flows. As noted, tissue requires oxygen and glucose. If the blood flow is not enough to supply oxygen and glucose, the tissue ceases to function.

Thus, while "adequate flow" seems to be a new concept in the discussion of blood flow to the brain, in reality it has been an unstated assumption all along whenever circulation has been used to determine life and death. Essentially the word "circulation" has been assumed to mean *adequate* circulation. Otherwise, a body being pumped with water would be considered a live human being.

Hence, circulation that is not adequate to support the function of the target tissue may not halakhically be considered circulation. Then the patient who fulfills the criteria and has no flow on studies could be considered dead based on the blood flow aspect of physiological decapitation.

The other approach to physiological decapitation is to derive tier 3 criteria not from actual blood flow, but from the outcome. Decapitation results in the cessation of neurological function. The group of patients described above, if they have no hypothalamic function on testing and a flat EEG, have no observable or measurable neurological function.[88] The lack of function then would be the equivalent of decapitation, and the person could be considered dead. The next step would be to decide whether the EEG or hypothalamic testing was actually necessary. That decision would hinge on whether halakha recognizes any of those findings as signs of life.

---

87. See "Anatomy and Pathophysiology" in "Part 3 – The Science of Brain Death," earlier in this essay.

88. "Measureable" here means by methods used outside the skull. Obviously it is possible to insert probes into the brain and try to determine if any cell is functioning. Since there are billions of cells in the brain, this would be quite an endeavor. Ultimately, it is necessary to decide if a single cell or a small group of cells in the brain deserve the label of human life.

C. Accepting the Judgment of Physicians

The third halakhic approach that's consistent with the neurological determination of death is stated by Rabbi Nachum Rabinovitch:

> Maimonides explains that the organism is no longer considered to be alive "when the power of locomotion that is spread throughout the limbs does not originate in one center, but is independently spread throughout the body." It follows that if the restoration of central control is feasible the commandment to save life applies. Obviously, then, the definition of death depends upon the availability of more sophisticated techniques of resuscitation. Here again, the applicability of such methods and the consequent decision as to the onset of death is determined according to the judgment of the physicians.[89]

Rabbi Asher Bush also hints at this approach in his paper discussing the definition of death:

> Rabbi [Mordechai] Eliyahu acknowledges that the permission to violate Shabbos to save a patient even for cases not mentioned in rabbinic sources should not be taken as a proof of the authority halakha grants expert doctors, given that Rambam started by writing, "Shabbos is suspended when it comes to endangered lives (דחויה היא שבת אצל סכנת נפשות)," so even a reasonable doubt would provide sufficient justification to permit violation of Shabbos. However, he does find the case of not executing the killer of a טריפה more compelling in the deference to be shown to medical authorities.
>
> Following this same line of thinking that the Torah has given this authority to doctors, [Rabbi Eliyahu] comments that we should view the patient who has been revived through CPR as one who never died and not as one who died and was revived.

---

89. Nachum L. Rabinovitch, "What Is the Halakhah for Organ Transplants?" *Tradition* 9, no. 4 (spring 1968): 20–27.

This, he says, is because the doctors have told us that it is so. And following this logic, he writes, it is only because doctors say this patient can be revived that he is viewed as alive, but if they say he cannot be revived, as in a case of "brain death," in such a case he is to be regarded as dead.[90]

In other words, the halakha, when dealing with issues of human life and death, takes into account the opinions of the medical authorities. Ostensibly, according to this opinion, death by neurological criteria would be accepted as halakhic death due to its acceptance by the medical authorities.

Death Defined by Cessation of Circulation

Many published halakhic positions continue to define death by cessation of circulation. As best as I can determine, these positions are logically untenable.[91] Like circulation-based definitions of death in the medical/ethical literature, they actually fail to define both circulation and what constitutes a human body, and are not internally consistent when applied to situations such as organ transplantation and conjoined twins.

In the world outside halakha, many advocates of non-neurologically based definitions of death appear to have specific religious beliefs, usually of a fundamentalist variety. Obviously matters of belief sometimes cannot be influenced by external factors, and those believers may have to either live with incoherence or give up their beliefs. In contradistinction, the

---

90. Asher Bush et al., *Halachic Issues in the Determination of Death and in Organ Transplantation: Including an Evaluation of the Neurological "Brain Death" Standard* (2010), 80–81, http://www.rabbis.org/pdfs/Halachi_%20Issues_the_Determination.pdf. Unfortunately, in my opinion, this paper failed in the most basic task of defining life and death by refusing to address the necessary anatomic and/or functional basis of a human being. This failure, combined with its many errors, misstatements, and obvious bias, made the study a great disappointment. For a thorough critique, see Noam Stadlan, "Death by Neurological Criteria: A Critique of the RCA Paper and the Circulation Criteria," http://torahmusings.com/2010/12/death-by-neurological-criteria/.

91. For an in-depth review of two such opinions, see my paper "Conceptual and Logical Problems Arising from Defining Life and Death by the Presence or Absence of Circulation," *Me'orot* 8 (5771/2010–11), http://www.hods.org/pdf/Problems-Defining-Life-and-Death-by-Circulation.pdf.

halakhic positions presented above, identifying life with the presence of neurological function, avoid the logical pitfalls while maintaining fealty to halakha and the halakhic process.

CONCLUSION

To quote Michael B. Green and Daniel Wikler (as paraphrased by Bertha Alvarez Manninen):

> To state that an ailing patient, Jones, is still alive, is in fact to make two claims; the second of which is usually taken for granted. One is that the patient is alive. The other is that the patient is (remains) Jones…. If we do establish that the patient, even if alive, is not Jones, and if no one else is Jones, then we will have established that Jones does not exist. And this, of course, establishes that Jones is dead.[92]

The basis of the neurological definition of death is that a collection of human tissue is no longer a human being when a certain amount of neurological function has been irreversibly lost. At that point, circulatory and respiratory status becomes moot.

---

92. Michael B. Green and Daniel Wikler, "Brain Death and Personal Identity," *Philosophy and Public Affairs* 9, no. 2 (winter 1980): 105–33; Bertha Alvarez Manninen, "Defining Human Death: An Intersection of Bioethics and Metaphysics," *Reviews in the Neurosciences* 20 (2009): 283–92.

Chapter 4

Dead Enough

Howard R. Doyle

But legally, I suppose, a man is dead when he has undergone irreversible changes of a type that makes it impossible for him to seek to litigate.

SIR PETER MEDAWAR[1]

PREFACE

A fifty-two-year-old man was brought to the hospital complaining of weakness on his left side. His speech was slurred, the left side of his face was partially paralyzed, and he did not seem aware of the left side of his body. A CT (computed tomography) scan[2] confirmed he had suffered an extensive stroke on the right side of his brain, in the region supplied by the middle cerebral artery. Too much time had elapsed since his symptoms started, so he could no longer receive drugs that would dissolve the blood clot; he was admitted for observation. Seventeen hours later a physician noticed he was lethargic, and ordered

---

1. Peter B. Medawar, *The Uniqueness of the Individual* (New York: Basic Books, 1957), 19.
2. In this test, a series of x-rays are taken from many different angles, producing cross-sectional images of the bones and soft tissues.

another CT scan. The stroke was larger. The right cerebral hemisphere was severely swollen, and parts of it had herniated,[3] compressing the brainstem. He was unresponsive, and his right pupil was widely dilated. After an urgent intubation he was placed on a ventilator, followed by vigorous treatment of the brain swelling.

By the afternoon of the second hospital day (approximately twenty-three hours after herniation), he wasn't triggering the ventilator – he made no effort to breathe – and a neurologist performed a brain death evaluation following a standardized institutional protocol. The patient had flaccid quadriparesis[4] and didn't respond to pain. He didn't trigger the ventilator, and both pupils were dilated and didn't react to light. The corneal, oculocephalic, oculovestibular, cough, and gag reflexes were absent. His blood pressure and temperature were normal. The urine toxicology screen was negative, and he hadn't received neuromuscular blocking agents or central nervous system depressants since admission. However, upon learning that the serum sodium was 173 mEq/L (milliequivalent per liter) – he had severe hypernatremia[5] – the neurologist decided to postpone a formal determination of death until this abnormality was at least partially corrected.

While this was being done, the patient developed severe instability, with extreme fluctuations in blood pressure that required minute-by-minute adjustments to the drugs used to control it. [6] For this reason, he was transferred to the intensive care unit I direct. By forty-eight hours after herniation, his blood pressure had stabilized, requiring only small amounts of norepinephrine to maintain it within a normal range, and the serum sodium had decreased to 159 mEq/L. The remaining blood chemistries were unremarkable, and his temperature was normal. The same neurologist then performed a repeat brain death evaluation, confirming the findings of the first exam.

---

3. Meaning that the brain, as a result of high intracranial pressure, had moved from its usual position inside the skull.
4. Severe or complete loss of motor function in all four limbs.
5. An elevated sodium level in the blood.
6. A classic "adrenergic storm."

Because the patient was severely hypoxic[7] (PO_2 61 torr,[8] on 100% O_2), we couldn't carry out an apnea test, so a brain perfusion scan was done instead.[9] It showed no intracranial tracer perfusion, consistent with brain death. Six hours after the previous brain death evaluation, a second examination was performed by an intensivist; it again confirmed all the findings of the previous two exams. The patient was pronounced dead, fifty-four hours after herniation, and his daughter was asked to consent to organ donation. The consent was given the following morning.

While organ procurement was being arranged, the patient was observed to be coughing – nineteen hours after the declaration of death, and seventy-three hours after herniation. My first reaction was incredulity. In my profession, it is an article of faith that there can be no return of any degree of brain function in someone who has been diagnosed as brain dead after a proper evaluation. And that had been my experience, until that day. I proceeded to cancel the organ donation and called the daughter to explain that her father no longer met the legal criteria for brain death. Then I reached for the patient's chart. Over the years I have written many death pronouncements. That was the first time I had to write a life pronouncement.

Following a lengthy discussion about his dismal prognosis in terms of a meaningful neurological recovery, his family concluded that he wouldn't want to be kept alive under those circumstances. We removed the ventilator the following day. He was still coughing.

INTRODUCTION

As a former liver transplant surgeon who now takes care of not only transplant recipients, but also the type of patient likely to become their donor, I have firsthand experience with the tug-of-war – both internal and external – that can arise when trying to balance our obligation to

---

7. When the brain is deprived of adequate oxygen.
8. PO_2 means partial pressure of oxygen; one torr is approximately equal to the fluid pressure of one millimeter of mercury.
9. In this test, 99mTc-DTPA is administered intravenously, and sequential images of the brain are obtained with a gamma camera. Areas in which there is blood flow appear dark.

those in dire need of an organ with our duty to protect their would-be donors.[10] Brain death was created, in large measure, to do away with these moral ambiguities, and has carried out its appointed task well for several decades. It will probably continue to deliver this service for some time, as long as not too many dead people develop intractable cough.[11]

One need not be a utilitarian to consider organ donation good, and transplantation would look drastically different today if not for the adoption of brain death. Yet a close inspection reveals it to be a construct held together more by dogma than by scientific fact. The question is not whether brain death remains a valid concept, but whether clinging to this fiction is the only way to morally justify the taking of vital organs.

Discussions about brain death can be had at several levels. At a strictly philosophical level, we can dispute the validity of the different brain-based formulations, or whether death can even be defined on the basis of degrees of brain function. We can also question the biological rationale behind any of these concepts, or critically examine whether the way we determine that death has occurred is consistent with how we purport to define it. I will leave the philosophical discussions to the philosophers, and concentrate on some of the more problematic aspects of brain death from a clinician's point of view.

THE BRAIN AS THE CENTRAL INTEGRATOR

The most widely accepted definition of death is that it consists of the "permanent cessation of functioning of the organism as a whole" – that is, the organism as an integrated, functioning unit. The rationale for equating the death of the brain with that of the entire organism has rested on the idea that the brain is the central integrator of the body. Without the brain, which "integrates, generates, interrelates, and controls complex

---

10. Although it is a commonplace that while taking care of patients who seem headed for brain death, we mustn't think about those who might benefit from their organs, this works more often in theory than in practice.

11. This case isn't unique. Several weeks later, a supervisor of our regional organ procurement organization tactfully inquired why I was being so meticulous – and time-consuming – in pronouncing the death of another patient under my care. When I related my recent experience, he remarked, "I know, Doctor. This happens to us more often than we would like to admit."

bodily activities," the organism as a whole cannot long survive. This "biological argument" was first advanced on a large scale a full decade after brain death had gained wide acceptance, and became orthodox.[12] There was evidence to support this central integrator hypothesis. In their landmark report, Pierre Mollaret and Maurice Goulon described twenty-three patients who, aside from being in a profound coma, had lost the automatic (vegetative) functions of the brain, including the control of breathing and blood pressure, temperature regulation, and the ability to maintain their bodies' chemical composition. Another characteristic of this *coma dépassé* – the forerunner of the concept of brain death – was its ineluctable progression to cardiac arrest within days, despite the support provided.[13] This uniformly rapid demise was expected, given that progressive circulatory collapse was a necessary component of the newly described syndrome. However, it also appeared to be the case in patients fulfilling the Harvard ad hoc committee's criteria, which didn't require hemodynamic instability.[14]

In the years immediately following the report, different groups described how somatic death also invariably followed a declaration of

---

12. This standard view maintains that human death is strictly a biological phenomenon, indistinguishable from the death "of a dog or a cat." See James L. Bernat, Charles M. Culver, and Bernard Gert, "On the Definition and Criterion of Death," *Annals of Internal Medicine* 94, no. 3 (1981): 389–94. See also the President's Commission for the Study of Ethical Problems in Medicine and Biomedical and Behavioral Research, *Defining Death: A Report on the Medical, Legal and Ethical Issues in the Determination of Death* (Washington, DC: US Government Printing Office, 1981).

13. Pierre Mollaret and Maurice Goulon, "Le coma dépassé (Mémoire préliminaire)," *Revue Neurologique* 101 (1959): 3–15. When Mollaret and Goulon wrote their seminal paper, the term "coma" described a condition in which patients could not be aroused and reacted to pain – or other noxious stimuli – to varying degrees, but the vegetative functions of their brains were largely preserved. In contrast, patients in *coma dépassé* went beyond a complete inability to respond to their environment, as they had also lost the brain's vegetative functions. Hence the term *coma dépassé*, which translates roughly as "beyond coma."

14. See "A Definition of Irreversible Coma: Report of the Ad Hoc Committee of the Harvard Medical School to Examine the Definition of Brain Death," *JAMA* 205, no. 6 (1968): 337–40. Hemodynamic instability is a condition in which a person requires support (pharmacological or mechanical) to maintain normal blood pressure and/ or adequate cardiac output.

brain death, usually within one week.[15] This close temporal association helped overcome any apprehensions people might have had, and the brain death concept quickly became an established fact.[16]

On closer inspection, however, things are less clear. In a 1981 study, Jennett et al. analyzed 609 cases of brain death in three neurosurgical units in Britain, from 1962 to 1980. Of these, 283 (47%) sustained cardiac arrest after the ventilator was removed; the remaining 326 did so while still receiving mechanical ventilation, after a median time of 3.5 to 4.5 days (depending on the unit). The authors chose the median to summarize their results because of the skewed distribution of the time to asystole (no heartbeat, aka flat line), which was "prolonged in a few cases." In fact, 14% of the cases had a time to asystole that exceeded three days, but the authors gave no further details regarding the length of their somatic survival times.[17]

In 1998, Dr. Alan Shewmon published a detailed study showing that somatic death need not shortly follow brain death. After an extensive review of the literature, plus his own experience, he collected 175 cases with a time to asystole of one week or greater. Of these, approximately

---

15. See Georges Ouaknine et al., "Laboratory Criteria of Brain Death," *Journal of Neurosurgery* 39, no. 4 (1973): 429–33; Julius Korein and Micheline Maccario, "A Prospective Study on the Diagnosis of Cerebral Death," *Electroencephalography and Clinical Neurophysiology* 30 (1971): 103–4; Karla Ibe, "Clinical and Pathophysiological Aspects of the Intravital Brain Death," ibid.: 272; Donald P. Becker et al., "An Evaluation of the Definition of Cerebral Death," *Neurology* 20, no. 5 (1970): 459–62; Bryan Jennett, John Gleave, and Peter Wilson, "Brain Death in Three Neurosurgical Units," *BMJ* (*Clinical Research Edition*) 282 (February 14, 1981): 533–39. Somatic death denotes the cessation of function of the rest of the body, ushered in by the cessation of circulation. It is a rather unfortunate choice of words, as they suggest that the brain and body (soma) are separate physical entities.

16. Bryan Jennett and Catherine Hessett, "Brain Death in Britain as Reflected in Renal Donors," *BMJ* (*Clinical Research Edition*) 283 (1981): 359–62; James L. Bernat, "The Definition, Criterion, and Statute of Death," *Seminars in Neurology* 4 (1984): 45–51; David R. Field et al., "Maternal Brain Death During Pregnancy: Medical and Ethical Issues," *JAMA* 260, no. 6 (1988): 816–22; Kerri M. Robertson and D. Ryan Cook, "Perioperative Management of the Multiorgan Donor," *Anesthesia Analgesia* 70 (1990): 546–56; Betsy E. Soifer and Adrian W. Gelb, "The Multiple Organ Donor: Identification and Management," *Annals of Internal Medicine* 110, no. 10 (1989): 814–23.

17. Jennett, "Brain Death in Britain," 536.

eighty patients survived at least two weeks, approximately twenty-four at least four weeks, approximately twenty at least eight weeks, and seven at least six months.[18] The longest survivor, pronounced brain dead at age four, was close to nineteen years old at the time of publication.[19] Significantly, in nineteen of fifty-six cases with enough information, cardiac arrest was not spontaneous, but followed the discontinuation of treatment.

There are significant problems with this study. The relatively few cases, coming mostly from small case series, and the fact that the author excluded the majority of cases before conducting a statistical analysis – selecting those that in his judgment had enough information – make any inference eminently suspect. The reliability of the diagnosis of brain death is also difficult to establish through a retrospective review – as we will discuss later, the quality of brain death determinations is uneven, to put it delicately. And there is publication bias – cardiac arrest shortly after brain death certification is not news.[20]

These and other criticisms were quickly pointed out to the author, sometimes with a vehemence bordering on ferocity.[21] Despite the study's weaknesses, this collection of counterexamples could not be summarily dismissed by those who based their rationale for equating brain death with death on a supposedly rapid, inexorable progression to asystole. And while one could question the accuracy of the diagnosis in some cases, as the author pointed out, "If patients were 'brain dead'

18. D. Alan Shewmon, "Chronic 'Brain Death': Meta-Analysis and Conceptual Consequences," *Neurology* 51, no. 6 (1998): 1538–45. The numbers are approximate because two references presented the survival data as the mean plus the standard deviation.

19. Susan Repertinger et al., "Long Survival Following Bacterial Meningitis-Associated Brain Destruction," *Journal of Child Neurology* 21, no. 7 (2006): 591–95. At age twenty-four, twenty years after being pronounced dead, this patient finally had a cardiac arrest after his mother decided to discontinue aggressive treatment.

20. The rarity of these reports, compared to the number of brain deaths diagnosed over the years, is used to downplay their significance, arguing that these events are so rare that they can be safely ignored. However, we simply don't know how many cases there have been, because most editors and referees – not to mention the physicians involved – assume these represent botched brain death determinations.

21. For the critiques of Antonio Lopez-Navidad, Eelco F. Wijdicks and James L. Bernat, and Claudio Crisci, see "Correspondence," *Neurology* 53, no. 6 (1999): 1369–70.

enough to qualify as organ donors, they were surely 'brain dead' enough to qualify for this study."

Orthodoxy aside, by the time Shewmon published his paper, the central integrator hypothesis no longer had currency with many working in the field. It couldn't be reconciled with brain dead pregnant women supported for weeks to months until delivery,[22] or with a preserved ability to detoxify and recycle cellular waste, fight infection, maintain body temperature, heal wounds, process nutrients, and undergo sexual maturation and proportional growth – among other things. In 2008, the President's Council on Bioethics published a white paper addressing the ongoing controversy in the diagnosis of death, explicitly acknowledging:

> If being alive as a biological organism requires being a whole that is more than the mere sum of its parts, then it would be difficult to deny that the body of a patient with total brain failure can still be alive, at least in some cases.[23]

This is a remarkable, even courageous statement, contradicting a dogma that had held sway for over a quarter century. It raises a troubling question, however. If it is possible to be alive – in the sense of being an integrated organism – after meeting the diagnostic criteria for brain death, why should this state be considered equivalent to the death of the organism? The President's Council goes to great lengths to address this issue.

After discarding "the false assumption that the brain is the 'integrator' of vital functions," it tackles the definition of death, arguing that to determine "whether an organism remains a *whole* depends on recognizing the persistence or cessation of the fundamental vital *work* of a living organism – the work of self-preservation, achieved through the organism's need-driven commerce with the surrounding world."[24] This commerce depends on three fundamental capacities:

---

22. For an experiment related to this question and the intersection of modern and talmudic medicine, see Prof. Avraham Steinberg's essay in this volume.
23. *Controversies in the Determination of Death: A White Paper by the President's Council on Bioethics* (Washington, DC, 2008), 57, http://bioethics.georgetown.edu/pcbe/reports/death/.
24. Ibid., 60. Emphasis in the original.

1. openness to the world, that is, receptivity to stimuli and signals from the surrounding environment;
2. the ability to act upon the world to obtain selectively what it needs;
3. the basic felt need that drives the organism to act as it must, to obtain what it needs and what its openness reveals to be available.

The council then argues that breathing and consciousness are especially important forms of need-driven commerce, and the irreversible loss of these two constitutes death. However, of all forms of commerce, why this particular combination should be sufficient to define death is not explained. For all its efforts, the council's new definition is neither simple nor elegant, the common attributes of any enduring explanation of nature. In the end, the inevitable impression is that council members started from the conclusion – brain death is a valid criterion for death – and worked backward.[25]

THE BRAIN, THE WHOLE BRAIN

As in most countries that accept brain death, the US has adopted the whole-brain criterion, requiring the irreversible loss of "all functions of the entire brain, including the brainstem." Sensibly enough, a function is defined as cellular activity that is organized and directed – randomly firing brain cells don't count.[26] But while the definition of death is clearly stated in the law, the method of ascertainment – the diagnostic procedure – is not. The determination of whether an individual satisfies the definition of death is "made in accordance with accepted medical standards," and it is possible to meet those standards without necessarily satisfying the definition.

---

25. Ibid., 61–65. A thorough critique of the President's Council's white paper is beyond the scope of this essay. For further discussion, see Franklin G. Miller and Robert D. Truog, "The Incoherence of Determining Death by Neurological Criteria: A Commentary on 'Controversies in the Determination of Death: A White Paper by the President's Council on Bioethics,'" *Kennedy Institute of Ethics Journal* 19, no. 2 (2009): 185–93; D. Alan Shewmon, "Brain Death: Can It Be Resuscitated?" *Hastings Center Report* 39, no. 2 (2009): 18–24.
26. President's Commission, *Defining Death*.

There are several examples of residual brain function in individuals pronounced dead by neurological criteria, with the preservation of neurohormonal regulation being the best documented. One function of the brain is to maintain blood volume and tonicity,[27] by regulating the amount of water lost in the urine. This function is the result of the coordinated action of at least two groups of cells in the hypothalamus that detect changes in blood tonicity. They in turn signal cells that produce the hormone vasopressin – which regulates water reabsorption in the kidneys – and are located in separate regions of the hypothalamus. If tonicity drops, the production of vasopressin increases, the kidneys reabsorb more water, and urine output decreases. The reverse is true when the blood becomes hypertonic.[28]

A deficiency in vasopressin production thus leads to greatly increased production of highly dilute urine, a condition known as diabetes insipidus, which, theoretically at least, should accompany brain death. However, the incidence of diabetes insipidus can range from as high as 87% to as low as 8.5%.[29] In at least one study, eleven patients with

---

27. Tonicity is a semi-quantitive measure of the response of cells or tissues to the fluid surrounding them, and it is related to osmolarity (the osmotic pressure exerted by the fluid, which itself depends on the amount and properties of the substances dissolved in it). If the serum is hypertonic, water will tend to leave the cells, dehydrating them; the opposite is true if the serum is hypotonic. Serum tonicity is generally maintained within a very narrow range.

28. Vasopressin is produced in the supraoptic and paraventricular nuclei. The cells that detect changes in tonicity, so-called osmoreceptors, are located in the organum vasculosum of the lamina terminalis, and in the median preoptic nucleus. See Michael J. McKinley et al., "Vasopressin Secretion: Osmotic and Hormonal Regulation by the Lamina Terminalis," *Journal of Neuroendocrinology* 16 (2004): 340–47; Charles W. Bourque, "Central Mechanisms of Osmosensation and Systemic Osmoregulation," *Nature Reviews Neuroscience* 9 (2008): 519–31.

29. Kristin M. Outwater and Mark A. Rockoff, "Diabetes Insipidus Accompanying Brain Death in Children," *Neurology* 34, no. 9 (1984): 1243–46; Debra H. Fiser et al., "Diabetes Insipidus in Children with Brain Death," *Critical Care Medicine* 15, no. 6 (1987): 551–53; Ake Grenvik et al., "Cessation of Therapy in Terminal Illness and Brain Death," *Critical Care Medicine* 6, no. 4 (1978): 284–91; Hans-Joachim Gramm et al., "Acute Endocrine Failure After Brain Death?" *Transplantation* 54 (1992): 851–57.

diabetes insipidus had normal or increased levels of vasopressin.[30] Some have explained these figures by postulating that the pituitary – the gland that releases vasopressin, among other hormones – has a dual blood supply, with part coming from outside the dura mater.[31] Therefore, the explanation goes, the pituitary can continue functioning thanks to stimuli coming from other parts of the body.[32] The problem with this theory is that for vasopressin production to remain normal, it is not enough for the pituitary to remain viable. As discussed, the cells that control production, and the ones that make the hormone, are in the hypothalamus, *which is decidedly a part of the brain.*

Another example is the persistence of electroencephalographic evidence of cortical function. For example, in a series of fifty-six consecutive patients who met brain death criteria, eleven showed cortical activity on the electroencephalogram. In two of these cases, the electroencephalographic patterns resembled physiologic sleep; in one case it persisted for a week. Autopsies showed extensive necrosis of the brainstem, with sparing of the cortex. Rather than raise questions in the authors' minds about the accuracy of the diagnosis in these cases, they concluded that the electroencephalogram shouldn't be used in brain death determinations, because it's potentially misleading.[33]

Consider also the preservation of thermoregulation. Taking the definition of brain death at face value demands that patients exhibit either poikilothermia or hyperthermia.[34] However, many patients undergoing

---

30. This condition, known as nephrogenic diabetes insipidus, stems from resistance to the action of vasopressin by the kidneys. M. Hohenegger et al., "Serum Vasopressin (Avp) Levels in Polyuric Brain-Dead Organ Donors," *European Archives of Psychiatry and Neurological Sciences* 239 (1990): 267–69.
31. The tough, fibrous sac that surrounds the brain
32. Eelco F. M. Wijdicks, ed., *Brain Death* (Philadelphia: Lippincott Williams and Wilkins, 2001), 30.
33. Madeleine M. Grigg et al., "Electroencephalographic Activity After Brain Death," *Archives of Neurology* 44 (1987): 948–54. These patients would not have been diagnosed as brain dead in countries requiring the EEG and isoelectric tracing for confirmation.
34. Poikilothermia refers to the equilibration of body and ambient temperatures; hyperthermia refers to a physiological response in which body temperature is high but (unlike a fever) heat-dissipating mechanisms are preserved.

brain death determinations don't require warming or cooling blankets at the time of certification, as would be the case if there were a loss of thermoregulation. A case in point is the patient described at the start of this essay, who maintained a normal temperature until the ventilator was disconnected.

The maintenance of core body temperature is a crucial homeostatic function, a complex process involving the preoptic area and dorsomedial nucleus of the hypothalamus; the periaqueductal gray area and raphe pallidus in the brainstem; skin vasoconstriction or vasodilatation, depending on the need to conserve or lose heat; and the production of heat through shivering and non-shivering thermogenesis.[35] It is, by anyone's definition, a brain function. Nevertheless, preservation of thermoregulation is quietly acknowledged and ignored, just as the physiological response of the brain dead donor during the organ procurement operation is dismissed as irrelevant. It is well known that in the absence of anesthesia, the blood pressure and heart rate usually increase in response to the skin incision,[36] evidence that the painful stimulus is being processed at some level. This fact has prompted some anesthesiologists to recommend, incongruously, the administration of anesthesia to the putative corpse.[37]

The response to these findings has been to say that certain brain functions can be preserved even after brain death. Or that the only relevant functions are those that can be assessed at the bedside (that is, if it requires a laboratory test, it's not relevant). Or that when we say, "all functions," we really don't mean "all." To quote the President's Council on Bioethics:

35. Kei Nagashima et al., "Neuronal Circuitries Involved in Thermoregulation," *Autonomic Neuroscience* 85, nos. 1–3 (2000): 18–25; Eduardo E. Benarroch, "Thermoregulation: Recent Concepts and Remaining Questions," *Neurology* 69, no. 12 (2007): 1293–97; Igor B. Mekjavic and Ola Eiken, "Contribution of Thermal and Nonthermal Factors to the Regulation of Body Temperature in Humans," *Journal of Applied Physiology* 100 (2006): 2065–72; Joseph A. DiMicco and Dmitry V. Zaretsky, "The Dorsomedial Hypothalamus: A New Player in Thermoregulation," *American Journal of Physiology – Regulatory, Integrative and Comparative Physiology* 292 (2007): R47–63.

36. Randall C. Wetzel et al., "Hemodynamic Responses in Brain Dead Organ Donor Patients," *Anesthesia and Analgesia* 64 (1985): 125–28.

37. Peter J. Young and Basil F. Matta, "Anaesthesia for Organ Donation in the Brainstem Dead – Why Bother?" *Anaesthesia* 55 (2000): 105–6.

In any event, whether or not the word "total" is justified, the patient diagnosed with total brain failure is in a condition of profound incapacity, diagnostically distinct from all other cases of severe injury. Whether this state of profound incapacity warrants a determination of death remains a matter of debate, with advocates of the neurological standard arguing that it does, while critics maintain that it does not.[38]

Whether we agree with this latest concept, total brain failure is indeed a matter of debate. However, the disputation starts from the premise that the diagnosis is accurate, something that cannot be taken for granted, as we will see.

UNEQUAL DEATHS

The diagnosis of brain death requires the presence of the elements originally proposed by the Harvard ad hoc committee, namely, coma, absence of brainstem reflexes, and apnea. There must be a demonstrable, irreversible condition that explains the clinical picture, and there should be no factors that can potentially confound the exam. A number of confirmatory tests can be used to support the diagnosis.[39] In 1995, the American Academy of Neurology (AAN) published guidelines for the diagnosis of brain death in adults, and they constitute the basis for standards adopted by individual states in the US.[40] Other countries have independently developed similar standards.

---

38. *Controversies in the Determination of Death*, 38.
39. "Guidelines for the Determination of Death: Report of the Medical Consultants on the Diagnosis of Death to the President's Commission for the Study of Ethical Problems in Medicine and Biomedical and Behavioral Research," *JAMA* 246, no. 19 (1981): 2184–86.
40. For details, see Dr. Zelik Frischer's essay in this volume. For the AAN guidelines: http:// www.aan.com/go/practice/guidelines. For a discussion of their development, see Eelco F. M. Wijdicks, "Determining Brain Death in Adults," *Neurology* 45, no. 5 (1995): 1003–11. The standards were updated in 2010 to conform to the evidence-based format. See Eelco F. M. Wijdicks et al., "Evidence-Based Guideline Update: Determining Brain Death in Adults: Report of the Quality Standards Subcommittee of the American Academy of Neurology," *Neurology* 74, no. 23 (2010): 1911–18. Whether these reissued guidelines are really evidence-based is debatable. See D. Alan Shewmon, Joseph L. Verheijde, and Mohamed Y. Rady, "Correspondence," *Neurology* 76, no. 3 (2011): 308; author reply, 308–9.

The AAN guidelines detail how the physical examination and apnea test should be conducted. They are, however, vague when defining conditions that can interfere with a proper evaluation. In the Prerequisites section, they stipulate there should be "exclusion of complicating medical conditions that may confound clinical assessment (no severe electrolyte, acid-base, or endocrine disturbance)." The problem, and it is not trivial, is that we do not know what "severe," "intoxication," or "poisoning" means in the context of brain death. The case described at the beginning of this essay, in which the examination was delayed because of severe hypernatremia, illustrates this point.

Hypernatremia is common in patients evaluated for brain death. Most have sustained severe neurological injuries that cause the brain to swell, and treatment of this swelling almost invariably leads to hypernatremia. Sufficiently elevated sodium concentrations can themselves be a cause of muscle weakness, and even coma, in patients whose brains are otherwise normal.[41] This makes it necessary to ensure that the patient is not severely hypernatremic before proceeding with a brain death evaluation. However, what constitutes severe hypernatremia is open to interpretation, and brain death evaluations are often carried out in the presence of electrolyte abnormalities that would be considered significant in patients with normal brains, let alone severely injured ones.[42]

---

41. Hypernatremia can become symptomatic after serum sodium exceeds 160 mEq/L. (See Horacio J. Adrogue and Nicolaos E. Madias, "Hypernatremia," *NEJM* 342, no. 20 [2000]: 1493–99; Kenji Hiromatsu et al., "Hypernatremic Myopathy," *Journal of Neurological Sciences* 122 [1994]: 144–47.) Therefore, we felt obliged to partially correct the electrolyte disturbance of our patient – from 173 mEq/L to 159 mEq/L – before proceeding with the brain death evaluation. However, whether a serum sodium of 160 mEq/L – or slightly less – does or doesn't cause symptoms in patients with severely injured brains is not at all clear. We assume it doesn't, because we often see stroke victims who have levels in this range and appear to be unaffected. Howbeit, by definition these patients have a lesser degree of neurological injury, and no data support extrapolation to patients who seem brain dead. (There is no evidence against it, either; this is a data-free zone.)
42. There used to be a controversy regarding the possible deleterious effects of donor hypernatremia after liver transplantation – some believed that severely elevated serum sodium made the transplanted liver more likely to fail. This controversy has waned over the years. However, I have participated in several discussions regarding whether to accept a liver from a donor with a terminal serum sodium close to, or in excess of, 170 mEq/L.

Other metabolic disturbances can interfere with a brain death evaluation. Consider, for example, renal failure, not uncommon in the setting of, say, severe trauma. Uremia was a common cause of coma before the advent of dialysis, and it is still an important contributor to so-called toxic-metabolic encephalopathy, the catchall term we use to describe the majority of cases of coma in critically ill patients with no structural brain pathology.

The uremic state is complex, and its impact on consciousness is due to a combination of factors. As a result, we lack the means to quantify the contribution of renal dysfunction in coma patients. Laboratory tests used to assess renal function show no correlation with mental status, and the same is true for other disorders, making it difficult to determine whether a given metabolic abnormality is severe enough to confound a brain death evaluation.

How to assess the combined effect of two or more conditions – critically ill patients usually have more than one thing wrong with them – is simply not known. And while the electroencephalogram shows characteristic changes in toxic encephalopathy – or other states, such as non-convulsive seizures – this test is not required in the US. Documenting the presence of an acute central nervous system catastrophe that's consistent with the diagnosis of brain death, as specified in the AAN guidelines, would protect patients from being mistakenly pronounced dead when they may be suffering in part from a severe metabolic disorder. However, those conducting the evaluation must adhere to the standards, and also have enough experience to judge whether the severity of the brain injury is consistent with the diagnosis. This is not always the case.

The problem gets even more complicated because several drugs used in the management of the critically ill – sedatives, analgesics, and anticonvulsants – depress the central nervous system, and the guidelines require only that a prerequisite for a brain death evaluation is that there be no drug intoxication or poisoning. Easier said than done. Drugs tend to accumulate in tissues, and their concentration in the blood doesn't necessarily reflect that of the target tissues. The suggestion to use the pharmacokinetic properties of the drug as a guide, and wait two or three half-lives before undertaking the examination, ignores the fact that these parameters differ in the critically ill, the elderly, the very young, and, for some medications, the obese – especially after prolonged administration.

Take midazolam, a drug with a short duration of action and a half-life of one to four hours in healthy individuals.[43] In the critically ill this can be increased by a factor of ten, and some patients may take more than twenty-four hours to wake up after stopping the medication.[44]

A frequent scenario is that of a patient placed in a barbiturate-induced coma to lower the metabolism of the brain and intracranial pressure, or to treat seizures that don't respond to other anticonvulsants.[45] Enough pentobarbital will not only induce coma but also flatten the EEG as much as one might wish, making it necessary to establish that the clinical picture is not due in part to the residual effects of the drug before proceeding with a brain death determination. Measuring the concentration of the drug in the blood would seem to be the most direct way to accomplish this, but pentobarbital levels are not available in most hospitals. Where I work, a major university hospital in New York

43. This is the so-called terminal half-life, measuring the decrease in blood concentration after the initial phase of equilibration.
44. See David J. Greenblatt et al., "Effect of Age, Gender, and Obesity on Midazolam Kinetics," *Anesthesiology* 61 (1984): 27–35; Joseph G. Reves et al., "Midazolam: Pharmacology and Uses," *Anesthesiology* 62 (1985): 310–24; Hans Oldenhof et al., "Clinical Pharmacokinetics of Midazolam in Intensive Care Patients, a Wide Interpatient Variability," *Clinical Pharmacology & Therapeutics* 43 (1988): 263–69; Audrey Shafer, Van A. Doze, and Paul F. White, "Pharmacokinetic Variability of Midazolam Infusions in Critically Ill Patients," *Critical Care Medicine* 18, no. 9 (1990): 1039–41; Anne S. Pohlman, Kevin P. Simpson, and Jesse B. Hall, "Continuous Intravenous Infusions of Lorazepam Versus Midazolam for Sedation During Mechanical Ventilatory Support: A Prospective, Randomized Study," *Critical Care Medicine* 22, no. 8 (1994): 1241–47.
45. See Lawrence F. Marshall, Randall W. Smith, and Harvey M. Shapiro, "The Outcome with Aggressive Treatment in Severe Head Injuries. Part II: Acute and Chronic Barbiturate Administration in the Management of Head Injury," *Journal of Neurosurgery* 50, no. 1 (1979): 26–30; Gary L. Rea and Gaylan L. Rockswold, "Barbiturate Therapy in Uncontrolled Intracranial Hypertension," *Neurosurgery* 12, no. 4 (1983): 401–4; Michael C. Smith and Barry J. Riskin, "The Clinical Use of Barbiturates in Neurological Disorders," *Drugs* 42 (1991): 365–78; Manuela Cormio et al., "Cerebral Hemodynamic Effects of Pentobarbital Coma in Head-Injured Patients," *Journal of Neurotrauma* 16, no. 10 (1999): 927–36.

City, the samples have to be sent to a reference laboratory. The results are available only after two days.

Even if blood levels were readily available, interpreting the results wouldn't be straightforward. While Britain's Code of Practice suggests values of thiopental and midazolam above which an evaluation should not be undertaken,[46] in every other country the decision to proceed is left to the examining physicians. A. Earl Walker and Gaetano F. Molinari, writing for the investigators of the largest prospective study on brain death ever conducted, pointed out:

> Unfortunately, the brain's precise tolerance of variable degrees and duration of intoxication, anoxia, and acidosis are not determined for the normal adult, and even less is known regarding the susceptibility of children and older people. Accordingly, even if the presence of a drug or drugs in the blood can be established, without knowledge of precise, time-integrated, dose-response curves for each agent, the actual blood level may be of relatively little value in the assessment of the total problem.[47]

Thirty years on, our knowledge of the effects of drugs and metabolic disturbances on the types of injured brains that would trigger a brain death evaluation has not improved significantly.

Once the decision to proceed with a brain death determination is made, the diagnostic process itself varies from country to country. The number of physicians required to evaluate the patient ranges from one to four, or it may not be specified in the regulations. In some countries only physicians with specific specialty training can carry out the exam. The us, on the other hand, leaves that unregulated. In some states a physician isn't necessary – a registered nurse or a physician assistant can do it – and most require no specialized training, leaving it to individual hospitals to

---

46. *A Code of Practice for the Diagnosis and Confirmation of Death* (London: Academy of Medical Royal Colleges, 2008), 14.

47. A. Earl Walker and Gaetano F. Molinari, "Criteria of Cerebral Death: A Critique," in *The nincds Collaborative Study of Brain Death* (ed. National Institute of Neurological and Communicative Disorders and Stroke; Bethesda: National Institutes of Health, 1980), 181–203.

decide who is qualified. As a result, brain death determinations are often entrusted to inexperienced personnel, including physicians-in-training working under varying degrees of supervision.[48]

Many countries do not specify which brainstem reflexes should be tested; of those that do, some require as few as two to as many as a half-dozen. More important, the apnea test – a central element of the diagnosis – may not be required, or there may be no guidelines regarding how to do it properly.

A recent survey of some of the best-known neurologic institutions in the US found significant variability in their compliance with the AAN guidelines. Of forty-one hospitals participating in the survey, three had no guidelines whatsoever. Less than half specified that metabolic and endocrine disorders should be absent before starting the evaluation. Remarkably, only 27% stipulated that there should be an absence of spontaneous respiration. One hospital required no apnea test. And only 17% instructed that the test be repeated if the results were inconclusive.[49]

Similar findings have been obtained in other studies.[50] In one of them, only 42% of the responding hospitals had a policy excluding examiners from participating in the transplant.[51] Considering that these are "leading neurologic institutions," our expectations regarding the quality of brain death determinations in the average hospital should not be unrealistically high.

48. See Walter F. Haupt and Jobst Rudolf, "European Brain Death Codes: A Comparison of National Guidelines," *Journal of Neurology* 246 (1999): 432–37; Eelco F. M. Wijdicks, "Brain Death Worldwide: Accepted Fact But No Global Consensus in Diagnostic Criteria," *Neurology* 58, no. 1 (2002): 20–25; David J. Powner, Michael Hernandez, and Terry E. Rives, "Variability Among Hospital Policies for Determining Brain Death in Adults," *Critical Care Medicine* 32, no. 6 (2004): 1284–88.
49. David M. Greer et al., "Variability of Brain Death Determination Guidelines in Leading US Neurologic Institutions," *Neurology* 70, no. 4 (2008): 284–89.
50. Christopher J. Doig et al., "Brief Survey: Determining Brain Death in Canadian Intensive Care Units," *Canadian Journal of Anesthesia* 53, no. 6 (2006): 609–12; Eun-Kyoung Choi et al., "Brain Death Revisited: The Case for a National Standard," *Journal of Law, Medicine & Ethics* 36 (2008): 824–36; Wijdicks, "Brain Death Worldwide"; Powner et al., "Variability Among Hospital Policies."
51. Powner et al., "Variability Among Hospital Policies."

The period of observation between exams varies considerably around the world: from as short as thirty minutes to as long as three days, depending on the underlying cause. Some US institutions have eliminated the second exam altogether.[52] This policy is of more than academic interest, as we will see in the next section. And as the case described earlier clearly illustrates, the period of observation can be decisive for the determination of whether brain functions are truly lost. As a result of these different standards, individuals may be dead in one country – or even in one hospital – and alive in another. This absurd state of affairs has led to calls for national and even international standards for the diagnosis of brain death.[53] Whether or not this regulation ever comes to pass, the reality is that, at least in the US, guidelines are mostly dead letters.

THE IRREVERSIBILITY MIRAGE

Natural processes are irreversible. When a radioactive element decays, the nucleus shrinks, giving off a particle, or radiation, in the process. A shattered glass doesn't reassemble spontaneously. Humpty Dumpty cannot be put back together. In thermodynamic terms, an irreversible process leads to increased entropy; rewinding the tape would require entropy to decrease, in violation of the second law of thermodynamics.[54]

Biological systems are not exempt from the second law, and one initial conceptual framework of brain death viewed it as a point of no return, beyond which the organism could no longer resist entropy and its attendant disintegration, regardless of any external efforts to stave it off.[55] However, this view assumed that the brain was the central integrator – a hypothesis that, as discussed, has been discredited. We thus need to define irreversibility in the context of brain death.

---

52. Ibid. See also Dana Lustbader et al., "Second Brain Death Examination May Negatively Affect Organ Donation," *Neurology* 76, no. 2 (2011): 119–24.

53. James L. Bernat, "How Can We Achieve Uniformity in Brain Death Determinations?" *Neurology* 70, no. 4 (2008): 252–53.

54. Strictly speaking, the tape can be rewound, but only at the expense of an increase in entropy somewhere else.

55. Julius Korein, *The Problem of Brain Death: Development and History* (New York: New York Academy of Sciences, 1978), 19–38.

Theoretically, this definition should be straightforward. Neurons are exquisitely sensitive to ischemia (restriction of blood supply), with cell death starting within minutes of the cessation of intracranial circulation. Most conditions leading to the clinical picture of brain death are accompanied by severe brain swelling, which increases intracranial pressure. If this increase is of sufficient magnitude, intracranial blood flow ceases, causing global cell death. Therefore, demonstrating a lack of intracranial blood flow would establish the irreversibility of the process.[56]

As always, in practice it's more complicated. The gold standard, the four-vessel angiogram, is invasive, demands specialized facilities and personnel as well as the administration of contrast material – which can harm the kidneys and jeopardize transplantation – and entails the risks inherent in transporting a potentially unstable patient to the angiography suite. Other techniques can be used to determine whether blood is flowing through the brain, but they all have limitations. They also require expertise to perform and interpret accurately, and these resources may not be available in every hospital, or during off hours.

Those in favor of these ancillary tests point out the uneven quality of brain death evaluations, as conducted in the real world, and are more sanguine regarding the tests' limitations.[57] Those opposing the tests focus instead on their weaknesses, while maintaining that clinical examinations done by experts are essentially infallible.[58] Are they?

Can a bedside examination alone prove irreversible loss of function? Let us ignore for a moment the obvious dearth of experienced clinicians – which is why many guidelines require no specialized training for those involved – and examine if this faith is justified.

To evaluate the claims made regarding the accuracy of the method we use to diagnose brain death, it's helpful to understand how

56. Incidentally, this would put us back in a thermodynamic framework, since the brain would have reached a state of maximal entropy, regardless of what the rest of the organism might be doing.
57. James L. Bernat, "On Irreversibility as a Prerequisite for Brain Death Determination," in *Brain Death and Disorders of Consciousness* (ed. Calixto Machado and D. Alan Shewmon; New York: Kluwer Academic/Plenum Publishers, 2004), 161–67.
58. Eelco F. M. Wijdicks, "The Case Against Confirmatory Tests for Determining Brain Death in Adults," *Neurology*, 75, no. 1 (2010): 77–83.

this method developed. When developing a diagnostic test, we measure its performance by comparing its predictions to a gold standard. For example, in the case of a new, rapid HIV test, we would compare its results with those of the more laborious, not readily available test that detects viral genetic material in blood. In the case of brain death, researchers used cardiac arrest as the gold standard. *The NINCDS Collaborative Study of Brain Death* – the largest prospective validation of diagnostic criteria – reported that the combination of coma, apnea, and electrocerebral silence had a true positive rate of 99%.[59] The key question is: a true positive rate for what?

As it turns out, these criteria accurately identified patients who subsequently sustained a cardiac arrest, either spontaneously or because their physician withdrew life support. Without getting into the debate about diagnosis versus prognosis, the logic behind the NINCDS study, and every one after that, is hopelessly circular. Once patients are declared brain dead, their organs and/or ventilators are usually removed in short order, after which these people are dead by anyone's definition. This death, in turn, confirms the accuracy of the diagnostic procedure, because the lost functions never return. If a junior researcher were to propose a similar study, he would be advised to review the concept of causality.

In light of the preceding discussion, can an expertly conducted bedside examination establish irreversibility? No. At best, it can predict that the loss will be permanent.

Leaving the language of thermodynamics aside, recall that an irreversible process is one in which the system cannot be restored to its original state; it simply cannot be done. Contrast this process with one that leads to a permanent state, that is, it lasts, or is designed to last, indefinitely. This doesn't mean the system can't be brought back to its original state. A change may be permanent yet still reversible.

In the context of brain death, if the loss of function is due to neuronal death, the new state is surely irreversible. On the other hand, if the

59. The acronym stands for National Institute of Neurological and Communicative Disorders and Stroke. See "An Appraisal of the Criteria of Cerebral Death: A Summary Statement, a Collaborative Study," *JAMA* 237, no. 10 (1977): 982–86; *NINCDS Study*.

cells are still alive but unable to function, the process is not, at least in principle, irreversible. The fact that an individual in such a state goes on to sustain a cardiac arrest – either spontaneously, after withdrawal of the ventilator, or following organ procurement – proves only that the loss of function was *permanent*. And the probability that a condition is permanent is inversely related to the time we're willing to wait before acting.

These are not theoretical musings. When blood flow to a given area of the brain ceases, an infarction (tissue death due to lack of oxygen) quickly develops, its size dependent on the blood vessel involved, the collateral circulation, and other factors. Surrounding this infarction is a region that receives too little blood for the brain cells to function, but enough to survive, at least for some time. This is the ischemic penumbra (the area surrounding the ischemic tissue).[60] The fundamental problem with relying solely on clinical examination is precisely that it cannot distinguish between infarcted brain and brain that is in penumbra.

The potential importance of this point for the management of those presumed brain dead cannot be overemphasized. Patients can recover, to a greater or lesser extent, from what was initially a dense neurological deficit, after receiving clot-dissolving drugs. More important, we can protect the penumbra brain and limit the extension of the infarct, such as by hypothermia, paralysis, or barbiturate-induced coma. These measures are instituted as a matter of course in comatose patients with severe brain injuries but residual brainstem function. On the other hand, if brainstem reflexes are absent the focus changes entirely, and all interventions that might interfere with the brain death determination cease or are not started. Penumbra brain becomes dead brain.[61]

What proportion of patients currently diagnosed as brain dead would have some degree of recovery if treated aggressively? That question will never be answered given the need for transplantation organs. Nevertheless, and in contrast to the debates surrounding what "all

---

60. Jens Astrup, Bo K. Siesjö, and Lindsay Symon, "Thresholds in Cerebral Ischemia: The Ischemic Penumbra," *Stroke* 12, no. 6 (1981): 723–25; Myron D. Ginsberg, "Adventures in the Pathophysiology of Brain Ischemia: Penumbra, Gene Expression, Neuroprotection – The 2002 Thomas Willis Lecture," *Stroke* 34, no. 1 (2003): 214–23.
61. Cicero Galli Coimbra, "Implications of Ischemic Penumbra for the Diagnosis of Brain Death," *Brazilian Journal of Medical and Biological Research* 32 (1999): 1479–87.

functions" means, irreversibility is central to the definitions of death.[62] Simply repeating that the current system is infallible in proving irreversibility does not make it so.

THE RED QUEEN'S CHALLENGE

The generally accepted narrative is that the concept of brain death evolved separately from transplantation, and that the adoption of the former was not intended to advance the latter.[63] However, while the first premise is correct – brain death is mentioned as early as 1800, by the French physiologist Bichat[64] – its adoption had everything to do with promoting the nascent discipline of transplantation.

In its seminal report, the Harvard ad hoc committee stated that a new definition of death was needed for two reasons. First, thanks to advances in resuscitation, there were now patients with beating hearts but irreversibly damaged brains. These patients burdened their families, the hospitals, and those who needed the beds they occupied. Second, the criteria for the definition of death were obsolete and could "lead to controversy in obtaining organs for transplantation."[65] Whether the members of the committee were more concerned with one or the other is a matter of debate, but transplantation was clearly never far from their thoughts.

In his initial letter to the prospective members of the committee, the dean of Harvard Medical School expressed his belief that "with its pioneering interest in transplantation," the Harvard faculty was better equipped to tackle the problem than any other group. Successive drafts toned down the emphasis on transplantation, for fear of a public backlash, until only one sentence remained, in the introduction. Nevertheless, when writing the following year about the scarcity of organs, the chairman of the committee said:

62. Whether we use the whole-brain, brainstem, or higher-brain criterion.
63. Calixto Machado et al., "The Concept of Brain Death Did Not Evolve to Benefit Organ Transplants," *Journal of Medical Ethics* 33 (2007): 197–200.
64. Xavier Bichat, *Physiological Researches Upon Life and Death* (trans. Tobias Watkins; 1st American ed.; Philadelphia: Smith & Maxwell, 1809), 138, 278.
65. "Irreversible Coma," 337.

Yet, as was evident in the preceding section [a discussion of the ad hoc committee's report], we have available a powerful means of overcoming the grave shortages.[66]

Diagnosing death had never been an urgent matter, but things were now different. In the words of the medical director of the American Heart Association:

> Until recently [when to turn off the ventilator] was not critical, but we've got a whole new ballgame now, because two hours can make the difference in whether an organ will be viable for transplant.[67]

If further clarification was needed, it was provided by a state medical society when it invited a well-known theologian to a symposium it was sponsoring:

> The purpose of this symposium is to more clearly define "The Moment of Death," so that those sick people who need transplanted tissues will not be sacrificed because of a lack of a clear definition as to when the donor has died.[68]

---

66. Henry K. Beecher, "Scarce Resources and Medical Advancement," *Daedalus* 98 (1969): 275–313. For a discussion of the evolution of the brain death concept and the role played by transplantation in its swift adoption, see Howard Doyle, "Reinventare La Morte: Dal Coma Dépassé Ai Criteri Dell'Harvard Ad Hoc Committee," in *Ripensare La Morte* (ed. Howard Doyle, Giovanni Boniolo, and Ignazio Rabbi Marino; Rome: Pensiero Scientifico, in press); an English version is available from the author. See also Martin S. Pernick, "Back from the Grave: Recurring Controversies over Defining and Diagnosing Death in History," in *Death: Beyond Whole-Brain Criteria* (ed. Richard M. Zaner; Dordrecht, the Netherlands: Kluwer Academic Publishers, 1988), 17–74; Mita Giacomini, "A Change of Heart and a Change of Mind? Technology and the Redefinition of Death in 1968," *Social Sciences in Medicine* 44 (1997): 1465–82; Martin S. Pernick, "Brain Death in a Cultural Context: The Reconstruction of Death, 1967–1981," in *The Definition of Death: Contemporary Controversies* (ed. Stuart J. Youngner, Robert M. Arnold, and Renie Schapiro; Baltimore: Johns Hopkins University Press, 1999), 3–33.
67. Robert Reinhold, "Doctors Need a New Definition of Death," *New York Times*, August 11, 1968.
68. Paul Ramsey, *The Patient as Person: Explorations in Medical Ethics* (2nd ed.; New Haven: Yale University Press, 2002), 104.

Is any of this relevant to this discussion? It is, insofar as it sheds light on the brain death debate, whose purpose is not so much to argue the soundness of the concept as it is to protect its conclusion, to wit, that brain death is the appropriate criterion for death.

In pursuit of this defense, greater or lesser degrees of violence are perpetrated against logic. For example, a brain function is considered relevant only if it can be tested solely by means of a bedside examination,[69] a dubious ad hoc qualification that ignores the preservation of neurohormonal function. More creatively, the ability to regulate body temperature or respond physiologically to pain is used to illustrate, without any hint of irony, how a dead brain can still do some work.[70] As for the problematic requirement of irreversibility, this is addressed by begging the question.

The defense has also required the dismantling of the theoretical foundation upon which the brain-based criterion once rested. The "cessation of functioning of the organism as a whole" is now dismissed as a "false assumption," and a looser concept, the "fundamental vital work of a living organism," is offered in its stead. Felicitously, the old criterion for death emerged unscathed from this otherwise tectonic shift, avoiding awkward questions about the validity of previous death declarations.

Like the Red Queen, who must run ever faster just to stay in place, for the last four decades we have continuously moved the goalposts so the brain death fiction could survive.

DEAD ENOUGH

Is death strictly a biological phenomenon? Does the death of a human mean the same as the death of a dog or cat, as boldly stated thirty years ago?[71] How far down the phylogenetic tree would a supporter be willing to take this argument? Is death, instead, the destruction of consciousness? The departure of a soul? And why should the ability to

---

69. James. L. Bernat, "How Much of the Brain Must Die in Brain Death?" *Journal of Clinical Ethics* 3, no. 1 (1992): 21–26.

70. The case of thermoregulation is indeed ironic, since it was singled out as an example of brain function in the original theoretical analysis of brain death. Bernat, Culver, and Gert, "Definition and Criterion," 1981.

71. Ibid.

breathe be more important than all the other vegetative functions put together? More important, does any of this matter? It does, of course, and it does not.

To most of us, human death is one of the great mysteries, which will never be solved to everyone's satisfaction. But as far as organ donation is concerned, this is beside the point.

As the previous discussion makes clear, I do not believe that patients who meet the accepted criteria for brain death are dead – biologically, metaphysically, ontologically, *and* socially dead. But I also do not believe a death so absolute is necessary for vital organ donation to be ethical. The donor need only be *beyond harm*. Or, stated differently, he should be dead enough.

To many, these words will sound jarring, but the reality is that this is what we've been doing for four decades. Our unwillingness to discuss it in public, for fear of jeopardizing organ donation, doesn't change this reality. Organ transplantation saves thousands of lives around the world every year, and brain death is the noble lie that makes this possible; but it's still dishonest. We ought to ask ourselves if the truth should still be held hostage to this noble purpose.

Chapter 5

Non-Heart-Beating Organ Donation: The Ethical Challenges Involved

Kenneth Prager

INTRODUCTION

Organ donation can involve either a living or dead organ donor. Living organ donation is limited almost entirely to the donation of a kidney. A much smaller number of living organ donors donate a portion of their liver.

All heart, lung, and pancreas transplants and the vast majority of liver transplants are made possible by the removal of these organs from donors who have been pronounced dead. About half the kidneys transplanted in the US are taken from such "cadaveric" donors.

Approximately 90% of cadaveric organ donations come from patients who have been declared brain dead. Brain death, whole-brain death, and brainstem death are accepted legally as death throughout the United States. The other legal definition of death in the US is the cardiopulmonary one, based on the permanent cessation of cardiac activity and breathing.

Because of the severe shortage of transplantable organs, the US Organ Donation Breakthrough Collaborative (ODBC) was instituted in 2003 at the request of the secretary of health and human services. The initiative was a concerted effort by the donation and transplantation community to bring about a major change in order to improve the organ donation system. In addition to promoting efforts to increase the number of brain dead patients who would become organ donors, the ODBC sought to implement donation after cardiac death (DCD), or non-heart-beating organ donation (NHBD).

NON-HEART-BEATING DONORS VS. BRAINSTEM-DEAD DONORS

Prior to the widespread introduction of brainstem death into law in the 1970s, all organ transplants from cadaveric donors came from NHBD. With the acceptance of the brainstem death definition, surgeons preferred to remove organs from these patients as their hearts were still beating and circulation was still maintained. These organs were in better condition than those removed from non-heart-beating donors, which were likely damaged by the lack of oxygen between the time of cessation of heartbeat/declaration of death and the retrieval of organs.

NHBD CANDIDATES

Medically and ethically, successful NHBD requires appropriate candidates:

NHBD from Severely Brain-Damaged Patients

NHBD usually occurs when the relatives of a patient who has sustained severe and irreversible brain damage request that life support be withdrawn. Although these patients do not fulfill the criteria of brainstem death, they have sustained massive brain damage either following cardiac arrest and cessation of blood flow to the brain for a critical period, or because of strokes, intracerebral hemorrhages, or severe brain trauma. They have no prospect of ever regaining a quality of life they would have considered acceptable. Most of these patients, if they were to survive to hospital discharge, would face a life on a ventilator and with a feeding tube in a nursing home with minimal or no consciousness.

NHBD from Dying Patients

Other NHBD candidates may not have sustained severe brain damage but are being kept alive with life support and have zero chance of leaving the hospital alive. Some of these patients have profound heart, lung, or liver failure, and their dying is prolonged by ventricular assist devices, ventilators, and a variety of potent medications that cannot heal them. Often these patients are suffering, and usually they are minimally conscious because of the severity of their illnesses and sedation.

Once again, the family members of such a patient decide he or she should be removed from life support because treatment is not helping, only prolonging the dying process.[1] Often, patients have written or stated clearly that they would never want to prolong their dying in such a hopeless situation, or to be kept alive indefinitely in a completely helpless state with severe brain damage.

CONSENT OF FAMILY AND DOCTORS

When family members request removal of life support, the attending physicians make sure the request is appropriate based on the patient's prognosis. This point is critical.

In general – including cases where no organ donation is involved – there must be unanimity among the physicians that, regardless of the aggressiveness of treatment, and whether or not life support is continued, the patient will die in the hospital, or the patient cannot regain what he or she would consider a minimally acceptable quality of life. The decision to remove life support should not be made without detailed and extensive discussion between the patient's family and physicians on this point. If the patient has written or clearly stated his or her wishes, these directives are most helpful in making this extremely difficult decision.

There should be unanimity not only among the doctors but among those family members closest to the patient, including his or her

---

1. Patients cannot decide themselves, because they're too ill, cannot communicate, and are usually either heavily sedated or minimally conscious.

legally appointed health care proxy, if such a designation has been made. Though in most states a decision to remove life support can be made by a legally appointed health care agent or by the closest family member, for the sake of family harmony it is desirable that there be unanimity before such a request is carried out.

The decision to remove life support in cases of NHBD is much simpler for the family than in cases where such a request is made based on quality of life. Removal of life support in potential NHBD occurs where there is absolute certainty that the patient will die imminently in the hospital after this support is removed. Even if life support is continued, it is certain that the patient will not survive to discharge regardless of aggressiveness of treatment. These patients are hanging on by a thread. So tenuous is their hold on life, even with life support, that they are expected to die within an hour or so once such support is removed. For these patients, medical technology is serving only to prolong the dying process rather than offering any hope of improvement or even of achieving medical stability so that they can be discharged to a nursing facility on life support.

If such a patient is identified and the family requests removal of life support, and if the patient will likely stop breathing and suffer cardiac arrest relatively quickly – usually within an hour – after life support is stopped, family members are asked to allow their loved one to become an organ donor after death (which will be pronounced based on the cardiopulmonary criteria noted above). Usually a representative from the Organ Donor Network makes this request, and only after the patient's medical suitability to donate has been evaluated.

In many if not most cases of NHBD, the patient has previously expressed a desire to be an organ donor. Even when such a declaration has not been made, families that permit NHBD via their relatives find great comfort in knowing that after the death of their loved ones, human lives can be saved.

NHBD – THE USUAL PROCESS

If the family agrees to organ donation, the patient is taken to the operating room (OR) while still alive but unconscious. There he is prepped and draped preparatory to organ removal if death occurs within an hour or so after removal of life support. Families may accompany patients to the OR to be with them until the moment of death, should it occur, or to accompany them back to their rooms if they don't die.

At the appropriate time, the patient is removed from life support. Usually this procedure involves disconnecting the patient from the ventilator and/or stopping medication, called pressors, to maintain the patient's blood pressure. All the steps that follow should be identical to those that would be taken if the patient were not to be an organ donor. Namely, the physician who accompanies the patient to the OR stays with the patient to be sure he is comfortable after ventilator support is stopped. If patient respiration appears labored, morphine is administered.

If, within an hour, the patient stops breathing and goes into cardiac arrest, the physician notes the time. After five minutes with absence of breathing and circulation, the patient is pronounced dead on the basis of cardiopulmonary criteria. The family, if still present, leaves the OR, and the surgeons enter to remove the organs destined for transplantation. The surgeons are not in the room with the patient while he is alive. There is complete separation between the team treating the living patient and the doctors involved in transplant.

Excursus – How Long until Death Is Declared?

Although most medical centers wait five minutes after cardiopulmonary arrest to pronounce death, some medical centers wait two. The rationale for the shorter period is that there has not been any documented case of cardiopulmonary autoresuscitation after two minutes of cessation of breathing and heart activity.

UNCONTROLLED NHBD

Procedure

Far less common are cases of NHBD in which a patient dies spontaneously, without the removal of life support. In these cases, a patient has a witnessed cardiac arrest, and cardiopulmonary resuscitation (CPR) commences. CPR continues until the resuscitation team sees no sign of cardiac activity or breathing for a suitable period, and pronounces the patient dead.

At this point, in countries where this procedure of "uncontrolled" NHBD is used, the team recommences cardiac compression and ventilation, endeavoring to keep the patient's kidneys perfused with oxygenated blood in order to maintain their viability until the organ transplant team arrives. When that team arrives, it places a catheter in the patient's aorta via the groin and flushes a large quantity of cold saline into the kidneys to preserve their viability.

Relatives of the deceased are contacted and permission requested to allow organ donation. If the relatives agree, the body is taken to the OR, where the kidneys are removed for transplant.

Difficulties

Only a few countries in Europe have adopted this alternative NHBD procedure. Additionally, only kidneys and heart valves can be retrieved in these uncontrolled situations, whereas under controlled NHBD, lungs and occasionally livers as well as kidneys can be used. Finally, many centers won't even accept organs procured under these circumstances, because of the high risk of organ damage from lack of oxygen.

Benefits

Nevertheless, from an ethical standpoint many feel more comfortable with uncontrolled NHBD, because life support is not removed from the patient/donor, who instead dies "naturally."

Uncontrolled organ donation is currently being tried in New York City, but no organ retrieval has yet occurred.

HALAKHIC QUESTIONS

NHBD presents several halakhic issues inapplicable to brain death:

Controlled NHBD

Since almost all NHBD must occur in a controlled fashion, namely, after planned removal of life support, is such removal ever permitted?[2] If so, how much time must elapse after cessation of circulation and breathing before a person may be pronounced dead and organ retrieval may

---

2. This question, of course, arises in non-NHBD cases as well, as removal of life support occurs for quality-of-life reasons.

commence? This question is tremendously important, since the more time passes, the less chance of organ viability.

Uncontrolled NHBD

In the case of uncontrolled death leading to kidney donation, should the requirements for the declaration of death be any different? Additionally, what is the status of a "person" who has been declared dead but whose organs are being perfused by cardiac compression and ventilation?

NHBD for Brainstem-Dead Patients

According to those halakhic authorities who reject the brainstem-based death definition,[3] would it be permissible to turn the potential brainstem-dead donor into a non-heart-beating donor by removing ventilator support, which would quickly lead to cardiac and respiratory arrest, followed by organ removal from someone who then fulfilled cardiopulmonary criteria for death?[4] To elaborate, could a brainstem-dead patient be defined as "dying" (*goses*), permitting removal of the ventilator, which could be viewed as impeding the soul's departure from the body?

And if these authorities reject this approach as well, would they perhaps allow such a patient to be moved to the OR when his or her vital signs were failing, on the supposition that cardiopulmonary arrest would soon occur – and then allow organ donation following cardiac arrest?

CONCLUSION

These are all complicated questions, dealing with the most sensitive and painful issues. I hope that clarification of the medical realities will clarify the halakhic options as well. It is vital that these deliberations be conducted with great care and thought, and in as timely a manner as possible. After all, an organ donated is a life saved.

---

3. Those who do accept the brainstem-based death definition have no need for the processes suggested in this section, since it goes without saying that a brain dead patient on a ventilator can provide more organs and in better condition than can NHBDs. Therefore, these suggestions should be seen as a last-ditch effort to retrieve whatever organs possible from patients whose families/proxies reject the brainstem-based definition of death.
4. See Rabbi Asher Lopatin's essay in this volume, where he makes a suggestion along these lines.

Section II

Halakha: General Responsa

Chapter 6

Jewish Law and
Medical Science

Yoel Bin Nun[1]

INTRODUCTION

Many people mistakenly believe that organ donation is the process of removing organs from the body of a dying person in the last moments of his or her life – God forbid! – an action that would be forbidden both halakhically as well as medically and legally.[2] The truth is quite the contrary. The entire medical establishment in our day agrees – and this rule is in force – that organs may be harvested only after the donor is

---

1. Translated from the Hebrew by Rabbi Zev Farber; the Hebrew version of the main essay (excluding the appendix) can be found on Rabbi Bin Nun's website: http://www.ybn.co.il/mamrim/m33.htm; for the Hebrew version of the appendix: http://www.ynet.co.il/articles/0,7340,L-4010683,00.html.

2. According to halakha, one may not take one life to save another (אין דוחין נפש מפני נפש). See m. *Oholot* 7; b. *Sanhedrin* 72b; Rambam, MT Laws of Murder 1:9. Also see Rabbi Yeḥezqel Landau, *Noda bi-Yehuda Tinyana* ḤM 59:

ואטו מי הותר להרוג את הטריפה	Is it somehow permitted to kill a dying person in
להציל את השלם? זה לא שמענו	order to save a healthy one? I have never heard
מעולם.	of such a thing.

deceased.[3] The question remains: How does one determine the moment of death, medically and halakhically?

Additionally, no one debates the fact that hundreds of deathly ill patients can be saved, and their lives significantly extended, through the transplantation of healthy organs from people who have just died. According to halakha, saving a life overrides the obligation to bury such people intact, just as it supersedes violation of the Sabbath and all other commandments, with the exception of the prohibition of murder, severe sexual immorality, and idolatry.[4]

Insofar as treating the deceased with respect, there is no greater honor than enabling him or her to save another's life with his or her own body. This seems especially true at the moment of death, when the deceased is standing before the heavenly court; this is a truly selfless gift, there is none greater, for the recipient will never be able to repay the donor.[5] Organ donation is a tremendous merit for the deceased and his or her family at this difficult hour. It's a real mitzva to inform family members of this merit – gently, conveying that one understands their terrible pain, but with exceptional clarity.

THE MOMENT OF DEATH AS DEFINED
BY THE BABYLONIAN TALMUD

The question of how one determines the moment of death was addressed explicitly by the sages in the Babylonian Talmud (*Yoma* 85a) about one

---

See also the following three volumes of *Sefer Assia*: 5 (5746/1985–86), 61–76; 7 (5754/1993–94), 177–87; and 9 (5764/2003–2004), 367–77. For the medico-legal standards, see the circulars of the director general of Israel's Ministry of Health: www.health.gov.il. The same rule is in force for the United States and other countries.

3. In sharp contrast, at the very beginning of the age of transplantation, hearts were removed from live donors, essentially killing them, since doctors felt that these people were about to die anyway. This is, in my opinion, a major reason for the widespread skepticism toward organ donation and the medical establishment even today. Yet the situation is very different nowadays, and nothing is ever done without the explicit agreement of the family, and only after an unambiguous declaration of death.

4. B. *Yoma* 82a, 85b; b. *Sanhedrin* 74a; Rambam, MT Laws of the Foundations of the Torah, ch. 5, and Laws of Shabbat, ch. 2.

5. "True kindness," or *ḥesed shel emet*, is when the kindness can never be repaid, since either the recipient or the benefactor has passed on.

thousand years before the issue was raised by the medical profession in the modern period.[6] By and large, the halakhic discussion has been based upon this pericope.

In the pericope preceding this one, the Mishna established that wherever it's possible to save another's life, Shabbat and Yom Tov should be violated in the attempt. Our mishna (*Yoma* 8:7) follows immediately after the articulation of this principle:

מי שנפלה עליו מפולת: ספק
הוא שם ספק אינו שם, ספק חי
ספק מת, ספק עובד כוכבים ספק
ישראל - מפקחין עליו את הגל.
מצאוהו חי - מפקחין עליו, ואם
מת - יניחוהו.

Regarding someone on whom debris has fallen [on Shabbat or a holiday], and it is unclear whether he is trapped in the rubble or not, and it is further unclear [assuming he is trapped] whether he is alive or dead, and whether he is a gentile or a Jew – they clear the rubble to rescue him. If they find him alive, they continue clearing the rubble; dead – they leave him [until after Shabbat or the holiday].

On this mishna, the Babylonian Talmud comments:

מצאוהו חי פשיטא! לא, צריכא,
דאפילו לחיי שעה.

If they find him alive – obviously [they clear the rubble]! No, this comment is necessary to teach [that we clear the rubble on Shabbat] even if it will buy the person only a few moments of life.

---

6. Galen, the great physician of ancient Greece (a contemporary of Rabbi Yehuda ha-Nasi, and referenced favorably as a medical authority by many *Rishonim*), was concerned about mistaken declarations of death, and warned of accidently burying someone alive. Galen recommended waiting three days to make sure. See Samuel Weiss, "Determining the Moment of Death in Medicine, Ethics, and Halakha" (Ph.D. diss., Hebrew University and Hadassah Medical Center, 5743), 29 [Hebrew]. Nevertheless, the issue became a matter of law only in 1772, when the duke of Mecklenburg imposed the three-day rule and required a declaration of death by qualified physicians.

תנו רבנן: עד היכן הוא בודק?
עד חוטמו, ויש אומרים: עד לבו.
[ס"א: טיבורו.]

Our rabbis taught: Up to where do we check [for signs of life]? Up to his nose. Some say: Up to his heart. (Some texts read: his navel.)[7]

•

נימא הני תנאי כי הני תנאי,
דתניא: מהיכן הולד נוצר?
מראשו, שנאמר: "ממעי אמי
אתה גוזי", ואומר: "גזי נזרך
והשליכי". אבא שאול אומר:
מטיבורו, ומשלח שרשיו אילך
ואילך.

Shall we say the above argument is similar to the [following] argument? For we learned: From what point is a fetus formed [in the womb]? From its head, for it says: "from the innards of my mother You sheared me" (Ps. 71:6), and it says: "shear your locks and cast them away" (Jer. 7:29). Abba Shaul says: From its navel; and it sends forth roots in all directions.

אפילו תימא אבא שאול, עד
כאן לא קא אמר אבא שאול
התם אלא לענין יצירה, דכל
מידי ממציעתיה מיתצר, אבל
לענין פקוח נפש - אפילו אבא
שאול מודי דעקר חיותא
באפיה הוא, דכתיב: "כל אשר
נשמת רוח חיים באפיו".

[No.] Even Abba Shaul [would agree here]. Abba Shaul refers only to the point of formation of the fetus, since everything forms from its center. But as far as saving a life, even Abba Shaul would agree that the core of life is in the nose, as it is written, "All in whose nostrils was the breath of life" (Gen. 7:22).

אמר רב פפא: מחלוקת ממטה
למעלה, אבל ממעלה למטה,
כיון דבדק ליה עד חוטמו שוב
אינו צריך, דכתיב: "כל אשר
נשמת רוח חיים באפיו".

Rav Pappa said: The dispute is when [uncovering the person] from bottom to top, but from top to bottom, once one checks the person's nose [for signs of breath], one need check no further, as it says: "All in whose nostrils was the breath of life."

The dispute among the authorities in this pericope is itself a dispute among the tannaitic authorities elsewhere (b. *Soṭa* 45b), specifically

---

7. This is the text of most manuscripts as well as most *Rishonim*.

with regard to measuring the distance from a corpse found in a field to the nearest city, part of the laws of the *egla arufa*:

מאין היו מודדין? רבי אליעזר אומר: מטיבורו. רבי עקיבא אומר: מחוטמו. רבי אליעזר בן יעקב אומר: ממקום שנעשה חלל, מצוארו.	From where did they measure? Rabbi Eliezer says: From his navel. Rabbi Akiva says: From his nose. Rabbi Eliezer ben Ya'aqov says: From the spot at which he became a corpse, from his neck.

The Talmud comments on this dispute:

במאי קמיפלגי? מר סבר: עיקר חיותא באפיה, ומר סבר: עיקר חיותא בטיבוריה.	About what [principle] are they arguing? One believes the source of life is in one's nose, and the other believes the source of life is in one's navel.

לימא כי הני תנאי: "מהיכן הולד נוצר? מראשו, וכן הוא אומר: 'ממעי אמי אתה גוזי', ואומר: 'גזי נזרך והשליכי וגו'. אבא שאול אומר: מטיבורו, ומשלח שרשו אילך ואילך!"	Shall we say that this is similar to the following argument: It was taught: "From what [part of the body] does the fetus form? From its head, for it says: 'from the innards of my mother You sheared me' (Ps. 71:6), and it says: 'shear your locks and cast them away' (Jer. 7:29). Abba Shaul says: From its navel; and it sends forth roots in all directions"?

אפילו תימא אבא שאול, ע"כ לא קאמר אבא שאול אלא לענין יצירה, דכי מיתצר ולד ממציעתיה מיתצר, אבל לענין חיותא דכולי עלמא באפיה הוא, דכתיב: "כל אשר נשמת רוח חיים באפיו...[מתו]".	[No.] Even Abba Shaul [would agree here]. Abba Shaul refers only to the formation [of the fetus], since a fetus forms from its center. But regarding life, everyone agrees that [the source of life] is in the nose, as it is written: "All in whose nostrils was the breath of life ... [died]."

The Talmud attempts to link the Mishna's dispute with the issue raised by Abba Shaul regarding where the formation of a human begins.

As in *Yoma*, this attempt is rejected, and the pericope ends with a quote from Genesis about the breath of life being in a person's nostrils. Rambam codifies the halakha like Rabbi Akiva (MT Laws of Murder 9:9), that one measures from the nose.[8]

The discussion in the *Yoma* pericope focuses on the conflict between saving a life and observing the Sabbath. The essential resolution that guides this discussion is that saving a life overrides Sabbath observance, and that even the *possible* saving of a life overrides the observance of the Sabbath or the Day of Atonement. This resolution had great historical significance insofar as the Oral Law is concerned, since a number of Jewish sects during the Second Temple period rejected this conclusion. Instead they prohibited the waging of war on the Sabbath,[9] and the desecration of the Sabbath in order to save someone's life in general.

All of the above applies to saving a life but not to dealing with corpses. Though halakha attaches importance to the honorable treatment of the dead, and requires that they be buried immediately, it is forbidden to desecrate the Sabbath for this burial. Therefore, it is halakhically necessary to determine the moment of death clearly and precisely, since until that point one must desecrate the Sabbath to extend a person's life, even if only by a matter of moments. Afterward, however, it is forbidden to violate the Sabbath in any way, since the person one is attempting to save is already deceased.

At this juncture, it behooves us to return to the dispute in *Yoma*.[10] We can suggest a connection between the position that one must check the person's nose and the position of Rabbi Akiva in *Soṭa* (which the halakha follows) that one measures from the nose.[11] Similarly, we can

---

8. Rambam also codifies Rabbi Akiva's position that if head and body have been separated, one brings the body to the head for burial (MT Laws of Murder 9:9), since the head is the essential feature of the person (*Commentary on the Mishna, Soṭa* 9:4).

9. See Jubilees 50:6–13; *Damascus Document* 10:14–11:18. For the opposing view, see I Maccabees 2:31–41; see also Shlomo Goren, *Meshiv Milḥama* I, 54–69.

10. As will be noted later, in the Jerusalem Talmud the dispute is amoraic, and in the Babylonian Talmud, tannaitic.

11. See Rabbi Joseph Karo's *Kesef Mishneh* (his commentary on Rambam's *Mishneh Torah*), Laws of Murder 9:5; see also Rabbi Shalom Mordechai Schwadron, *Responsa of Maharsham* 6:124.

connect the opinion that one checks up to the navel (or the heart) with Rabbi Eliezer's view that one measures from the navel.

The pericope in *Yoma* clearly prefers the position that one need only check the person's nose and that if there is no breath, one does not violate the Sabbath to remove the body. As Rashi (ad loc.) states:

ואם אין חיות בחוטמו, | If there is no life in his nostrils, i.e., if he
שאינו מוציא רוח, ודאי | doesn't exhale, he is certainly dead, and they
מת ויניחוהו. | leave him [until after the Sabbath or holiday].

The presumption of the passage itself stands out clearly in its explanation of the opinion of Abba Shaul, who believes that the fetus is formed from the navel outward. Even so, the Talmud suggests: "when it comes to saving someone's life – even Abba Shaul would admit that the essence of a person's life is in his nostrils, for it is written: 'All in whose nostrils was the breath of life…[died].'" Rav Pappa sums up the presumption of this pericope similarly: "Rav Pappa said: The debate is when [uncovering the person] from bottom to top, but from top to bottom, once one checks the person's nose [for signs of breath], one need check no further, as it says: 'All in whose nostrils was the breath of life…[died].'"

THE HALAKHA AS CODIFIED

Let us look at Rambam's codification of the laws found in this pericope (MT Laws of Shabbat, ch. 2).

א) דחויה היא שבת, אצל סכנת | 1) Shabbat is overridden by life-and-death
נפשות, כשאר כל המצוות; | considerations, like all other mitzvot.
לפיכך חולה שיש בו סכנה - | Therefore, when a person is dangerously
עושין לו כל צרכיו בשבת, על | ill on Shabbat, one should provide for all
פי רופא אומן של אותו מקום. | his needs, as directed by a local expert
ספק שהוא צריך לחלל עליו את | physician. If it is uncertain whether Shab-
השבת, ספק שאינו צריך, וכן | bat need be violated or not, or if one
אם אמר רופא לחלל עליו את | physician says Shabbat must be violated
השבת, ורופא אחר אומר אינו | and another physician says it needn't
צריך - מחללין עליו את השבת: | be – one violates Shabbat, for the pos-
שספק נפשות, דוחה את השבת. | sible danger to life overrides Shabbat.

טז) מפקחין פיקוח נפש בשבת,
ואין צריך ליטול רשות מבית
דין; והמקדים להציל הנפש, הרי
זה משובח.

16) One may save a person's life on Shabbat, and one needn't obtain permission
from the court first; the quicker one is to
save a person's life, the more praiseworthy.

יח) מי שנפלה עליו מפולת - ספק
הוא שם, ספק אינו שם - מפקחין
עליו; מצאוהו חי - אף-על-פי
שנתרוצץ, ואי אפשר שיבריא,
מפקחין עליו ומוציאין אותו,
לחיי אותה שעה. בדקו עד
חוטמו, ולא מצאו בו נשמה -
מניחין אותו, שכבר מת.

18) Regarding someone on whom debris
has fallen [on Shabbat or a holiday], and
it is unclear whether he is trapped in the
rubble or not, they clear the rubble to rescue him. If they find him alive, even if his
body is crushed, and there is no chance
he will recover, they continue clearing the
rubble and remove him [from the rubble]
for those few moments of life. If they
check up to his nose and find no breath,
they leave him [until after Shabbat or the
holiday], since he is already dead.

This is the ruling of Rabbi Joseph Karo in the *Shulḥan Arukh* as
well (OḤ 329):

ג) מי שנפלה עליו מפולת, ספק
חי ספק מת, ספק הוא שם ספק
אינו שם, מפקחין עליו, אף על
פי שיש בו כמה ספקות.

3) Regarding someone on whom debris has
fallen [on Shabbat or a holiday], and it is
unclear whether he is alive or dead, and it
is further unclear whether he is trapped in the
rubble or not, they clear the rubble to
rescue him, even if there are several doubts.

ד) אפילו מצאוהו מרוצץ, שאינו
יכול לחיות אלא לפי שעה,
מפקחין, ובודקין עד חוטמו. אם
לא הרגישו בחוטמו חיות, אז
ודאי מת, לא שנא [אם] פגעו
בראשו תחילה, לא שנא [אם]
פגעו ברגליו תחילה.

4) Even if they find his body crushed, and
there is no chance he can live more than
a few moments, they continue clearing
the rubble, and check [for vital signs] up
to his nose. If they detect no evidence
of life in his nostrils, then he is certainly
dead, and it doesn't matter whether they
reached his head first or whether they
reached his feet first.

It seems clear from both of these sources that the only real factor in determining whether a person is alive or dead is whether he or she is breathing.

THE MOMENT OF DEATH AS DEFINED
BY THE JERUSALEM TALMUD

All of the above is in keeping with the approach of the Babylonian Talmud, which establishes that there is a debate, and that the talmudic passage and halakhic decisors follow the opinion that the breath of the nostrils is decisive, and if no breath is found, the person is certainly dead and is left until after Shabbat.

In the Jerusalem Talmud's pericope (*Yoma* 8:5), however, there is no clear proof of a debate. This passage may be understood as saying that there is no difference of opinion at all. Indeed, this is the interpretation offered by Rabbi Moshe Margalit in his commentary, *Pnei Moshe*, on this pericope.[12]

The Jerusalem Talmud states:

עַד אֵיכָן? תְּרִין אֲמוֹרִין: חַד
אָמַ[ר]: עַד חוֹטְמוֹ, וְחוֹרְנָה אֲמַר:
עַד טִיבּוּרוֹ.

Up to what point [must one check]? There are two opinions recorded. One says: Up to his nose. The other says: Up to his navel.

מָאן דְּאָמַר עַד חוֹטְמוֹ - בְּהוּא
דַּהֲוָה קַיָּים. וּמָאן דְּאָמַ[ר] עַד
טִיבּוּרוֹ - בְּהוּא דַּהֲוָה רַבּוּן/רָכִין.

According to the person who says, "Up to his nose" – the reason is that he is *qayam*. According to the person who says, "Up to his navel" – the reason is that he is *rabun/rakin*.

---

12. Rabbi Moshe Margalit (Margolies; d. 1781) lived in Lithuania at the time of Rabbi Eliyahu Kramer, the Vilna Gaon. Rabbi Margalit wrote a detailed commentary on the Jerusalem Talmud, based on his thorough knowledge of all the rabbinic texts at his disposal, including a manuscript of the Tosefta. He also familiarized himself with the natural sciences in order to make his commentary as accurate as possible, as can be seen most clearly in his treatment of *Seder Zera'im*, the agricultural laws.

Rabbi Margalit explains:

ולא פליגי, דמאן דאמר עד
חוטמו מיירי בהוא דהוה קיים,
כלומר שחזק וקשה הוא, ונרגש
בבדיקת חוטמו, אם יש בו איזה
חיות; ומאן דאמר עד טיבורו,
בהוא דהוה רכין, שהוא רך
כשממשמשין בו, ואינו נרגש
בחוטמו, ובודקין אותו עד
טיבורו, שאפשר, שעוד ירגישו
בו חיות.

They aren't arguing. The one who says "Up to his nose" is referring to someone who is stable, meaning he is strong and hardy,[13] and this can be felt when checking his nose to see if there is any sign of life. The one who says "Up to his navel" refers to someone who is soft, i.e., he feels limp to the touch, and nothing can be felt from his nose, so one checks until his navel, for perhaps some sign of life can still be felt.

According to this interpretation, there would seem to be no room for the position of Rav Pappa in the Babylonian Talmud, or for the decision of the *posqim*, since everything depends on what's possible to check in different situations, and one should always make sure the person is dead before leaving him or her, by checking the nose as well as the chest. This explanation, suggested by Rabbi Margalit, was adopted by a number of authorities who objected to heart transplants.[14] However, the Jerusalem Talmud never mentions the heart as a vital organ that requires checking. The checking of the navel simply means checking for a breath under the diaphragm, as explained by medical professionals as well as Torah scholars.[15]

RASHI AND CHECKING FOR HEARTBEAT

In fact, checking the heart is mentioned only in Rashi's text of the Babylonian Talmud. Rashi explains in his commentary:

---

13. Meaning, his body underneath the rubble is still strong.
14. See Eliezer Waldenburg, "The Prohibition of Transplanting the Heart or Liver from One Person to Another," *Sefer Assia* 7 (5754/1993–94), 149–62 [Hebrew].
15. See Avraham Steinberg, "Determining the Moment of Death and Heart Transplantation," *Sefer Assia* 7 (5754/1993–94), 209–230 [Hebrew]; see also Rabbi Steinberg's comments in *Sefer Assia* 3 (5743/1983), 405 [Hebrew], as well as the extensive summary in his *Encyclopedia of Halakha and Medicine* (2nd ed., 2006), vol. 6, 816ff. [Hebrew].

בליבו יש להבחין אם יש בו   With his heart it is possible to tell if there
חיות, שנשמתו דופקת שם.   are any vital signs, since his life force
                         (*neshama*) pulses from there.

Rashi's words can be understood in two ways. The first way is to understand heart as chest, meaning that one can see the person's vital signs (i.e., breaths)[16] are pulsing. This explanation would be like all the other possibilities explored above, that everything is dependent upon breathing. Alternatively, Rashi may be expressing an entirely different opinion here, that the heart must be checked to see if it's beating.

Be that as it may, even if one were to interpret Rashi as referring to heartbeat, nothing would change in halakha. The *Yoma* pericope discounts this position, and the same is true for the post-talmudic halakhic literature. In fact, if the Talmud and the major halakhic authorities all discounted this view, it is no longer possible for any later authority to disregard the Talmud's universally accepted ruling. In fact, if an authority were to rule that one must violate Shabbat for a person whose heart was still beating, though he or she was no longer breathing and could never breathe again – this violation would be a desecration of Shabbat and require atonement!

REGULAR CASES OF DEATH

Still, some argue that the Talmud's case of a person caught under the rubble of a collapsed building is unique, since it stands to reason that if he isn't breathing, he has died, unlike in regular instances of death. However, if this case were truly exceptional, the halakhic authorities who codified the law should have stated clearly in the laws of Shabbat that, in general, if one finds a person's body on Shabbat, one must violate Shabbat when necessary to check the heart or navel.

Ḥatam Sofer
Rabbi Moshe Sofer forcefully rejected this idea in a famous responsum (*Ḥatam Sofer* YD 338):

---

16. Understanding the term "life force" (*neshama*) as breathing (*neshima*).

ולומר נפל מפולת שאני
כאשר כ' ידידי נ"י תמי' גדולה
בעיני וכי קרא נשמת רוח
חיים במפולת מיירי ועוד דבר
ידוע בהיפוך כי המתים מיתה
פתאומיות יש לחוש יותר
שנדמה כמת מחמת בהלה
וכעין חולה שיתוק שקורין
(שלאג) ואפ"ה כשפסקה
נשמתו שוב אין מחללין שבת.

And to suggest that a case of fallen debris is different, as my colleague has suggested,[17] seems very surprising to me. Is the verse about the breath of life discussing collapsed buildings or avalanches? Furthermore, the opposite is well known to be true. When someone dies suddenly, there is reason to worry that the person only appears to be dead due to shock, as in the illness of paralysis that's called *Schlag* [= stroke]. Even so, when his breath has stopped, one no longer violates Shabbat [to save him].

וע"כ כלל הוא לכל המתים
שזהו שיעור המקובל בידינו
מאז היתה עדת ה' לגוי
קדוש וכל הרוחות שבעולם
אם ימלאו חפניהם רוח לא
יזיזונו ממקום תורתינו
הקדושה!

Therefore, the general rule for all [examinations of] the dead is that this has been the accepted evaluation among us ever since the assembly of God became a holy nation; and all the winds in the world – if [our opponents] fill their hands with wind – will not move us from the position of our holy Torah.

והנה כן משמע ברמב"ם
{הלכות אבל פ"ד ה"ה}:
"והמעמיץ (= המעצם עיניו של
נפטר) עם יציאת נפש הרי זה
שופך דמים אלא ישהה מעט
שמא נתעלף" - והנה היה לו
להודיע אימת יציאת הנפש,
ואיזה שיעור וגבול יש לו, אלא
על כורחך סמך עצמו על מה
שכתב בהלכות שבת {פ"ב
הי"ט} במפולת, שבודקין עד
חוטמו ושם ניכר יציאת הנפש,
ועל זה כתב כאן שאחר כך
ישהה מעט זמן שמא נתעלף,
ואז מותר לעמץ (= לעצם) עין.

This is implied in what Rambam wrote (MT Laws of Mourning 4:5): "One who closes the eyes [of the dead] as he is dying is as if shedding blood. Instead, one should wait a bit, since perhaps he has only fainted." It would have been incumbent upon [Rambam] to tell us when the soul departs and to quantify and specify how this is determined. Rather, he must have been relying on what he wrote in the Laws of Shabbat (2:19) with regard to the collapsed building, that one checks his nose, and that's where one can determine if his soul departed. It is regarding this that he wrote that one should wait a bit in case he only fainted, and only then may one close the eyes of the deceased.

---

17. Rabbi Sofer is writing to Rabbi Tzvi Hirsch Chajes.

Rabbi Sofer is responding specifically to the attempt by the scholar Rabbi Moses Mendelssohn to permit a body to sit without burial for three days, as the duke of Mecklenburg had requested, based on advice from medical experts. These physicians claimed that a significant number of people had been burying their relatives alive. Therefore, the kaiser ruled that one must not bury a relative for three days, at which point the body will begin to show signs of decomposition and blackening.

Looking carefully at this responsum, one sees that Rabbi Sofer does not intend to argue with the kaiser, or against the rule in those countries. Rather, he was arguing against the attempt to fit the halakha in with the kaiser's order, as was the way of the Enlightenment scholars.

At the end of the responsum, Rabbi Sofer adds an extra point:

כל שאחד שמוטל כאבן דומם ואין בו שום דפיקה ואם אח"כ בטל הנשימה אין לנו אלא דברי תורתינו הקדושה שהוא מת ולא ילינו אותו והמטמא לו אם הוא כהן לוקה אחר ההתראה.	Anyone lying still as a stone, with no heartbeat, and whose breathing then terminates – all we have are the words of our holy Torah that he has died, and he should not be left out [unburied] – and if a *kohen* allows himself to be defiled by his corpse, he will receive lashes after proper warning.

This description of death is perfectly accurate for the vast majority of dying patients, even today. The heart stops beating and supplying blood to the brain. After a few minutes, if there is no attempt at resuscitation, the brain begins to stop functioning. When the brainstem dies, since it controls respiratory function, breathing stops and the person dies.

However, there are a minority of cases in which the process is reversed, due to an external injury or some sort of internal collapse, and the brain dies first. When the brain dies, the effect extends to the respiratory center, causing a permanent cessation of respiratory function, though the heart is still beating. In premodern days this state would last only a few minutes, since without respiration the heart would receive no oxygen and die.

Does Rabbi Sofer mean that in this latter case, it is not the breath that determines whether the person remains alive, but rather the heartbeat, in opposition to the Talmud and the explicit halakhic rulings that he himself defends in this same responsum with such force? If so, he certainly would have made that clear. Furthermore, in his own summary of the talmudic pericope, he quotes the verse "All in whose nostrils was the breath of life ... [died],"[18] adding:

דהכל תלוי בנשימת האף,	For everything depends on respiration, as explained in b. *Yoma* [85a] and codified by Rambam and *Tur Shulḥan Arukh*.
וכמבואר ביומא [פ״ה ע״א],	
ופסקו רמב״ם, וטוש״ע.	

It seems clear that Rabbi Sofer did not intend to suggest the possibility of an alternative criterion to breathing.[19]

Maharsham

Others who oppose relying fully on the pericope in *Yoma* have claimed that this text discusses a case where there is no opposing evidence from another part of the body that the person is alive. However, where there is a pulse, and one can see that the heart is still beating, it would be impossible to rely on this pericope and upon the halakhic authorities who codified it. Rather, we would be required to follow common sense and take the heartbeat into consideration, though this factor was codified neither by the Talmud nor by any halakhic authority until Rabbi Tzvi Ashkenazi (*Ḥakham Tzvi*).

Rabbi Ashkenazi held this position since he believed that all life stemmed from the heart, mainly because this was the dominant view of the medical professionals of his time. Nevertheless, contemporary

---

18. Already in describing the creation of man, the Torah states: "and He [God] blew the breath of life into his nostrils, and man became a living soul" (Gen. 2:7). Nevertheless, the Talmud chose to emphasize the parallel verse in the flood story (ibid. 7:22), perhaps because it offers a definition of death.

19. This was how Rabbi Shaul Yisraeli (*Barkai* 4 [5747]: 32) explained the passage in the *Ḥatam Sofer* as well.

medical authorities and scholars have already explained that the reality
as understood by modern medicine is very different from what Rabbi
Ashkenazi describes.[20]

However, in his own responsum on the subject (6:124), it would
appear that Rabbi Shalom Mordechai Schwadron (Maharsham) of
Berezhany understood the pericope differently. Many authorities who
oppose organ donation base themselves on this responsum.

מכתבו הגיעני, ובקראי בו	I received your letter,[21] and as I read it,
עמדתי מבהיל ומחריד בדבר	I stood in bewilderment regarding your
שאלתו	question:

---

20. Rabbi Tzvi Hirsch Ashkenazi (1660–1718) was an important rabbi and halakhic authority in Altona, Amsterdam, and Lvov. In his work *Ḥakham Tzvi* (74, 77), he deals
with the kosher status of a chicken without a heart. After consulting with medical
experts, he decides that since the chicken couldn't possibly have lived without a
heart, the chicken must have had one, and it is therefore kosher. During the course
of his medical discussion, he describes the workings of the heart, which he believes
controls breathing through the conduit of the lungs. With reference to the requirement in *Yoma* to check the nose for breathing, he writes:

הוא משום שדרך החוטם יוצא	This is because the warm air from the heart exits
האויר החם מן הלב, ונכנס בו אויר	through the nostrils, and the cold air then enters
קר לקרר הלב, ואם אין לב אין	through it to cool the heart; hence if there's no
נשימה.	heart, there's no breath.

This description of cardiac function is clearly inaccurate; as everyone knows
nowadays, the heart pumps blood, not air. Nevertheless, Rabbi Shmuel ha-Levi
Wosner accepts this ruling (Wosner, "Regarding Heart Transplantation (A Prohibition)," *Sefer Assia* 7 [5754/1993], 163–65 [Hebrew]). Rabbi Prof. Avraham Steinberg
disagrees ("Determining the Moment of Death and Heart Transplantation," *Sefer
Assia* 7, 220–21 [Hebrew]), quoting important halakhic authorities who base their
decisions on modern biology. He shows that breathing actually depends on the brain,
not the heart. Furthermore, the heart is not even mentioned in the rabbinic texts
insofar as the determination of death is concerned. Rabbi Prof. Steinberg's position
was adopted by Rabbis Shaul Yisraeli and Zalman Nehemia Goldberg and by Chief
Rabbis Avraham Shapira and Mordechai Eliyahu.

21. The letter was sent by a certain Rabbi A. A. Waldman.

באחד שהלך לפנות לביהכ״ס
ומצאוהו שם כמת, וכל
התרופות שעשו ופעולת
הרופאים לא הועילו, ואמרו
שמת הוא, וכשלקחו אותו
לטהרו נשמע ממנו קול כמו
חארטשען כמו בגוסס ויען
שהי׳ בעש״ק ומיהרו לקברו
שלחו אחר רופאים בשתיקה
ואמרו כי הוא מת אלא שהקול
נשמע ע״י שאינו מכיל הרעי
בקרבו וע״י אכילה ושתי׳
שבמעיו, וניסו כמ״פ בנוצה
בחוטמו ולא נראה שום
נשימה, רק א׳ אמר שכמדומה
שדופק גיד א׳ תחת הארכובה
ושאר אנשים ניסו ואמרו
שאינו כן, והגם שהי׳ בשרו
חם לא השגיחו ע״ז וקברוהו,

A man went to the synagogue, and [later] he was found there dead. All the medicines they administered and the procedures that the doctors attempted were of no use, and they declared him dead. When they took his body to purify it, they heard a sound like the groaning of a dying man. However, since it was the eve of the Sabbath, and they were in a rush to bury him, they sent for physicians quietly. [The physicians] said that he was dead and that the sounds were just the gases from undigested waste in the intestines. They tested him several times by placing a feather in his nose, and there was no sign of breath. One person remarked that there seemed to be a pulse from one spot under the elbow, but the others tested and said it was untrue. Finally, though his flesh was still warm, they paid no attention to this and buried him.

ועתה ח״א מערער שלא
יפה עשו שלא שאלו
מהב״ד שבעיר והרופאים
אינם נאמנים בזה ושצריכים
לעשות תשובה...

And now, one member of the community has been complaining that they didn't behave properly, since they didn't consult the local court, and doctors aren't to be trusted with this, and that they need to repent....

...צדקו דברי דודאי קי״ל
דעיקר חיותא באפי׳ כיון
דממעלה למטה א״צ לבדוק
רק עד חוטמו, אבל היינו
בסתמא אם ליכא הוכחה
להיפוך סמכי׳ על בדיקת
חוטמו דהוי רוב גמור ואפי׳
מיעוטא ליכא אא״כ על צד א׳
מאלף דהוי מיעוטא דמיעוטא
דאין לחוש לכך גם בפ״נ...

...he would seem to be correct. Certainly it is true that a person's life is mainly in his nostrils, for when we uncover him from the top down, we stop checking once we reach his nostrils, for that [would accurately determine death] in the vast majority of cases, leaving an irrelevant – maybe one in a thousand – minority, for which we should have no concern, even for saving a life.

אבל אם רואים איזו סימן של
חיות בשאר איברים ואיתרע
רובא לפנינו י"ל דלא סמכינן
אבדיקת חוטם .... וה"נ
בנ"ד שנשמע קול הברה
מה דלא שכיח בשאר מתים
י"ל דבכה"ג אין לסמוך על
בדיקת חוטם....

But if they see any sign of life in any of his other limbs, then the argument from the majority is compromised, and it can be argued that we do not rely on checking the nostrils [for signs of breathing].... So in our case, where a sound was heard, which is unusual with other corpses, one could argue that in this case one should not have relied upon the breathing test....

ואם היה ערב שבת ומיהרו
לקברו לבל ילין המת הרי
אם מלינו לכבודו של מת
ליכא איסור ואין לך כבודו
יותר מזה שיש חשש אולי
עודנו חי, ודברי הרופאים אין
מכריעין בכל כה"ג....

And if it was the eve of the Sabbath, and they rushed to bury him so as not to leave out the body, in truth, if they leave the body out to honor him, there is no sin – and there is no greater honor than to be cautious and make sure the person isn't still alive, and the words of doctors are not definitive in this regard....

אך לפמ"ש רו"מ שטלטלוהו
אח"כ הרבה ולא נשמע יותר
שום קול יש הוכחה שכבר
מת ממש.... כיון שבדקו
בכל מיני נסיונות ובהסכמת
הרופאים אין לחוש יותר.

However, according to what my honorable colleague has written, that they moved him around a lot afterward, and no further sounds were heard, this is proof that he had certainly died.... Since they checked into it with all kinds of tests, and received confirmation [of his death] through doctors – there is no reason to be concerned further.

This responsum appears to represent a different understanding of the pericope in *Yoma*, which supports and even describes precisely the position of those who oppose organ donation. In truth, Maharsham's position is very difficult, since it seems to be the exact opposite of Rabbi Sofer's in his understanding of the pericope in *Yoma*. If Rabbi Schwadron is correct, why did no authority record in the laws of Shabbat that if there is any sign of life in any of a person's limbs, one should not rely on Rav Pappa but should desecrate the Sabbath to save this person? It can't be that there were no such cases in antiquity, because there certainly were.

This fact is explicit in Tractate *Semaḥot* 8:1:

יוצאין לבית הקברות, ופוקדין
על המתים עד ג' ימים, ואין
חוששין משום דרכי האמורי.

One should go out into the cemetery and examine the dead for three days, and one should not worry that this is an idolatrous practice.

מעשה שפקדו אחד וחיה
[עוד] כ"ה שנים, ואחר-כך מת;
[ופקדו] אחר, והוליד ה' בנים,
ואחר-כך מת.

There was a case in which they examined someone [who turned out to be alive], and he lived [another] twenty-five years and only then died. In another case, [the person subsequently] fathered five children before he died.

Actually, this statement of the sages in *Semaḥot* precipitated Rabbi Mendelssohn's claim that it was forbidden to rush a burial, since only in the time of the Second Temple and talmudic periods did they bury in caverns,[22] as described in the Mishna (*Bava Batra*, ch. 6), such that they could check on the bodies. However, we bury in the ground, as was done in Babylonia,[23] so we cannot examine bodies after burial. Hence, Mendelssohn argued, we should worry that people may have been buried alive; this is why the law was made in the time of the kaiser. This is exactly the position Rabbi Sofer attacked with such vehemence, in accordance with the pericope in *Yoma* and the authorities who codified it.

It turns out that the responsum of Rabbi Schwadron is diametrically opposed to that of Rabbi Sofer, both insofar as the point of the question and the concerns in the response, as well as in his interpretation of the pericope in *Yoma* and the authorities who codify the halakha.

---

22. See Amos Kloner and Boaz Zissu, *The Necropolis of Jerusalem in the Second Temple Period* (Leuven: Peeters, 2007).

23. Rambam (MT Laws of Mourning 4:4) writes that we cover the body in dirt even in the caverns; this matches the Babylonian Jewish practice. Rabbi Yehoshua Falk-Katz, in his glosses on the *Ṭur* (*Perisha* YD 94:3), adds that it would be impossible to watch over a body for three days without such a practice. His position is quoted by Rabbi Shabtai Kohen in his glosses on the *Shulḥan Arukh*, *Siftei Kohen* (*Shakh* YD 394:2). See also Rabbi Moshe Sofer, *Ḥatam Sofer* YD 338.

Moreover, one must ask with regard to Rabbi Schwadron: How is it that he accepted what was reported to him in the letter, that they moved the body a great distance, and since they heard no other noise, they considered it sufficient proof that the man was certainly dead? Should the rabbi not have cried out – as people do nowadays – that anyone who touches a dying person is as if he or she has shed blood? How could Rabbi Schwadron accept this confirmation of death by way of excessive physical contact?

However, if one thinks it through carefully, there's really no problem. Why would our ancestors check the bodies of the deceased? Clearly, if they saw some sort of movement in the limbs or heard a sound, they would remove the person from the rubble and try to revive him or her with whatever resuscitative practices they had. On this point, Rabbi Schwadron is no doubt correct. If one sees the person moving an arm or leg or making a sound, one should not rely on checking for breathing with a feather under the nose, since these movements mean the brain is still alive, as the brain is the source of movement and voice.

Furthermore, the very fact that they heard a sound raises the concern that the person's breathing had not yet really terminated. Therefore, the essential condition for determining death according to *Yoma* would not have been fulfilled. However, if the person continues to lie still as a stone – as Rabbi Sofer so eloquently put it – and there is no movement or sound whatsoever, then he or she is dead, and it would be permitted to move or adjust his or her body in order to make sure. The fact that they heard one isolated sound – if there is even a medical explanation for it – and then checked again and again and found no indication of movement or any further sounds, whatever the person was originally, he or she was certainly deceased by this point.

THE MODERN DETERMINATION OF BRAIN DEATH

The above is precisely the halakhic justification for the medical procedure used today to determine brain death.[24] Doctors check all the bodily reflexes that can demonstrate life in the brainstem – via the pupillary

---

24. It's based on the Hadassah protocol, which was submitted to the Chief Rabbinate of Israel during its deliberations on this matter. This was the baseline rule until the legislation put forward by Knesset member Otniel Schneller, discussed later in this essay.

reflex test, cold caloric testing, etc.[25] – and if these exams produce even one sign of life, the patient may not be declared brain dead.

Afterward, the doctors check for signs of life by administering the apnea test, in which the patient, after preoxygenation of his or her blood, is removed from the respirator, and they watch for any sign of attempts at spontaneous respiration. If there is any life whatsoever in the breathing center found in the brainstem, the patient will attempt to breathe. If there is no attempt, it is clear that the patient will never breathe again and is certainly deceased; both Rabbi Sofer and Rabbi Schwadron would agree to this. Hence, in this case there is absolute accord between medicine and halakha.

Nonetheless, those who object to this definition claim: "But the heart's still beating, and heartbeat is an essential characteristic of life! What's the difference whether there's some sort of reflex motion or sound or whether the heart is pumping, which is certainly a more significant demonstration of life?!" However, there is a clear counterclaim as well.

Oholot and Convulsions

The Mishna in *Oholot* (1:6) distinguishes between signs of life originating in the brain and various convulsions and random paroxysms of the muscles even after the brain has died.

אדם אינו מטמא עד שתצא נפשו.	A person doesn't defile [i.e., isn't considered dead] until his soul has departed.
ואפי[לו] מגוייד ואפי[לו] גוסס - זוקק ליבום, ופוטר מן היבום, מאכיל בתרומה, ופוסל בתרומה.	Even if he is sliced up, even if he is in his death throes – his being alive obligates a woman in levirate marriage or exempts a woman from levirate marriage, allows others to partake of *teruma* or bars them from partaking of *teruma*.
וכן בהמה וחיה אינן מטמאין עד שתצא נפשם.	The same is true for animals, domesticated or wild – they don't defile until their souls have departed.

25. For details, see Dr. Zelik Frischer's essay in this volume.

הותזו ראשיהם, אף על פי
שמפרכסים - טמאין, כגון זנב
של לטאה שהיא מפרכסת.

If their heads have been severed, even though they are convulsing – they defile, as this is like the tail of a lizard, which continues to convulse.

Rambam codifies this as halakha (MT Laws of the Impurity of the Dead 1:15).

המת אינו מטמא עד שתצא נפשו.
אפילו מגוייד או גוסס, אפילו
נשחטו בו שני הסימנים - אינו
מטמא עד שתצא נפשו, שנאמר:
"בנפש האדם אשר ימות".

A body doesn't defile until its soul has departed. Even if one has been sliced up or is dying, even if the trachea and esophagus have been severed – he doesn't defile until his soul has departed, as it says: "when the soul of a man has died" (Num. 19:13).

נשברה מפרקתו ורוב בשר
עימה, או שנקרע כדג מגבו, או
שהותז ראשו, או שנחתך לשני
חלקים בבטנו - הרי זה מטמא,
אף-על-פי שעדיין הוא מרפרף
באחד מאבריו.

If the nape of the neck was broken, and most of its flesh along with it, or he was torn asunder from behind, like a fish, or his head was severed, or he was cut in two at his waist – he does defile, even if one of his limbs is still flailing.

The Status of Heartbeat in a Brain Dead Patient

Certainly in their day, these convulsions could not have lasted more than a few minutes. However, if one attaches the person to a respirator, the machine can enable the cardiac muscles to contract, and the heart can keep beating for hours or days, and in certain cases for weeks or months.[26] Thus the question must be asked, does the rule established by the sages (until Rabbi Moshe Sofer), that only the cessation of respiratory function defines death, still apply?[27]

---

26. D. Alan Shewmon, "Chronic 'Brain Death': Meta-Analysis and Conceptual Consequences," *Neurology* 51, no. 6 (1998): 1538–45.

27. Those who oppose transplantation and maintain that life is defined by the heart are forced to interpret the passage in *Yoma* in a rather limited way, adding conditions

The heart can continue beating even outside the body if placed in a solution allowing the cardiac muscle to contract.[28] In the case of brain death – a state nothing like either clinical death, on the one hand, or persistent vegetative state, on the other – the body is essentially dead, according to both halakha or medicine, and would be lying still as a stone if a machine weren't breathing on behalf of the patient, keeping the heart beating. Absent a functioning brain, this artificial system (of a heart beating because of a respirator) will eventually crash, but if not for the machine, the heart would have crashed in minutes.[29]

THE DECISION OF THE CHIEF RABBINATE

This is the situation that confronted Israel's Chief Rabbinate in 5747 (1987).[30] Soon afterward, under its scrutiny, two experiments were performed involving a pregnant ewe whose head and brain were removed from its body – dead without question. Nevertheless, the heart continued to pump and the respiration was controlled by machine. The fetus was successfully carried to term and born.[31] This outcome proved to anyone objective that it's possible to keep an organism's appendages and organs alive – even without a head or brain – with the proper machinery.

In light of all the above – the pericope in *Yoma*, the mishna in *Oholot*, the codification of the halakhic decisors, the responsum of Rabbi

---

and exceptions that are referenced neither in the primary source nor in the halakhic authorities who later codified it.

28. This can be – and has been – witnessed by anyone dissatisfied with theoretical musings and seeking the facts without undue emotion or preconceived notions. It can easily be demonstrated with the heart of an animal and can be witnessed firsthand by anyone who cares to see it.

29. A Ḥaredi physician who objects to the brainstem-based death criteria privately admitted to me that he knows of no case in which a person "woke up" from this state, or even began to move a hand or finger, or showed any improvement at all!

30. During the winter of 5745, the heads of the Israeli medical establishment asked the Chief Rabbinate for a ruling on transplantation. The rabbinate appointed a committee of rabbis and physicians, and confirmed its findings on Rosh Ḥodesh Marḥeshvan 5747. The decision was published in *Tchumin* 7 (5746): 187–92; *Barkai* 4 (5747): 11–14; and *Assia* 42–43 (5747/1986–87): 70–81. For a detailed discussion of this ruling, see Rabbi Ariel Picard's essay in the organ donation volume.

31. See Rabbi Prof. Avraham Steinberg's essay in this volume.

Moshe Sofer, and the careful testing of medical professionals,[32] meeting the requirements of Rabbi Schwadron – the chief rabbis decided, together with other prominent halakhic decisors, that once the irreversible death of the *brainstem* is conclusively demonstrated,[33] death is complete, even if the heart still beats, and it is therefore permitted to remove organs (even the heart, lungs, or liver) from a brainstem-dead person in order to save lives. When the brainstem is dead and autonomous respiration has permanently and irreversibly ceased, the soul has departed and the body is dead, even if certain organs are still alive. This is what is written in the Torah and what the sages and *posqim* have concluded: *neshama* (soul) = *neshima* (breath)![34]

This decision is aligned precisely with the Talmud and halakha and bears no resemblance at all to a "forced permissive argument" (היתר דחוק). All the objections to this decision are themselves far from being in line with the Talmud and the halakha, and rely upon theories and concerns – and mainly upon distrust of doctors. Doctors are, of course, relied upon for every other medical need, and when deciding about the necessity of violating Shabbat or Yom Kippur. Everybody knows how dedicated and reliable most physicians are, and I have never heard of a rabbi or halakhic authority claiming that one shouldn't go to a doctor for medical needs. Nonetheless, when it comes to this question of defining the moment of death, suddenly all doctors are ideologically anti-halakha, or motivated by a desire for fame or money, supporting the "questionable" practice of organ donation for these spurious reasons alone.

Despite this pernicious indictment of the medical community, it was the doctors themselves, together with Israel's Ministry of Health, who introduced the requirement that there be no connection whatsoever between the attending physician and the doctors who declare a person dead, and between either of these and the doctors who harvest the organs.[35] Additionally, the supposed "fame" that comes with organ

---

32. Following the Hadassah protocol, which was explained to the Chief Rabbinate.
33. I.e., not just brain death, which has no halakhic definition.
34. For a similar formulation, see Rabbi Yaakov Love's essay in this volume.
35. According to the regulations of Israel's Ministry of Health.

transplantation is long gone,[36] together with the grave errors that plagued the earliest transplants. It was these that caused the doubts expressed by rabbis and halakhic authorities,[37] as well as by the community at large, during the early years of transplant surgery.

The Cost of Ignoring the Chief Rabbinate's Decision

On the other hand, people's lives are hanging in the balance. Every year, seventy to eighty people die in Israel for lack of transplantation organs,[38] and it is very difficult for Israel to receive surplus organs from the outside world. Since Israelis do not generally donate organs, Israel is ineligible to receive surplus organs, except under very unusual circumstances.

In addition, it is a terrible sin to take or purchase organs from certain countries (mainly China), since there's a real concern that opponents of the government are being murdered, and their organs sold.[39] Participating even passively in such an act is a grievous violation of Torah law.

Considering the above, the question of saving lives cannot be avoided. Anyone who forbids organ donation due to frivolous concerns and gut feelings as opposed to relying on solid halakhic analysis, grounded in the Talmud and subsequent halakhic literature, is causing the death of dozens of critically ill men and women every year! Furthermore, those who are truly skeptical and object to defining brainstem death as death, claiming that it is in fact not the operative definition in halakha, are consequently *forbidden* to receive donated organs in order to save their own lives. Hence, they will, in fact, be causing the death of many of their own followers, whom they could save by allowing them to receive organs.

---

36. This point was emphasized by Rabbi Shaul Yisraeli at the beginning of his article (*Barkai* 4, 32).
37. Mostly those who have steadfastly refused to express an opinion on these matters to this day.
38. According to Israel's National Transplantation Center, especially in recent years.
39. The Chinese government persecutes countless members of the Falun Gong movement, essentially for their religious views. Tortured in concentration camps, many of these Chinese have their organs forcibly removed and sold while they're still alive. These atrocities were revealed to the world by a few survivors who escaped these camps. An international inquiry confirmed the reports.

Since this last point has been disputed, I will clarify. In Israel, it has already been decided by the great Rabbi Shlomo Zalman Auerbach that receiving organs if one considers organ donation to be murder is forbidden according to halakha.[40] Outside of Israel, there is also the very grave concern that the receipt of organs by such a person will desecrate God's name. I have already heard of gentile physicians who speak angrily about observant Jews who want to receive organs but won't donate.

The Chief Rabbinate was well aware of the awesome responsibility on all sides, and had already taken into account halakhic issues surrounding the "reliability" of doctors, which in halakha is always defined as "uncertain."[41] Medicine is constantly in flux, and things believed to be certain today could become uncertain tomorrow. Therefore, with regard to desecrating Shabbat, where even a possible threat to life overrides Shabbat, it is enough to receive a medical opinion in order to move ahead with any action deemed necessary by doctors. However, such an opinion is not necessarily sufficient when it comes to deciding whether to continue or discontinue treatment and life support, and whether to declare a person dead. Accordingly, the Chief Rabbinate endorsed brainstem death on three conditions:[42]

1. The administering of a diagnostic test that would demonstrate – in addition to clinical tests – that there is no blood flow to the brain, particularly in the brainstem. At the time, the Auditory Brainstem Response (ABR) test[43] was the preferred one, although nowadays

---

40. Avraham Steinberg, *The Encyclopedia of Halakha and Medicine* (2nd ed., 2006), vol. 6, 886 [Hebrew].

41. For instance, Rabbi Avraham Yitzhak Kook (*Da'at Kohen* 140–42) ruled that *metzitza* after circumcision be done with a pipette, lest direct oral contact endanger the infant. However, Rabbi Kook refused to do away with *metzitza* altogether, since the sages said it protected the infant.

42. I am discussing here only the controversial conditions; others were readily accepted by the medical and legal community.

43. Also known as Brainstem Auditory Evoked Response (BAER) or Brainstem Auditory Evoked Potentials (BAEP); see appendix 2 of the decision of the Chief Rabbinate, which was written by Prof. Harvey (Chaim) Sohmer, an auditory neurophysiologist with expertise in this area. For details about this and other confirmatory tests, see Dr. Zelik Frischer's essay in this volume.

the method of choice is the Transcranial Doppler (TCD), which provides an excellent picture of blood flow in the brain. With this requirement in place,[44] the Torah principle of "a person shall be put to death based on the testimony of two witnesses" (Deut. 17:6) is actually fulfilled twice over.[45]

2. The participation of a representative of the Chief Rabbinate in the process of declaring the person brain dead.[46]

3. A committee of rabbis and doctors that would oversee the implementation of the above requirements and ensure that everything was done according to halakha.

Unfortunately, these three conditions were rejected, leading to a lack of vital cooperation – for twenty years and counting – between rabbis and doctors. The medical community wasn't ready to accept these conditions, and negotiations dragged on for years. In the meantime, the opposition, which denies the legitimacy of the Chief Rabbinate's decision, has gained ground, and as a result, people who desperately need organs wait with little hope.

MY OWN INVOLVEMENT

This situation gives me no peace and robs me of sleep. I cannot help but think about Jephthah's daughter,[47] and the midrashic statement (Genesis

---

44. It should be noted that confirmatory testing wasn't required by the Ministry of Health, and it is performed only when requested by the family, often at the instigation of rabbis and Torah-learned doctors who are experts in this field. However, this situation changed when the law accepting brainstem death as death was passed. Pushed forward by Knesset Member Otniel Schneller, this law incorporated the conditions stipulated by the Chief Rabbinate, such as confirmatory testing. Important halakhic authorities supported the legislation, including Rabbi Ovadia Yosef, who had never before publicized his opinion.

45. Via the examination undertaken by two doctors, who are there neither to harvest organs nor as part of the attending medical team, as well as via the confirmatory test, administered by yet another medical professional.

46. The Chief Rabbinate stopped short of requiring an actual rabbi to participate, since an observant doctor who understood the halakhic requirements as expressed by the Chief Rabbinate would be acceptable too.

47. Judg. 11:30–40; also see b. *Ta'anit* 4a.

Rabba 60:3) that Phineas the son of Eleazar, the high priest, could have undone her father's vow according to halakha, based on the technicality of regret:[48]

אלא פנחס אמר, הוא צריך לי	However, Phineas said: "He needs me;
ואני אלך אצלו?...ויפתח אמר,	why should I go to him?" ...Jephthah
אני ראש קציני ישראל, ואני	said: "I am the head of the Israelites;
הולך אצל פנחס? בין דין לדין	why should I go to Phineas?" Between
אבדה הנערה ההיא...ושניהם	the two of them, the girl was lost... and
נענשו בדמיה.	both were punished for her blood.

In this case, it was the Chief Rabbinate that suggested options, but no one on the right or the left paid attention. What was there to do?

A few years ago, I went to meet Professor Jonathan Halevy together with Rabbi Menachem Burstein, whose founding of the Puah Institute[49] had already proven that he was a major force in building bridges between doctors and rabbis, even when it came to emotionally charged subjects such as in vitro fertilization in hospitals. We suggested forming a training program similar to Puah to familiarize rabbis with both the halakhic and medical realities of brain death determination and organ donation. Professor Halevy agreed immediately, but it didn't work out.

We returned to him some time later with a design for an intensive, four-day course at the Schlesinger Institute (adjacent to Jerusalem's Shaare Zedek Medical Center), under the guidance of Rabbi Dr. Mordechai Halperin, who has spent much of his career working on these questions as a part of the Chief Rabbinate's own research – from the very beginning of the process until today. The course would be under the auspices of the Sephardic chief rabbi at the time of the historic decision

---

48. I.e., had Jephthah known his daughter would emerge first, would he have made the vow? And if a pig or dog had come out first, what would he have done?

49. Puah is an acronym for *Poriyut u-Refu'a al-pi Halakha*, fertility and medicine in accordance with Jewish law. The institute assists anyone with gynecological or fertility problems, handling around 165 inquiries a day – free of charge. Its scholars author responsa related to medicine and Jewish law, teach approximately three thousand classes per year, and organize important conferences for rabbis, doctors, and the public. For more information: http://www.puahonline.org/.

of 5747, Rabbi Mordechai Eliyahu, who stood behind this decision like the Rock of Gibraltar, declaring it the indisputable halakha without hesitation.[50] With God's help, the course began, and all the participants felt the electricity in the air and the light from Above. There was now some hope for a historic breakthrough in the area of rabbinic and medical cooperation surrounding organ donation and brainstem death.

A number of lives have already been saved thanks to this course. Furthermore, every hospital knows that if a patient's family seems amenable to organ donation and wishes to participate under the guidance of halakha – in line with the 5747 decision of the Chief Rabbinate – we can assist. The excellent cooperation between rabbis and doctors that has developed since this course cannot be overstated. Our experience underlines the fact that there is no substitute for direct communication, friendly and intimate, between colleagues, especially between doctors and rabbis, as there are a great many similarities between the problems they face and the way they solve them. In all my experience, I have never come across a doctor refusing to administer a confirmatory test, as requested by the Chief Rabbinate. In fact, I've seen a readiness to finally build the necessary bridge between doctors and rabbis – despite all the differences and disagreements between the two – in order to save lives. All concerned want to prevent any further deaths in Israel for lack of available organs.

Over the past few years, Knesset member Otniel Schneller took upon himself the task of pushing forward a law regarding brainstem death, encapsulating the conclusions reached after protracted negotiations between the rabbinic and medical communities. With that begins the extraordinary effort to explain to the public about the importance of this mitzva, and answer all questions regarding this most serious of subjects.

What's at stake is nothing less than the saving of hundreds of lives. Dozens of men and women die every year due to unavailability of organs, a direct result of people's unwillingness to donate the organs of their own loved ones who have been declared brain dead and eligible for harvesting. The rabbinic establishment that supports the Chief Rabbinate's decision

---

50. For more on Rabbi Eliyahu's thinking, see Rabbi Yitz Greenberg's essay in this volume.

must act quickly and decisively to educate the public about halakha and organ donation. We cannot waste a moment waiting for some sort of universal agreement between all rabbis and halakhic authorities, especially since many of them have little faith in the medical establishment and fear that the prospective donor may actually still be alive.

Most of these rabbis know nothing about brain function; hence their uncertainty about brainstem death and whether it really counts as death. I have seen and heard how they all require the few rabbis who are also medical professionals to explain this process – ironically, the same experts who taught this material to us at the course in Shaare Zedek Medical Center.

Despite this pushback from the community of objectors, my good friend Rabbi Burstein is optimistic. Based on his successful experience with fertility issues, he believes the entire Torah world could eventually unite around this great mitzva. I share this hope, since "great is peace" (Numbers Rabba 11:7) and "truth and peace should be loved" (Zech. 8:19).

APPENDIX: REFLECTIONS AND Q/A

The Phenomenon of Emotional Rejection

Organ transplantation is a medical miracle, beyond natural human ability. The human immune system naturally rejects any foreign body introduced into it, including organs. Until the medical community learned how to weaken the body's natural immune response, organ transplantation was impossible. Contrariwise, if the immune system is overly weakened, one may die of any number of illnesses that can attack a body without immunity.

It's necessary to be exact, to find the proper, delicate balance. The immune system must be weakened enough not to reject the transplanted organ, yet remain strong enough to retain its natural defenses against other threats. The wisdom that the Creator placed in man outdoes even the natural order He created, allowing us an amazing ability to save human life through organ transplantation.

Ironically, the natural *emotional* rejection of organ donation is similar. A whole series of natural and religious emotions arise and gush forth to reject the fantastic idea that one can take organs from a brain dead body and transplant them into an ill patient to save his or her life. Unless we deal with these emotional objections, we cannot save lives.

Emotional rejection has great importance, just like physical rejection. One should not dismiss the phenomenon or treat it lightly. Without it, we would be unable to deal properly with the dead and treat their bodies with due respect. Dealing with death is first and foremost an emotional exercise. It would be wrong to belittle the intense pain felt by family members when facing life's hardest decision. As opposed to the long argument presented in the main essay, below I will try to offer short answers to questions family members often ask.

Questions and Answers

(1) *Question*: The first and most poignant question is always: Is our loved one really dead? What if there's some mistake? Might he still possibly survive? He's still breathing. She's still warm. Her heart is still beating. He looks exactly the way he did yesterday, when we brought him to the hospital with his head injury. Maybe the doctors are giving up too fast? Perhaps prayer, crying out to God, and giving charity can save her, just as we've been hoping throughout the many days and nights we've been sitting by her bedside during the various medical interventions. The heart refuses to accept the terrible decree, and our hearts are beating together with that of our loved one – perhaps a miracle could occur?

Answer: In truth, my dear friends, there have been cases where people have awakened from comas and even from persistent vegetative states, since their brains were still living. However, no person has ever awakened from brain death, even if it does take a while before the final collapse of the other bodily systems. Brain death is irreversible and much more serious than cardiac arrest. If a heart stops pumping, it can be made to pump again, even outside the person's body, inside a dish – it has been done! But not the brain. The death of the brain is final.

(2) *Question*: But does halakha really recognize brain death?

Answer: Yes! The Torah has defined life as breath – only this is determinative. When man was created in the Garden of Eden, the Torah states that God "blew the breath of life into his nostrils, and man became a living soul" (Gen. 2:7). When describing the destruction of the generation of the flood, the Torah states: "All in whose nostrils was the breath of life…died" (Gen. 7:22). Respiration is what connects the soul to the body, and when respiration ceases irreversibly, the soul has left the body and the person is dead, even though other parts of the body may still be functioning. Such a person is not dying, but is already dead.

This is what the Talmud decided. One is not required to check the heartbeat when attempting to extricate a person from collapsed rubble; rather, one need check only his or her nose, to see if there is breath. This is also the conclusion found in all works of halakha, and this was the practice of our ancestors; they would place a feather under a person's nose and check for signs of breathing. Whoever wasn't breathing was considered dead.

Breathing is controlled by the brainstem. Hence, if the brainstem is dead, there will be no more respiration in that body until the day of resurrection. When expert physicians check for respiratory function, they are looking for signs of spontaneous attempts at breathing by way of the apnea test. The respirator is disconnected from the patient – after raising the oxygen levels of the blood in order not to cause any damage – and they wait until the level of CO_2 in the blood is such that if there were any spark of life left in the person at all, he or she would attempt to breathe. If no attempt is made, the breathing center is dead, and the soul has departed. Whoever continues to treat this person is treating a corpse.

If an apnea test cannot be administered, several other tests are used to ascertain the status of the person. Additionally, the Chief Rabbinate, which allows for the declaration of death based on neurological criteria, requires confirmatory testing to ensure that there is no electrical activity in or blood flow to the brain. The way medicine determines death based on the brain has been accepted as the definition of death according to the Torah and the halakha by the Chief Rabbinate (the previous one as well as the current) and even by the important halakhic authority Rabbi Ovadia Yosef, and has been legislatively sanctioned in Israel as the law of the land.

(3) *Question*: But we've heard that great and important halakhic authorities disagree with this position, and say it would be a violation of a severe

prohibition to remove an organ for donation before the donor's heart died, even if the law of the land permits it.

Answer: No one in our day can make good decisions in all Torah matters. Even the greatest and most talented doctor isn't qualified to administer a particular form of medicine if he or she hasn't specialized in it. The same is true for Torah scholars, and there is no one among them who knows everything.

In this particular subfield of medicine and halakha, there are only two experts in Israel, people who really know all the halakhot and responsa and also understand the workings of the brain. I am referring to Rabbi Prof. Avraham Steinberg and Rabbi Dr. Mordechai Halperin, both of whom work in Shaare Zedek, and are Torah scholars as well as medical authorities.

Of course, other rabbis and doctors know a lot about this subject. Nevertheless, I have seen and heard chief rabbis Avraham Shapira, Mordechai Eliyahu, Ovadia Yosef, and Shlomo Amar consulting with these two rabbi-doctors, asking about every little detail.

I did the same as well. A few years ago – as detailed above – when I wanted to expand the group of rabbis dealing with this topic, I organized a course at Shaare Zedek under the guidance of these two rabbi-doctors, and we learned from them and their expertise for four solid days. At the end of the course, we received Rabbi Eliyahu's official approval in writing. Since then, I've been present in many hospitals across Israel to assist in these agonizing situations. Whenever a particularly difficult question arises we consult with Rabbi Prof. Steinberg and Rabbi Dr. Halperin, exactly as the chief rabbis have done for years.

With all due respect, any rabbi who offers an opinion on this subject without fully grasping its complexities cannot authoritatively decide the halakha. This is no different from my policy of not offering halakhic rulings on proper slaughtering or checking for *treifot* – I simply lack sufficient expertise in these areas. Whoever has not learned how the brainstem is built and how it functions, or doesn't know the location of the control center for respiratory function and how exactly physicians check if a person is alive or dead – such a person's decisions carry little weight, even if he is an expert and acknowledged halakhic authority in other matters.

Every rabbi or halakhic authority of whom people ask questions about these areas is required to turn to Rabbi Dr. Halperin and/or Rabbi Prof. Steinberg and to work within the parameters of their advice. If he doesn't, he's acting incompetently and has no right to offer a halakhic opinion on the subject. This is no different from the fact that it would be forbidden for a doctor, smart and talented as he or she might be, to perform neurosurgery if this was not his or her area of specialization, and if he or she wasn't licensed to do so. The rabbis who went through our training course consult only with these two experts, and that's how former Sephardic chief rabbi Amar functioned as well, in all cases and with every question. Since this type of expertise is rare, the rabbis who took the course feel an obligation to visit all the hospitals throughout Israel and come at the behest of anyone who asks, free of charge.

(4) *Question*: But we've heard that it's impossible to trust doctors when it comes to harvesting organs, since what they really want is to advance medicine as much as they can and in any way possible. We've heard that they're not careful about halakha, even when asked to be, and that when they see a person close to death – with no chance of recovery – they'll declare that person dead in order to retrieve his or her organs and save someone else's life.

Answer: In recent years, ever since completing the course, I've been present at many hospitals on numerous occasions. I've seen with my own eyes the careful work of the attending physicians, the physicians who make the determination of brain death, and the physicians who harvest the organs. I can tell you with no uncertainty that there is no truth to these rumors.

These allegations originate in events that occurred years ago, at the very beginning of organ transplantation in Israel and the world at large. Because of these concerns, there is a strict separation between the medical team that attends the patient and the medical team that makes the brain death determination, and there is no connection between either of these groups and the team that harvests the organs.

In every case I've observed, I've found total honesty and complete transparency on the part of the physicians and the medical establishment. I have encountered only genuine professionalism – strict observance of protocol coupled with a deep commitment to saving lives. Anyone treated in a hospital relies on these physicians, and for good reason. It is wrong to believe the malicious gossip about them.

(5) *Question*: But we feel a sacred responsibility to return the body of our loved one to God complete, the way it came to us. It is difficult for us to think about removing organs from his body, or bringing her to the grave with a body not intact. How will our loved one rise again at the time of resurrection without a heart or a liver, without lungs, kidneys, or even a cornea?

Answer: All these body parts decompose in the grave together with the rest of the body, leaving only the skeleton. There is no intact body in the grave. A person can be whole in his or her actions and merits before God, but the body will decompose nonetheless. To imagine that the Creator of the world and humanity would resurrect a person with "missing pieces" just because organs were removed from his or her corpse – this borders on the heretical!

God can resurrect people whose bodies were entirely burnt, where nothing whatsoever remains of them. All our holy brethren who died glorifying the name of the Lord – during the Holocaust as well as other tragic events – will be resurrected. What counts is not the intactness of the person's body but the perfection of his or her behavior when alive and the accumulation of merit. It is clear that saving another person's life is a tremendous mitzva, and it is even permitted to violate Shabbat to do so. Therefore, it is also a mitzva to donate organs and transplant them, even on Shabbat itself.

There is no greater merit to the deceased than the use of his or her organs to save someone else's life. Precisely when he or she is standing before the heavenly court to be judged for his or her actions in this world, the willingness of the deceased to donate organs can help atone for past sins. This act of donation even brings merit to the deceased's entire family. All the prayers and learning of Mishna done on behalf of the deceased's soul, with all their importance, pale in comparison to the enormous value accrued to the deceased's soul through the donation of his or her organs after death.

CONCLUSION

Since the death of the brainstem means the irreversible cessation of respiration, and respiration (*neshima*) equals life (*neshama*), this is the point when organs are harvested. The family has the opportunity to participate in this process on behalf of their deceased loved one, helping him or her fulfill one last mitzva. All that the family members need to understand is that the doctors are there to determine whether the patient is breathing autonomously and whether there is any blood flow to the brain, and they have tests to determine both these things. Anyone with further questions should feel free to contact me or any of the rabbis in or out of Israel who've been trained in these areas and can offer informed guidance.

Chapter 7

The Talmud's Understanding of Life and Death

Yaakov Love

APOLOGY

The question of the halakhic definition of death has been presented to me among others, many of whom are far more qualified than I to answer. "The laws of life [and death] are not like monetary laws" (m. *Sanhedrin* 4:5) and certainly not like *issur ve-heter*. I should not, and will not, offer practical answers, but rather halakha in the form of various ideas that have come to me in my studies. I pray that I not err and that my words are acceptable to "those who don't discern between *abba* and *abba*" (*Ta'anit* 23b).

I. YOMA AND SOṬA

Let us examine a talmudic passage in b. *Yoma* (85a):

תנו רבנן: עד היכן הוא בודק? Our rabbis taught: Up to where do we
עד חוטמו, ויש אומרים: עד לבו.[1] check [for signs of life in one who is
being dug out of debris on Shabbat,
when unnecessary moving of the debris
or the body is forbidden]? Up to his
nose. Some say: Up to his heart.

Rashi comments:

עד היכן הוא בודק - אם דומה Up to where do we check? – If the person
למת שאינו מזיז איבריו, עד היכן is like a dead man, who isn't moving his
הוא מפקח לדעת האמת? limbs, up to where do we dig to know
the truth?

In other words, if, as we're digging the person out, we see motion in the
now uncovered limbs, we must assume he is alive. Evidently the need
to check the heart or nose indicates that no such motion is perceived.[2]

---

1. In most manuscripts of the Babylonian Talmud, this phrase appears as *ad ṭabburo* (up
   to his navel), referring to the rise and fall of the chest while breathing, and making
   this debate equivalent to the one in the Jerusalem Talmud. Most *Rishonim* cite this
   version of the Babylonian Talmud as well. Nevertheless, this section of the essay is
   predicated on Rashi's text, the one in the standard printing of the Babylonian Talmud,
   which has *libbo*, his heart.

2. The heart is obviously not part of the "motion of limbs" to which Rashi refers,
   since – at least according to one opinion – that's what we're checking for. Rabbi
   Moshe Sofer (*Ḥatam Sofer* Y D 338) describes this victim as "lying still as a stone, with
   no heartbeat (שמוטל כאבן דומם ואין בו שום דפיקה)." Until we know whether there is
   "life," all motion must be considered. Once the absence of life is determined, some
   motion may be ignored, since it is considered postmortem spasms. Rambam (M T
   Laws of the Impurity of the Dead 1:15) writes:

   או שהותז ראשו...הרי זה מטמא ...or if his head was severed...he causes defile-
   אף על פי שעדיין הוא מרפרף באחד ment [as a corpse], even if one of his limbs is
   מאיבריו. still flailing.

   If Rashi's "limbs" include the heart or other vital organs, Rambam's "limbs" should
   too. So according to Rambam, when death is assured (here, because of decapitation),
   the heart's fluttering makes no difference. One could claim that Rashi means one
   thing and Rambam another. Nevertheless, I prefer to say they agree. If so, motion
   of the heart cannot determine life. See also b. *Soṭa* 45b, where, according to one

The Talmud continues:

נימא הני תנאי כי הני תנאי, דתניא: מהיכן הולד נוצר? מראשו.... אבא שאול אומר: מטיבורו....	Shall we say the above argument is similar to the [following] argument? For we learned: From what point is a fetus formed [in the womb]? From its head.... Abba Shaul says: From its navel....
אפילו תימא אבא שאול, עד כאן לא קא אמר אבא שאול התם אלא לענין יצירה, דכל מידי ממציעתיה מיתצר, אבל לענין פקוח נפש - אפילו אבא שאול מודי דעקר חיותא באפיה הוא, דכתיב: "כל אשר נשמת רוח חיים באפיו".	[No.] Even Abba Shaul [would agree here]. Abba Shaul refers only to the point of formation of the fetus, since everything forms from its center. But as far as saving a life, even Abba Shaul would agree that the core of life is in the nose, as it is written, "All in whose nostrils was the breath of life" (Gen. 7:22).

What does the argument about heart or head have to do with that of navel or head? "Heart" is occasionally used by Hazal to mean the chest. This usage would perhaps explain Rashi (s.v. *hakhi garsinan*), who correlates breath with the heart.[3] Since "heart" may include the entire trunk, it may also include the navel. If so, it isn't the heartbeat we're checking for, but rather the rise and fall of the trunk with respiration.[4]

---

opinion, a decapitated person can still run. His heart, in fact, can still pump. What he cannot do is breathe. There we follow Rabbi Akiva, but I'm not sure that means running is impossible; chickens do it all the time (though I've read that birds depend less on oxygen than humans).

3. See also Rashi, b. *Shabbat* 134a, s.v. *dela minsheta*. Note also the alternate use of *neshama* and *neshima*.

4. One can also explain Rashi's correlation of the heart with respiration if we understand that medicine then was based on Galen's science. Galen (second to third centuries) believed that the right side of the heart delivered air to the body and that the heartbeat mirrored respiration. (Nonetheless, I'm not sure the heartbeat could be detected, so the heartbeat Rashi refers to may well be the rise and fall of the chest/trunk.) It was Avicenna (980–1037) who proposed that the whole heart delivers blood and that the heartbeat was the sound of the opening and closing of valves.

However, I believe there is another explanation. For this reading, we need to look at another passage, in b. *Soṭa* 45b. The discussion refers to a murder victim found between two cities. The Torah (Deut. 21) requires that we measure the distance from the victim to both cities, with the nearer city performing the ritual of *egla arufa*.

The Mishna discusses a case in which the head of the victim and his or her body were found separated:

מאין היו מודדין? רבי אליעזר
אומר: מטיבורו. רבי עקיבא
אומר: מחוטמו.

From where did they measure? Rabbi Eliezer says: From his navel. Rabbi Akiva says: From his nose.

The Talmud asks:

במאי קמיפלגי? מר סבר: עיקר
חיותא באפיה, ומר סבר: עיקר
חיותא בטיבוריה.

About what [principle] are they arguing? One believes the source of life is in one's nose, and the other believes the source of life is in one's navel.

לימא כי הני תנאי: "מהיכן הולד
נוצר? מראשו.... אבא שאול
אומר: מטיבורו...".

Shall we say that this is similar to the following argument: "From where is the fetus formed? From its head.... Abba Shaul says: From its navel...."?

אפילו תימא אבא שאול, ע"כ
לא קאמר אבא שאול אלא
לענין יצירה, דכי מיתצר ולד
ממציעתיה מיתצר, אבל לענין
חיותא דכולי עלמא באפיה
הוא, דכתיב: "כל אשר נשמת
רוח חיים באפיו וגו'".

[No.] Even Abba Shaul [would agree here]. Abba Shaul refers only to the formation [of the fetus], since a fetus forms from its center. But regarding life, everyone agrees that [the source of life] is in the nose, as it is written: "All in whose nostrils was the breath of life."

We see not only the similarity to the text in *Yoma*, but also the difference. In *Soṭa* the original argument is one of head versus navel, paralleling the argument to which we wish to compare it. What we have in *Yoma* is the common talmudic occurrence of the transfer of a *sugya* from one place to another. In our case, it is from *Soṭa* to *Yoma*. Though Talmud critics, and often *Rishonim*, frequently state that a given *sugya* is "not in its place" in one of the two sites, I believe there is a reason for the Talmud's citing the *Soṭa* passage in *Yoma*.

After the Talmud in *Yoma* makes it clear that "everyone" would agree that "life" is in the nose, how does it explain the opinion that we must uncover and check only up to the heart? And if we believe there is indeed an argument on the subject, why can't Abba Shaul side with that opinion?[5] This was a problem for the Talmud, which makes its next statement very important:

אמר רב פפא: מחלוקת ממטה למעלה, אבל ממעלה למטה, כיון דבדק ליה עד חוטמו שוב אינו צריך, דכתיב: כל אשר נשמת רוח חיים באפיו.	Rav Pappa said: The dispute is when [uncovering the person] from bottom to top, but from top to bottom, once one checks the person's nose [for signs of breath], one need check no further, as it says: "All in whose nostrils was the breath of life."

The passage in *Soṭa*, which tells us that "all agree," is the perfect bridge between the argument itself and Rav Pappa's need to answer our question and explain that the argument applies only when there's no evidence of life in the heart. In that case, the question is whether we should be satisfied with that and forbid further removal of the debris, or whether we still need to check the nose. When the nose has been checked and there is no sign of breath, all see no reason to check further down.[6]

---

5. True, if the *sugya* was transferred willy-nilly, this isn't really a problem. In any event, the fact that it was transferred means that there is no real correlation between navel and heart and therefore no proof of whether "heart" means heart or chest/trunk when explaining the Talmud.

6. The question we asked in *Yoma* might rightfully be asked in *Soṭa* as well: If everyone agrees that life is in the nose, what do we do with Rabbi Eliezer? And if Rabbi Eliezer believes life is in the navel, why can't Abba Shaul believe that as well? I think that – contrary to the case in *Yoma*, which is a practical ruling (*halakha le-maʿaseh*) – in *Soṭa* we needn't answer the implied question about Rabbi Eliezer. *Egla arufa* is a law applicable only in messianic times at best. Perhaps it even "never was and never will be" and is mentioned only for us to be rewarded for its study (b. *Sanhedrin* 71a); both Rabbi Akiva and Rabbi Eliezer, right or wrong, will receive their reward.

II. THE TALMUD AND THE ḤATAM SOFER

The *Rishonim* depended on the science of their time in interpreting the Talmud,[7] so we too must reconcile the text with our own science. Even how Rav Pappa himself understood the reality of the subject is somewhat immaterial.

If he believed that it was movement of the chest or trunk (i.e., evidence of breath) that we were checking for, then today as well, we would give much weight to obvious respiration and treat the patient as alive. Alternatively, if he believed it was actually heartbeat that we were seeking – or even if he didn't – we would certainly do all we could to (re)instigate respiration in someone found to have a pulse.

In other words: Rav Pappa didn't believe that one who demonstrably lacked respiration at the nose still needed to be checked at the chest. Nevertheless, this would not be our practice today. Whether Rav Pappa was simply not cognizant of the heartbeat, or considered it a sign of respiration, we would rely on our science over his. Nowadays, if someone were found under a pile of debris, and he exhibited no breathing, he would certainly be checked at least for a carotid pulse. In such a case, where a pulse was found, we would certainly try to save him.[8]

This is probably the idea behind Rabbi Moshe Sofer's statement (*Ḥatam Sofer* YD 338):

כל שאחר שמוטל כאבן דומם	Anyone lying still as a stone, with no
ואין בו שום דפיקה ואם אח״כ	heartbeat, and whose breathing then
בטל הנשימה אין לנו אלא דברי	terminates – all we have are the words
תורתינו הקדושה שהוא מת.	of our holy Torah that he has died.

---

7. As mentioned, either Rashi sees checking the "heart" as checking the chest for movement, or he considers heartbeat a sign of respiration. Either way, his commentary is based on the science of his time.

8. Surely even Rabbi Avraham Yeshaya Karelitz (the *Ḥazon Ish*), who believes that the science of "years of Torah" directs halakha, wouldn't demand that we stop checking at the non-breathing nose on Shabbat and not look for a carotid pulse. Rabbi Moshe Feinstein also states that if an ECG shows cardiac activity, we certainly try to save the person (IM YD 2:174). The Talmud and *Rishonim* discuss the heart (or the chest), not a pulse, because they misunderstood the workings of the heart, or at least of circulation as we know it.

We cannot rely on lack of breathing alone where we can find a pulse. Rabbi Sofer stated earlier in the same responsum that when the Torah forbade us to leave a corpse without burial,

ע"כ אז נמסר לנו שיעור מיתה אולי הי' אז מסורת מבעלי טבעיים הראשונים אעפ"י שנשכח מרופאי זמנינו....

Perforce the measure of death was then conveyed to us. Perhaps there was a tradition from the early naturalists – though it was lost to our contemporary physicians....

אם לא היה להם מסורת מהטבעיים ע"כ קבל מרע"ה השיעור מהלכה למשה מסיני.

If there was no such tradition among the naturalists, Moses our teacher must have received it as a *halakha le-Moshe mi-Sinai*.

או שסמכו עצמן אקרא כל אשר רוח חיים באפו.

Or they [the sages] supported [this position] with the verse "All in whose nostrils was the breath of life."[9]

Rabbi Sofer takes for granted that breath becomes the operative criterion only if there is no pulse. How does he understand the passage in *Yoma*? If "all agree" that when starting to remove the debris from the head, we stop when there is no sign of breathing at the nose, why aren't we checking a bit further for a pulse? If the sages weren't familiar with the pulse per se, why not continue till the heart? Could it be Rabbi Sofer believes that the sages, like Rashi, not only were unfamiliar with the pulse, but believed that the motion of the heart was a function of breathing, so there would be nothing to gain from further examination?

From where did Rabbi Sofer introduce the idea of the pulse? Is the Talmud useless to us now that we understand the workings of the heart and the circulatory system? Wouldn't the halakha of saving a life (*piqu'ah nefesh*) be transmitted along with not standing over the blood

---

9. Cf. *Derashot ha-Ran* 5 (alternate text), s.v. *u-khemo she-nitztavinu*; I wonder if Ran would include things learned by Ḥazal from science among those we must believe. The passage in the *Ḥatam Sofer*, however, may refer only to science at the time of the giving of the Torah.

of one's fellow (Lev. 19:16), just as it was with the law requiring burial of a body (Deut. 21:23)?[10]

Apparently, in Rabbi Sofer's case, where we have a completely uncovered body that we can check for both breathing and a pulse, either one would be evidence that the other has perhaps stopped only temporarily, that it is not *irreversible* (in contemporary terminology). As mentioned, we would share this reasoning. The Talmud, on the other hand, refers to a case in which we have access only to one or the other. If the heart has stopped (from the legs up), we must check further for breathing. If breathing has stopped – which, in talmudic times, may have been confirmed by checking the nose – there is no reason to check further, since the Talmud believes that either heart motion itself is only a function of breathing, or heartbeat is not a sign of life but only a sign that the person may be breathing.[11]

Ultimately, Rabbi Sofer did quote the verse from *Yoma* as the Torah's criterion for life. We have thus reconciled the Talmud with the *Ḥatam Sofer* and medical reality. There is no reason to interpret the Torah or the Talmud as inconsistent with science.

III. PRACTICAL APPLICATION

How does the case we need to deal with compare to the Talmud? What we have is someone who cannot, and according to our science will not, breathe on his or her own.[12] The person's heart, however, can be kept beating and pumping by supplying oxygen. The heart doesn't beat because of the central nervous system; it has its own built-in pacemaker, which works on its own electrical source.[13] Breathing, on the other hand,

---

10. Rambam in his *Commentary on the Mishna* (*Ḥullin* 2:1) seems familiar with the carotid pulse. In explaining the term *veridin*, he states: "They are the two pulsing arteries that extend within the neck along both sides of the trachea." (This description accords with Avicenna.) Though it's possible to explain that when checking from the feet up, the carotids are to be examined as well, when checking from the head down Rambam decides that we needn't go beyond the nose. Pulse/heartbeat is evidently to be ignored. True, having reached the nose, one could detect a pulse at the ear, but Rambam makes no mention of this.

11. Rabbi Feinstein seemingly draws the same conclusion (IM YD 2:174). I believe Rabbi Sofer would agree.

12. I refer to someone who has undergone the full battery of tests for brainstem death.

13. This is not the place to expand on the sinoatrial (SA) and atrioventricular (AV) nodes.

depends on the brainstem. A heart that has stopped can be restarted. If autonomic breathing has stopped, it cannot be restarted.

In his *Commentary on the Mishna* (*Oholot* 1:6), Rambam explains why movement after decapitation is no sign of life and is only like a lizard's tail severed from the body. He writes:

ויארע זה למקצת מיני בעלי	This [movement] occurs in some living
החיים אם לא היה הכח המניע	beings when the force of motion doesn't
מתפשט בכל האברים מיסוד	spread to all the limbs from a single root
ומוצא אחד אלא יהיה מפולג	and initiation but rather is dispersed
בכל הגוף.	throughout the body.

Rambam is clearly differentiating between nervous spasms, which are local, and life, which is dependent on the central nervous system.

In the *Mishneh Torah* (Laws of the Impurity of the Dead 1:15), Rambam states:

המת אינו מטמא עד שתצא	A body doesn't defile until its soul has
נפשו. אפילו מגוייד או גוסס,	departed. Even if one has been sliced up or
אפילו נשחטו בו שני הסימנים	is dying, even if the trachea and esophagus
- אינו מטמא עד שתצא	have been severed – he doesn't defile until
נפשו, שנאמר: "בנפש האדם	his soul has departed, as it says: "[Whoever
אשר ימות."	touches a corpse] when the soul of a person
	has died [shall be defiled]" (Num. 19:13).

נשברה מפרקתו ורוב בשרה	If the nape of the neck was broken, and
עמה, או שנקרע כדג מגבו	most of its flesh along with it, or he was
או שהותז ראשו, או שנחתך	torn asunder from behind, like a fish, or
לשני חלקים בבטנו - הרי זה	his head was severed, or he was cut in two
מטמא, אף-על-פי שעדיין	at his waist – he does defile, even if one of
הוא מרפרף באחד מאיבריו.	his limbs is still flailing.

The word "limbs" in this context refers to organs both internal and external, including the heart.

As we've seen, any movement not connected to the central nervous system, such as that of the heart after decapitation or the breaking of the nape of the neck, is considered "flails." The person is dead in keeping with the halakha in *Yoma* because breathing is impossible.[14] The heart, especially in the case of decapitation, can continue beating, as explained. In theory, if vessels are connected at the neck and oxygen is supplied, the heart can beat indefinitely.

As to whether physiological "decapitation" is the same as physical decapitation, it seems that it isn't decapitation per se that renders the person "dead," but rather the inability to breathe. There is no decapitation in *Yoma*, and the common denominator in Rambam's list is not the lack of a head, but the inability to breathe.

Finally, I defer to the great Rabbi Moshe Feinstein in his *Iggerot Moshe* (YD 3:132 and 4:54). Although Rabbi Feinstein seems to require the test for brain (stem) death in order to confirm that the person is dead, his description of the condition as "it is as if the head were severed with force (וזהי כאילו הותז הראש בכח)" is unnecessary – and unnecessarily exhaustive – unless he agrees that brain death is indeed equivalent to decapitation. In the latter source, he explicitly equates them.[15]

IV. TAKING BUT NOT GIVING

Yet another question has been discussed: If someone believes that only cessation of both respiration and circulation define death, may he accept an organ that was removed from a donor after brainstem death?

It appears to me that if the recipient is the only one for whom the organ(s) will be removed – which would rarely if ever be the case[16] – it

---

14. Breathing is also impossible when one has been cut in two below the diaphragm.
15. This statement seems to have been added, but it is substantiated by the former responsum.
16. In his essay in the organ donation volume, Rabbi Dr. Eugene Korn argues that heart transplantation is always a case of organ removal for a specific patient. He writes:

> The defense of [receiving but not donating] is often phrased as, "Why shouldn't the potential recipient be saved by the transplant after the heart has been removed by others, even if it was done unethically? It's not always wrong to benefit from unjust gains." However, this is an inaccurate description of what actually takes place. Each heart extraction is recipient-specific: The doctor removes the heart only after the particular recipient consents to receive it and for the explicit purpose of implanting it into that one recipient. Because the removal of the heart

would be wrong for him to request or sanction the removal in any way. Whether or not the rules of "an appointed messenger committing a sin on one's behalf (*shaliaḥ li-dvar aveira*)" apply, the potential recipient would be an accessory to murder.

If, however, the organ would be removed in any event – for another local patient or for shipment – we can see the removal as being ex post facto, and "nothing stands in the way of saving a life (*ein davar omed bi-fnei piqu'aḥ nefesh*)" (t. *Shabbat* 9:22). What about the question of *eiva*, causing ill will, by using donated organs but not donating? The sages didn't apply the idea in all cases,[17] so we certainly cannot assume they would have applied it where *piqu'aḥ nefesh* was involved.[18] "*Nothing stands in the way of saving a life,*" probably not even *eiva*.

V. SAVING THE LIVING AT THE EXPENSE OF THE DYING

The permissibility of taking organs can be strengthened by looking at the little-known and even less-quoted opinion of Rabbi Yisrael Lifshuetz (*Tiferet Yisrael, Boaz*, end of m. *Yoma*).

---

is done *for the specific recipient upon his willingness to receive it,* the recipient is an essential factor in the extraction. The causal connection between recipient and extraction is explicit and definite. The claim that the recipient is not a material cause of removing the heart is false. Because of this strong causal connection, if the removal of the heart entails possible murder, the recipient is an indirect agent of that murder. [Note: This is unlike transplanting an organ drawn from an organ bank, which is not recipient-specific. Such an organ is removed from the donor before a recipient is identified, after which it is held in the bank until a single recipient is selected. Hence the actual recipient is not a material cause of removing that specific organ.]

Assuming these facts are correct, it would indeed be forbidden to receive a heart if one believes its removal from a brain dead patient to be murder. I thank my student Rabbi Zev Farber for calling my attention to this passage in Rabbi Dr. Korn's essay.

17. See especially b. *Bava Qamma* 38a regarding goring oxen; who can say that it was not because of *Ḥazal's* integrity in not changing the law that it was not reported?

18. Some understand the permission to receive an organ as based on reliance on Rabbi Feinstein to save the recipient's life, even though we cannot rely on his opinion for the removal of the donor's organs. In the case above, where I believe it is wrong to sanction removal, depending on Rabbi Feinstein's view to accept the organ would be, in fact, relying on that view to do the removal! Other than the supposed idea of *eiva*, I cannot see why all wouldn't agree in the second case.

ונראה לי דאיכא למימר
דאף על גב דקיימא לן
דחיישינן לחיי שעה, היינו
באין חיי קיום כנגדו, אבל
ביש חיי קיום כנגדו וודאי
דדם חיי קיום שלו סומק
טפי מדם חיי שעה של
חבירו שאינו סומק כל כך,
ואפילו ספק חיי קיום עדיף
מוודאי חיי שעה, ויכול
להציל את עצמו בו.

It seems to me that one can argue that although we're concerned about short-term life, this is only when it's not up against stable life. However, when it's up against stable life, certainly the blood of the person with stable life is "redder" than the blood of the person with short-term prospects, which isn't so red. Even [the life of] a person with only a possibility of stable life is preferable to [that of a person] who will survive only a short while, and [the former] may save himself at [the latter's] expense.

Rabbi Lifshuetz deems it permissible to save someone who could live a "normal" life at the expense of someone who will imminently pass on. Given that someone who is brainstem dead will not survive more than a few days, according to this opinion it would be permitted even ab initio to remove his organs in order to save the recipient. It would certainly be permitted to accept the organs post facto, since according to Rabbi Lifshuetz the procedure itself was permitted.

This opinion should not be taken lightly. Regarding the principle that "We don't follow the majority when it comes to saving lives" (b. *Yoma* 84b),[19] in his *Beit Yosef* (OḤ 618) Rabbi Joseph Karo quotes the opinion of Rabbeinu Yeruḥam that it also applies to an argument of the *posqim*.

בענין מחלוקת הפוסקים
באומדנא דחולה אי
אזלינן ביה בתר רוב
דעות דלדידן לא נפקא
לן מידי דאפילו תהיה
מחלוקת פוסקים אם היה
בא מעשה לידינו היינו
מאכילין אותו דספק
נפשות להקל.

Regarding the issue of when there is a debate among halakhic authorities, in a case of establishing a presumption about an ill person [on Yom Kippur], whether we follow the majority opinion – to us this is a non-issue, for even if there is a debate among authorities, if such a question came before us we would feed the ill person, since any case of doubt in a situation of possible lifesaving is decided leniently.

---

19. לא הלכו בפקוח נפש אחר הרוב.

164

Rabbi Shlomo Kluger (*Ḥokhmat Shlomo* OḤ 328, s.v. *notnin kli*) accepts this principle as well. Constructing an argument that would allow the violation of Shabbat in order to save a person's eyesight, Rabbi Kluger references Rabbi Yehuda's position that a blind person is exempt from mitzvot,[20] and notes that Rabbeinu Yeruḥam, as quoted by Rabbi Karo (*Beit Yosef* OḤ 473), follows this position as a matter of halakha. Rabbi Kluger argues that since we allow the violation of Shabbat in certain cases in order to enable someone to observe the coming Sabbaths, saving a person's eyesight accomplishes this goal, since if the person were to go blind, he would be exempt from observing Shabbat. Although Rabbi Karo himself is rather surprised at Rabbeinu Yeruḥam's stance, maintaining that we do not follow this position, Rabbi Kluger writes:

וניהו דרוב הפוסקים חולקים עליו, מכל מקום אין הולכין בפקוח נפש אחר הרוב.	Though most halakhic authorities argue with [Rabbeinu Yeruḥam], nevertheless, we don't follow the majority when it comes to saving lives.

Considering this principle, it is not inconceivable that we could follow Rabbi Lifshuetz's opinion here.[21]

FURTHER THOUGHT

Finally, I would like to pose a hypothetical question to those who require cessation of both respiration and circulation. No matter how aggressive their maintenance, brainstem-dead patients eventually succumb. I also assume that removal of such a patient's heart in order to install an artificial one would be permitted.[22] Would it then be permitted to remove the brainstem-dead patient's heart and install a mechanical one so that a recipient could benefit from the heart?

---

20. His position is explained in b. *Bava Qamma* 86b and b. *Qiddushin* 31a.
21. True, the rules of reliance on a minority opinion generally don't apply to an opinion unmentioned by the *posqim*. However, this inapplicability itself may apply only where we wish to overturn a ruling that otherwise would be decided according to the majority. When majority rule is inapplicable, such as when saving a life, perhaps it makes no difference which minority opinion we use. This question would depend on whether the rejection of an obscure opinion is merely an exclusion from the rule or whether it is because the opinion is regarded as nonexistent.
22. This procedure would possibly even keep the patient "alive" longer.

Chapter 8

Death Is a Process

Joseph Isaac Lifshitz

Writing this essay, I find myself troubled. As in many ethical dilemmas, questions regarding the moment of death do not distinguish good from evil, for the choice is between two evils. The price of a mistake in this area is too high, whether one is for or against the Harvard criteria. Nonetheless, I contend that the question that's commonly asked – is the precise moment of death determined by the death of the heart, the brain, or the brainstem? – is incorrect. This question assumes that such a moment even exists. I would like to suggest that death is not a momentary event, but rather a process. Therefore, what needs to be examined is not one particular organ or another, but rather the body as a whole.

I. HISTORY

Before delving into this idea, I would like to touch upon the history of the acceptance of brain death as one decisive moment, with the Harvard criteria being an indicator of such.

Traditionally, there have been two signs of life – breath and heartbeat. For most of history, there was no possibility of life without both.

That's why halakhic sources are very poor regarding the definition of the moment of death: Whenever a person lacked either one of these signs, he was declared dead.

Modern halakhic decisors have tried to find halakhic sources that define death. Most opinions connect death to respiration, while a minority connect it to heartbeat. While these arguments remained primarily theoretical, during the latter half of the twentieth century they began to have serious ramifications.

In 1968, an ad hoc committee at Harvard Medical School published a pivotal report defining the criteria for irreversible coma. The Harvard criteria gradually gained consensus, moving toward what we now consider brain death. Today, both the legal and medical communities around the world use the concept of brain death as a legal definition of death, allowing a person to be declared dead even if life support maintains the body's metabolic processes.

Rabbis resisted the Harvard criteria. In 1985, however, an oral ruling by Rabbi Feinstein (which followed a similar one in 1976) finally accepted the Harvard criteria.[1] They were endorsed by the Israeli rabbinical court as well.

The criteria were accepted because brain death was deemed halakhically similar to beheading. Halakhic sources define a beheaded person as dead, even if we recognize some movement of his or her body. Rabbi Feinstein's halakhic authority was so immense that his ruling changed the opinion of many rabbis worldwide.

II. PROBLEMATIZING BRAIN DEATH

These rabbis and doctors sought to establish the moment of death for a very practical reason: to harvest organs. One may harvest organs only from a dead patient. Nevertheless, despite the urge to find this moment, searching for it should proceed with some skepticism and doubt.

---

1. Rabbi Moshe Feinstein, IM YD 3:132. Some questioned the authenticity of Rabbi Feinstein's 1985 ruling. See, for instance, Rabbi Shlomo Zalman Auerbach as cited in Shabtai A. HaKohen Rappaport, "Rabbi Moshe Feinstein on Brain Death," *Sefer Assia* 7 (5754/1993–94), 148 [Hebrew]. Unfortunately, they ignored his 1976 decision, which shows a consistent line of reasoning. For a detailed analysis of Rabbi Feinstein's position, see Rabbi Daniel Reifman's essay in this volume.

Whereas science once assumed that death occurred once breathing ceased, we know now that organs stop functioning at different times. A decision that the brain is the crucial organ, rather than the heart, lungs, or liver, should be approached cautiously.

The difference between past and present is not only practical but conceptual. The ancients assumed that a vital essence, powered by God, spread vitality throughout the body. This essence was situated in the heart. As Rambam described it:

> And just as in the body of man there are ruling parts and ruled parts requiring for their continued existence the governance of the ruling part governing them, so are there in the world as a whole ruling parts – namely, the fifth encompassing body – and ruled parts requiring a governor – they are the elements and what is composed of them. And just as the ruling part, which is the heart, is always in motion and is the principle of every motion to be found in the body, whereas the other parts of the body are ruled by the heart, which in virtue of its motion sends towards them the forces they require for their functions, so heaven in virtue of its motion exerts governance over the other parts of the world and sends to every generated thing the forces that subsist in the latter.[2]

Such a perception of a hierarchy of vitality doesn't exist anymore. Of course, we do have a concept that God gives life, but we don't point to any one organ as a mediator between Him and our bodies. We understand now that the body functions as a complex organism. The perception of the brain as a replacement of what the heart used to symbolize is an anachronism. I wouldn't define death as the degeneration of every tissue in the body, but we should assign equal value to all the main systems in the body – vascular, nervous, and pulmonary.

Therefore, I propose that although a person defined as dead according to the Harvard criteria is in the process of dying, he is not

---

2. Moses Maimonides, *The Guide of the Perplexed* (trans. Shlomo Pines; Chicago: University of Chicago Press, 1963), 1:72, 186–87.

completely dead until the heart, as the last main organ of the vascular system, stops beating.

Halakha is comfortable with the concept of processes, as can be demonstrated in many other areas. Death is an excellent example of a process. The moment of death isn't always well defined, and we shouldn't force it when it doesn't exist, however tempting that may be.

I know my conceptualization here differs greatly from the majority opinion. Nevertheless, the gravity of the subject requires me to voice my view.

III. LIFE AS A PROCESS

The moment of birth is very well defined in Jewish law – when the baby's head is out, he is defined as a complete human being. But what is the definition of the fetus in the womb? Without entering into a discussion of abortion in Jewish law, I would like to claim that the fetus is understood as a life in process. It is not considered a complete living being, yet it's not just the flesh of the mother either.

Contingent definitions exist in halakha. A famous example is that of day and night. Day and night change shifts in the twilight zone. Rabbi Yosef Rozin (1858–1936) contends that twilight is a halakhic model of a doubtful reality (*Tzofnat Pa'ane'aḥ*, Shabbat 5:4). Unlike halakhic doubts stemming from a lack of information, twilight is intrinsically doubtful. Night and day mingle, so this period can be defined as neither.

A contingent reality is defined as a doubt because contingency contradicts the nature of law. A legal system is built on definitions, whereas reality contains many gray areas, to which clear definitions don't always apply. Halakha, as a legal system, suffers from the same problem. The solution to this problem lies in defining a contingent situation as a doubt.

There are numerous contingent situations in halakha. For example, halakha grapples with the status of incense that slips through the priest's fingers. Incense held between his fingers and palm becomes sanctified. Incense that falls from his hand does not. But what about incense between the fingers? Ritva (b. *Yoma* 47b) accords such incense "possible" (*safeq*) sanctity, positing the same type of definition as twilight. The incense case is a spatial contingency. Twilight is a temporal one, and it's understood as a process.

Another contingent definition in halakha is that of partial amounts (*ḥatzi shiur*). Insofar as the minimal requirements for receiving a punishment, halakha clearly defines every prohibited act. In prescribing proper behavior, however, halakha has no precise measurements.

That is why, according to Rambam, the milk and eggs of non-kosher animals are also not kosher. Though the Torah seemingly prohibits only the flesh of these animals, the prohibition extends to their milk and eggs, which are considered *ḥatzi shiur*.[3]

Rabbi Avraham Sternbuch defines a fetus similarly.[4] Although a fetus is not considered a human being according to the Mishna in *Nidda* (3:7), it is in the process of becoming one, and therefore it is defined as *ḥatzi shiur*. Consequently, killing a fetus is considered murder, yet, as in all cases of *ḥatzi shiur*, the offender receives no punishment.

A dying person is the same as a fetus but at the other end of the spectrum. One shouldn't touch such a person, though he's in the midst of an irreversible process. If we conceive of death as the degeneration of the body's main systems, a person whose brain is dead but whose heart still beats should not be considered dead. Instead, he or she is dying.

IV. MOVEMENT AND LIFE

One of the sources quoted most often in reference to brain function is Rambam's mention of a man whose neck is broken and cut off but whose body is still moving.[5] His movements are commonly compared to the reflexes of a lizard's tail, as the Mishna states.[6]

Rabbi Menaḥem ha-Me'iri suggests standards for deciding when reflexes indicate death and when they don't. If the neck is broken and the majority of the tissue around it is cut off as well, the person is dead, even if movement can be observed in the remainder of the body. In any other case, as long as there is movement, the person is alive.[7]

---

3. Rambam, MT Laws of Forbidden Foods 3:6.
4. See Rabbi Yeḥiel Ya'aqov Weinberg, *Seridei Eish* 3:127 (Jerusalem: Mossad Harav Kook, 1977), 347 n. 2.
5. Rambam, MT Laws of the Impurity of the Dead 1:15.
6. Rabbi Joseph Karo, *Kesef Mishneh*, Laws of the Impurity of the Dead 1:15, following m. *Oholot* 6:1.
7. Rabbi Menaḥem ha-Me'iri, *Beit ha-Beḥira*, b. *Yoma* 23a.

The dual requirement of a broken neck and severed tissue is well documented. In addition to being codified by Me'iri, it is recorded by Rabbi Aḥa in the *She'iltot* (*Emor* 103), by Rabbi Yitzḥaq Alfasi (Rif) in his *Halakhot* (*Ṭuma* 2b), and by Rambam in the *Mishneh Torah* as well (Laws of the Impurity of the Dead 1:15).[8]

Nevertheless, Rabbi Moshe Feinstein claims (IM YD 3:132) that a broken neck signifies death because the brain's neural connection to the body is missing. Therefore, if there's any other proof that the brain has ceased to send messages to the body and is considered dead, halakha would not require a broken neck and amputated tissue.

Rabbi Feinstein clearly believes the brain to be the dominant organ, as he deduces from the source that discusses the broken neck. However, an alternative possibility seems plausible as well: Someone with a broken neck and severed neck tissue is considered dead because the head is *actually separated* from the body. Such a person is essentially decapitated.

Let me expand on this point. A living person is dependent on a fully functioning system with all its complexity; the various body parts must work together. True, a disconnection between organs is a problem, perhaps a fatal one, indicating that the person is dying. Nevertheless, it doesn't mean he's already dead. In the case of the severed head, actual death is defined not by the fact that information from the brain is no longer being delivered, but by the head's literal detachment from the body.

That's why Rambam cited the case of a broken neck combined with severed tissue. A broken neck alone doesn't define a person as dead. Only actual decapitation signifies death. A broken neck indicates that the person is dying, not that he or she is dead.

CONCLUSION

According to contemporary common sense, brain death indicates the death of a person as an intelligent being with awareness and responsibility. Other organs may serve important functions but they are never as representative of such a being as is the brain. Nevertheless, the question remains: Is this the concern of halakha?

---

8. See also Rabbi Yeḥezqel Landau, *Noda bi-Yehuda Qamma* EH 64.

Halakhic definitions depend on halakhic tradition, which is not always parallel to contemporary common sense. According to halakha, a living human being is perceived as a complex system in which all body parts function together. Some are crucial, whereas others (such as a limb or kidney) serve a local purpose but the body can survive without them.

The key organs of the body – such as the heart, liver, and brain – function together. In the process of death, they die but not necessarily simultaneously. The death of one shows that the process of dying has begun, but not that the person is dead. Complete death is defined in halakha either by the death of all primary organs or by the head's detachment from the body, with the latter no longer one system. However, if a person's heart and lungs are functioning, and the head is intact but the brain has stopped functioning, he or she cannot be defined as dead but rather, in the process of dying. During this process, the person's heart or other organs may not be harvested.

Chapter 9

Brain Death or Cardiocirculatory Death?

Dov Linzer

ARTICULATING THE PROBLEM

The question of the halakhic definition of death, and whether the death of the lower brain or brainstem qualifies, has been dealt with extensively in recent publications, including all the excellent essays here. The relevant sources from the Talmud, *Rishonim*, and *Aharonim* have all been thoroughly analyzed. With all the wealth of material that's been written, I think it's helpful to take a step back and see how the debate has been, and should be, framed.

It goes without saying that brainstem death is not addressed in the Talmud. By attempting to define brainstem death as halakhic death per se, *posqim* have left themselves open to the attack that there is no direct evidence for this definition in the Talmud. Many try to prove the definition based on a mishna (*Oholot* 1:6) in which a decapitated animal, although its limbs may still be twitching, is considered dead. The use of such a proof makes brainstem death look rather questionable.

We have, it seems, a new definition, adopted from the larger, secular society, without precedence or basis in the Talmud. Rejection of brainstem death is seen as the standard, traditional position, and those who accept the new definition must therefore defend it.

A DEFINITION BASED ON THE TALMUD

This controversy obscures what should be the more straightforward point, made by a number of authors in this collection. Simply stated, the definition of death in the Talmud (b. *Yoma* 85a), and *Shulḥan Arukh* (OḤ 329:4, 330:5) – and used throughout the generations[1] – is cessation of breathing. This definition coincides perfectly with brainstem death. When brainstem death occurs, the brainstem no longer controls the autonomous nervous system, and the person cannot breathe.

What takes longer is for the blood to stop circulating, since the heart has its own internal pacemaker and will continue beating briefly after brainstem death. Prior to modern medical innovations, however, cessation of circulation followed soon and inexorably after cessation of respiration. The time gap between the shutdown of these two systems has been artificially and significantly extended nowadays, given our ability to keep the lungs pumping with a ventilator.

When a person is in this state – her autonomous breathing has stopped, but because of the ventilator she is still breathing, and thus her heart is still pumping – the critical questions arise: May the ventilator be removed? May her organs be donated? In short, when respiration has stopped but circulation continues, is a person alive or dead? To consider this person alive is to reject brainstem death, but it is also to reject cessation of autonomous breathing as the sole criterion of death.[2] This

---

1. See, for example, Rabbi Moshe Feinstein, IM YD 3:132.
2. Some would argue that artificial respiration, once begun, should be considered the body's own respiration, and thus a person on a respirator is breathing. This is again an innovative argument, both textually and – from my perspective – logically. The person himself is not breathing. Consider the *reductio ad absurdum*: If a brain dead person, whose lungs and heart had stopped their autonomous functions, was made to both breathe and circulate blood through artificial means, would such a person be considered alive? Those who would give weight to nonautonomous breathing again bear the burden of both logical and textual proof. Rabbi Moshe Feinstein, for one, was quite clear that only autonomous breathing matters (IM YD 3:132).

person is alive only if a new criterion is added: Death requires cessation not only of respiration, but also of circulation.

The framing of this debate, then, needs to be reversed. The question is not "What sources or arguments justify the brain death definition?" but rather, "What sources or arguments justify adding a new criterion, cessation of circulation, to the standard halakhic definition of death?"[3]

How do *posqim* explain the addition of the circulation criterion? Sources, of course, are brought to support this position, most notably responsa by Rabbi Tzvi Ashkenazi (*Hakham Tzvi* 77) and Rabbi Moshe Sofer (*Hatam Sofer* Y D 2:338). However, as the essays in this volume and in the excellent new book on this topic by Rabbi Prof. Avraham Steinberg[4] make clear, it is highly questionable whether these sources are using cessation of circulation as a criterion for death. Instead, they seem to assume that either (a) circulation is part of the respiratory system (as the Greeks believed), or (b) cessation of circulation confirms that one has truly and irreversibly stopped breathing. Certainly, an argument can be made that cessation of circulation is intended by these later sources as an actual criterion of death, but *the burden of proof is on those who would introduce this criterion.* On what basis should we abandon the definition as found in the *Shulhan Arukh*, used throughout the generations, and reaffirmed by modern *posqim* such as Rabbi Moshe Feinstein?

---

3. The fact that cessation of respiration is the most obvious position can be seen in a "slip" made by *Yated Ne'eman*. On January 21, 2011, a vitriolic article in *Yated* attacked the "Rabbinic Statement Regarding Organ Donation and Brain Death," which was signed by over one hundred rabbis, many of world-renowned stature. In a statement meant to decimate the brain death position, the article triumphantly declared:

> In short, most *gedolei ha-posqim* consider the time of death to be defined by lack of independent respiratory activity, i.e., cessation of breathing.

A few days later, *Yated* realized that this definition was equivalent to the brainstem death standard and that the paper was actually supporting the position it had rejected. *Yated* then corrected this "error." In fact, we are now told, most *gedolei ha-posqim* require cessation not only of respiration, but also of circulation.

4. Avraham Steinberg, *Respiratory-Brain Death* (ed. Yigal Shafran; trans. Fred Rosner; Science, Halacha and Education Series; Jerusalem: Merhavim, 2012).

A NEW DEFINITION

Sources aside, some may argue that it makes rational or intuitive sense that as long as the heart is pumping and blood is circulating, the person should be deemed alive. As to the Talmud's emphasis on breathing, they would contend that it is meant not as a definition, but merely as an indicator. In talmudic times, cessation of circulation followed inexorably and almost immediately after cessation of breathing, so that the latter could be used to indicate death, even if the true definition lay elsewhere.

However, once we begin to use intuition or reason to move beyond the straightforward criterion in the Talmud, we should also consider the intuition that brain death, per se, should be defined as death. To my way of thinking, a person whose upper brain has irreversibly ceased to function and whose brainstem has irreversibly ceased to maintain the autonomous functions of the body, and whose body would have shut down completely if not for mechanical ventilation, is dead. The above seems like a reasonable definition of death, and it can even be supported by analogy to the aforementioned mishna regarding the decapitated lizard.

I believe that what makes it hard for people to consider such a person dead is not just the fact that the body – with the help of a ventilator – is continuing to perform its autonomous functions, but the fact that this person does not look dead. The doctors may tell us she is brain dead, but her heart is pumping, her chest is rising and falling, she looks no different than if she were in a coma, or asleep. If this emotional response is what is informing this position, we should make that explicit, but for me the arguments for a brain death definition are more persuasive than this argument based on appearance.

Consequently, we are left with two choices: We can assume the Talmud is giving us a definition of death, i.e., cessation of autonomous breathing. The burden of proof would then be on those requiring cessation of circulation as well. Alternatively, we can assume the Talmud is giving us only an indicator of death, and then we have to be guided by intuition and analogies.

Some will opt for the respiration and circulation criteria, finding support in a particular reading of certain responsa. Others, including myself, will opt for a brain death definition, supported by the analogy to the decapitated lizard. If we're dealing with a new definition, I see no textual or intuitive reason to prefer the respiration-circulation definition over the brain death one.

BOTTOM LINE

I respect both sides of this debate, and many revered *posqim*, far beyond my stature, have ruled on both sides. What needs to be clear, though, is that given where the sources lie, the position of either cessation of respiration (a criterion satisfied by brainstem death) or of brain death per se is of equal, if not greater, weight than the position requiring cessation of both respiration and circulation.

Either way, there are lives at stake – the life of the dying or dead person, and the lives of those who can be saved if this person's organs can be donated to them. All who deal with such questions must do so with the greatest solemnity and *koved rosh*; for those who would rule on such issues, a full knowledge and understanding of all the relevant sources and opinions is a prerequisite.

I hope this book, and others like it, will help clarify the issues, lead to a more informed laity and rabbinate, and bring us all closer to the truth and to God's will in these matters, as in all others.

Chapter 10

Updating the Brainstem Death Definition[1]

Yosef Carmel

As an author of responsa, I have dealt with the question of brain death and brainstem death on several occasions. Following in the footsteps of Rabbi Shaul Yisraeli and his writings on this subject,[2] and after much research and thought, I will summarize my perspective on the issue.

I. THE BASIC HALAKHA

From the main pericopae in the Babylonian Talmud, and from the opinions expressed by the *Rishonim*, it seems that the basic criterion for determining death according to halakha is lack of respiration. All the tests described by the Talmud seem to be aimed toward determining whether a person is breathing. Even when pulse seems to be

---

1. A version of this essay originally appeared in Hebrew in *Be-Mareh ha-Bazak* 7:86. The English version was translated and adapted from this responsum by Rabbi Zev Farber.
2. See *Be-Mareh ha-Bazak* 2:81.

mentioned, with the goal of ascertaining whether the heart is still beating, the discussion is still connected to the issue of respiration. As is clear from the responsum of Rabbi Tzvi Ashkenazi (*Ḥakham Tzvi 77*), in the past the heart was thought to function as of the respiratory system.

Additionally, the Jerusalem Talmud makes no mention of checking for heartbeat in its version of the pericope in *Yoma*, and according to the text and discussion of a number of *Rishonim*, this test does not seem to have appeared in the Babylonian Talmud either. Either way, according to Rambam's *Mishneh Torah*, the *Ṭur*, and the *Shulḥan Arukh*, checking for breath is the definitive way to determine whether a person is alive.

Undoubtedly, the intent of these authorities is that respiration has ceased irreversibly. This is why many discussions (especially among the later authorities) describe secondary indications, such as a person being "still as a stone," etc. These factors help determine that the loss of respiration is irreversible rather than "apparent" or temporary. Certain later authorities who require a lack of heartbeat are also attempting to ensure that the loss of respiration is irreversible.

II. ENSURING COMPLIANCE WITH HALAKHA

All contemporary authorities agree on one thing: Since some physicians may declare a person dead based on non-halakhic criteria, it is necessary to ensure, as a precondition for agreeing to donate organs, that this declaration be made in accordance with halakha.

Therefore, all these authorities[3] require the participation of a rabbi in the process of the declaration of death, or at least the participation of physicians who have been trained by rabbis who are licensed to provide this training. It is, in fact, this reasonable suspicion – which I will discuss later – that caused Rabbi Yosef Shalom Elyashiv and Rabbi Shmuel ha-Levi Wosner, as well as Rabbi Eliezer Waldenburg, to add conditions above and beyond what the talmudic pericopae would require.

---

3. Including Rabbis Shaul Yisraeli, Avraham Shapira, Mordechai Eliyahu, and Zalman Nehemia Goldberg, Sephardic chief rabbis Ovadia Yosef and Shlomo Amar, and the office of the Ashkenazic Chief Rabbinate.

III. ORGAN TRANSPLANTS ARE NO LONGER DANGEROUS

That which was claimed by certain halakhic authorities in the past – that the donation of vital organs constitutes "double murder" – is no longer relevant, at least from the recipient's perspective. The issue nowadays centers exclusively on the donor and depends on one's halakhic position, and on one's confidence that the halakha will in fact be followed during the process.

Medically speaking, organ donation is the opposite of "double murder." It has long saved many lives. The survival rate for organ recipients is excellent; most even regain considerable quality of life. Though it's forbidden to kill one person to save another – or even many others – if we can ensure that the organs will be taken from the person after he is determined to be dead according to halakha, there is a mitzva to do so and save lives. This conclusion is unavoidable, and it places a heavy weight upon halakhic authorities, who need to offer practical guidance.

IV. TAKING BUT NOT GIVING

Some have suggested to me, in the name of well-known halakhic authorities, that it would be permissible to receive donated organs even though it is forbidden to donate them. It was precisely with regard to such statements that the phrase "Sages, be cautious with your words" was coined.[4]

Not only would publishing a statement like this be an unparalleled desecration of God's name, but it could lead to crises of life-and-death proportions, including increased anti-Semitism and even a worldwide ban on Jews' receiving organs. Even worse, this ban would be understandable, humane, and correct, since whoever does not donate should not be allowed to receive donations.

Decisions like this one are exceedingly dangerous. There is no place in halakha or Jewish ethics for such an idea, and it is forbidden to propagate such a policy, even in fora presumed to be inaccessible to the general public.

---

4. M. *Avot* 1:11, in the name of Avtalyon.

V. SURVIVING BRAIN DEATH?

Some claim that people who were once designated as brain dead are now alive and among us. If one follows the definition accepted by Rabbi Shaul Yisraeli and other authorities of similar disposition, this claim is false. The requirements according to the protocol established by the Chief Rabbinate of Israel in its day, and recently ratified by the Knesset, are designed to prevent such an occurrence.

Furthermore, even after declaration of death based on cardio-pulmonary criteria – as accepted by all halakhic authorities – there have been cases of people returning to the land of the living. This is because of human error in medical analysis, which we must certainly work diligently to avoid, but which has little relationship to the overall principles at work.

Human fallibility is, in fact, the basis of Rabbi Moshe Sofer's important responsum on this topic (*Ḥatam Sofer* YD 338). In his day, there was much misdiagnosis, prompting rampant fear of being buried alive. Therefore, certain observant Jews – first and foremost Rabbi Moses Mendelssohn – suggested that the Jewish community follow the duke of Mecklenburg's policy and wait three days before burying anyone, just in case. Nevertheless, Rabbi Sofer argued stalwartly that "all the winds in the world" couldn't blow halakha off its path of immediate burial.

VI. LIVING BRAIN CELLS IN A BRAIN DEAD PATIENT

Researchers recently discovered that a certain percentage of brain cells in a brain dead patient are still alive. Yet these findings have little if any relevance to the status of brain death in halakha, for several reasons.

1. Dead bodies also have a number of living cells that survive even after burial.

2. Even after a declaration of death by cardiopulmonary criteria, many heart cells remain alive. Yet nobody claims the deceased is not dead! So what's the difference between cardiopulmonary death and brain death?

3. The requirement that each and every brain cell be dead has no basis in classical halakhic sources. This criterion does appear in the writings of Rabbi Shlomo Zalman Auerbach and, perhaps, in

those of Rabbi Moshe Feinstein as well. However, its appearance seems to reflect their desire to ensure that cessation of respiration is truly irreversible. Accordingly, no one would make this demand once the barrage of tests required by Rabbi Yisraeli's protocol – and now adopted as law by the Knesset – has been conducted, for it is then certain that the patient is brain dead and the cessation of respiration is irreversible. Therefore, Rabbi Auerbach's and Rabbi Feinstein's requirement of total cellular lysis is no longer necessary.

4. There is no precedent in halakha for dealing with microscopic findings, as has been discussed at length in contemporary halakhic literature.[5]

5. The tests showing live brain cells after the declaration of brain death were not done on the brains of people who were declared dead based on the protocol of Rabbi Shaul Yisraeli and the Chief Rabbinate.

6. These studies don't discuss the state of the brain on a macroscopic level. Presumably, had they examined people who'd been declared dead based on Rabbi Yisraeli's protocol and the Knesset's law, they would have seen liquefied brains, as required by Rabbis Auerbach and Feinstein.

VII. AN INTERNATIONAL SOLUTION

I would like to suggest that the rabbis of America and other diaspora communities adopt the language of the new Knesset legislation and publicize their support of this position. The law recognizes brain death as legal death when irreversible cessation of respiration has been demonstrated, as determined by very strict medical criteria.[6] Additionally, the law mandates the participation of rabbis and/or doctors trained in the halakhic requirements as set forth by the Chief Rabbinate.[7]

---

5. See, for example, Rabbi Ovadia Yosef, *Yabi'a Omer* 4, YD 20.
6. For more on the method of determining brain death, see Dr. Zelik Frischer's essay in this volume.
7. For more on the Knesset law and the various proposals that led to it, see the essays of Rabbi Yoel Bin Nun and Rabbi Prof. Daniel Sinclair in this volume.

Whoever wishes to rely upon the great halakhic authorities who back this decision is, without a doubt, on solid ground. For this reason, I propose that we support this decision. The law even allows a person to be strict (or lenient, depending on how one thinks about it) and follow the positions requiring cardiac death. Such a person may request that medical attention be continued even after brain death. Hence, this law's sensitivity to all sides should make it universally acceptable.

ADDENDUM

I would like to add that there is a way of allowing organ donation even according to Rabbi Shlomo Zalman Auerbach and those who follow him (assuming that this process would be acceptable to the medical establishment). According to Rabbi Auerbach, if an "ill" patient has been declared brain dead and is no longer breathing on his or her own,[8] but is breathing solely by means of an artificial respirator, it would be permitted to disconnect said patient from the machine.[9]

Once the person is removed from the respirator, his or her heart will soon stop beating. He or she is then considered dead by all halakhic authorities. After a brief waiting period (not too short, to ensure irreversibility, but not too long, such that the organs become useless) the person may be returned to the machine, to protect the internal organs such that they can be useful for transplantation.[10] At this point, in my opinion, even Rabbi Auerbach would allow organ harvesting from the body of such a patient.

---

8. Although doctors assess breathing by administering the apnea test, according to Rabbi Auerbach one could, in theory, simply put a feather under the person's nose – the classic rabbinic method.
9. See Rabbi Shlomo Zalman Auerbach, *Minḥat Shlomo* II (86:5, p. 263).
10. For a similar argument, see the essays by Rabbi Asher Lopatin and Dr. Kenneth Prager in this volume.

Section III

Halakha: A Look at the Posqim

Chapter 11

Rabbi Moshe Feinstein on Brainstem Death: A Reassessment

Daniel Reifman

INTRODUCTION

If there's one thing that unites virtually all sides in the fractious halakhic debate over brainstem death, it is the critical significance of the position of Rabbi Moshe Feinstein. Rabbi Feinstein was one of the earliest *posqim* to weigh in on this issue, and one of very few with sufficient stature to potentially resolve the debate. That his position has become the subject of intense dispute is thus particularly unfortunate. Since his death in 1986, both camps have expended a remarkable amount of energy in posthumously "recruiting" Rabbi Feinstein to their side.

Though Rabbi Feinstein's responsa have been picked over endlessly in the course of the debate, there remain not only a number of persistent misconceptions about his position, but also several passages that scholars on both sides have virtually ignored. In this essay, I will argue that Rabbi Feinstein's position is fully consistent with the standard of brainstem death currently accepted by the medical community, and that the passages scholars have overlooked provide important conceptual grounding for that position. I will further propose that the outsized attention accorded to Rabbi Feinstein's position is justified not only by his inestimable status as a *poseq*, but also by his extremely incisive analysis of this issue. Both in his conceptual analysis and in his use of sources, Rabbi Feinstein challenges the deeply ingrained views that have that come to dominate the debate over brainstem death and medical halakha in general.

I. "TRULY THE MURDER OF TWO INDIVIDUALS"

The simplest reason for the controversy over Rabbi Feinstein's position is that he refused to fully explain himself. In a June 1968 responsum (IM YD 2:174), written just months after the first successful human heart transplant in Cape Town, South Africa, Rabbi Feinstein denounced the procedure as "truly the murder of two individuals" – the donor whose heart is excised, and the recipient whose functioning (if severely diseased) heart is exchanged with another of dubious value. Clearly Rabbi Feinstein felt that the criteria doctors were using to establish the donor's death were inadequate.

However, rather than present the halakhic reasoning behind his position, Rabbi Feinstein insisted that the only response to be published in his name was a brief statement prohibiting the procedure and excoriating the doctors who were promoting it. He stated that any attempt to explain his position might lead people to question some of his proofs, thus opening the door to permitting a procedure that he considered outright murder. The responsum continues with a lengthy analysis of various issues related to the determination of death and end-of-life treatment, but at no point in any of his responsa pertaining to end-of-life issues does Rabbi Feinstein explicitly relate his halakhic analysis to his initial assertion prohibiting the removal of the donor's heart.[1]

---

1. It is widely acknowledged that in later years, Rabbi Feinstein gave oral approval to individuals seeking various cadaveric organ transplants (Moshe D. Tendler, "Rabbi Moshe Feinstein and Brainstem Death," *Le'ela* [March 1996], 31). However, these reports don't explain what changed in Rabbi Feinstein's thinking and thus don't help us understand his initial objection.

There is, of course, much more to discuss about Rabbi Feinstein's position. Despite his stubborn silence on the issue of heart transplants, he subsequently wrote two responsa, in 1970 and 1976, on how halakha determines death. These texts form the main basis of the dispute over his opinion on brainstem death. Nonetheless, the effect of Rabbi Feinstein's uncharacteristically opaque initial response is considerable, particularly since he reiterated this assertion – again without elucidation – in a brief 1978 responsum (IM ḤM 2:72), which postdates all his other responsa on this matter. Between 1968 and 1978, the medical community made considerable advances in defining and standardizing the concept of brainstem death, and, as will be seen, Rabbi Feinstein's writings – particularly his 1976 responsum – reflect some of this analysis. However, opponents of brainstem death reason that had Rabbi Feinstein accepted it, he would not have repeated in 1978 that heart transplants constitute "double murder."

This interpretation strikes me as an example of hindsight bias, the way our historically conditioned expectations color our understanding of a text. Knowing as we do that the use of new immunosuppressants would revolutionize organ transplantation in the early 1980s, we read Rabbi Feinstein's 1978 responsum as though it related to that incipient phenomenon. Yet when this responsum was penned, all but a handful of medical centers had issued a moratorium on heart transplants due to the abysmal survival rate of the recipients, and few in the medical community predicted that the procedure would soon be viable. Indeed, the thrust of the 1978 responsum – and the reason for its brevity – is that Rabbi Feinstein simply concurred with doctors' concern for the welfare of the heart recipient, and therefore agreed that the procedure should remain off-limits.[2]

Hence, even as doctors continued to study the ramifications of brainstem death for other purposes (such as removing the patient from life support), almost no one had reassessed its implications for cadaveric

---

2. On this point, see the interview with Rabbi Binyamin Walfish in this volume. Rabbi Walfish offers a very similar analysis of the position of Rabbi Joseph Soloveitchik, who initially opposed heart transplants as "double murder" but changed his mind after the introduction of immunosuppressants.

organ transplantation. Whatever Rabbi Feinstein meant in referring to heart transplants as "double murder" in 1968, an issue we will consider presently, it is likely that when he repeated this statement in 1978, he was merely expressing his continued opposition to the procedure without considering its precise implications for the status of a brainstem-dead heart donor.[3]

In the remainder of this essay, we will not discuss the responsa (1968 and 1978) in which Rabbi Feinstein directly addresses the permissibility of heart transplants. Rather, we will focus exclusively on the two responsa (1970 and 1976) in which he explains the *reasoning* behind his position regarding the determination of death.

II. REJECTION OF THE "BRAIN DEATH" STANDARD

If there is any passage in Rabbi Feinstein's subsequent responsa that could be understood as clarifying his forceful 1968 statement, it is the opening paragraph of his 1970 responsum (YD 2:146), addressed to Rabbi Chaim Dov Ber Gulevsky, where he refers to "what the doctors say – that indications of life and death are found in the brain." As in

---

3. Opponents of brainstem death have also noted that the volume of *Iggerot Moshe* in which the 1978 responsum appears was published in 1985, when heart transplantation was quickly becoming an accepted procedure. Again, they suggest that had Rabbi Feinstein endorsed the removal of organs from brainstem-dead patients, he wouldn't have approved this responsum for publication. See J. David Bleich, "Of Cerebral, Respiratory and Cardiac Death," *Tradition* 24, no. 3 (spring 1989): 59–60; Asher Bush et al., *Halachic Issues in the Determination of Death and in Organ Transplantation: Including an Evaluation of the Neurological "Brain Death" Standard* (2010), 54, http://www.rabbis.org/pdfs/Halachi_%20Issues_the_Determination.pdf; David Shabtai, *Defining the Moment – Understanding Brain Death in Halakhah* (New York: Shoresh Press, 2012), 251.

This objection ignores the fact that by 1985, Rabbi Feinstein's responsum was out of date in a much more important way: The medical consensus against the procedure that the responsum prominently cites had evaporated. Moreover, most scholars acknowledge that by 1985, Rabbi Feinstein himself had given oral approval to potential heart recipients, indicating at the very least that his stated opposition to heart transplants was no longer valid. One can only conclude that Rabbi Feinstein didn't revise his responsa for publication, so the publication date offers no evidence as to his intention.

his initial statement, Rabbi Feinstein immediately rejects the doctors' position:

מה שאומרים הרופאים שסימני חיות ומיתה הוא בהמוח שאם לפי השערותיהם אין המוח פועל פעולתו הוא כבר נחשב למת אף שעדיין הוא נושם. ...

Regarding what the doctors say – that indications of life and death are found in the brain; that if according to their assessment the brain isn't functioning, [the patient] is considered dead, even if he's still breathing....

האמת ודאי שלא זה שפסק המוח לפעול הוא מיתה דכל זמן שהוא נושם הוא חי, רק זה שפסק המוח לפעול פעולתו הוא דבר שיביא למיתה שיפסוק לנשום, ואפשר כיון שעדיין הוא חי שאיכא מיני סמים בעולם מהידועים לאינשי או שעדיין אינם ידועים שיעשו שהמוח יחזור לפעול פעולתו. ...

The truth is that cessation of brain function isn't death, since as long as one is breathing, he's alive. Rather, the cessation of brain function is what causes death, since [the patient] will stop breathing, and it is possible that since he's still alive, there are types of drugs – either those that are known to man or those as yet unknown – that would cause the brain to function again....

לכן פשוט שההורגו הוא רוצח וחייב מיתה. ...דהא לא הוזכר בגמ' ובפוסקים שיהיה סימן חיות במוח, ולא שייך לומר נשתנו הטבעים בזה, דגם בימי חז"ל היה המוח פועל הפעולות כמו בזמננו וכל חיות האדם היה בא ממנו ומ"מ לא היה נחשב מת בפסיקת פעולת המוח, וכמו כן הוא ברור שגם בזמננו הוא כן.

Therefore, it is clear that one who kills such an individual is a murderer and liable for capital punishment.... For neither the Talmud nor the *posqim* mention that indications of life are found in the brain. And it is impossible to say nature has changed, for even in the time of the sages the brain worked as it does now, and all human life depended on it, and even so one wasn't considered dead upon cessation of brain function. So it's clear that the same is true in our time.

The central point that emerges from this passage is that Rabbi Feinstein's objection to doctors' use of loss of brain function to determine death is that the patient is still breathing. On a purely technical level, then, if the doctors' position that Rabbi Feinstein presents here is the same one he was referring to in his 1968 statement, he was clearly objecting to the diagnosis of death based on *partial* loss of brain function (e.g., cerebral function), since complete loss – specifically the loss of brainstem function – is inconsistent with continued autonomous respiration.[4] The notion of brain death that he rejects here is thus distinct from the standard that has become widely accepted in the medical community.

More conceptually, Rabbi Feinstein rejects brain death in that he doesn't regard brain function as the definitive indicator of life and death; that is, he rejects the medical definition of death as the cessation of neurological functions. Rather, he asserts that halakha regards autonomous respiration – over and above all other physiological functions – as the definitive indicator, a tenet he reiterates repeatedly in both his responsa on this topic. His rationale is purely textual. The Talmud (b. *Yoma* 85a, a source he analyzes at length later in the responsum) establishes that

---

4. This point has been made repeatedly by Rabbi Feinstein's son-in-law, Rabbi Moshe Tendler. See Moshe Tendler, "Determining the Moment of Death and Organ Transplants: Physiological 'Decapitation,'" *Emeq Halakha* (Jerusalem: Dr. Falk Schlesinger Institute of Medical-Halachic Research, 1989), 215 [Hebrew]; Moshe D. Tendler, "Halakhic Death Means Brain Death," *Jewish Review* 3, no. 3 (January 1990/Kislev 5750): 20, http://thejewishreview.org/articles/?filename=tendler3_3&route=from search.

There is no basis to explain that Rabbi Feinstein's statement here – כל זמן שהוא נושם הוא חי (as long as one is breathing, he's alive) – is referring to anything other than autonomous respiration. Nowhere in this responsum does he mention mechanical ventilation, and when he does address it in his 1976 responsum, he explicitly states that it doesn't render the patient alive:

אבל איכא חולים גדולים שלא יכלו	However, there are critically ill patients who
לנשום והניחו הרופאים בפיהם	cannot breathe, and the doctors place in their
מכונה שנושם ע"י זה, שע"י המכונה	mouths a machine that allows them to breathe,
הוא שייך שינשום אף שהוא כבר מת	such that by use of this machine one can breathe
דנשימה כזו הוא לא מחשיבו כחי.	even if he's dead, since this sort of breathing doesn't render him alive.

Contrast with J. David Bleich, *Bi-Netivot ha-Halakha* 3 (New York: KTAV, 2000), 108; and Shabtai, *Defining the Moment*, 367–69, who suggest that even if a patient is incapable of autonomous ventilation (i.e., actively drawing air into the body), the passive process of gas exchange in his lungs should qualify as "breathing."

regardless of how a victim buried in rubble is uncovered, it is both necessary and sufficient to examine his nose for signs of breathing. Neurological function, on the other hand, does not feature in halakhic literature as an indicator of death.

Needless to say, many scholars interpret this passage to mean that Rabbi Feinstein considered neurological criteria irrelevant to the determination of death.[5] They then acknowledge that this position seems to conflict with his 1976 responsum (IM YD 3:132), where he explicitly endorses the use of a cerebral blood flow scan to allow removing a patient from a ventilator. We will address this responsum – and these scholars' interpretations of it – below. But a more serious problem with this understanding of Rabbi Feinstein's position is that it ignores the continuation of his 1970 responsum.

Just a few paragraphs after the above passage, Rabbi Feinstein writes:

אבל ברור ופשוט שאין החוטם האבר שהוא נותן החיות בהאדם, וגם אינו מאברים שהנשמה תלויה בו כלל, אלא דהמוח והלב הם אלו הנותנים חיות להאדם וגם שיהיה לו שייך לנשום ע"י [ח]וטמו, ורק הוא האבר שדרך שם נעשה מעשה הנשימה שבאין ע"י המוח והלב.

However, it is abundantly clear that the nose isn't the organ that gives life to a person, nor is it an organ on which life depends. Rather, the brain and the heart are the organs that give life to a person and enable him to breathe via the nose, and the nose is only the organ through which the respiration that comes from the brain and the heart occurs.

ואית לנו הסימן חיות רק ע"י החוטם אף שלא הוא הנותן ענין הנשימה, משום שאין אנו מכירים היטב בלב ובטבור וכ"ש שאין מכירין במוח.

We have no indication of life other than nasal [activity] – even though the nose isn't what generates respiration – since we cannot easily detect activity in the heart or abdomen, and all the more so in the brain.

---

5. For example, see Avraham Steinberg, "Determining the Moment of Death and Heart Transplants," *Or ha-Mizrah* 38 (1987): 61 [Hebrew]; Bleich, "Of Cerebral," 59; and Bush et al., *Halachic Issues*, 49.
6. The text has פוטמו, but this is clearly a typo.

וכוונת הקרא דנשמת רוח חיים באפיו לא על עצם רוח החיים שזה ודאי ליכא בחוטם, אלא הרוח חיים שאנו רואין איכא באפיו אף שלא נראה באברים הגדולים אברי התנועה, וגם אחר שלא ניכר גם בדפיקת הלב ולא ניכר בטבור, שלכן נמצא שלענין פקוח הגל בשבת תלוי רק בחוטם.

And the verse "All in whose nostrils was the breath of life" (Gen. 7:22) isn't referring to the [source] of the breath of life – for that's definitely not in the nose. Rather, [it is saying that] the breath of life that's visible to us is located in the nostrils, even if it's not visible in the larger, moving organs or apparent in the heartbeat or abdomen. Therefore the matter of clearing the heap [of rubble] on Shabbat depends only on nasal [activity].

The same idea is restated twice later in the responsum:

... דהא ודאי לכו"ע הרי עיקר חיותא שאנו רואין הוא בחוטמו, ועיקר חיותא ליתן החיות והכח בהאברים הוא הלב והמוח ...

...for surely everyone agrees that the primary manifestation of life that we see is nasal [activity], and the primary manifestation of life that gives life and strength to all the limbs is the heart and the brain...

... שודאי הלב הוא עיקר נותן החיות, וכן ודאי המוח נמי הוא עיקר נותן החיות שבכלל זה הוא גם הנשימה דרך החוטם.

...for it is certain that the heart is the main provider of life, and so, too, it is certain that the brain is also the main provider of life – which includes breathing via the nose.

These passages, typically given short shrift by expositors of Rabbi Feinstein's position, clearly establish that he regards all three factors – heart function, brain function, and respiration – as germane to halakha's understanding of life and death. Obviously, then, when Rabbi Feinstein rejects the secular medical notion of brain death, he *does not mean* that neurological criteria are irrelevant to the determination of death.

III. THE RELATIONSHIP BETWEEN BREATHING AND BRAIN/HEART FUNCTION

Yet Rabbi Feinstein's integration of these three factors is unclear. First, he systematically refuses to single out either the heart or the brain as the primary source of life,[7] undermining the simple dichotomy that has framed the contemporary debate. More problematically, however, his description of the relationship between breathing and heart/brain function seems deeply counterintuitive: If the brain and heart are the sources of life, why is breathing the definitive *indicator* of life?

One possible explanation is that respiration is not inherently significant, but merely serves as a reliable external indicator: Because we lack the tools to detect heart and brain activity, we use respiration as a litmus test. This interpretation is suggested not only by Rabbi Feinstein's language in the above passage ("we have no indication of life other than nasal [activity]...since we cannot easily detect activity in the heart or abdomen, and all the more so in the brain"), but also by the well-known responsa of Rabbi Tzvi Ashkenazi (*Ḥakham Tzvi* 74, 77) regarding a case in which the heart of a slaughtered chicken couldn't be located.

Rabbi Ashkenazi argues that the chicken should not be considered a *treifa*, since the heart must have gone missing after the slaughter. His reasoning is simply that the heart is essential for life, so had the heart gone missing beforehand, the chicken could not have been alive at the time of slaughter. In addressing why the Talmud in *Yoma* rules that death is determined by the absence of breathing rather than heartbeat, Rabbi Ashkenazi explains that breathing is always perceptible, whereas a weak heartbeat may not be. Based on this approach, if we were to possess more advanced means of detecting brain and heart activity, respiratory activity would be irrelevant.

However, in another oft-overlooked section of this responsum, Rabbi Feinstein himself dismisses this understanding of the relationship between heart activity and respiration:

---

7. Contrast with Bleich ("Of Cerebral," 60), who cites the first passage in which Rabbi Feinstein identifies both the heart and the brain as life-giving organs and then incongruously concludes that "[t]hose comments certainly reflect a clear recognition that the primary vital force in the human organism is the beating of the heart."

ואין צורך להסבר החכ״צ
שפעמים א״א לשמוע דפיקת
הלב מפני שהלב תחת החזה
ומרוב חולשה א״א להכיר
אם עודנו בחיים, וכוונתו
מפני שהדפיקה היא נמוכה
ביותר, דאף אם נימא שנפסק
הדפיקה ממש עדיין הוא נותן
כח חיות מעט להגוף דלכן
הוא נושם בחוטמו עדיין.
ומש״כ הרמב״ם דאם ינוח
הלב כהרף עין ימות ויבטלו כל
תנועותיו, אין כוונת הרמב״ם
על הפסק דפיקה אלא על
הפסק עבודתו ליתן חיות
להאברים, שהדפיקה הוא
רק סימן לעבודת הלב ואירע
שעובד הלב עבודתו ולא ניכר
סימן זה דדפיקה כשהלב הוא
בחולשה, והפסק עבודתו
לגמרי ניכר בפסיקת הנשימה
מהחוטם.

ואולי מה שהוצרך החכ״צ
לסברתו הוא מחמת שסובר
דאם אך הלב לא הפסיק
עבודתו היה ודאי נשמע
הדפיקה, לכן כתב שכל זמן
שנושם בחוטמו איכא ודאי
דפיקה בלב אבל מאחר שעובד
בחולשה הוי קול הדפיקה
נמוך מאד עד שלא נשמע כלל
מאחר שהוא תחת החזה, ואף
שאין הכרח לזה אפשר שהוא
כן. וזהו כוונת החכ״צ.

And there's no need to invoke the Ḥakham Tzvi's explanation that sometimes it's not possible to hear the heartbeat since the heart is beneath the chest, and due to its weakness it's impossible to tell if it's still alive – meaning that the heartbeat is very faint. For even if we assume that the heart had actually stopped beating, it would still be providing minimal life force to the body, which is why the individual is still breathing. And regarding that which Rambam wrote – that if the heart stops, the individual will die instantly, and all his movements will cease – he is referring not to the cessation of the heartbeat, but rather to the cessation of [the heart's] function in providing life to the limbs, for the heartbeat is only an indication of the heart's functioning, and when the heart is weak it may happen that it is performing its function without this indication being discernible, but the complete cessation of heart function is discernible in the cessation of breathing through the nose.

And perhaps what drove the Ḥakham Tzvi to his explanation is his assumption that unless the heart stopped functioning, the heartbeat would still be audible. Therefore he wrote that as long as the individual breathes through his nose, the heart is certainly still beating, but since the heart is weak, the sound of the heartbeat would be very faint to the point where it is imperceptible, since it is beneath the chest; and even if this isn't necessarily the case [that the heart would still be beating imperceptibly], it is possible that it is so. That's what the Ḥakham Tzvi meant.

198

Rabbi Feinstein's assumptions in this passage are a bit unsettling. He seems to say that the heart's physiological function – providing life force to the body – is not dependent on its beating, an idea that modern medicine utterly rejects. Yet this assumption is not integral to Rabbi Feinstein's approach; he freely concedes (in the second paragraph) that the Ḥakham Tzvi may be correct in assuming that the heart continues to beat as long as it functions. Whether or not there is ever an actual (i.e., biological) divergence between heartbeat and heart function, Rabbi Feinstein insists on making a *conceptual* distinction between the two when it comes to determining death. The aspect of cardiac function that's relevant to the determination of death is not the heartbeat per se, but rather the heart's ability to provide life force to the rest of the body; respiration is the final manifestation of that life force.[8] Thus, when we conclude from the Talmud that absence of breathing is the definitive indicator of death, what we mean is that the heart's inability to provide life force to the body is *determined* – not merely indicated – by its failure to support autonomous respiration.

Rabbi Feinstein's understanding of Rabbi Ashkenazi's responsum stands in stark contrast with the approach taken by numerous opponents of brainstem death, who equate Rabbi Ashkenazi's insistence that life depends on the heart with the notion that the heartbeat is a dispositive sign of life, even in the absence of autonomous respiration.[9] Some have even imputed this understanding to Rabbi Feinstein

---

8. Rabbi Shlomo Goren makes the same distinction. See Shlomo Goren, "Discontinuing Life Support for a Terminal Patient," in Goren, *Torat ha-Refu'a* (ed. Yisrael Tamari; Jerusalem: Ha-Idra Rabba, 2001), 63 [Hebrew].
9. For instance, see Eliezer Waldenburg, *Tzitz Eliezer* 9:46; and Shmuel ha-Levi Wosner, "On Heart Transplants," *Assia* 42–43 (5747/1986–87): 92–94 [Hebrew]. See also J. David Bleich, "Establishing Criteria of Death," *Tradition* 13, no. 3 (winter 1973): 96; J. David Bleich, "Survey of Recent Halakhic Periodical Literature," *Tradition* 16, no. 4 (summer 1977): 133, 137; J. David Bleich, "Signs of Death," *Ha-Pardes* 51, no. 4 (1977): 16 [Hebrew]; and Bleich, "Of Cerebral," 57.

himself,[10] though he *explicitly rejects* just such an interpretation, which Rabbi Gulevsky proposes in his question:

ולא מובן לי היכן ראה כתר"ה מה שמסיק, נמצא שלהחכ"צ ישנו סימן אחד של חיות וזה הלב ולפי"ז אדם שהלב פועם דינו כחי ואדם שהלב נפסק דינו כמת אולם בלי נשימה הלב אינו פועל והוא מת תיכף, דאין זה כוונת החכ"צ אלא כדכתבתי שהחיות לכל האברים נותן הלב כדהביא מזוהר ומרמב"ס במו"נ, וגם זה שאיכא ענין הנשימה ע"י החוטם הוא מהלב, וכשפוסק הלב מלעבוד לגמרי נפסק תנועת כל האברים וגם הנשימה מהחוטם נפסק, אבל כל זמן שעובד הלב אף בחולשה גדולה באופן ששאר אברים לא מתנוענעים איכא עדיין חיות בנשימה דהחוטם שהוא אבר האחרון מלהפסיק.

And I don't understand on what basis you [i.e., Rabbi Gulevsky] concluded: "It emerges that for the Ḥakham Tzvi there is but one indication of life, and that is the heart, so according to this an individual whose heart is beating is considered alive, and one whose heart has stopped is considered dead, though without respiration the heart cannot function, causing [the individual] to die imminently." For this isn't the intention of the Ḥakham Tzvi, but rather, as I wrote above, [he means] that the heart provides life force to all the organs, as he cited from the *Zohar* and Rambam in *The Guide of the Perplexed*. And even nasal respiration is [enabled by] the heart, and when the heart stops functioning completely, all limbs stop moving, and breathing through the nose stops as well. But as long as the heart is functioning – even with great weakness, such that the rest of the limbs aren't moving – life is still present in respiration, since the nose is the last organ to cease.

---

10. Abraham S. Abraham, "Determining the Time of Death," *Assia* 42–43 (5747/1986–87): 82–83 [Hebrew]; Bleich, "Of Cerebral," 60; Joshua Kunin, "Brain Death: Revisiting the Rabbinic Opinions in Light of Current Medical Knowledge," *Tradition* 38, no. 4 (winter 2004): 49; Bush et al., *Halachic Issues*, 27, 29; Shabtai, *Defining the Moment*, 226. Elsewhere Shabtai asserts that "Rabbi Feinstein does not, however, explain how

Based on Rabbi Gulevsky's understanding of the *Ḥakham Tzvi*, absence of respiration indicates death only because heart function will quickly cease without it. Rabbi Feinstein counters by reversing the direction of causation: What's important is not that absence of breathing causes the heart to stop beating, but rather that absence of heart function invariably causes cessation of autonomous respiration (along with all external bodily movement).

The difference between these two formulations is crucial. If autonomous respiration is significant only insofar as it sustains the heartbeat, then any alternate means of sustaining heart function – such as providing mechanical ventilation and parenteral nutrition (the heart will continue beating autonomously when supplied with oxygen and nutrients) – would be just as effective in keeping the patient "alive." But according to Rabbi Feinstein's explanation, autonomous respiration *defines* heart function: Because respiration is *necessarily* the *last* physiological function to cease, it determines what it means for the heart to provide life force to the rest of the body.

This explanation of the relationship between breathing and heart function suggests that the absence of observable autonomous respiration indicates that meaningful, life-giving heart function has ceased, and that any heart activity observed henceforth is no indication of life.

IV. HEART ACTIVITY IN THE ABSENCE OF AUTONOMOUS RESPIRATION

Before reaching any firm conclusion, however, we need to consider an earlier passage in this responsum, in which Rabbi Feinstein addresses a case in which residual heart activity is detected in the absence of respiration:

---

he understood [Rabbi Ashkenazi's] ruling" (ibid., 259), though Rabbi Feinstein clearly does just that in offering an alternative to Rabbi Gulevsky's interpretation. Among these scholars, only Abraham notes Rabbi Feinstein's explanation of Rabbi Ashkenazi's position, but concedes that he doesn't understand his point.

אבל לדמות לזה חשיבות
מיתה לומר דהאדם לומר
שאף שרואים הרופאים ע"י
עלעקטריק ראדיאגראם
שאיכא תגובות לב נחשב מת,
נראה לע"ד שאינו כן. דהחת"ס
בתשובה הובא בפ"ת יו"ד סימן
שנ"ז סק"א כתב דהא דאיתא
במסכת שמחות פ"ח ה"א
פוקדין על המתים עד ג' ימים
ומעשה שפקדו אחד וחי [ועוד]
כ"ה שנים, הוא שאיכא מציאות
רחוק מאד דלכן אין בזה משום
דרכי האמורי, אבל הוא רחוק
אפילו ממיעוטא דמיעוטא דלכן
אין לחוש לזה ומותר לקוברו
תיכף כשפסקה נשימתו דאף
שהוא ענין פק"נ אין לנו לחוש
לדבר רחוק כזה.

But to compare this to the determination of death, to say that an individual is considered dead even if the doctors see cardiac activity on an electrocardiogram, seems in my humble opinion incorrect. For the Ḥatam Sofer – in a responsum cited in Pithei Teshuva YD 357:1 – interpreted what it says in Semaḥot 8:1 – "One should examine the dead for three days, and there was a case in which they examined someone [who turned out to be alive], and he lived [another] twenty-five years" – to mean that there's a very remote possibility that [a person can survive without breathing for up to three days] …, but it is so remote that we need not be concerned about it, and one may bury a person as soon as he stops breathing, for though it's a matter of life and death, we need not worry about such a distant possibility.

וא"כ במי שרואין העלעקטריק
ראדיאגראם שיש לו איזה חיות
הרי על אופן זה ליכא שוב אפילו
רוב לומר שהוא מת, ואולי גם
מיעוט ליכא והוא החי ממש
אף שאינו נושם, כאיש ההוא
שנקבר בהכוך מחמת שפסקה
נשימתו וחי אח"כ כ"ה שנה,
מאחר דאיכא עכ"פ איזה
מציאות, וזהו ג"כ היחידי דאיכא
במציאות זה. ולכן יהיה אסור
לקבוע לאיש כזה ואדרבה יהיו
מחוייבים להשתדל ברפואות
אם אפשר ומסתבר שגם בשבת.

If so, in the case of one who shows signs of life on an electrocardiogram, there's no majority (or even significant minority) of such people who are considered dead, and therefore he's considered to be alive even though he's not breathing – like the individual who was buried in the crypt because he had stopped breathing and went on to live another twenty-five years – since there was such a case, even if this is the only such case that ever occurred. Therefore it is forbidden to determine [death] for such a person; on the contrary, they must try to treat him medically, if possible, even on Shabbat.

In this passage, Rabbi Feinstein grapples with a problem addressed by earlier authorities, including Rabbi Moshe Sofer (*Ḥatam Sofer* Y D 338): Despite the conclusion of the pericope in b. *Yoma* (85a) that absence of breathing is necessary and sufficient to establish death, a few halakhic sources – most prominently Tractate *Semaḥot* 8:1 – suggest that individuals can survive for extended periods without breathing.[11] Like Rabbi Sofer, Rabbi Feinstein dismisses these instances as so rare that in routine cases, they need not be taken into account. However, he insists that if there are other signs of continued vitality, such as heart activity detected on an electrocardiogram, the possibility that the individual might survive becomes far more plausible, and hence he must be treated as living.

At a minimum, this passage establishes that the tentative conclusion we drew above is not completely correct: Though Rabbi Feinstein considers cessation of breathing to be the decisive indicator of death, we cannot categorically dismiss all subsequent heart activity as inconsequential. However, the question remains: What *is* the significance of such residual heart activity? This issue is of paramount significance within the debate over brainstem death, since, as mentioned, artificial ventilation of a brainstem-dead patient (along with parenteral nutrition) allows the heart to continue beating independently. Would Rabbi Feinstein consider this continued heartbeat sufficient reason not to declare death? Several scholars have inferred as much, reasoning that if Rabbi Feinstein hesitates to declare death due to heart activity so minimal that it is detectable only on an electrocardiagram (ECG), all the more so that the regular heartbeat of a brainstem-dead individual would be cause for concern.[12] A few scholars have even presented this not as an inference, but as the explicit meaning of Rabbi Feinstein's words.[13]

---

11. Likewise, Rabbi Meir (m. *Yevamot* 16:3) cites a case in which "a man fell into a large cistern and emerged after three days"; Rashi (b. *Yevamot* 121a, s.v. *ishto asura*) explains that Rabbi Meir considers the possibility that someone might be able to survive in water for a day or two. These sources are obviously inconsistent with modern medicine, which asserts that depriving the brain of oxygen almost invariably results in death within minutes.

12. Bleich, "Survey of Literature," 132–33; Shabtai, *Defining the Moment*, 226, 241; and Naftali Moses, *Really Dead? The Israeli Brain-Death Controversy 1967–1986* (2011), 164–65.

13. Abraham, "Determining the Time," 83; and Bush et al., *Halachic Issues* 49.

Regarding this latter interpretation, there is little to say. This passage is clearly not addressing the case of a patient on a ventilator: If it were, not only would reference to an ECG be utterly extraneous (since artificial ventilation allows the patient to maintain a regular heartbeat and pulse), but nowhere in this responsum does Rabbi Feinstein address the issue of mechanical ventilation, a topic he takes up with regard to the determination of death only in his 1976 responsum.[14] However, the suggestion that we should extrapolate from Rabbi Feinstein's case of minimal heart activity to all other instances of continued heart function also presents difficulties. First, it puts this passage at odds with the one cited above, in which Rabbi Feinstein rejects Rabbi Gulevsky's suggestion that heart activity alone definitively indicates life. More important, in the very same paragraph, Rabbi Feinstein explains that halakha does not impart significance to phenomena below the level of unaided human perception. (Thus, for example, the presence of microscopic nicks in the blade of a knife does not render it unfit for use in ritual slaughter, and there is no problem with the fact that we constantly ingest microorganisms that don't meet the criteria of kosher animals.) Based on this logic, heart activity detectable only by an ECG is not halakhically comparable to a full-fledged heartbeat or pulse; even if Rabbi Feinstein considered heart function an independently sufficient sign of life, such faint heart activity would not qualify.

If so, what is the rationale behind Rabbi Feinstein's ruling? The simplest explanation is suggested by the very source he cites: We are concerned that this patient could, like the person referred to in *Semaḥot*, turn out to be the rare individual who recovers from his current condition. However, this concern is generated only by the extraordinary phenomenon of a positive ECG reading in a non-breathing patient: The highly unexpected nature of this result suggests that the observable absence of other vital signs may not tell the whole story, and that our diagnosis of death may be incorrect.[15] This cannot be said of the

---

14. Rabbi Feinstein also refers implicitly to mechanical ventilation in his 1968 responsum (§3), where he addresses whether one may use "artificial means" to prolong the life of a terminally ill patient.

15. Rabbi Feinstein's concern in this passage appears virtually identical to that expressed by Rabbi Shalom Mordechai Schwadron in his *Responsa of Maharsham* 6:124. This responsum addresses a case in which members of the *ḥevra qaddisha* feared that they

heartbeat of a brainstem-dead patient, which is perfectly consistent with our expectations for someone in this condition. To the extent that we hope against hope that a patient diagnosed as brainstem-dead might make a miraculous recovery (there are, after all, a handful of well-publicized instances of this happening), these hopes are based on the possible inaccuracy of the diagnostic tests that were administered, not on the persistence of his heartbeat.[16]

According to this explanation, Rabbi Feinstein's ruling regarding heart activity detected in a non-breathing and non-ventilated patient represents the exception, not the rule, and does not reflect the idea that heart activity in and of itself is a dispositive sign of life. Rather, residual heart activity is significant precisely because it suggests that the cessation of other vital signs (such as respiration) may be temporary, just as they were for the individual in *Semaḥot*. This point brings us to Rabbi Feinstein's 1976 responsum (IM YD 3:132), in which he directly addresses the question of how to determine whether autonomous respiration has irreversibly ceased.

V. THE PURPOSE OF ASSESSING BRAIN ACTIVITY

As stated, Rabbi Feinstein's 1976 responsum, addressed to his son-in-law, Rabbi Dr. Moshe Tendler, deals with the problems of diagnosing death amid mechanical ventilation. Here, too, his point of departure is that death is diagnosed by the absence of autonomous respiration, which poses a difficulty in individuals connected to a ventilator. Rabbi Feinstein maintains that the general practice of removing the ventilator in order to assess the patient's autonomous respiratory ability is

---

hadn't conclusively established someone's death in their haste to bury him before Shabbat. Initially Rabbi Schwadron validated their concern based on their report that the person had emitted some sort of sound during the purification process. The rabbi explains that one may not rely on the cessation of breathing to establish death when the a person exhibits a symptom "not commonly found among deceased persons." (Ultimately he reassured them that they had acted appropriately, since they'd observed no further indications of life during their subsequent handling of the body.) For a discussion of Rabbi Schwadron's responsum, see the essay by Rabbi Yoel Bin Nun in this volume.

16. For more discussion of possible recovery and what functionality, if any, can be recovered, see Dr. Howard Doyle's essay in this volume.

forbidden, presumably because the act of disconnecting a still-living patient might inadvertently cause his death.[17] As a result, Rabbi Feinstein allows such an assessment only when the ventilator must be removed for other reasons, such as maintenance or the replacement of the oxygen tank.[18]

The problem is compounded, however, in cases where the patient's condition is the result of an accident or other sudden event:

אבל זהו באינשי שנחלו בידי
שמים באיזו מחלה שהיא אבל
באלו שהוכו בתאונת דרכים
(בעקסידענט ע״י הקארס) וע״י
נפילה מחלונות וכדומה שאירע
שע״י התכווצות העצבים באיזה
מקומות הסמוכים להריאה
ולכלי הנשימה אינם יכולין
לנשום וכשיעבור איזה זמן
שינשומו אף רק ע״י המכונה
יתפשטו מקומות הנכווצים
ויתחילו לנשום בעצמם שאלו
אף שאין יכולין לנשום בעצמן
וגם לא ניכרין בהם עניני חיות
אחרים אפשר שאינם עדיין
מתים.

But all this is in reference to people suffering from disease, but regarding those injured in a car accident or a fall from a window and the like, it may occur that they can't breathe due to the contraction of the nerves near the lungs and respiratory organs, but after breathing for some time by means of a machine [i.e., respirator] these contracted nerves will expand, and they'll begin breathing independently. Regarding these individuals, even if they can't breathe independently, and no other indicia of life are visible, they may not yet be dead.

---

17. Rabbi Feinstein doesn't elaborate on this point. Rabbi Shabtai Rappaport suggests that Rabbi Feinstein considers oxygen an essential substance that one may not withdraw from a dying person, lest its removal bring about his death. See Shabtai A. HaKohen Rappaport, "Rabbi Moshe Feinstein on Brain Death," *Sefer Assia* 7 (5754/1993–94), 148e–g [Hebrew].

18. Obviously this recommendation is irrelevant to contemporary ventilators, which don't rely on oxygen tanks and don't normally need to be removed for service. However, there are other ways for doctors to assess the patient's ability to breathe

וכיון שאתה אומר שעתה איכא
נסיון שרופאים גדולים יכולין
לברר ע״י זריקת איזו לחלוחית
בהגוף ע״י הגידים לידע שנפסק
הקשר שיש להמוח עם כל הגוף
שאם לא יבא זה להמוח הוא
ברור שאין להמוח שוב שום
שייכות להגוף וגם שכבר נרקב
המוח לגמרי והוי כהותז הראש
בכח, שא״כ יש לנו להחמיר
באלו שאף שאינו מרגיש כבר
בכלום אף לא ע״י דקירת מחט
ואף שאינו נושם כלל בלא
המכונה שלא יחליטו שהוא
מת עד שיעשו בדיקה זו שאם
יראו שיש קשר להמוח עם הגוף
אף שאינו נושם יתנו המכונה
בפיו אף זמן גדול, ורק כשיראו
ע״י הבדיקה שאין קשר להמוח
עם הגוף יחליטו ע״י זה שאינו
נושם למת.

And since you (Rabbi Tendler) say
there's now a test with which expert
doctors can determine – by means of
injecting [a radioactive nucleotide solu-
tion] into the blood vessels – whether
the connection between the brain and
the body has been severed, for if [the
radioactive solution] doesn't reach the
brain, it is clear that the brain has no
more bearing on the body and also that
the brain has rotted completely, and it
is as if the head were forcibly severed
from the body; if so, we must be stringent with such a patient, such that even
if he's completely unresponsive – even
to a pinprick – and even if he doesn't
breathe independently at all, we may
not determine that he is dead until
they perform this test. For if they see a
connection between the brain and the
body – even if he's not breathing – they
should put the ventilator in his mouth,
even for a long time; and only when
they determine by means of this test
that there is no longer a connection
between the brain and the body, then
they may determine – based on lack
of independent respiration – that he
is dead.

---

independently while complying with Rabbi Feinstein's restriction, such as providing
oxygen through a thin tube inserted into the trachea while disconnecting the main
tube of the ventilator (Edward Reichman, personal communication). Contrast with
Bleich, "Survey of Literature," 133.

וגם הערת דבאלו שלקחו מיני
סם וכגון הרבה כדורי שינה
שעד שיצא הסם מהגוף אינם
יכולין לנשום, שלכן יש להצריך
שהמכונה תהיה בפיו זמן ארוך
עד שיהיה ברור שכבר אין הסם
בגוף שיכולין הרופאים לבדוק
זה בטפת דם שיוציאו ממנו, ואז
יוכלו שלא להחזיר את המכונה
לפיו עוד הפעם ויראו שאם אינו
נושם כלל הוא מת ואם נושם
אף רק בקושי הוא חי ויחזירו
המכונה לפיו עוד הפעם.

You've also noted that some have taken various drugs, such as an overdose of sleeping pills, and cannot breathe until the drugs leave their body. Therefore one must require that the [respirator] remain in [such a person's] mouth for an extended period, until it is clear that the drugs are no longer present in his body, which the doctors can check by extracting blood. And then they may refrain from returning the [respirator] to his mouth [once it is removed for servicing] and observe him, for if he doesn't breathe at all, he is dead, but if he breathes – even if only with difficulty – he is alive, and they must return the [respirator] to his mouth once again.

Rabbi Feinstein is aware that numerous conditions may cause cessation of autonomous respiration, not all of them permanent. If there is reason to suspect that the condition preventing autonomous respiration is temporary (e.g., the thoracic cavity may be compressed, or the patient has overdosed), Rabbi Feinstein insists that additional tests be performed to confirm the individual's death. Here Rabbi Feinstein introduces the notion of testing for brain activity, specifically via a radionuclide cerebral blood flow scan.[19]

Some scholars conclude that this position departs from Rabbi Feinstein's 1970 responsum, where he ostensibly rejects the brain death standard espoused by the medical community.[20] But as emphasized above, what the 1970 responsum actually says is that brain and heart function are the sources of life, while respiration is the definitive indicator of when the heart and brain stop providing life force to the body. Hence the most cogent explanation for Rabbi Feinstein's

---

19. For more on this test and how it works, see Dr. Zelik Frischer's essay in this volume.
20. Steinberg, "Determining the Moment," 61–2; and Kunin, "Revisiting Rabbinic Opinions," 49.

requirement of the blood flow scan is to clarify whether cessation of breathing stems from the brain not providing life force to the body or from a peripheral condition. Not only does this explanation make his ruling here consistent with the premises laid out in his previous responsum, but it is also the straightforward meaning of his language in the above passage, where he states that even once the test establishes a lack of blood flow to the brain, death is determined only "based on lack of independent respiration."

In addition, this responsum bolsters our conclusion regarding the significance of cardiac activity: Nowhere here does Rabbi Feinstein mention heart activity, though he is addressing the case of an artificially ventilated patient. Since there would be no reason to continue ventilating a patient whose heart had already stopped, Rabbi Feinstein's omission of any reference to heart function *strongly suggests* that he does not consider heart activity after the cessation of autonomous respiration to be a dispositive sign of life. Were this merely an argument from silence, one could argue – with considerable difficulty – that Rabbi Feinstein is referring to an idiosyncratic case in which, for some reason, doctors have continued to ventilate a non-heart-beating patient, and he makes no mention of this fact because he takes for granted that any heart activity would indicate life.[21] However, Rabbi Feinstein's endorsement

---

21. Dr. Abraham ("Determining the Time," 83) suggests this interpretation of Rabbi Feinstein's ruling, in part because it matches his understanding of Rabbi Feinstein's 1970 responsum (see note 10 earlier in this essay). However, while Abraham finds it incredible that Rabbi Feinstein would contradict an earlier responsum, he finds it equally incredible that Rabbi Feinstein would require neurological confirmation – even as an added stringency – for the death of an accident victim with no autonomous respiration or heartbeat.

In contrast, Rabbi Bleich ("Of Cerebral," 59–60) does find this a reasonable understanding of Rabbi Feinstein's ruling. Likewise, both the RCA Vaad Halacha (Bush et al., *Halachic Issues*, 53) and Rabbi Shabtai (*Defining the Moment*, 240–41) propose that Rabbi Feinstein is referring to a non-heart-beating patient, and that his position here correlates with the notion expressed in his 1970 responsum that the heart may continue to provide life force to the body even after it has stopped beating. However, none of these authors explains how the radionuclide scan would be expected to work were the heart not pumping blood through the body. (Rabbi Bleich also suggests an alternative explanation of Rabbi Feinstein's ruling – see the appendix to this essay.)

of the radionuclide scan confirms that he *is* referring to a typical case where the patient's heart is beating, since this test relies on blood flow from the heart.[22]

However, some opponents of brainstem death draw on the language of this responsum to formulate another argument. They note that Rabbi Feinstein assumes that the blood flow scan establishes "that the brain has no more bearing on the body and also that the brain has rotted completely, and it is as if the head were forcibly severed from the body." This wording echoes a claim articulated by Rabbi Tendler himself elsewhere, that the medically accepted standard of "whole-brain death" – defined as the complete destruction of the entire brain (i.e., including the brainstem) and established by the complete cessation of all brain functions – should be considered a halakhically acceptable standard of death, because it constitutes "physiological decapitation."[23]

The problem with Rabbi Tendler's assertion is that some of the medical assumptions it relies on have now been called into question. In the past two decades, research has shown that the brain may retain significant structural integrity even after clinical brainstem death, and that the hypothalamus often continues various homeostatic functions (such as regulation of body temperature), occasionally for extended periods. Hence, opponents of brainstem death argue, the standard medical tests used to establish this condition no longer meet the bar set by Rabbi Feinstein, and his endorsement of the radionuclide scan may no longer be relied upon.[24]

This argument has been challenged by Rabbi Dr. Edward Reichman,[25] who notes that it assumes that Rabbi Feinstein considers

---

22. Mordechai Halperin, "Rabbi Moshe Feinstein's Position on Brain Death," *Sefer Assia* 7 (5754/1993–94), 69 [Hebrew].

23. Frank J. Veith et al., "Brain Death: I. A Status Report of Medical and Ethical Considerations," *JAMA* 238, no. 15 (1977): 1651–55; and Fred Rosner and Moshe David Tendler, "Definition of Death in Judaism," *Journal of Halacha and Contemporary Society* 17 (1989), 24–25.

24. Abraham S. Abraham, *Nishmat Avraham* YD 339:2; J. David Bleich, "Brain Death: Medical Myth and Semantic Sleight of Hand," *Le'ela* (March 1996), 36–37; and Kunin, "Revisiting Rabbinic Opinions," 55–56.

25. Edward Reichman, "Don't Pull the Plug on Brain Death Just Yet," *Tradition* 38, no. 4 (winter 2004): 63–69.

brain criteria an independent indicator of death, distinct from cessation of breathing. As noted, this assumption takes Rabbi Feinstein's endorsement of the radionuclide scan out of the context of the rest of his writings on this topic. Whereas Rabbi Tendler himself frames his analysis as a defense of a brainstem death standard, of which cessation of respiration is only one component, Rabbi Feinstein repeatedly states that cessation of respiration – not of brain function – is the definitive indicator of death. Hence, according to Rabbi Feinstein, the radionuclide scan need confirm only that the brain is incapable of supporting autonomous respiration. Any aspect of brain function or integrity that doesn't relate to the patient's ability to breathe independently would not be considered life-giving, and would therefore be irrelevant to the halakhic determination of death.

On this basis, Reichman maintains that Rabbi Feinstein's explanation for the significance of the blood flow test – "that the brain has no more bearing on the body and also that the brain has rotted completely" – should *not* be considered an essential aspect of his rationale, even if he originally intended these words literally.[26] As far as Rabbi Feinstein's position is concerned, the medically accepted criteria used to establish brainstem death would be sufficient, since the new medical findings uphold the fact that patients diagnosed as brainstem dead are – without exception – incapable of autonomous respiration.

VI. THE CONCEPTUAL COMPLEXITY OF RABBI FEINSTEIN'S POSITION

We have suggested that the crux of Rabbi Feinstein's position is the way he situates three distinct physiological phenomena – respiration, heart function, and brain function – in relation to one another: Cessation of autonomous respiration is the definitive indicator of when the heart and the brain have stopped providing life force to the body. Not only have we documented this aspect of his position within the text of his responsa, we have also shown how it accounts for the cases in which he considers heart or brain function significant even in the absence of autonomous respiration.

---

26. Ibid., 65–66.

Nonetheless, it would seem that this element of Rabbi Feinstein's responsa has caused the most confusion about where he stands on brainstem death. Simply put, *Rabbi Feinstein does not recognize any one organ or bodily function as significant in and of itself.* Cessation of autonomous respiration is significant only insofar as it reflects cessation of heart/brain function, but heart/brain function is significant only insofar as it is manifest in autonomous respiration. Given the obvious circularity of this position, it is understandable that it would strike many readers – consciously or unconsciously – as illogical. I suggest that it is scholars' discomfort with this aspect of Rabbi Feinstein's position that has drawn them to passages in his responsa that focus on only one of these bodily functions (such as his ruling in the case of cardiac activity detected on an ECG), and caused them to overlook or misconstrue other passages (such as his interpretation of the Ḥakham Tzvi) which describe the complex, interdependent relationship between these functions.

The difficulty scholars have had in absorbing Rabbi Feinstein's logic is also evident in other aspects of the brainstem-death debate. For example, some thinkers have maintained that defining death as cessation of respiration precludes taking any brain or heart activity into account. Thus Rabbi J. David Bleich challenges the respiratory definition of death by citing the example of a polio victim dependent on an iron lung, who is permanently incapable of breathing and yet obviously not dead. In a similar vein, he cites Shmuel's statement in b. *Gittin* (70b) that a man whose trachea and esophagus have been severed may issue his wife a *geṭ*: Despite his presumed inability to breathe (and impending death), he is still considered to be alive.[27]

---

27. J. David Bleich, "Brain Death and Determining the Time of Death in Jewish Law," *Or ha-Mizrah* 36 (1987), 73–74 [Hebrew]; and Bleich, "Of Cerebral," 54, 57–58. Rabbi Bleich insists that the only plausible reason a polio victim or someone with a severed trachea would be considered alive is that he presents a heartbeat or other vital movement. Bleich dismisses an equally plausible reason – the fact that these people are fully conscious – by saying, "Nowhere in rabbinic literature is there the slightest hint that consciousness is an indicator of life" (Bleich, "Of Cerebral," 54; see also J. David Bleich, "Determining the Moment of Death by Terminating Brain Activity [A Response to Critiques]," *Or ha-Mizrah* 37 (1988): 82 [Hebrew]). Even if we accept his assertion that consciousness cannot be considered a factor in determining life and death unless

Yet these examples prove only that inability to breathe – even as a permanent condition – is relevant to the determination of death solely insofar as it reflects the failure of the heart and brain. In that sense, these cases are no different from those Rabbi Feinstein addresses in his 1976 responsum, where the patient's inability to breathe is caused by a mechanical or chemical problem rather than a neurological one. Rabbi Tendler puts this point succinctly: "The question isn't whether a person can or cannot breathe, but only *why* he can't breath[e]."[28]

Scholars' failure to grasp Rabbi Feinstein's logic is also apparent in a second common argument against the respiratory determination of death. Many have suggested that sources referring to cessation of breathing – such as the Talmud in *Yoma* – establish it only as an *indicator* of death, leaving open the possibility that death is *defined* by the cessation of other bodily functions, such as heart function or other lifelike muscle movement.[29] In light of Rabbi Feinstein's responsa, this point becomes both self-evident and irrelevant. It is self-evident because (in Rabbi Feinstein's words) "it is abundantly clear that the nose isn't the organ that gives life to a person, nor is it the organ on which life depends. Rather, the brain and the heart are the organs that give life to a person and enable him to breathe via the nose." It is irrelevant because the pertinent question is whether cessation of breathing constitutes the *definitive* indicator of death, to which Rabbi Feinstein answers – repeatedly and consistently – in the affirmative.

Thus, the importance of Rabbi Feinstein's responsa goes beyond his position on brainstem death: His conception of life and the human body is profoundly different from the one prevailing in much of the scholarship on this topic. Many scholars (mostly those who oppose brainstem death, but also some who support it) conceive of life as

---

it is explicitly identified as such in halakhic literature (a point we will address in more detail below), we might suggest that this is precisely what the Talmud in b. *Giṭṭin* 70b is doing – establishing consciousness as a dispositive sign of life!

28. Tendler, "Halakhic Death," 7.

29. The earliest articulation of this argument may be Bleich, "Establishing Criteria," 95–96. However, this argument has become so central to the rejection of brainstem death that it is made by almost every scholar who espouses that position.

"located in a particular part of the body,"[30] or speak of a particular process as *"the* primary vital force in the body."[31] Rabbi Feinstein, however, indicates that the significance of any physiological phenomenon is fundamentally dependent on *context*: It is significant only insofar as it fulfills its role in sustaining other organs.

What prevents this logical circularity from being problematic is the realization that *all biological systems are necessarily circular in this way.* Just as we do not accord the status of "life" to disembodied organs, we should not consider heartbeat or brain function significant unless it provides life force to the body as a whole. Again, Rabbi Tendler's formulation is apt: "The fact that a polio patient cannot breathe, but is yet alive, is based precisely on the fact that he is an organized system."[32] This is the black box we refer to as "life": an amalgam of biological functions that is somehow more than the sum of its parts.

VII. HALAKHIC SOURCES AND MODERN SCIENCE

No less than his conceptual analysis, Rabbi Feinstein's use of halakhic texts diverges from the way most scholars approach this issue. Proponents of a cardiac definition of death emphasize references to heart function in Rashi's commentary in *Yoma* and in the responsa of Rabbi Ashkenazi and Rabbi Sofer. Advocates of brainstem death, too, point to sources that seem to establish the brain as the decisive organ by which death is determined, particularly m. *Oholot* 6:1, which considers a decapitated animal dead even if it exhibits movement.[33] Rabbi Feinstein cites all these sources in his responsa, yet *none of them* serves as a basis for his position on how halakha determines death.

---

30. Noam Stadlan, "Conceptual and Logical Problems Arising from Defining Life and Death by the Presence or Absence of Circulation," *Me'orot* 8 (5771/2010–11): 67. For further discussion of Dr. Stadlan's position, see his essay in this volume.
31. Bleich, "Of Cerebral," 60.
32. Tendler, "Halakhic Death," 20.
33. This source was first cited in reference to this issue by Rabbi Gedalia Aharon Rabinowitz and Mordechai Koenigsberg, "Defining Death and Determining Its Time in Light of Halakha," *Ha-Darom* 32 (1970): 59–76 [Hebrew]. It also informs Rabbi Tendler's notion of "physiological decapitation."

Rabbi Feinstein's analysis of the mishna in *Oholot* occupies an entire section of his 1968 responsum (where he explains why the mishna's ruling regarding decapitation of animals would apply to humans as well), yet as we noted above, his 1970 responsum insists that brain function is never mentioned as an indicator of death within halakhic literature.[34] Likewise Rabbi Feinstein cites Rabbi Sofer's responsum in both his 1970 and 1976 responsa, yet he never mentions Rabbi Sofer's statement that cessation of heart function is needed to establish death.[35] Even the responsum of Rabbi Ashkenazi, which figures prominently in his 1970 responsum, enters Rabbi Feinstein's analysis only because he feels the need to correct Rabbi Gulevsky's interpretation; he relates to Rabbi Ashkenazi's responsum not as a basis for his position but as a source to be squared with it. In the end, the only halakhic sources that inform Rabbi Feinstein's position are those that establish cessation of respiration as the definitive indicator of death, most prominently the passage in *Yoma*.

In and of itself, a disagreement about the relevance of certain sources is hardly noteworthy; it is, in fact, an integral part of normative halakhic discourse. We can well understand why scholars try to ground their positions in earlier sources, and we can also understand why Rabbi Feinstein might find their inferences wanting. What is remarkable is the way Rabbi Feinstein recognizes both the heart and the brain as the sources of life, yet bases this recognition on nothing more than common sense. Again we refer to what is arguably the central point in Rabbi Feinstein's 1970 responsum (inasmuch as he asserts it three times): "However, it is abundantly clear (*barur u-fashut*) that the nose isn't the organ that

---

34. As noted, Rabbi Feinstein does state in his 1976 responsum that an absence of blood flow to the brain renders the patient "as if the head were forcibly severed from the body" – an oblique reference to the mishna in *Oholot*. However, as also noted, this doesn't seem to be Rabbi Feinstein's main rationale for using lack of brainstem function to determine the patient's death.

35. In his 1970 responsum, Rabbi Feinstein cites Rabbi Sofer's analysis of *Semaḥot* 8:1 but *not* his reference to the cessation of pulse, even though Rabbi Feinstein cites him specifically in the context of a case of residual heart function. In his 1976 responsum, Rabbi Feinstein refers generally to Rabbi Sofer's responsum as support for the notion that, in most cases, death may be established by repeatedly confirming that breathing has ceased. Contrast with J. David Bleich, *Time of Death in Jewish Law* (New York: Z. Berman Publishing, 1991), 174; and Bush et al., *Halachic Issues*, 49 n. 111.

gives life to a person, nor is it the organ on which life depends; rather the brain and the heart are the organs that give life to a person and enable him to breathe via the nose."[36]

Upon further reflection, we might question whether the central importance of both heart and brain function is as obvious as Rabbi Feinstein makes it out to be. Our conception of the body has changed radically and repeatedly since the time of the sages, so demonstrating timeless agreement on this point would seem to require a more rigorous and nuanced examination of the halakhic literature than Rabbi Feinstein provides. One might even find his conviction a bit disingenuous: If the primacy of the heart and the brain is so obvious, why *doesn't* it figure explicitly in the traditional sources?

I propose that Rabbi Feinstein's argument is motivated by a subtle agenda, which discourages him from delving into this point: He wants to avoid a contradiction between halakha and modern science. Rabbi Feinstein is aware that the halakhic sources don't attest to the significance that modern science accords to heart and brain function; however, given the lack of contradictory evidence, he would rather assume that what we regard as common sense was just as commonsensical in the eyes of the sages. As he writes at the start of his 1970 responsum (in the first passage cited above): "it is impossible to say nature has changed, for even in the time of the sages the brain worked as it does now, and all human life depended on it." In context, the point of this statement is to reject doctors' use of brain function instead of respiration to determine death. However, based on Rabbi Feinstein's subsequent exposition, the logic of this statement cuts both ways: If the nature of the human body has not changed, then just as the legal dicta of the sages are pertinent today, the scientific principles of modern medicine must be pertinent to our understanding of the sages' rulings.

Yet as this passage indicates, Rabbi Feinstein still makes a sharp distinction between truths learned from contemporary science and those grounded in halakhic sources. Ultimately death is determined *solely* by cessation of respiration, the only standard of death that is unambiguously

---

36. This point severely challenges Rabbi Bleich's assertion (cited above) that obvious signs of life, such as consciousness, cannot be halakhically valid unless they're explicit in halakhic literature.

affirmed in halakhic literature; we may not introduce an independent parameter based on contemporary medicine. But in a modern medical context, the very meaning of "cessation of respiration" becomes much more complex. The most significant aspect of Rabbi Feinstein's position is not that he identifies cessation of respiration as the definitive indicator of death, but that he *reinterprets* what this standard means by situating it within the paradigm of modern medicine. Based on modern medicine's understanding of the interdependence of respiration and both heart and brain function, Rabbi Feinstein effectively translates the traditional halakhic position – "Death is determined by cessation of respiration" – into modern medical terms: "Death is determined by the permanent cessation of heart and brain activity capable of supporting autonomous respiration."

APPENDIX: ALTERNATE INTERPRETATIONS OF RABBI FEINSTEIN'S 1976 RESPONSUM

In the main essay, I cited Rabbi Bleich's suggestion that Rabbi Feinstein endorses the use of the cerebral brain scan to determine death only when the patient's heart has already stopped beating.[37] Perhaps in light of the practical difficulties of this explanation (e.g., the brain scan relies on blood flow from the heart), Rabbi Bleich offers an alternate explanation of Rabbi Feinstein's ruling. In a 1977 essay, he explains that in the cases where Rabbi Feinstein permits not reattaching the patient to the respirator, his reasoning is based on a position expressed in his 1968 responsum, that it's not necessary to prolong the life of a *goses* (i.e., an individual in the last throes of life).[38] Commenting on this statement of Rabbi Feinstein's, Rabbi Bleich writes:

> If not only medicaments but also oxygen need not be administered to a *goses*, it would follow that a *goses* need not be attached to a respirator. This consideration is, however, germane only in the case of a patient actually in a state of *gesisa*.[39]

---

37. See note 21 earlier in this essay.
38. Rabbi Feinstein explains that in general, prolonging a dying person's life prolongs his agony (סתם עכוב יציאת הנפש הגוסס הוא בגוף ביסורים).
39. Bleich, "Survey of Literature," 132.

Rabbi Bleich elaborates on this approach in a 1991 essay, where he seems to concede that Rabbi Feinstein's 1976 responsum is addressing a case in which the patient's heart is still beating. Yet Rabbi Bleich insists that the responsum "addresses not determination of death, but criteria for withholding treatment from a terminally ill patient" – in other words, the question of when the patient is considered a *goses* such that one may withhold (though not withdraw) the supply of oxygen.[40]

Rabbi Bleich does not offer a line-by-line exegesis of the responsum, but it is difficult to see how this approach, as he presents it, could possibly be sustained. Contrary to Rabbi Bleich's assertion that the responsum doesn't address the determination of death, Rabbi Feinstein titles the responsum, "Establishing the Time of Death," and opens with the words "On the matter of determining when an individual is considered dead." In each case he addresses, Rabbi Feinstein states that cessation of autonomous breathing renders the patient dead; the term *goses*, in fact, does not appear in the entire responsum. The reason Rabbi Feinstein gives for not reattaching the ventilator when the patient exhibits no autonomous respiration for fifteen minutes is that we are "certain he is dead," not a *goses*. If the category of *goses* applies to any case in this responsum, it is to the patient who *does* exhibit autonomous breathing when the ventilator is removed for servicing. If this categorization is correct, Rabbi Feinstein does consider oxygen a necessary component of treatment even for a *goses*.

The implausibility of this explanation suggests that Rabbi Bleich may have in mind something closer to the interpretation offered by Rabbi Shlomo Zalman Auerbach in his assessment of Rabbi Feinstein's letter to Dr. Elliot Bondi,[41] which was intended to clarify his 1976 ruling. Rabbi Auerbach proposes that when the letter states that a patient who cannot breathe independently is "considered dead," it is relating *only* to the permissibility of not replacing the ventilator.[42] In other words, we are willing to rely on our diagnosis of death enough to discontinue treatment, but not enough to actively harvest the patient's organs.

---

40. Bleich, *Time of Death*, 173.
41. See Rabbi Charles Sheer's discussion of the Bondi letter in this volume. A photocopy of this letter appears in *Assia* 7, 148–148a.
42. Abraham, *Nishmat Avraham* Y D 339:2.

According to this interpretation, a patient who could not breathe independently would not be considered a *goses*, a category that is considered fully alive, but rather would fall within the range of a *safeq ḥai/safeq meit* – someone whose death is legally indeterminate. Hence, following Rabbi Auerbach's understanding, the reason one need not reattach the ventilator when the patient cannot breathe independently is not that he is considered a *goses*, but that with regard to the issue of withdrawing treatment, he is considered dead.

This explanation is certainly less problematic than Rabbi Bleich's formulation, yet nothing in Rabbi Feinstein's language indicates any hesitancy about considering such patients to be dead. Rabbi Auerbach acknowledges that his is not the simple meaning of the responsum; he proposes it only because he finds it hard to believe that Rabbi Feinstein would approve of harvesting the patient's organs without saying so explicitly, given that this was such a hot topic in 1984, when the letter to Dr. Bondi was written. To this there is little more to say: Rabbi Auerbach's assessment of Rabbi Feinstein's mindset may be correct, but to my mind it says more about his own, more stringent position on this issue.[43]

---

43. A two-part version of this essay (which was the third in a series) appears on the RCA's *Text and Texture* blog, http://text.rcarabbis.org/the-brain-death-debate-a-methodological-analysis-part-3a%E2%80%94rabbi-moshe-feinstein-by-daniel-reifman/; http://text.rcarabbis.org/the-brain-death-debate-a-methodological-analysis-part-3b%E2%80%94rabbi-moshe-feinstein-by-daniel-reifman/.

Chapter 12

Rabbi Joseph B. Soloveitchik on Brain Death and Organ Donation: A Testimony

Interviews with Marc Angel, Binyamin Walfish,
and Maurice Lamm

INTRODUCTION

In 2010, the Vaad Halacha of the Rabbinical Council of America issued a report on brain death.[1] The editor, Rabbi Asher Bush, writes there:

> As is well known, Rav Binyamin Walfish, former executive vice president of the RCA, reported that late in 1983 or early in 1984 he met with the Rav [Rabbi Joseph B. Soloveitchik], who according to this account ruled in favor of using brain death as a criterion

---

1. Asher Bush et al., *Halachic Issues in the Determination of Death and in Organ Transplantation: Including an Evaluation of the Neurological "Brain Death" Standard* (2010), http://www.rabbis.org/pdfs/Halachi_%20Issues_the_Determination.pdf.

for death, thus permitting the removal of vital organs for transplantation. While the Rav was not very active in public policy matters at that time due to age and health, shortly thereafter, his brother, Rav [Rabbi] Ahron Soloveichik, who himself had ruled that brain death was not at all to be considered as death, insisted that his brother never ruled in favor of it.... Indeed, Rav Marc Angel reported [RCA Record, September/October 1991] that he had received a letter from Rav Ahron Soloveichik and Rav Isadore Twersky, son-in-law of the Rav, stating that the Rav did not accept brain death as a definition of death.[2]

The document then quotes Rabbi Meir Twersky, Rabbi Yitzchok Lichtenstein, and Rabbi Haym Soloveitchik all saying that the Rav never said this. The document concludes its discussion of the Rav's position with the following:

> From the moment that public claims were made in the name of the Rav that he had accepted brain death as a criterion of death and permitted the removal of organs for transplant from such patients, his close family members have continuously protested the accuracy and veracity of such claims. This understanding is, in fact, supported by Rav [Dr. Moshe] Tendler himself, who stated in a lecture to the RCA in November 1991 that he had spoken with the Rav on numerous occasions and the Rav never accepted Rav Tendler's idea that brain death should be considered death. All of the above, along with the added information gained through our own research, leaves no doubt as to what the Rav did in fact say. This clarity is especially true for those of us who are *talmidim* of the Rav and knew of the cautious and judicious manner in which he dealt with all such grave matters, as well as being acquainted with the family members quoted herein, who have unanimously reported his opinion on this matter.[3]

---

2. Ibid., 76.
3. Ibid., 77.

Since the RCA document points to controversy about Rabbi Walfish's discussions with Rabbi Soloveitchik, it was decided to use the opportunity afforded by this essay collection to hear how Rabbi Walfish remembers what happened. We also took the opportunity to ask Rabbi Angel (president of the RCA when the controversy over brain death broke out) how the Rav's *pesaq* figured in the RCA's process of formulating its position on brain death as it eventually appeared in the 1991 Health Care Proxy, as well as to record a case dealt with by Rabbi Maurice Lamm, who describes his interactions with the Rav on this matter.

QUESTION 1

Rabbi Angel, was Rabbi Walfish's testimony taken in earnest? If it was, why was the Rav's position not included as part of the final RCA document?

RABBI ANGEL

First and foremost, I want to clarify what seems to be an ambiguity in the RCA document. It is true that I received letters from Rabbi Ahron Soloveichik and Dr. Isadore Twersky, and that I placed them on record, as was my obligation. However, this was not meant as a challenge to Rabbi Walfish. I never repudiated Rabbi Walfish's view on the Rav's position; on the contrary, Rabbi Walfish's testimony was an important part of our decision-making process.

Rabbi Walfish assured us that he had discussed the issue with the Rav, and that the Rav endorsed the brainstem death definition. We did receive strong letters from Rav Ahron and Dr. Twersky, vigorously protesting that the Rav had never said such a thing and that we should not quote his name as one who accepts the brainstem death definition. I discussed this with Rabbi Walfish, and he assured me that he was reporting accurately.

The truth is, I thought then and think now that Rabbi Walfish had it right. A number of years before this, when the Rav was still actively replying to halakhic questions, I had spoken with Rabbi Maurice Lamm, who had an actual case on his hands.[4] He told me that

---

4. The case is described by Rabbi Lamm below.

he had called the Rav and received a *pesaq* allowing for the donation of organs from a brain dead patient. Rav Ahron's response to this was that Rabbi Lamm didn't understand the Rav's *pesaq*, or that Rabbi Lamm didn't ask the question correctly. Neither possibility seems all that plausible to me.

Nevertheless, since Rav Ahron and Dr. Twersky made a public repudiation of our presentation of the Rav's opinion, we decided it would be futile to continue to use the Rav's name in support of the RCA position. Rabbi Walfish himself agreed to this as a practical matter. If we used the Rav's name, this would only raise more repudiations and controversy, and would divert us from more important things. We would be in a "they said/we said" controversy, and we probably would lose credibility, since Rav Ahron and Dr. Twersky were so vocal and well regarded by so many.

Finally, I thought (and still think) that truth is truth, regardless of which authorities endorse or repudiate it. I thought (and still think) our position was (is!) correct, and is not undermined by which *Gadol* is with us or against us or neutral on the subject.

QUESTION 2

Rabbi Walfish, can you describe your conversations with the Rav on this topic? Were there particular cases involved, or was it theoretical?

RABBI WALFISH

My first interaction with the Rav on this subject was when Dr. [Christiaan] Barnard was starting to do heart transplants. At the time, the Rav was the chairman of the Vaad Halacha. His reaction was to unequivocally claim that this was double murder. At the time, there were no real criteria for absolute death, and the only way one could determine whether a patient was dead was if he had stopped breathing and his or her heart had stopped beating. The donors in these cases were certainly breathing at the time of the transplant, even if assisted by machinery, and their hearts were still beating.

One of the first times I spoke with the Rav directly on this subject was after New York State added an addendum to the driver's license in the very early eighties, allowing a person to agree in advance to donate his or her organs. The RCA began receiving calls from a number of rabbis in New York asking whether this would be permitted. The Rav told me that he would allow this for cornea transplants but not heart transplants. For kidneys, he said it depended on the percentage of people who would choose a new kidney over dialysis (he believed that if the percentage was over 85% it would be permitted, otherwise not).

This was the status quo until around 1983–84, when we received a letter from Rabbi David Silver of Harrisburg. Rabbi Silver was concerned since the state of Pennsylvania was in the process of legislating a specific definition of death, and he wanted to know what the RCA's position was on the definition of death. So I called Rabbi Tendler to find out if there was anything new in this field, and Rabbi Tendler told me that in fact, if I hadn't called him he would have called me, since Harvard had just come out with a foolproof test for brainstem death: the apnea test.

To explain, the apnea test solved one of the fundamental problems we had in defining the life status of a person with assisted breathing. Until this test, it was impossible to determine whether the person's brainstem was alive but the person was too weak to breathe on his own, or whether the brainstem was dead, and, in essence, the machine was ventilating a corpse. The apnea test was designed to answer this question.

Rabbi Tendler suggested that we ask the Pennsylvania legislature not only to include this test as part of the definition, but to add a clause that if any more sophisticated tests are designed in the future, they should automatically be required as part of the process of declaring death.

I then went to the Rav and told him what Rabbi Tendler had advised us to do. The Rav asked me: "Is Rabbi Tendler sure this test is foolproof?" I answered in the affirmative and offered to have Rabbi Tendler call him and tell him directly. The Rav said this would not be necessary. He said that if Rabbi Tendler was certain, this was sufficient for him, since he [Tendler] was the expert in such matters. The Rav authorized me to send the letter to Rabbi Silver, telling him that brainstem death, if determined by the aforementioned test, was an acceptable definition of death as far as the RCA was concerned. I wrote the letter, and this was the status quo answer until the health care proxy process described above.

QUESTION 3

Rabbi Lamm, can you describe the case you had and your interactions with the Rav on this question?

RABBI LAMM

Although it has not been my wish to participate in the debate on the question of the time of death, I do feel the need to set the record straight insofar as my interactions with the Rav on this topic. I simply cannot accept the science of the RCA, or the recent description of the Rav's position. The following is what transpired – and no, the Rav did not misunderstand me, nor I him.

A young member of my shul, the Hebrew Institute of University Heights in the West Bronx, was in the last minutes of her demise, and unconscious. Her husband asked me to ask the Rav if she would be permitted to have one of her kidneys transplanted, and preferably both, as she was not expected to survive the operation. I thought then – in the late 1960s – that it was probably forbidden, as she would be deprived of living if she were to be without at least one kidney. However, I was asked to ask the Rav, and I did so.

Due to some recent unpleasant experiences, I wanted to ask the Rav directly. To explain, around this same time, I had asked Rabbi David Bleich a complex question originally posed by four religious cardiac surgeons who regularly prayed at our shul. Rabbi Bleich had responded with the one-word answer "*Retziḥa!*" – murder. This reinforced my decision to ask the Rav this question directly. I did, and the Rav *pasqened*, in no uncertain terms, that she be permitted to donate *both* her kidneys. I communicated this to her husband, and this was done – one was given to a seventy-year-old man who eventually died, the other to a sixteen-year old girl, who soon recovered.

I remember the incident distinctly, and I will continue to do so, no matter what Rav Ahron wrote, what Prof. Twersky surmised, or what all the other naysayers have claimed over the years. I cannot change my story. I was there; they were not.

QUESTION 4

Rabbi Walfish, why do you think it was so hard for all the Rav's family and students to believe your account? Can you explain the discrepancy between your testimony about the Rav's view and that of your detractors?

RABBI WALFISH

It was around the time of the debate about the health care proxy that Rabbi Ahron Soloveichik wrote the letter that his brother never accepted brainstem death – a claim that I, unfortunately, had to contest. It wasn't that I didn't trust Rav Ahron, but I assume that he must have spoken to his brother before the Harvard criteria were established, since it was the foolproof nature of the apnea test that changed the Rav's mind on this subject.

I have not spoken directly to the various students and relatives who claimed the Rav could not have said what I reported him to have said. However, in one case, where I did succeed in confronting a certain student who vociferously denied that the Rav accepted the Harvard criteria, I asked him point-blank what it was that the Rav had said to him and when it was that he'd said it. His response was that the Rav never spoke about this with him, but he was sure the Rav would never have said what I reported. I have no idea what to respond to such a claim.

It is certainly true that for a time the Rav was wary of organ transplants, and was absolutely opposed to heart transplants, calling them double murder. However, with the advent of the apnea test, where there was now a way to determine whether the patient was breathing or the machine was breathing, he changed his mind and accepted that this clear demonstration that the brainstem was dead was enough to declare a patient dead and permit his or her organs – even the heart – to be donated.

My assumption is that those relatives and students who claim that my report of the Rav's opinion must have been mistaken either spoke to the Rav about this before he learned of the Harvard criteria or never spoke to him at all. Either way, the facts as I have reported them in this interview are accurate, and even if certain people question this, the *Ribbono shel Olam* knows what occurred; more than this I cannot add.

Chapter 13

Rabbi Hershel Schachter on Vital Organs: A Response

Zev Farber

In an article written in 1989 (and subsequently expanded in a Hebrew article),[1] Rabbi Hershel Schachter attempted to demonstrate that brain death cannot be the proper definition of death according to halakha. The article, which brings up a number of points, is based primarily on two core arguments.

First, Rabbi Schachter argues from his reading of a biblical phrase that circulation is the definition of life according to the

---

1. Hershel (Tzvi) Schachter, "Determining Death," *Journal of Halacha and Contemporary Society* 17 (1989): 32–40; Tzvi Schachter, "Regarding the Laws of a Dead Person and a Person Certain to Die," *Assia* 49–50 (5750/1989–90): 119–37 [Hebrew], http://www.medethics.org.il/articles/ASSIA/ASSIA7/R007188.asp.

Torah.[2] Second, he argues from a talmudic text and its canonization in Rambam's *Mishneh Torah* that halakha recognizes more than one vital organ, each of which must be dead before the person may legitimately be declared dead. This short essay will focus on the second argument.

I. ARAKHIN

Mishna

The Mishna in *Arakhin* (5:2–3) discusses how much a person must pay the Temple if he vows the value of various body parts. The discussion revolves around the difference between vows of "evaluations of value" (*arakhin*) and vows of cost or worth (*damim*).[3]

---

2. The biblical phrase is "he has no blood" (אין לו דמים/דם), meaning that the killing is not actionable. The phrase appears twice in the Torah, regarding killing a burglar at night (Exod. 21:2) and killing a "manslaughterer" who has left the city of refuge (Num. 35:27).

With all due respect to Rabbi Schachter, interpreting the phrase to mean that blood circulation is the definition of life would seem to be reading too much into the text. Even if the point of the colloquialism is, as Rashi ad loc. suggests, that "a person without blood is as if he is already dead" (הרי הוא כהורג את המת שאין לו דם), this would mean only that lack of blood in the body indicates that the person is dead; it doesn't mean that having blood makes a person alive.

Furthermore, "circulation" is not addressed at all and seems to be an anachronistic retrojection. It is unclear that the rabbis of the Talmud and its medieval interpreters – such as Rashi, whose interpretation Rabbi Schachter follows in this case and in the other examples of blood being the "seat of the soul" that Rabbi Schachter quotes – know that blood circulates or even moves. This phenomenon was uncovered over time, beginning with the work of Andreas Vesalius in the sixteenth century and culminating with the work of William Harvey in the seventeenth.

Finally, the verse is never used this way in talmudic literature as far as I know; it certainly isn't used this way in the halakhic literature about determining death. If Rabbi Schachter is simply offering his own reading of the verse, this raises the issue of whether modern readings of verses have halakhic significance, a question best left to a different venue. Either way, if what is being discussed is a *peshat* (simple or contextual) reading as opposed to rabbinic exegesis, I would suggest that the verse is referring to the killer's blood, not the victim's, and means that the killer has no "bloodguilt," as per the JPS translation.

3. *Damim* literally means "blood," but it's also a rabbinic colloquialism for money.

(ב) "דמי ידי עלי" שמין אותו כמה הוא שוה ביד וכמה הוא שוה בלא יד.

(2) [If a person vows:] "The cost of my hand is upon me [to pay to the Temple]," they evaluate how much he's worth [if sold as a slave] with his hand, and how much he would be worth without his hand. [By subtracting the latter from the former, we get the value of his hand.][4]

זה חומר בנדרים מבערכין וחומר בערכין מבנדרים. כיצד? האומר "ערכי עלי" ומת יתנו היורשין. "דמי עלי" ומת לא יתנו היורשים שאין דמים למתים.

In this matter vows are treated with more severity than evaluations.[5] In a different matter evaluations are treated with more severity than vows. How so? One who says: "My value is upon me [to pay to the Temple]," and then he dies – the heirs must pay. "My cost is upon me," and then he dies – the heirs need not pay, for there is no cost evaluation for the dead.

"ערך ידי וערך רגלי עלי" לא אמר כלום. "ערך ראשי וערך כבדי עלי" נותן ערך כולו. זה הכלל דבר שהנשמה תלויה בו נותן ערך כולו.

"The value of my hand or the value of my leg is upon me" – he has said nothing. "The value of my head or the value of my liver is upon me" – he pays the value of his entire person. This is the principle: [If one pledges] something the soul is dependent on, he pays the value of the entire person.

---

4. The Talmud (b. *Arakhin* 19b) interprets this mishna to mean how much he would be worth not if his hand were removed, but if his original owner still owned his hand after the sale. This technicality is irrelevant for our purposes.

5. This is because evaluations relate either to the entire worth of a person or to nothing at all; there are no evaluations of the relative worth of body parts in halakha.

(ג) "חצי ערכי עלי" נותן חצי ערכו,
"ערך חציי עלי" נותן ערך כולו.
"חצי דמי עלי" נותן חצי דמיו,
"דמי חציי עלי", נותן דמי כולו.
זה הכלל דבר שהנשמה תלויה
בו נותן ערך כולו.

(3) "Half of my value is upon me" – he pays half his value. "The value of half of me is upon me" – he pays his entire value. "Half of my cost is upon me" – he pays half his cost. "The cost of half of me is upon me" – he pays his entire cost. This is the principle: [If one pledges] something the soul is dependent on, he pays the person's entire value.

According to the Mishna, the mechanism of offering the Temple one's *erekh* (evaluated value) works only when evaluating the entire person. Hence, if one offers one's value to the Temple, one must pay it. If one offers half one's value to the Temple, one must pay that as well. However, if one offers the *erekh* of one's hand or foot, one need not pay it, since there is no concept of *erekh* when it comes to limbs.

That said, the Mishna takes up two liminal cases:

(a) What if a person pledges the *erekh* of half of his or her body to the Temple? Is this like offering a collection of limbs, which have no *erekh*? Or is this like offering one's entire *erekh*, since if a person were to lose half of his body, he or she would die? The Mishna chooses the latter understanding, stating the rule that whenever one offers something without which a person cannot live, it is as if the person has offered his or her entire *erekh*.

(b) What if a person offers the *erekh* of his or her head or liver? Is this like offering one body part, which is an invalid *erekh* offering? Or is this like offering one's whole being, since without a heart or liver a person would die? As in the case of offering the *erekh* of half of one's body, the Mishna decides that this type of *erekh* offering is equivalent to offering one's life, since the organ in question is vital. In other words, the offering of the value of the body part is understood metonymously, with the "vital body part" standing in for the person's life as a whole.

Baraita

The rule that regular body parts cannot be the subject of *erekh* vows, but vital body parts can, receives support from a *derasha* in a *baraita* in b. *Arakhin* 4a.

"בערכך" - ערך כולו
הוא נותן ולא ערך
אברים, יכול שאני מוציא
אף דבר שהנשמה תלויה
בו? ת"ל: "נפשות".

"[When a person makes a vow, pledging] the
value…" (Lev. 27:2) – one pays his entire value, not
the value of specific organs. Is it possible that this
would exclude even vital body parts?[6] [The verse]
comes to teach: "[the value of] souls" (ibid.).

As in the Mishna, there is a division between a person's whole
value and the lesser value of a body part. Additionally, as in the Mishna,
a vital body part, without which a person could not live, is equated with
the person's overall value, not the value of his or her parts.

Rambam

In his *Commentary on the Mishna*, Rambam explains the purpose of the
principle here:

ואמרו זה הכלל, לכלול
כל אבר שאין קיום לאדם
בהעדרו אם אמר ערכו
עלי נותן ערך כולו.

They said, "This is the principle," to include any
other body part without which a person could
not live. If one were to say, "The value of said
body part is upon me," he would have to pay
the person's entire value.[7]

Rambam codifies this interpretation in the *Mishneh Torah* (Laws of
Valuations and Dedications 2:1–4).

(א) האומר ערך ידי או ערך
עיני או רגלי עלי או שאמר
ערך יד זה או עינו עלי לא
אמר כלום. ערך לבי או
כבדי עלי או ערך לבו של
פלוני או כבדו עלי נותן
ערך כולו, וכן כל אבר שאם
ינטל מן החי ימות אם אמר
ערכו עלי נותן ערך כולו.

(1) One who says, "The value of my hand or the
value of my eye or my leg is upon me," or one
who says, "The value of this one's hand or eye
is upon me," has said nothing. "The value of my
heart or my liver is upon me," or "The value of
so and so's heart or liver is upon me" – he pays
the person's entire value. Similarly, for any body
part whose removal would cause a person to
die, if one were to say, "The *erekh* of said part
is upon me," he pays the person's entire value.

---

6. Literally, "parts upon which the soul depends."
7. Rabbi Ovadia of Bartenura interprets this line the same way.

(ב) אמר חצי ערכי עלי
נותן חצי ערכו, ערך
חציי עלי נותן ערך כולו
שאי אפשר שינטל חציו
ויחיה.

(2) One who says: "Half my value is upon me" pays half his value. "The value of half of me is upon me" – he pays his entire value, since it is impossible for a person to lose half his body and live.

(ג) האומר דמי ידי עלי
או דמי יד פלוני עלי
שמין אותו כמה הוא
שוה ביד וכמה הוא שוה
בלא יד ונותן להקדש....

(3) One who says: "The cost of my hand is upon me," or "The cost of so and so's hand is upon me" – they evaluate how much he's worth with his hand, and how much he would be worth without his hand, and he consecrates [the difference]....

(ד) האומר דמי ראשי או
כבדי עלי או דמי ראשו
של פלוני עלי או לבו
או כבדו עלי נותן דמי
כולו, וכן האומר דמי
חציי עלי נותן דמי כולו,
אבל האומר חצי דמי
עלי נותן חצי דמיו.

(4) One who says: "The cost of my head or liver is upon me," or "The cost of so and so's head is upon me," or "[The cost of] his heart or liver is upon me" – he pays the entire cost [of the person]. So too, one who says: "The cost of half of me is upon me" – he pays the cost of the whole person. However, one who says, "Half my cost is upon me" – he pays half his cost.

One small detail stands out in Rambam's codification: In the case of the *erekh* vow, whereas the Mishna referred to the head and liver, Rambam replaced head with heart, but for the *damim* vow, he used all three examples—head, heart, and liver. In truth, as Rambam points out in his *Commentary on the Mishna*, the principle applies to any vital body part, and there is no reason, theoretically, to limit the organs to just head, heart, and liver. This is clear from the Mishna's own example of "half a person," since if the person were to be cut in half, death would result, even though he could be left with all three of the above-mentioned vital organs. Similarly, if one's digestive system is removed, one would be unable to live. The point seems to be that if one attempted to quantify the value (*erekh*) of a limb outside of its life-sustaining properties, this would be illegitimate in an *erekh* donation, although acceptable in a *damim* vow.

II. NAZIR

Tosefta

Similar to the Mishna's treatment of *erekh* vows is the Tosefta's treatment of the nazirite vow (t. *Nazir* 3:2–3).

(ב) מי שאמ': "הריני נזיר", | (2) Someone who said: "I am a *nazir*," and he
ושהא כדי דיבור, ושמע | paused [...], and his fellow heard and said:
חבירו ואמ': "ואני" -הוא | "And I" – [the first person] is bound [by the
אסור וחבירו מותר. | vow], and his fellow is unbound.

(ג) "הריני נזיר", ושמע | (3) "I am a *nazir*," and his friend heard and
חבירו ואמ': "פי כפיו ושערי | said: "My mouth is like his mouth, and my
כשערו" - הרי זה נזיר. "ידי | hair is like his hair" – he is a *nazir*. "My hand
כידו רגלי כרגלו" - הרי | is like his hand, and my leg is like his leg" – he
זה נזיר. "ידי נזירה ורגלי | is a *nazir*. "My hand is a *nazir*, and my leg is a
נזירה" - אין נזיר. "ראשי | *nazir*" – he is not a *nazir*. "My head is a *nazir*,
נזיר וכבידי נזירה" - הרי | and my liver is a *nazir*" – he is a *nazir*. This
זה נזיר. זה הכלל: דבר | is the principle: [If one takes a nazirite vow
שהנשמה תלויה בו נזיר | regarding] anything the soul is dependent
דבר שאין הנשמה תלויה | on, he is a *nazir*. [If one takes a nazirite vow
בו אין נזיר. | regarding] anything the soul is not dependent
| on, one is not a *nazir*.

Like the *erekh* vow, the *nazir* vow cannot be made on a person's parts. Therefore, to determine whether one means to actually make oneself into a *nazir*, the Tosefta claims that it depends which parts one dedicates. If the parts mentioned are vital, like the liver or head, the vow is understood metonymously, and the person is a *nazir*; if the parts are not vital, like hands or legs, the person is not a *nazir*.

Rambam

As he did for the laws of *arakhin*, Rambam codifies the rules about vows concerning body parts in his *Mishneh Torah* (Laws of the Nazirite 1:16).

האומר הרי ידי נזירה הרי רגלי
נזירה לא אמר כלום, הרי ראשי
נזיר כבדי נזירה הרי זה נזיר, זה
הכלל כל אבר שאם ינטל מן החי
ימות אם אמר הרי הוא נזיר הרי
זה נזיר.

One who says: "My hand is a *nazir*," "My leg is a *nazir*" – he has said nothing. "My head is a *nazir*," "My liver is a *nazir*" – he is a *nazir*. This is the principle: Any body part whose removal from a living person would kill him – if one says it is a *nazir*, the person is a *nazir*.

Again, just as in *arakhin*, Rambam claims that the definition of a vital organ or body part is that if it were to be removed from a living creature or person, said creature or person would die.

III. RABBI HERSHEL SCHACHTER'S ARGUMENT

In his 1989 article, Rabbi Hershel Schachter uses the Mishna and *Mishneh Torah* passages about *erekh* vows to prove that halakha recognizes three vital organs. In his later Hebrew adaptation, he expands this argument, leading with the passage about the *nazir*. Below I quote from his English article.

> The Talmud posits specific organs which are vital to life. Each one is an "*eiver she-ha-neshama teluya bah* [sic]," an organ upon which the soul depends. This is a *halakhic* concept. Rambam in quoting the Talmud names three such vital organs: the heart, brain, and liver. In determining the moment of "*yetziat neshama*," the departure of the soul, it would appear that one ought to consider the state of these three organs "upon which the soul depends." One could argue that if any *one* of these three vital organs is halakhically declared dead, then the entire body is pronounced dead. On the other hand, one could also claim that a person is not dead until *all* three vital organs are dead....
>
> If we accept the view that if any one of the vital organs is dead, the person is dead, it might result in some rather startling conclusion[s]: If a person's liver is removed...even though the person can still walk, and talk, and think, he would be considered halakhically dead!

The second option, namely, that a person is not considered dead until all the vital organs are "dead," might be a help to defining with precision a related halakhic concept, that of *goses*. The Rambam defines *goses* as one in whom the process of death has already begun.... [I]f we follow the reasoning discussed above, it would follow by definition that when any one of the vital organs is dead, the process of death has clearly already begun, but will not be completed until all of the vital organs have irrevocably ceased functioning.[8]

According to Rabbi Schachter, the rabbis have defined – halakhically – three particular organs as vital. This definition would leave modern-day halakhists with only two options: If any one of the three organs is dead, the person is dead – an absurdity, since a person can live a certain amount of time without a liver – or all three must be dead. If the latter is true, then someone who is brain dead but whose lungs are being pumped to keep his or her heart beating would still be alive. Rabbi Schachter defines such a person as a *goses* and spends the remainder of the article discussing the ramifications of such a definition.

IV. A CRITIQUE OF RABBI SCHACHTER'S POSITION

With all due respect to Rabbi Schachter, it would seem that his interpretation of the passage in *Arakhin* (and *Nazir*) is mistaken for several reasons.[9]

(A) No Specific List of Organs

The mishna is not actually offering a specific list of organs. Although it uses head and liver, these are just examples of organs without which a person will die. In fact, "head" in the mishna refers not only to the brain,

---

8. Schachter, "Determining Death," 37–40.
9. For a similar critique of Rabbi Schachter's analysis, albeit focusing on his Hebrew article, see Daniel Malaach, "Organs Upon Which the Soul Depends: Defining Death," *Assia* 65–66 (5759/1998–99) [Hebrew], http://www.daat.ac.il/daat/kitveyet/assia/malaach.htm.

but to the whole head.[10] The term *eiver* is better translated as "body part." This is easily demonstrated by the uses of the term "vital body part" in context and elsewhere in rabbinic literature.

In the very next mishna, also quoted above, a person's pledge of the value of half of his or her body is considered legitimate, since half of a person's body is certainly "vital." The mishna does not specify which half or what organs; it states only that no person could be chopped in half in any direction and remain alive. Similarly, the Talmud (b. *Arakhin* 20a) offers a very general interpretation of the phrase "vital body part" (*eiver she-ha-neshama teluya bo*):

זה הכלל: דבר שהנשמה תלויה	This is the principle: "Something the soul
בו כו'. לאתויי מן הארכובה	is dependent on," etc. – This comes to
ולמעלה.	include [the leg] from the knee up.

Certainly "[the leg] from the knee up" is not a classic "vital organ." Nevertheless, the Talmud's point is that if one were to cut off a person's thigh, the person would die. This is why an animal with a leg cut off at the thigh is considered a *treifa*, an animal that cannot survive.

Rabbi Schachter's inclusion of the heart as a vital organ belies his own point about an official "talmudic list." The mishna did not actually include the heart; Rambam introduced it. Rambam felt the introduction of heart into the list to be acceptable because he understood the principle referenced in the mishna to include any vital body part. For whatever reason, Rambam preferred heart as his example as opposed to head.

In fact, just looking at Rabbi Schachter's sources, one can't help but notice that the list of vital organs appears nowhere. The mishna lists head and liver, but not heart. Rambam lists heart and liver in one place, and heart, liver, and head in another. The Talmud suggests the thigh, and no source actually includes the brain. Bottom line: There is no "list" of vital organs to be found anywhere in rabbinic literature. Rabbi Schachter's list, which gathers examples from the Mishna and Rambam but ignores the Talmud and interprets head as brain, is incomplete.

---

10. Granted, a person cannot live without a brain, but that's not the example the Mishna uses.

(B) Rabbi Moshe Feinstein

To buttress his interpretation of the Talmud and Rambam as indicating that halakha recognizes three vital organs, Rabbi Schachter footnotes a responsum of Rabbi Moshe Feinstein (ıм оӊ 2:146, s.v. *aval barur u-fashut*). In this passage, Rabbi Feinstein explains why the primary test for vital signs in halakha is checking the nostrils for evidence of breathing:

<table>
<tr><td>אבל ברור ופשוט שאין החוטם האבר שהוא נותן החיות בהאדם, וגם אינו מאברים שהנשמה תלויה בו כלל. אלא דהמוח והלב הם אלו הנותנים חיות להאדם וגם שיהיה לו שייך לנשום ע"י [חוטמו], ורק הוא האבר שדרך שם נעשה מעשה הנשימה שבאין ע"י המוח והלב.</td>
<td>However, it is abundantly clear that the nose isn't the organ that gives life to a person, nor is it an organ on which life depends. Rather, the brain and the heart are the organs that give life to a person and enable him to breathe via the nose, and the nose is only the organ through which the respiration that comes from the brain and the heart occurs.</td></tr>
<tr><td>ואית לנו הסימן חיות רק ע"י החוטם אף שלא הוא הנותן ענין הנשימה, משום שאין אנו מכירים היטב בלב ובטבור וכ"ש שאין מכירין במוח.</td>
<td>We have no indication of life other than nasal [activity] – even though the nose isn't what generates respiration – since we cannot easily detect activity in the heart or abdomen, and all the more so in the brain.</td></tr>
<tr><td>וכוונת הקרא דנשמת רוח חיים באפיו לא על עצם רוח החיים שזה ודאי ליכא בחוטם, אלא הרוח חיים שאנו רואין איכא באפיו אף שלא נראה באברים הגדולים אברי התנועה, וגם אחר שלא ניכר גם בדפיקת הלב ולא ניכר בטבור.</td>
<td>And the verse "All in whose nostrils was the breath of life" (Gen. 7:22) isn't referring to the [source] of the breath of life – for that's definitely not in the nose. Rather, [it is saying that] the breath of life that's visible to us is located in the nostrils, even if it's not visible in the larger, moving organs or apparent in the heartbeat or abdomen.</td></tr>
</table>

With all due respect to Rabbi Schachter, I do not see how these words can be interpreted as a defense of his point. True, Rabbi Feinstein believes that the brain and the heart are vital organs, but he makes no mention of the liver. Furthermore, Rabbi Feinstein derives his "vital organ list" not from the text in *Arakhin*, but from the simple reality that the heart and brain are, in fact, vital organs.

Rabbi Feinstein is merely attempting to deal with the ironic fact that although the primary halakhic method of testing for life is to check the nostrils, the nostrils themselves are not vital organs. Rabbi Feinstein's point is that since the nostrils are the parts of the respiratory system to which we have access, we have no choice but to check them, even though he is well aware of the fact that the breathing center is in the brainstem. That's why, later in life, after being told about cerebral angiography,[11] Rabbi Feinstein accepted these tests as definitive, since now there was a way to check the brain itself.[12]

(C) Halakhic Reality

Rabbi Schachter is aware that placing the liver on par with the brain or the heart in its level of "vitality" flies in the face of medical reality. He parries this problem in footnote 22:

> It is irrelevant whether medical facts in the twentieth century support this conclusion, which is a legal, not a medical statement. Jewish law follows the principles [l]aid down by the Talmud; all halakhic categories have been fixed by the Talmud and are the basis for developing all further Torah decisions. Thus, those organs designated by the rabbis of the Mishna as the "vital organs" retain that *halakhic* status.

In essence, Rabbi Schachter claims that medical death has no bearing on legal death. Halakha can declare a person with no liver dead,

---

11. A test that determines whether there is blood flow to the brain, with no flow being a definitive sign of death. For details, see Dr. Zelik Frischer's essay in this volume.

12. For Rabbi Feinstein's letter to this effect, see the Chief Rabbinate of Israel, "Heart Transplantation," *Tchumin* 7 (5746): 187–92 n. 2 [Hebrew]; for a thorough discussion of Rabbi Feinstein's position on brain death, see Rabbi Daniel Reifman's essay in this volume. See also the essays by Rabbi Charles Sheer and Dr. Noam Stadlan here as well as those of Dina Najman and Rabbi Ariel Picard in the organ donation volume, which touch upon Rabbi Feinstein's position as well.

or, conversely, it can declare a person with no heart or brain alive. There are a number of problems with this argument.

First, although death is a process, and choosing a particular part of this process as "the moment of death" is a legal/halakhic issue, the choice must at least be reasonable.[13] To call someone without a liver dead seems more than a little unreasonable. Second, even if one were to accept the argument that halakha has absolutely free rein in determining death, it would seem that halakha does not function this way in practice.

The only talmudic example of examining a person for signs of life (b. *Yoma* 85a; j. *Yoma* 8:5) refers to checking for breathing or for either heartbeat or abdominal movement (depending on the text of the Talmud one is using, and which interpretation one follows). These tests are valid because they are the obvious ways one can check for vital signs in an unconscious person, not because the nose, abdomen, and heart are necessarily the main or only organs defining a person's life. As Rabbi Feinstein said, these are simply the avenues most accessible to us for making a life or death determination.

Consequently, while it is possible (although not necessary) to argue that a breathing test is required in order to declare a person dead, since this is what the Talmud states, this is hardly an endorsement of Rabbi Schachter's position. In fact, an apnea test is part of the process of virtually all cases of brain death declaration.[14] However, it is impossible to argue that halakha has officially declared the heart, brain, and liver to be *the* official trio of halakhically recognized vital organs simply by offering a creative reading of part of the mishna in *Arakhin* combined with Rambam's codification of the passage in the *Mishneh Torah*. In matters of life and death, one cannot make recourse to nonexistent lists and claim them to be halakhic reality.

Again, Rabbi Schachter's own words belie his point. He claims that "all halakhic categories have been fixed by the Talmud" but then

---

13. For an interesting exchange on this point, see the debate between Michael J. Broyde and Alexander Morgan Capron, "Correspondence," *NEJM* 345, no. 8 (2001): 616–18.
14. If an apnea test is impossible for various reasons, may one accept a brain death declaration without it? For halakhic authorities who accept brain death, this is a major question, even if failure on the reflex tests is accompanied by a confirmatory test.

includes Rambam's own expansion of this category to include the heart, while ignoring the Talmud's own inclusion of the thigh.

(D) Definition of Vital Body Parts

There are three distinct categories, or questions, relevant to determining death and the various talmudic pericopae that discuss vital body parts.

1. What body part or parts – if any – can be defined as coterminous with life?
2. What bodily functions are necessary to sustain life, such that absence of such functions (for the requisite amount of time) means the person is dead?
3. What wounds can be declared to be "mortal wounds"?

Starting with the second question, the pericope in *Yoma*, that discusses how to check for vital signs, deals with this issue. Lack of breathing (or heartbeat) would demonstrate to the people attempting to save the person that he is already dead. The pericope in *Arakhin* about offering the value of one's organs to the Temple seems a bit more amorphous. It would appear that it actually deals with both the second and third questions.

The point of the law in *Arakhin* is that halakha does not recognize *erekh* offerings of body parts. One can assess only the value of a person as a whole, not the value of any of his or her parts. However, once the "offered part" is vital, the offering of its value signifies the offering of the whole person's value.

From the two examples in the mishna, head and liver, one could understand the concept of vital body parts as belonging in the second category. A vital body part is not meant to be coterminous with life, nor does it cover any mortal wound. Instead, the concept refers to any body part without which a person cannot live. This designation would include most organs and significant body parts, like the head and the torso, as well as the vow about "half the body."

However, from the Talmud's inclusion of the thigh in this category, one gets a different picture. The thigh is not something a person cannot live without. However, cutting a person's leg off at the thigh would be so dangerous if not done with cauterization that one could practically consider the wound mortal. That's why such wounds disqualify an animal from kosher slaughter, since said animal has been "mortally wounded."

Although Rambam's codification of the body-parts rule seems to follow the second category, it would appear that Rashi prefers the Talmud's reading of the mishna, which follows the third category. This is evident from Rashi's treatment of the concept of "vital body part" in a different context (b. *Temura* 10b). In this passage, the Talmud discusses the law that if an animal's owner declares one of its body parts holy, the entire animal becomes holy – another example of a metonymously understood vow. It is suggested that this rule would apply only to a vital body part. Rashi (ad loc.) comments on this term:

| כגון אם הקדיש רגליה מן הארכובה | Such as if one were to consecrate |
| ומלמעלה.... | its legs from the knee up.... |

Of all possible examples, Rashi chooses the thigh, the most extreme example in its "lack of vital necessity" the Talmud offered for this category. Since the thigh is in no way a vital body part, Rashi must understand this term primarily as a part of the body whose removal would render the victim mortally wounded, as he would likely die as a result.

As opposed to Rambam and Rashi, Rabbi Schachter seems to interpret the talmudic pericope in *Arakhin* as defining what organs are coterminous with life. Even if one were to accept Rabbi Schachter's (artificial) list as the sum total of possible body parts/organs referred to by the Talmud in this context, it would mean only that these three organs are the only ones without which a person would die (category 2) – or even that their removal would normally kill a person (category 3). It would not mean that any one of these functioning organs defines a person as alive or even partially alive (category 1). Rabbi Schachter mischaracterizes the point of the talmudic passage.

Furthermore, the simple reading of the Talmud is that these organs are necessary for life, which is certainly true. However, this doesn't mean that the moment one of these organs is removed or dies, a person is automatically dead. A person will die without a liver, but one is not dead without a liver. These are two distinct concepts.

CONCLUSION

In the brain death debate, the question is whether a functioning brain is coterminous with life. Is a brain dead person on a ventilator alive or dead? This is an important question, but it is not touched upon by the pericopae in *Arakhin* or *Nazir* at all.

Chapter 14

Rabbi Shlomo Zalman Auerbach and the Sheep Experiments

Avraham Steinberg

In 1986, after the Chief Rabbinate of Israel ruled that respiratory-brain death criteria are acceptable halakhically, I approached Rabbi Shlomo Zalman Auerbach to learn his opinion on this fundamental and crucial halakhic issue. After lengthy hesitation, Rabbi Auerbach decided to look into the matter. Subsequently, I had the privilege of summarizing his halakhic opinion and – after his very careful review and corrections, and with his authorization – publishing it.[1]

---

1. See Avraham Steinberg, "Defining the Moment of Death: A Survey," *Assia* 53–54 (5774/1993–94): 13–16 [Hebrew], http://www.medethics.org.il/articles/DoD/DoD24.asp or http://www.daat.ac.il/daat/kitveyet/assia/kviat-2.htm. Rabbi Shlomo Zalman Auerbach's position has been discussed at length by many authorities in different venues. See, for example, the article upon which this essay

The purpose of this short essay is *not* to offer a reading of Rabbi Auerbach's views on brain death. Rather, my intent here is to detail an interaction I had with Rabbi Auerbach about a specific talmudic pericope, and how this interaction led to a fascinating scientific inquiry overseen by me, together with a number of distinguished colleagues – Rabbi Prof. Abraham S. Abraham, Rabbi Dr. Mordechai Halperin, and Rabbi Prof. Yigal Shafran – and conceived of by Rabbi Auerbach himself.

THE TALMUDIC PERICOPE IN *ARAKHIN*

In one of our many meetings before the above-referenced publication of his views, Rabbi Auerbach pointed out to me that there seems to be an explicit statement in the Talmud that, by implication, would contradict the idea that brain dead people are actually dead. The statement appears in the Babylonian Talmud and is a comment on the final mishna in the first chapter.

האשה שיצאה ליהרג - אין ממתינין לה עד שתלד. האשה שישבה על המשבר - ממתינין לה עד שתלד.	When a [pregnant] woman is to be executed, one does not wait for her to give birth. However, if [when she is condemned] she is already in labor[2] – [the court] waits for her to give birth.

Upon this mishna the Babylonian Talmud (b. *Arakhin* 7a–b) comments:

אמר רב יהודה אמר שמואל: האשה היוצאה ליהרג, מכין אותה כנגד בית הריון כדי שימות הוולד תחילה, כדי שלא תבא לידי ניוול.	Rabbi Yehuda said in the name of Shmuel: When a [pregnant] woman is being led out to her execution, [the court] strikes her abdomen to kill the fetus first, so that [her execution] not cause a repulsive spectacle.[3]

---

is based: Steinberg, "Defining the Moment," 5–16. See also the discussions of Rabbis Yosef Carmel and Asher Lopatin in this volume as well as that of Rabbi Ariel Picard in the organ donation volume.

2. Literally, "if she is sitting on the birthing stool."
3. Meaning that the baby's birth or miscarriage during the execution would be particularly gruesome.

למימרא, דהיא קדמה ומתה
ברישא, והא קיימא לן דוולד
מיית ברישא! דתנן: תינוק
בן יומו נוחל ומנחיל, ואמר
רב ששת: נוחל בנכסי האם
להנחיל לאחין מן האב, דווקא
בן יום אחד, אבל עובר לא,
דהוא מיית ברישא, ואין הבן
יורש את אמו בקבר להנחיל
לאחין מן האב!

Does this mean to say that she would die first? But didn't we learn that the fetus dies first?! For we were taught: "A one-day-old baby inherits and enables others to inherit." Rav Sheshet said: "He inherits the possessions of his mother, and he enables his brothers on his father's side to inherit." [This text] specifically references a one-day-old baby, but not a fetus. This is because a fetus would naturally die first, and a son doesn't inherit his mother from the grave, nor does he enable his brothers on his mother's side to inherit!

הני מילי לגבי מיתה, איידי
דוולד זוטרא חיותיה, עיילא
טיפה דמלאך המות ומחתך
להו לסימנין, אבל נהרגה - היא
מתה ברישא.

This is true in a case of natural death. Since the fetus' life force is so weak, the "drop" from the angel of death extinguishes its vitality.[4] However, in a case of violent death, she dies first.

והא הוה עובדא ופרכיס עד
תלת פרכוסי! מידי דהוי אזנב
הלטאה דמפרכסת.

But did it not once occur that [the fetus] kicked three times [after the mother had died]?! This is like the tail of a lizard that convulses [after it is cut off].

According to this source, Rabbi Auerbach argued, a fetus does not outlive its host. Since a fetus is considered dependent upon its mother, when she dies a natural death, the fetus automatically predeceases her; its life force is inherently weaker than that of its mother.

I countered that according to the next passage in this same talmudic source, there are exceptions to this rule:

---

4. Literally, the drop "slices the signature [organs]," a phrase generally used to describe slaughtering, the "signature organs" being the trachea and esophagus.

א״ר נחמן אמר שמואל: האשה שישבה על המשבר ומתה בשבת, מביאין סכין ומקרעים את כריסה ומוציאין את הוולד. פשיטא, מאי עביד? [ז:] מחתך בבשר הוא! אמר רבה: לא נצרכה, להביא סכין דרך רשות הרבים.

Rabbi Naḥman said in the name of Shmuel: "If a woman dies on Shabbat while in labor, a knife is brought, and her womb is sliced open and the fetus removed." Obviously! What would be the problem? [7b] It is simply slicing meat. Rava said: "This [statement] is necessary to permit the carrying of a knife through a public thoroughfare."

ומאי קמשמע לן? דמספיקא מחללינן שבתא, תנינא: מי שנפלה עליו מפולת, ספק הוא שם ספק אינו שם, ספק חי ספק מת, ספק כנעני ספק ישראל - מפקחין עליו את הגל!

And what does this teach us? That we violate Shabbat even when saving a life is not guaranteed?! But we were taught this [already]: "When someone is caught under falling debris [on Shabbat or a holiday], and it is unclear whether he is trapped in the rubble or not, and it is further unclear [assuming he is trapped] whether he is alive or dead, and whether he is a gentile or a Jew – the rubble should be cleared for his sake."

מהו דתימא: התם הוא דהוה ליה חזקה דחיותא, אבל הכא דלא הוה ליה חזקה דחיותא מעיקרא אימא לא, קמ״ל.

One may have suggested that in the case [of the rubble] there was an assumption of life, but in this case [of the trapped fetus], where there is no assumption of life, perhaps one would not be permitted to [violate the Sabbath]. Hence [the statement of Rabbi Naḥman in the name of Shmuel] teaches us that [violating the Sabbath would in fact be permitted to save the fetus].

Explaining why people would feel the need to perform an emergency cesarean section on a dead woman, Rashi writes:

דזימנין דמיקרי דהיא מייתא ברישא.

For it sometimes occurs that [the mother] predeceases [the fetus].

248

According to this explanation, Rashi appears to believe that although a fetus is generally known to predecease its mother, there are exceptions – such as in cases of trauma – in which the mother dies first; otherwise, why would it be permissible to desecrate Shabbat by bringing a knife through a public thoroughfare in order to perform an emergency C-section on a dead woman?! Therefore, I argued, perhaps it would make sense to suggest that a pregnant woman on a respirator would be another such exception?

Rabbi Auerbach responded that there is a difference between a woman in labor and a woman at an earlier stage of pregnancy. When a woman is in labor, her fetus is considered sufficiently separate from her that we deem it viable; hence Shabbat can be violated lest the fetus still be alive. However, before labor begins, the fetus is considered dependent upon the mother, and when she dies a natural death, the fetus automatically predeceases her, since its life force is weaker than hers.[5]

With this in mind, Rabbi Auerbach proposed that it would seem impossible for the Talmud to consider brain death to be death, since there have been cases in modern times in which the fetus continued to gestate and was delivered alive long after the mother was declared brain dead. Although most cases of brain death involve trauma, and the talmudic dictum is generally aimed at natural death, in cases of ventilated patients this difference would lose all relevance. This is because the reason the Talmud distinguishes between violent death and natural death is that since the former comes with no time for preparation from the body, the mother could die even faster than the fetus. However, since ventilated patients can survive quite a while, this talmudic distinction would fall away. Thus, following Rabbi Auerbach's interpretation, the

---

5. This understanding of this pericope – as hinging on a distinction between mothers before and during labor – is not the only one suggested in halakhic literature. See, for example, Rabbi Avraham Gombiner, *Magen Avraham* 330:10; Rabbi Ya'aqov Reischer, *Shevut Ya'aqov* 1:13; and Rabbi David ibn Abi Zimra, *Responsa of Radbaz* 2:695. See also Rabbi Natan ben Yeḥiel, *Arukh*, s.v. *d-f-n*. Nevertheless, as this was Rabbi Auerbach's interpretation, it was the starting point for designing the experiment discussed in this essay. For further reading on this debate, see Avraham Steinberg, *The Encyclopedia of Halakha and Medicine* (2nd ed., 2006), vol. 4, s.v. *leida*, pp. 294–95 nn. 369–71 [Hebrew].

talmudic principle just outlined – that a fetus generally predeceases its mother – could be a serious impediment to accepting any neurological death criteria as halakhically valid.

Despite the strength of this point in Rabbi Auerbach's eyes, further discussion and reflection led to an alternative hypothesis. Rabbi Auerbach suggested that one could, in fact, reconcile the talmudic position with the present-day reality if one assumed that the talmudic belief that the fetus generally predeceases its mother applied only in the past, before the advent of modern medicine. In our times, technology allows us to keep a body "alive" through artificial respiration and the like. Hence, Rabbi Auerbach proposed that perhaps the talmudic dictum applies only to a person who has died and has not been connected to any life-sustaining equipment, since this equipment may allow the body to simulate the aspects of life needed to sustain the fetus.

THE EXPERIMENT

Considering these two hypotheses, Rabbi Auerbach requested that my esteemed colleague Rabbi Prof. Yigal Shafran and I set up a scientific experiment to prove whether a fetus could continue gestating and be born alive in a dead mother whose death has been determined by indisputable halakhic criteria[6] while the body has been connected to artificial life support.

To me this seemed both a unique and exciting request. This was to be a modern scientific inquiry designed to test out a halakhic matter in an empirical fashion. The parameters of the experiment were devised by one of the leading halakhic authorities of the generation in order to evaluate the scientific reality behind a certain halakhic pronouncement. As far as I know, this has been the first and only example of such an experiment in the history of modern science.

Rabbi Shafran and I commenced designing the experiment according to Rabbi Auerbach's halakhic specifications. We fine-tuned the necessary conditions and medico-surgical techniques, in consultation

---

6. For example, someone who has been decapitated is halakhically considered dead, as stated in m. *Oholot* 1:6.

with experts in veterinary medicine,[7] intensive care, and obstetrics. We ended up conducting two experiments. Both were conducted at the largest veterinary hospital in Israel, located in Beit Dagan. The whole procedure was overseen by experienced doctors and veterinarians.

The First Experiment

The first experiment was conducted on Thursday, 4 Sivan 5752 (January 9, 1992). In addition to the surgical team, the designers and originators of the experiment were in attendance: Rabbi Shafran, Dr. Moshe Hersch of the Intensive Care Unit at Shaare Zedek Medical Center, and myself. Additionally, Rabbi Prof. Abraham and Rabbi Dr. Mordechai Halperin were present as observers.

A pregnant sheep was given general anesthesia to avoid causing it any pain.[8] The sheep was then intubated and attached to a respirator. An intravenous line was attached so fluid and medicine could be administered to the sheep. Additionally, a device designed to monitor the sheep's heartbeat and blood pressure was attached, as was a fetal heart monitor. (Throughout the experiment, the gas and electrolyte levels in the sheep's blood were constantly tested, as was its red cell count.)

The surgeons proceeded to dissect the soft tissues of the neck, revealing the large arteries. The arteries were tied to avoid massive blood loss and death. Then they were cut.

Next, the skull was sawed through, and the brain was suctioned out in its entirety. The brainless sheep was then left attached to respirator for three hours. Throughout that time, the sheep's heart continued to function normally; its heartbeat remained steady and its blood pressure normal, with virtually no drugs or other medical interventions required to maintain them. The fetal heartbeat also remained steady.

Though the conditions of the experiment as set forth by Rabbi Auerbach had been met, we decided to take it one step further and

---

7. Obviously we couldn't experiment on human subjects, but according to Rabbi Auerbach, since the physiology concerning the issues at hand is the same in animals and humans, the experiment could be carried out on an animal.

8. The sheep was anesthetized both out of consideration for medical ethics as well as in compliance with the halakhic prohibition of causing needless pain to animals (*tza'ar ba'alei ḥaim*).

remove the sheep's head entirely. To that end, first a tracheostomy was performed.[9] Next, a breathing tube was placed directly into the trachea through this new incision. Finally, the spinal column was cut at a height of the cervical vertebrae 1–2, and the head was removed.

The sheep's body maintained the same basic level of functionality – without a head – for twenty minutes. Then there was a sudden and dramatic drop in fetal heart rate. An emergency C-section was performed, and the lamb was removed, already lifeless. Resuscitative measures failed.[10]

After the experiment was completed, Rabbi Auerbach, Rabbi Shafran, Rabbi Prof. Abraham, and I met at Rabbi Auerbach's home to process the results. At first, we agreed that the experiment had confirmed that matters today were quite different than in talmudic times due to artificial respiration and other advanced technology. Nowadays, therefore, there should be no problem in positing that even if the mother is in fact dead – assuming the correctness of the neurological criteria for the purposes of this discussion – the fetus can remain viable in cases where the mother's body is maintained by mechanical means. The experiment seemed to have conclusively demonstrated this point; the sheep was certainly dead – having no brain or even a head – yet the fetus continued to live, at least for a while.

A Possible Objection

However, one of us raised the following objection: According to our own definition, the sheep was not considered alive, though its heart was beating. However, the only indication that the fetus was alive was its heartbeat. If heartbeat was not to be taken as conclusive proof that the sheep was alive according to the parameters of our experiment, how could we use this very same indicator to demonstrate that the fetus was alive? Perhaps the fetus was actually brain dead as well, but with a still-beating heart?

I responded by stating that the two matters were not at all analogous. The sheep was clearly dead, since its brain *and* head had been

---

9. A tracheostomy is a low incision on the anterior part of the neck, cutting into the trachea.
10. This type of sudden, unexplained drop in heart rate is well known in obstetrics. Sometimes the baby cannot be saved.

removed. Therefore, its heartbeat was meaningless, reflecting only that the animal was being maintained through mechanical respiration. However, there was no indication that the fetus was dead; nor was its body being maintained artificially in any way. Hence, there was no reason to postulate the unlikely possibility that the fetus was essentially a heartbeating cadaver, like its mother. Rather, the fetal heartbeat proved that the lamb was, in fact, still alive after its mother had already died.

Nevertheless, to remove all doubt with regard to the important conclusions derived from the experiment, we decided to conduct a second one.

The Second Experiment

The second experiment was conducted on Wednesday, 17 Shevat 5752 (January 22, 1992), with the same medical staff and observers.

The first steps of the process were similar to those of the first experiment, but instead of beginning by suctioning out the brain, the surgeons immediately removed the head. For the next twenty-five minutes, the heart functioned properly, and blood pressure and pulse were stable, as was the fetal heart rate. Then a C-section was performed. The lamb was removed from the brain dead sheep. The lamb was alive and in decent health and was sent to a farm. It was still alive and well at the time of the original Hebrew documentation of this experiment (1994).

Having conducted this second experiment, all – including Rabbi Auerbach – were convinced that although the pericope in *Arakhin* declared that a fetus could not outlive its mother, this statement applied only under ordinary circumstances of death. However, if the deceased mother's body was maintained by artificial respiration and other advanced medical care, it was possible – as conclusively demonstrated by our experiments – for the fetus to continue gestation and even be delivered alive.

SUMMARY

As I stated in the introduction, this essay is not an attempt to outline the halakhic position of Rabbi Shlomo Zalman Auerbach. This has been done in a number of settings, and the interested reader has many avenues through which to explore and analyze Rabbi Auerbach's various pronouncements on the subject. The purpose of this essay is to detail the sheep experiments and explain why they were performed and what they accomplished. This, I feel, is important for three reasons.

First, the entire process is a fascinating chapter in halakha and science, and I want the English-speaking Jewish world to become acquainted with it. Second, the experiments have direct bearing on the crucial issue of halakha and brain death, which is still hotly debated as of this writing. Third, beyond the issue of brain death and organ donation in halakha, these experiments serve as a useful heuristic paradigm for resolving questions of science and halakha in general. In this case, scientific experimentation emerged as an effective method of determining the relevance of a particular talmudic medical pronouncement in a world of quickly evolving technological and scientific advances unimaginable in the talmudic era.[11]

---

11. This essay was translated and adapted by Rabbi Zev Farber. For a more scientific description of the experiment, see A. Steinberg and M. Hersch, "Decapitation of a Pregnant Sheep – A Contribution to the Brain Death Controversy," *Transplantation Proceedings* 27, no. 2 (1995): 1886–87.

Chapter 15

Non-Heart-Beating Donation from Brain Dead Patients: Rav Ahron Soloveichik's Solution

Asher Lopatin

I. THE POSITION OF RABBI AHRON SOLOVEICHIK

Rabbi Ahron Soloveichik is generally seen as a great opponent of using brain death to define the end of life. Both the recent study of the Vaad Halacha of the Rabbinical Council of America (RCA) and rabbis such as Rabbi Yitzchak Breitowitz understand Rabbi Soloveichik to require cessation of both heartbeat and breathing as well as brain death. Rabbi Soloveichik believes this is the *pesaq* of Rashi, Rambam, and both Rabbi Joseph Karo and Rabbi Moshe Isserles in the *Shulḥan Arukh*.

For decades, Rabbi Soloveichik argued against defining death merely on the basis of cessation of brain activity, and it seemed that his *pesaq* would not allow for the donation of organs such as the liver and kidneys, which must still be functioning in order to be transferred to another, living body.

The past fifteen years have seen the emergence of a new form of donation: non-heart-beating donation (NHBD), also known as donation after cardiac death (DCD).[1] At first glance, NHBD seems even more controversial than brain death, and it is certainly treated so by the RCA's Vaad Halacha. However, NHBD might actually bring together opponents and proponents of brain death within the Orthodox community, and allow the harvesting of organs only after meeting Rabbi Soloveichik's stringent death criteria. Moreover, it mirrors, with some important modifications, the decisions of Rabbi Shlomo Zalman Auerbach in dealing with a brain dead patient.

II. THE NHBD PROCESS

Protocols for NHBD developed by the University of Pittsburgh Medical Center (1992) generally work in the following way: The patient agrees in advance to a Do Not Resuscitate order (DNR), organ donation, and the withdrawal of life support if it is determined that he or she will not recover.[2] Once the physicians make this determination, they prepare for organ retrieval, even bringing the patient to the operating room.

Now comes the controversial element. Life support – respirator and/or ventilator – is removed, and the doctors await the cessation of cardiac function. If the heart stops, they wait two to five minutes, not resuscitating, and then declare the patient dead. The first team of doctors then leaves the room, and the transplant team enters and immediately begins removing whatever organs remain viable. In some cases, this team will even resuscitate the heart in order to be able to harvest it, and to keep the other organs fresh.[3]

Controversy

Even in the medical community, which generally accepts brain death as death, NHBD is controversial, mainly because it doesn't rely on brain death. The respirator is removed *before* the patient is brain dead, and

---

1. Regarding this procedure and the ethical concerns it entails, see Dr. Kenneth Prager's essay in this volume.
2. We'll return to this point in the last section.
3. See Raymond J. Devettere, *Practical Decision Making in Health Care Ethics* (Washington, DC: Georgetown University Press, 2010), 139.

the heart is not resuscitated when it stops, even though it almost certainly could be.

Thus, some see NHBD as "standing by" while a person is dying. Though the heart and lungs may have stopped functioning, the brain remains alive as the physicians watch the patient die. This is because the patient is declared dead based on cardiopulmonary criteria, which define death as the moment the heart cannot naturally resume functioning on its own.

Reframing

Halakhically, however, removing life support may not be as controversial as it seems. If the patient relinquishes in advance all rights to a respirator and/or ventilator if and when diagnosed as brain dead, or upon some other medical condition, disconnecting the patient from life support would involve only an abstention from the mitzva of saving a life,[4] rather than active (or even passive) murder.

Furthermore, I would argue that if NHBD is practiced only on brain dead patients, it could become the method of choice according to all opinions[5] and even allow organ donations according to the strict view of Rabbi Soloveichik. Indeed Rabbi Breitowitz implies as much in discussing the position of Rabbi Auerbach, who did allow the removal of the respirator tube from a brain dead patient. [6]

III. RIGHTS TO THE RESPIRATOR

Rabbi Moshe Feinstein

A number of *posqim* allow for disconnecting the respirator, because they see this act as simply removing an impediment to the dying person's natural death, not as actively hastening it. However, Rabbi Moshe Feinstein prohibited such a move.

---

4. "Do not stand idly by the blood of your fellow" (Lev. 19:16).
5. Although admittedly, NHBD would limit the amount of organs that can be used, since during the few minutes that the person is without heartbeat, some begin to degrade.
6. Rabbi Yitzchak Breitowitz, response to letter regarding his article "The Brain Death Controversy in Jewish Law" (*Jewish Action* 52, no. 2 [spring 1992]), *Jewish Action* 53, no. 3 (summer 1992), 80 n. 3.

I would like to suggest that Rabbi Feinstein might have allowed the removal of the respirator if the patient, through an advance directive, specifically transfers all rights of use of the respirator to the medical team upon reaching a certain medical marker – brain death or otherwise. Once that transfer occurs, the only obligation to maintain respiration would be the commandment of saving life.

Once the halakhic force becomes this positive commandment rather than the prohibition of murder, we can prioritize other patients who may need the respirator as well, and remove it from the brain dead or otherwise compromised patient. Perhaps we should also take into account the suffering of the patient whose life is unduly lengthened by the respirator. The obligation not to murder is clear and unbendable, but the obligation of saving a life is complex, and triage can be applied.

Rabbi Feinstein prohibited the removal of the respirator before NHBD existed, so he had no way of adding the saving of other lives to the equation. Perhaps if the respirator would be used for another patient, and the NHBD organs would save yet another, Rabbi Feinstein would have allowed the removal of this device.

Two People in a Desert: Rabbi Soloveichik's Deduction

In determining if disconnecting a respirator is murder or just a failure to save life, the importance of who owns – or has rights to – this equipment reflects the thinking of Rabbi Soloveichik as well. His analysis is based on the famous ruling of Rabbi Akiva in b. *Bava Metzia* 62a:

שנים שהיו מהלכין בדרך, וביד אחד מהן קיתון של מים, אם שותין שניהם - מתים, ואם שותה אחד מהן - מגיע לישוב. דרש בן פטורא: מוטב שישתו שניהם וימותו, ואל יראה אחד מהם במיתתו של חבירו. עד שבא רבי עקיבא ולימד: וחי אחיך עמך - חייך קודמים לחיי חבירך.

Two people are traveling, and one has a jug of water. If they both drink, they'll both die. If one drinks, he'll arrive safely at the next inhabited area. Ben Peṭora taught: "Better that both drink, and let not the one see the death of his fellow." But when Rabbi Akiva arrived, he taught: "'And your fellow shall live with you' (Lev. 25:36) – your life takes precedence over your fellow's."

Rabbi Akiva reasons that since giving one's fellow water is "only" saving a life – a case of "do not stand idly by"[7] if ever there were one – this commandment is pushed off in order to save one's own life. One need not give up one's own life to fulfill the mitzva of saving life.

Clearly, if there were any question of murder in such a case, one would not be permitted to put his life ahead of another's. He would be required to at least share the water, if not let the other person drink it all. However, since the water is his, his drinking it doesn't constitute the murder of his fellow.

Rabbi Soloveichik pointed out that if the fellow *took* the water from its owner – even to save his own life – that would be murder. However, the owner was permitted to drink all the water to save *his* own life. As I understand it, this is because, with regard to the fellow, there was only an obligation to save life, which could be obviated by the water owner's need to save his own life.

Therefore, in our case, if the patient no longer has rights to the respirator, because he has transferred them to the hospital in advance, a doctor's assigning the machine to someone else is only an avoidance of the obligation of saving life. Such an act is offset by the need to save someone else. It is akin to taking the water away from the fellow; it is not murder.

Removing the Respirator as Strangulation

Some have claimed that removing the respirator and/or ventilator is akin to actively suffocating the patient, one of the descriptions of murder listed in Rambam's *Mishneh Torah* (Laws of Murder 2:1). Yet this difficulty can be alleviated by placing an oxygen mask on the patient after the respirator is removed, to demonstrate that no oxygen is denied him.

Furthermore, it seems to me, Rambam sees air as the God-given property and right of every human. No one may deny anyone else air. However, a machine that pumps air into a person may be owned by individuals – it is not the shared property of mankind. Rather, it is akin to the bottle of water in the desert.

---

7. See note 4 earlier in this essay.

IV. HALAKHIC NHBD

The removal of the respirator, then, as is done with NHBD, would be allowed as long as the patient has forfeited all rights to the machine. However, the patient cannot be declared dead, according to Rabbi Soloveichik, until the cessation of the vital bodily systems, i.e., until cardiopulmonary death and brain death. Therefore, halakhic NHBD à la Rabbi Soloveichik would allow the harvesting of organs only after the patient is diagnosed as dead based both upon cardiopulmonary and neurological criteria.

According to this logic, if a patient is declared dead based on neurological criteria, then halakhic NHBD can be used to create consensus among halakhic authorities. Upon removal of the respirator – as requested in advance by the patient, such that this act is not murder – the patient will be not only brain dead, but dead based on cardiopulmonary criteria as well.

Once the person is brain dead and the respirator is removed, we need wait only for breathing to stop – as should happen immediately if the person is brain dead – and then for the heart to stop soon afterward (for merely thirty seconds, as Rabbi Auerbach writes). Then, since all three systems – cardiac, respiratory, and neural – have stopped, that person should be considered dead according to almost all major positions, including Rabbi Soloveichik's; the body is just a body, no longer a living human being. Even if the hospital can restart the heart – as some claim – the person is still dead. The person has died, and now the body and organs are merely pieces of equipment – precious equipment, but not living. Any movement, including heartbeat, is equivalent to *pirkus be-alma*,[8] random movement.

SUMMARY

Rabbi Ahron Soloveichik's definition of death – combined with viewing removal of a respirator as a lack of saving the patient, rather than murder – allows for an almost universally acceptable halakhic ruling along with the practical and ethical ability to donate and receive almost every organ in the body that would have been harvested through

---

8. See b. *Ḥullin* 21a.

the halakhically controversial brain death definition of death. Patients must, however, issue an advance directive regarding when they relinquish respirator rights. Moreover, while there is some debate over how many organs can be harvested by NHBD (especially after brain death is declared), as medicine advances, no doubt many more organs will become available. Most important, halakhic NHBD may permit organ harvesting even according to those who oppose relying on brain death and/or removing respirators from patients who have rights to them.

Section IV

Historical and Ethical
Considerations

Chapter 16

A Life of Halakha or a Halakha of Life?

Irving (Yitz) Greenberg

INTRODUCTION: THE PURPOSE OF TORAH AND HALAKHA

Rabbi Joseph B. Soloveitchik on Life vs. Death

It was the Rav, writing in *Halakhic Man*, who opened our eyes to the Torah's and halakha's primary commitment to life. In section 7 of this classic work, he expands on the centrality of life to *qedusha*, sanctity. He stresses the importance of opposing death as a core concern of halakha; this approach is distinctive to Jewish religion. He writes:

> Many religions view the phenomenon of death as a positive spectacle, inasmuch as it highlights and sensitizes the religious consciousness.... Death is seen as a window filled with light, open to an exalted, supernal realm. Judaism, however,...abhors death, organic decay, and dissolution. It bids one to choose life and sanctify it.... [H]alakhic thought

sees in death a terrifying contradiction to the whole of religious life.[1]

Reflecting his absorption of modern values, the Rav makes clear that religious life is centered on "...this world...physical, concrete reality.... Holiness means the holiness of earthly, here-and-now life."[2] Rabbi Soloveitchik continues:

> The saving of a life overrides the commandments of the entire Torah, "'and he shall live by them' (Lev. 15:5) – and not die by them..." (b. *Yoma* 85b). *This law is the watchword of Judaism.*[3]

The Rav is particularly troubled that some may hesitate or resist saving a life lest this act violate some existing mitzva (such as Shabbat). Therefore he quotes verbatim from the *Tur* (OH 328):

> An authority who allows himself to be consulted [when a life is in danger on Shabbat] is reprehensible, and he who consults with him [rather than speedily acting to save the life in danger] is a murderer.

Rabbi Soloveitchik also quotes Rambam at length, for he elaborated the urgency of overriding mitzvot in order to save a life. Rambam condemned those who discourage lifesaving behavior by asserting that such actions violate a commandment, and he labels them nothing less than "heretics."[4] Rambam denounced such people as guilty of turning the Torah into the curse that the prophet Ezekiel placed on the sinners

1. Joseph B. Soloveitchik, *Halakhic Man* (Philadelphia: Jewish Publication Society, 1983), 31. By implication, one should work to decrease death and increase life.
2. Ibid., 32. Of course, Rabbi Soloveitchik believes in the World to Come, but he understands it as a place one receives reward.

   The receiving of a reward is not a religious act. Therefore, halakhic man *prefers the real world to a transcendent existence* because here, in this world, man is given the opportunity to create, act, accomplish, while there, in the World to Come, he is powerless to change anything at all. (ibid.; italics added)
3. Ibid., 34; italics mine.
4. Rambam, MT Laws of Shabbat 2:3.

of Israel: "Wherefore I also gave them statutes that were not good, and ordinances by which they would not live" (Ezek. 20:25).

If this were not enough, the Rav restates his own view (incorporating some of Rambam's language, which he just quoted!):

> The teachings of the Torah do not oppose the laws of life and reality, for were they to clash with this world and were they to negate the value of concrete, physiological-biological existence, then they would *contain not mercy, loving-kindness, and peace but vengeance and wrath....* This law that *piqu'aḥ nefesh,* saving a life, overrides all the commandments and its far-reaching effects are indicative of the high value which the halakhic viewpoint attributes to one's earthly life.[5]

Over the years, the Rav taught a whole generation that halakha is not merely a set of abstract legal statements; nor does carrying out halakhic observances constitute merely following the instructions of a legal code. The halakha embodies the worldview and purpose of the Torah. That purpose is to perfect creation, i.e., to fill it with life sustained at the highest level of dignity. Halakhic rulings and behavior are intended "to replenish the deficiency in creation" and to make the real world "conform to the ideal world." The human makes these repairs through human creativity, and this is "the central idea in the halakhic consciousness – the idea of the importance of man as a partner of the Almighty in the act of creation."[6]

Over the years, I have come to understand two further implications of the Rav's teaching. (1) The primary goal of the Torah – as expressed in the account of creation and the messianic prophecies – is to repair the deficiency in creation by overcoming death, or at least by extending life and expanding the realms where it is stronger than its enemies. These enemies are sickness, poverty, hunger, injustice, war, etc., which are allied with death.[7] (2) When one asks a halakhic question, the criterion for the answer is not, primarily, precedent or existing

---

5. Soloveitchik, *Halakhic Man,* 34–35; italics indicate direct quotes from Rambam.
6. Ibid., 99.
7. The prophets identify these enemies and predict their defeat in the messianic era. See, for example, Isaiah 29:18; 32:3–4; 35:5–6 (sickness); 66:12 (poverty); 49:8–10 (hunger); 11:5, 9 (injustice); 2:3–4 (war).

norms. The prime criterion is to uphold life – or save it. This is why I'm convinced that the recognition of brain death as a halakhically valid criterion confirming the cessation of life is correct. Therefore, I believe that this conclusion – which permits the transplantation of the heart of a brain dead person to save another life – will win out in the coming years.

God of Love

Let me start at the beginning. God, who is the Living God/God of Life (*Elohim Ḥaim*), the Ruler who lusts for life (*Melekh ḥafetz ba-ḥaim*),[8] created the world – which He loves and considers "very good" (Gen. 1:31).

> God is good to all, and His maternal love (*raḥamav*) is over all His creatures. (Ps. 145:9)

God's greatest love and delight is in life and all living things. It is God who, in creating, calls forth life;[9] God is delighted with every appearance of life, blesses it, and asks for more.[10] This reaction is specific to the appearance of life. Then God lovingly sustains all living things.[11] Out of love, God provides light and warmth for the earth and all that live on it.[12] To get close to God, one must attach to life. The Rav points out that the House of God in our midst, the *Mishkan/Beit ha-Miqdash*, is totally devoted to life; no death – or even a person rendered impure by contact with death – is allowed in.[13] Thus, the Rav makes clear that being/working on the side of life is the desired religious response to God's commitment to life.[14] By this logic, the halakha "in all its multifold aspects and manifestations" operates to sustain or increase life, to "fully

8. High Holy Day liturgy.
9. See Gen. 1:11, 20, 24, 27.
10. See ibid. 1:23, 28.
11. The daily liturgy repeated refers to God as *Mekhalkel ḥaim be-ḥesed*.
12. *Daily Prayer Book* (trans. Philip Birnbaum; New York: Hebrew Publishing Company, 1977), 71, 337.
13. Soloveitchik, *Halakhic Man*, 31, 32, 35–37.
14. Ibid., 31, 33, 34–35, 37, 39.

realize all the potentials of life"[15] (or to protect it against its enemies: death and its allies).[16]

To those who object to my using Scripture to define the purpose of halakhic observances, I remind them of the Rav's comments:

> The halakha sees the *whole Torah* as consisting of basic laws and halakhic principles. Even the scriptural narratives serve the purpose of determining everlasting law.... Therefore, if the Torah spoke at length about the creation of the world and related to us the story of the making of heaven and earth and all their hosts, it did so ... in order to teach *practical* halakha. The scriptural portion of the creation narrative is a legal portion in which are to be found basic, everlasting halakhic principles, just like the portion of *Qedoshim* or *Mishpatim*.[17]

I. REVERENCE FOR LIFE

In Judaism, the centrality of life is expressed in laws that concretize the reverence for life and uphold its dignities. The value of all created things – even those without life – is embodied in the law of *bal tashḥit*. One is forbidden to use them up for no purpose, i.e., waste them. Regarding animals, however, since life is more treasured than inanimate materials, the halakha adds another restriction – *tza'ar ba'alei ḥaim*. Even if animals are legitimately used for a human purpose – such as food, work, or transportation – one may not cause these creatures unnecessary pain.[18]

The highest form of life – the human being – is created in the image of God. This characteristic imbues every human with three

---

15. Ibid., 49, 132.
16. See also ibid., 99–115.
17. Ibid., 100–101; italics added.
18. Similarly, in the laws of *kashrut*, even after a living creature or a whole organism dies, it isn't nullified even in a mixture a thousand times greater in volume. A living creature – or even a residual, whole body of one – evokes the awe and "weight" of life itself; therefore, it is never nullified. A piece of nonkosher meat, on the other hand, has no such resonance. It is merely part of a dead animal and *is* nullified if embedded in a kosher product sixty times its volume.

inherent dignities, as defined by the Mishna in a case of capital punishment: *infinite value,*[19] *equality,*[20] and *uniqueness.*[21]

These are not abstract concepts. From these dignities, a host of laws flow. From these dignities stem the wide-ranging obligations of *kevod ha-briyot* (respect for human beings), which, according to the Talmud, override even Torah prohibitions.[22]

The Rav indicates that *kevod ha-briyot* is the basis of many laws in the Torah.[23] He even suggests that all the ethical commandments, the interpersonal mitzvot, are based on this value. In turn, he interprets Ramban as basing the *kevod ha-briyot* of all humans (not just Jews) on the even more fundamental principle of *tzelem Elokim*, that the human being is created in the image of God.[24] I apply the Rav's thought by deriving all ethical commandments from the principle of the dignities of a *tzelem Elokim.*[25]

From infinite value and equality comes the obligation of *tzedaka.* From the same equality principle comes the notion that the highest form of charity lies in providing the poor with a job or a loan rather than just food or some other gift.[26] From uniqueness flows the prohibition of counting people in a census. From all three comes the command to "love your neighbor as yourself" (Lev. 19:18). From the intrinsic dignity of infinite value and equality comes the prohibition of saying something degrading about someone – even if it's true (*lashon ha-ra*).

As an extension of respect for human dignity, the halakha developed practices regarding the handling of a dead body. It is important to

---

19. "Anyone who saves one life is as if he has saved an entire world" (b. *Sanhedrin* 37a).

20. "No one may say: 'My father is greater than yours'" (ibid.).

21. "The Holy One, Blessed Be He, has fashioned every person in the form of the first human being, yet none of them resembles the other" (ibid.).

22. See b. *Berakhot* 19b, which allows the violation of such prohibitions only via *shev ve-al ta'aseh* (sinning by inaction), not by *qum ve-aseh* (direct action).

23. See Joseph B. Soloveitchik, "A Mission," in *Yemei Zikaron* (Jerusalem: World Zionist Organization, 1986), 9 [Hebrew].

24. Soloveitchik, "Mission," 9.

25. As Ben Azzai comments in j. *Nedarim* 9:4, *tzelem Elokim* is the fundamental principle from which all mitzvot can be derived or understood. See *Pnei Moshe* and *Qorban ha-Eida* ad loc.

26. See Rambam, MT Laws of Gifts to the Poor 7–10 [10:7–14].

understand that death ends the status and full dignity of a living human being. The corpse has none of those three primary, intrinsic human dignities. Unless otherwise contaminated, a living person is ritually pure, whereas a dead body is the ultimate paradigm of ritual impurity (אבי אבות הטומאה). One is not permitted to desecrate Shabbat in order to protect a dead body, but to protect a living person one must.[27]

Nevertheless, the dead person is the remnant of a living image of God, just as the corpse is the shell of a creature that was infinitely valuable, equal, and unique. Therefore, the halakha developed laws to uphold the residual dignity of the person. One is required to bury the body as soon as possible. Since the deceased is no longer the vital, dignified person he or she was, keeping this person in the community is prohibited, as is "beautifying" or cosmetically treating the corpse for public display. Such actions are a form of mockery (called *lo'eg la-rash* – teasing/tormenting a poor person, in this case, the dead), for the corpse is a woefully inadequate representation of the living person.

On the other hand, from the moment of death until burial, the body must not be left unattended. This act of watching over the body until it reaches the grave is a gesture of loving-kindness, as is the preparation of the body for burial (including *ṭahara*, washing and purification). Similarly, it is a mitzva to escort the dead body to burial, as it is for the family to sit seven days (*shiva*) in mourning for the deceased.

The most distinctive statements of respect for the residual dignity of the deceased (affirming the great value of the living) are two laws dealing with the dead body. One is the prohibition of *nivul ha-meit* – sullying/degrading/negatively modifying the body. To cut off limbs, to in any way carve, cut, or mark up the body, is a desecration/degradation of the dead.[28] Compounding this restriction is the law of *issur hana'a* – a prohibition of using the body or its parts, even for utilitarian purposes. (In the nineteenth century, people snatched bodies from graves and sold them for use in experiments or medical training.)

The halakha is very clear here. So is the theological reasoning. Profiting from the body or its parts is a way of saying – in the very last

---

27. See b. *Shabbat* 85a.
28. B. *Bava Batra* 154a; b. *Ḥullin* 11a.

contact between the living and the dead – that the deceased had only cash value. It denies this human being's intrinsic dignity – let alone his or her infinite value. Deriving benefit from the dead is equivalent to saying: This is my last chance to get anything out of this person.

True honor should be not-for-profit; respect for the dead is rooted in love and relationship. Hence the mitzva that all acts of caring for the dead be done without pay, showing that this care is being provided by someone who loved or related to this *tzelem Elokim*.

The *issur hana'a*, then, affirms the value of the living person. In the generation after the *Sho'ah* – after the Nazis sought not only to wipe out the Jews but to degrade them – the statement made by the laws of *nivul ha-meit* and *issur hana'a* is even clearer. The final expression of contempt and debasement before killing the Jews was to shave off their hair (for use in textiles), and afterward the Nazis robbed the corpses of their gold teeth. The bodies were burned, the ashes used for fertilizer and for road traction in winter. In essence, the Nazis were saying that the Jews weren't human beings; they were "things," to be exploited to the last drop.[29] The countertestimony in the laws of *issur nivul ha-meit* and *issur hana'a* – in upholding human dignity in life and death – shines all the more nobly by comparison.[30]

---

29. The rumor that the Nazis used Jewish body fat to make soap seems to be unfounded. Nevertheless, the prevalence of the story reflects the widespread recognition that the Nazis tried to dehumanize the Jews and turn them into objects, stuff. On this Nazi policy, see Irving Greenberg, *The Jewish Way: Living the Holidays* (New York: Summit Books, 1988), 316–17.

30. The Talmud bases the laws of respect for the dead on biblical verses. Thus, the commandment of immediate burial and the prohibition of mutilating a corpse are adduced from the Torah's prohibition of keeping the body of an executed criminal hanging all night. Rather, "you shall surely bury him the same day" (Deut. 21:22–23). The Talmud reasons that if such respect is to be shown to an executed criminal, it must a fortiori be shown to a regular person (see b. *Sanhedrin* 46b). Similarly, the prohibition of benefit from the dead is derived by a linguistic comparison of the death of Miriam and the law of the *egla arufa* (b. *Avoda Zara* 29b). These *derashot*, in turn, are drawn upon in modern responsa to make distinctions and rule in medical ethics cases.

Nonetheless, I follow Rabbi Soloveitchik's view that halakhic man partners with God in repairing the world, and that "the telos of the halakha *in all its multifold aspects and manifestations*" (emphasis added) is to make the real world "conform to the ideal world." The *derashot*, then, should be seen as *asmakhtot* (mnemonic connections).

II. CHANGING THE BALANCE OF FORCES
BETWEEN LIFE AND DEATH

The laws of *kevod ha-meit* were articulated by the sages to protect human dignity after death. In their age, one could do little to save the living from death, so it was all the more important to uphold the dignity of human beings after they passed away. In modern times, however, especially through science and medicine, people have taken up what the Rav calls "the mandate from the Almighty" to perfect creation; in medicine, particularly, this means to advance and extend life.

This profoundly religious quest, as defined in Judaism, constitutes the pursuit of the realization of the human task – both to self-realize through developing human capabilities and to help perfect the world. As Rabbi Soloveitchik puts it:

> The objective…can be only one, namely, that which God has put up before him, to be "man," to be himself. Man is a dignified being and to be human means to live with dignity.[31]

The Rav translates this dignity directly into upholding life, and into medical action to save lives:

> Man of old who could not fight disease and succumbed in multitudes to yellow fever or any other plague with degrading helplessness could not lay claim to dignity. Only the man who builds hospitals, discovers therapeutic techniques, and saves lives is blessed with dignity.[32]

To achieve these cures, the human must be creative. He must gain "mastery over his environment" and assume responsibility for the world. "Only when man rises to the heights of freedom and action and creativity of mind does he begin to implement the mandate of dignified responsibility entrusted to him by his Maker." What is the doctor/scientist/researcher doing? "He engages in creative work, trying to imitate his Maker (*imitatio*

The overarching goal is to advance life and show respect for a person's *tzelem Elokim* even after death.

31. Joseph B. Soloveitchik, "The Lonely Man of Faith," *Tradition* 7, no. 2 (1965): 13.
32. Ibid., 13–14.

Dei)."[33] This is one of the highest expressions of religious life. In this manner, the human fulfills *ve-halakhta bi-derakhav*, acting like God.[34]

III. HEART TRANSPLANTS: THE PROBLEM OF TRADITIONAL THINKING

Heart transplants represent an amazing extension of doctors' capacity to save lives – all the more dramatic because cardiac disease is the leading cause of death in the United States and in most developed countries. One instinctively thinks of heart surgeons as Godlike, for since the beginning of humanity, no one has survived once the heart was removed.

Of course, some will acknowledge this feat as an extraordinary fulfillment of our divine mandate to increase human dignity and take responsibility by curing disease, rolling back death, and extending life. Such proponents will therefore be supportive halakhically.[35] This viewpoint was best expressed by Rabbi Chaim David Regensberg of Chicago, in a posthumously published article:[36]

The transplantation of a new heart into a person's body took the world by storm and surprise, though organ transplants are nothing new. For years now [doctors] have been successfully transplanting vital organs – such as the kidneys – into human bodies. Nevertheless, successful heart transplantation feels unique.

השתלה של לב חדש בגוף האדם הסעיר והפתיע את כל העולם, למרות שהשתלת אברים אינו נושא חדש, וכבר כמה שנים שמצליחים להשתיל בגוף האדם אברים שהנשמה תלויה בהם כגון כליות וכדומה, בכל זאת יש לנו הרגשה מיוחדת להצלחת ההשתלה של הלב.

---

33. Ibid., 15. For the Rav, the two creation stories in Genesis represent two aspects of humanity. Adam the First is called upon, by his nature and by God, to master the world; he is driven to perfect it. Adam the Second is called upon, by his nature and by God, to live more inwardly, relating to God and to fellow human beings. Adam the Second is redeemed by "surrender" and acceptance of what is in relationship with God rather than by changing the world. Of course, the Rav calls for realizing the Adam the Second aspect of the human as well, but mastering the physical world and improving life are unquestionably a central religious calling of humanity.

34. See Deut. 28:9 and 10:12, and the various midrashim on these verses.

35. See Soloveitchik, "Lonely Man," 14–15, cited earlier in this essay.

36. Chaim David Regensberg, "Heart Transplants," *Halakha u-Refu'a* 2 (1981): 3–8 [Hebrew].

Our emotional relationship with the heart is evidently considerable. As Rabbi Yehuda ha-Levi said, "The heart is the king of the organs." The entire world stood stunned by this important achievement, not only because it advanced medical science as part of the biological revolution taking place in medicine, but because we feel ourselves standing on the brink of new horizons. [Heart transplants] open the gates of knowledge before us, so we recognize the greatness of humanity and creation. With great feeling we read the verse "How great are Your deeds, O Lord" (Ps. 104:24), how wondrous Your creation. We cannot even guess where this scientific advance will take us. "My soul praises the Lord; …You wear splendor and glory" (ibid. 104:1)

כנראה שהיחס שלנו אל הלב הוא רב, כמאמרו של ר' יהודה הלוי - הלב הוא מלך האברים. וכל העולם עומד משתומם לתופעה חשובה זו, לא רק בשביל הקידמה המדעית במישור הרפואי, מהמהפיכה הביולוגית של מדע הרפואה, אלא הוא מרגיש שאנו עומדים בפני התגלות אופקים חדשים, הוא פותח לפנינו שערי בינה להכיר בגדלות האדם והבריאה, ובהרגש רב אנו קוראים "מה רבו מעשיך ה'" מה נפלאים מעשיך. וטרם אנו יכולים לעמוד ולצפות עד היכן תוליך התקדמות מדעית זאת. "ברכי נפשי את ה' הוד והדר לבשת".

Others will be troubled by humans' exercising such Godlike powers. These reservations are likely part of the resistance to this treatment on the part of many *posqim*. These authorities are less sympathetic to the needs of medicine and more focused on protecting inherited halakhic values such as prohibiting *nivul ha-meit* or upholding the inherited definition of death.

Heart transplants raise additional halakhic issues beyond dignity and respect for the dead body. Most troubling is how to establish the state of death. In talmudic times, death was established primarily by cessation of breathing.[37] The person's nose (חוטמו) would be checked. If there was no breath, then the person would be declared dead. Conversely, if there was breath, everything possible to save his or her life had to be done,

---

37. B. *Yoma* 85a; j. *Yoma* 8:5. The Talmud discusses the need to check the vital signs of a person crushed by a collapsed building on Shabbat or Yom Tov. If the person is alive, the holy day must be violated to save him or her; if the person is not, he or she should be left until day's end. Of course, as long as the person's condition is unknown, he or she is dug out, but once enough of the person is uncovered to check for vital signs, this examination must take place.

even violating the Sabbath. The Talmud also discusses an alternative test: checking either the heart (ליבו) or the chest (טיבורו), depending on the manuscript of the Babylonian Talmud one uses (the Jerusalem Talmud has only the latter). Whether this test suffices to declare a person dead is debated, and whether heartbeat without breathing signifies life is a key problem in the talmudic passage.[38]

Throughout history, this question has been academic, but in modern times a person no longer breathing can be hooked up to a ventilator, and the heart can keep beating. If this heartbeat means the person is still alive, the heart would have to stop in order to declare the person dead. This position would make heart donation impossible.

To continue functioning in a new body, the organ to be transplanted must be harvested quickly; organs deteriorate rapidly once oxygen is no longer being brought to them by breathing and blood circulation. The heart deteriorates precipitously after death. Were doctors to wait until it stopped and all breathing ceased for several minutes, the heart would no longer be usable.

Today doctors keep a patient on a ventilator when there is no longer spontaneous breathing, and keep the heart pumping until the moment of excision.[39] However, many halakhists object that one of the

---

38. This essay is not the place to lay out the discussion. For more details, see the essays by Rabbis Yoel Bin Nun and Yaakov Love in this volume, and by Dina Najman and Rabbi Ariel Picard in the organ donation volume.

39. The advance of medicine – in particular, the invention of mechanical ventilators that could keep patients breathing after all normal functions ceased – necessitated a new definition of death. Many people died while on a ventilator, yet their breathing continued, driven by the machine. At what point could you turn off the ventilator on the grounds that the person was deceased beyond hope of recovery? In 1968, a Harvard Medical School committee published its findings under the title "A Definition of Irreversible Coma: Report of the Ad Hoc Committee of the Harvard Medical School to Examine the Definition of Brain Death" (*JAMA* 205, no. 6: 337–40). The committee defined permanent loss of brain function (= irreversible coma) as decisive proof of death. In 2008, after reviewing various positions and medical controversies, the President's Council on Bioethics adopted the Harvard criteria when confirmed by a flat electroencephalogram (EEG) twice within twenty-four hours. If not for this definition, essentially only the living could donate organs, and heart transplantation would therefore be impossible. Now, however, organs could be harvested before they deteriorated, i.e., immediately after brain death was established, while breathing and circulation were maintained artificially.

halakhic criteria of death (cessation of heartbeat) is not fulfilled before the removal of the heart, and therefore its removal constitutes the killing of the donor. In this view, cardiac transplantation is nothing less than murder.[40] Traditionalists – in medicine as in theology – charge that the new definition was not objective, that it was motivated by the desire to harvest organs for transplantation.[41]

The "brain death" definition of death was particularly ill-received by some (most?) traditional *posqim*. Many were repelled by the thought that classic halakhic rulings would be overruled, even in the name of *piqu'aḥ nefesh*. They dug in to uphold the tradition – whatever the cost in preventing the saving of lives. The problem they saw was that the classic halakhic criteria for death – irreversible cessation of breathing and circulation – were not being met before harvesting. Of course, this was a catch-22; if those criteria were met, the chances of successful transplant were drastically reduced.

Although neither a *poseq* nor a physician myself, it would seem to me that the best response to the gap between the new brain death criteria and the talmudic requirement would have been to say that the sages used their best judgment to establish death, based on the limited scientific capacity of their time.[42] Detecting breathing or heartbeat in a person lying under a pile of stones by holding a feather or some other indicator under the nose is hardly a precise or reliable procedure. Additionally, the realities before modern medicine were very different. Before

---

40. An ancillary prohibition is invoked as well. The heart donor is by definition close to death, and it is forbidden to treat a *goses* in any way – even minimally and with intention to heal – lest one hasten the person's death (*Shulḥan Arukh* YD 339:1).

41. See Dick Teresi, *The Undead: Organ Harvesting, the Ice-Water Test, Beating-Heart Cadavers – How Medicine Is Blurring the Lines Between Life and Death* (New York: Pantheon Books, 2012). Teresi argues that professional pressures to declare patients dead are undercutting the integrity of these decisions.

42. See, for example, b. *Pesaḥim* 94b, where Jewish and gentile sages debate (1) whether the celestial sphere revolves and the planets and stars are fixed (the gentile sages), or the sphere is fixed and the heavenly bodies revolve (the Jewish sages); (2) whether the sun travels beneath the sky by day and above the sky by night (the Jewish sages) or beneath the sky by day and below the earth by night (the gentile sages). Rabbi Yehuda ha-Nasi uses scientific observations to resolve the argument and in the second case accepts the conclusion of the gentile sages based on scientific evidence. Nobody in that passage claims that the sages' views are revelation-based and therefore authoritative. (Need I add that both sides' views are pre-Copernican and incorrect by the standards of contemporary science?)

the advent of ventilators, there was no question of "Who's breathing, the patient or the machine?" and no way to maintain the pumping of the heart after the cessation of respiration.

Posqim should have welcomed the kind of precision and analysis now available through electroencephalograms or nuclide scans – not to mention that contemporary medicine has established that the brain controls all higher-level coordinated activities.[43] The latter fact means that cessation of brain activity as measured by EEG or nuclide scans is the definitive way of establishing irreversible death, more precise than checking for breath or pulse.

Some *posqim* did take this approach, notably Rabbi Regensberg, in the article quoted above:

אולם בימינו שיש לנו אמצעים
להפעיל שוב את הלב אחר שפסק
לפעול ולהפעיל שוב את הריאות
אחר שפסקו לנשום שוב אין
לסמוך על בדיקת הנשימה, ובזמן
הזה קובעים על פי פעילות המוח
ואם המכונה הנקראת עלקטרא
ענסעפאלא גראם, היא שלילית
שכל פעילות המוח הופסקה
ואין הוא ממשיך להשפיע על
הגוף והגוף עצמו אבד לו לגמרי
הרגשתו, הרי מצב האדם כמו
'פסיק רישא' ואז אנו קובעים
בבטחה את מותו של האדם הזה.

However, in our day we have ways of restarting the heart after it has stopped, and of restarting or continuously pumping the lungs after they have ceased to function. For this reason we can no longer rely on checking for breath. Instead, nowadays, we determine [death] based on brain function, so if the machine known as the electroencephalogram shows that all activity in the brain has ceased and that it no longer has any effect on the body, and the body has lost all sensation, this situation is comparable to that of a beheaded person, and thus we determine with certainty the death of the person.

Rabbi Regensberg recognizes that scientific advances have made the breath test obsolete. He accepts that brain death constitutes more accurate and definitive proof of death and that an EEG can fulfill the halakhic need for such proof before transplantation. Such an approach advances lifesaving by enabling organ transplantation on a grand scale.

---

43. To put it bluntly, the Talmud's criteria are more limited and less developed than contemporary science and sometimes conflict with it.

Yet many *posqim* objected to brain death as an acceptable definition of death to be honored in halakhic rulings.[44] This rejection reflects three powerful forces in the culture of *posqim*: Orthodoxy's inbuilt resistance to change; lack of scientific training, which makes *posqim* less understanding of medical procedures as well as of medicine's potential accomplishments;[45] and suspicion (or even hostility) regarding doctors.

---

44. See, for instance, Rabbi Eliezer Waldenburg, "The Prohibition of Transplanting the Heart or Liver from One Person to Another," in *Establishing the Moment of Death* (ed. Mordechai Halperin; Jerusalem: Dr. Falk Schlesinger Institute of Medical-Halachic Research, 2006), 84–96 [orig. *Sefer Assia 7* (5754/1993–94), 149–62] [Hebrew].

45. In an article prohibiting heart transplants, Rabbi Shmuel ha-Levi Wosner writes:

...השתלת לב (או כבד)...היא פעולה	...the transplantation of a heart (or liver)...
נגד מציאות בריאת האדם ושינוי	is a procedure contradicting the reality of the
גמור במעשה בראשית להעביר אברי	creation of humanity and a complete change in
הנפש מאדם לחברו נגד השגחת	the laws of creation to move the life-giving or-
הבורא בבריאת האדם - מי התיר	gans from one person to another, thereby going
להם לעסוק בזה?	against divine providence in the creation of the human. Who gave them permission to do this?

Wosner, "On Heart Transplants," *Assia* 42–43 (5747/1986–87): 92–94.

Compare Rabbi Shlomo Goren's enthusiastic discussion:

השתלת לב מלאכותי באדם שהיה	The transplanting of an artificial heart into a
חולה אנוש בסולט-לייק סיטי	deathly ill person in Salt Lake City, in the Unites
בארצות הברית עוררה בצדק	States, has rightly aroused breathless excitement
התרגשות עוצרת נשימה בעולם	all over the world. At this point, now that more
כולו, כעת לאחר שעברו כבר למעלה	than three weeks have passed, and the patient,
משלושה שבועות והחולה ד"ר בארני	Dr. Barney Clark, is alive and well, and improv-
קלארק חי וקיים, ומתאושש קימעא	ing a bit every day from his critical condition
קימעא ממצבו הקריטי שהיה נתון בו	before and after the transplant – one can guess
לפני ההשתלה ואחריה אפשר כבר	that this will not turn out to be a failed or one-
להניח שלפנינו לא נסיון נפל או חד	time attempt. Rather, we are standing on the
פעמי. אלא אנו עומדים בפני מהפך	brink of a serious and bold revolution in medi-
רציני ונועז בעולם הרפואה המהווה	cine that is nothing less than a breakthrough in
פריצת דרך לחיים ארוכים יותר לבני	human longevity, since heart disease nowadays
האדם. באשר מחלות הלב מהוות	is the main cause of death. I'm sure that all of
כיום את הגורם הראשי לתמותה.	humanity is joined in prayer and hope that this
בטחוני שכל האנושות שותפה	blessed trial will be just the beginning and will
לתפילה ותקוה, שהנסיון המבורך	turn into a common and safe treatment for any
הזה יתפתח וישתכלל, יצלח ויהפך	heart requiring replacement or repair.
לאמצעי ריפוי שכיח, בטוח, והולם	
כל לב הזקוק לחידוש ולריפוי.	

Rabbi Shlomo Zalman Auerbach captured the attitude of "no change" when he articulated the halo effect: *Anything* the rabbis said (even scientific judgments) is sacred and unchangeable. In conversation with Rabbi Prof. Abraham S. Abraham, he said the following:

...מכיון שאין שום הגדרה כזאת
[של מוות גזע המוח] בש"ס אין
אנו יכולים לחדש הגדרה כזו
בימינו, ורק כשתקום סנהדרין
יהיה בכוחם לקבוע אם מוות גזע
המוח נקרא מוות, או לא. ועד
אז, אמר לי הגאון זצ"ל, אסור
להוציא ממנו לבו או כל אבר
אחר כל זמן שלבו עוד פועם
בקרבו.

...since there is no definition like this [i.e., brainstem death] in the Talmud, we cannot create any such definition in our day. Only when a new Sanhedrin is formed will [it] have the authority to determine whether brainstem death is defined as death or not. Until then...it is forbidden to remove a person's heart or any other organ as long as the person's heart beats inside him.[46]

I would argue that such attitudes and claims flow from non-halakhic factors. They are the outcome of the yeshivish cultural environment in which most *posqim* are trained and live. In this setting, interpretations of sacred texts are real; scientific facts are not. The definition of death then becomes the conclusion derived from a talmudic passage, not the result of a medical finding or the correlative of a specific physical state.

Goren, "On Artificial Hearts in Halakha," in Goren, *Torat ha-Refu'a* (ed. Yisrael Tamari; Jerusalem: *Ha-Idra Rabba*, 2001), 95 [Hebrew]. Goren clearly recognizes the religious value of this revolutionary medical development.

The transplant occurred on December 2, 1982. Barney Clark, in fact, survived only 112 days, and in a second attempt, patient William Schroeder survived 620 days. Both were given Jarvik-7 hearts. In current medical practice, artificial hearts are used only as short-term solutions while awaiting a donor heart. For more information, see http://www.wired.com/thisdayintech/2009/12/dayintech_1202jarvikheart/.

Although the artificial heart never proved to be the panacea Rabbi Goren had hoped, the difference in attitude toward scientific advancement between him and Wosner couldn't be starker. Sadly, Goren himself suffered from heart problems and died of a heart attack in 1994, at age seventy-seven.

46. Abraham S. Abraham, *Nishmat Avraham* YD 339. This source is quoted in Asher Bush et al., *Halachic Issues in the Determination of Death and in Organ Transplantation: Including an Evaluation of the Neurological "Brain Death" Standard* (2010), 63 n. 160, although the reference there is incorrect.

The fact that a textual deduction cuts off a medical procedure and condemns any number of patients to die (in the absence of the treatment) is of little import. The *posqim* are conditioned to ignore the human consequences of their rulings. Moreover, there is no accountability if the rulings don't work in real life or prove ruinously expensive. Given the scant self-awareness and methodological sophistication in their culture, most *posqim* insist that their thinking is pure halakha. They often contend that those sympathetic to halakhic change are the ones importing outside cultural values. As Rabbi Yisrael Salanter once said: The greatest *negia* (distorting bias/self-interest) is *tzidkus* (the conviction that one is pure and righteous).[47]

Most halakhists' treatments of the issue portrayed doctors as ready – even driven – to snatch organs from living (but deathly ill) people for the benefit of younger, more vital patients. The claim was that physicians gave less weight to the life of a very sick person than to a more vital person – whereas the halakha treats all life, even that of the terminally ill, as infinitely sacred. While there's no reason to romanticize all doctors as idealists, it is equally prejudicial to imply that as a class, physicians are prepared or even likely to harvest organs and end lives prematurely for the sake of another person's cure. Not to mention that major bodies of laws and medical ethics prohibit such behaviors.

Compounding their rejection of standard medical procedures, many *posqim* asserted that the talmudic definition of death was revelatory in nature, that it was the word of God. This conviction turned halakhists into infallible judges of science and attributed divine authority to talmudic statements that were manifestly human.[48] The *posqim's*

---

47. Quoted in Dov Katz, *Tnu'at ha-Musar*, vol. 1 (Tel Aviv: Bitan ha-Sefer, 1952), 309.

48. I acknowledge that Rabbi Moshe Sofer made the same claim in his treatment of the criterion of death (*Ḥatam Sofer* YD 138). However, his statement is part of his overall ideology that "anything new is prohibited by the Torah." This position grew out of a community policy of rejecting any halakhic modification of custom – even where the traditional halakha itself had been flexible – lest any new thinking or change in practice strengthen Reform Judaism and assimilation. While this outlook can be justified as a defensive strategy in the nineteenth century, it's not workable or good for the advancement of Judaism in the twenty-first. We are long past the absolute power of modernity. Many Jews are open to reengaging or deepening their halakhic

fundamentalism is the climax of the "no change" ideology and of the
Ḥaredi claim – developed in the past two hundred years – of the inerrant
authority of the *Gedolim*, who speak with the power of *ru'aḥ ha-qodesh*
(holy spirit), not of their own intellect.[49]

The obvious self-interest that blinds people into making such
extravagant pronouncement should be rejected – at least by the Modern Orthodox and Jews in general, whose education has shown them
that the accuracy of the sages in science and in such matters as history
is not necessarily governed by the standard of contemporary research.

This stance takes nothing away from our commitment to the
divinity of the Torah or the Oral Law.[50] If the sages were here before
us, I would wager that they would be the first to affirm that they reasonably used the science of their day to establish facts as best they could.
They too would affirm that the products of ancient medicine or Greek
science should not be given absolute or eternal validity by mistakenly
wrapping them in the mantle of sacred revelation.

In the *Guide for the Perplexed*, Rambam writes that one should
accept the results of one's scientific study and follow the most convincing
science in explaining natural facts (in this case, the motion of heavenly
bodies). He praises the sages for yielding on an astronomical question

---

observance. But they won't accept erroneous scientific statements in the name of the
Torah; nor will most believe the manifestly incorrect claim that nothing can change
or ever has changed in the Jewish tradition.

49. On *Da'at Torah* and the authority of the *Gedolim*, see Jacob Katz, "*Da'at Torah*: The
Unqualified Authority Claimed for Halakhists," *Jewish History* 11, no. 1 (1997): 41–50;
Lawrence Kaplan, "*Daas Torah*: A Modern Conception of Rabbinic Authority," in
Rabbinic Authority and Personal Autonomy (ed. Moshe Sokol; Orthodox Forum;
Northvale, NJ, and London: Jason Aronson, 1992), 1–60; and Gershon Bacon,
"*Da'at Torah* and the Birth Pangs of the Messiah," *Tarbiz* 52 (1983/5743), 497–508
[Hebrew]. In the nineteenth century, the embattled Catholic Church declared itself
unchanging as well, citing papal infallibility. However, this claim was restricted to
matters of faith as opposed to science and medicine.

50. See Moses Maimonides, *The Guide for the Perplexed* (trans. M. Friedländer), II:8,
45, and III:14, 55–59. See also Rabbi Avraham ben ha-Rambam's *Milḥamot Hashem*
(ed. Rabbi Reuven Margoliot), where he represents his father as believing that one
should follow the best contemporary science and philosophy, and that the sages
followed their contemporary science, so no one should ascribe prophetic authority
to their scientific views. Rather, one should accept the truth whatever its source.

and following the views of the (gentile) scholars, because "everyone accepts that which appears to him established by proof."[51] He points out that certain talmudic statements on astronomical matters are erroneous in light of contemporary science. Says Rambam,

> You must not…expect that everything our sages say…[should be correct by contemporary scientific standards], for mathematics were not fully developed in those days; and their statements were not based on the authority of the prophets, but on the knowledge which they either themselves possessed or derived from contemporary men of science.[52]

It follows that one should not reject the conclusions of science on the grounds that all the statements of these rabbis have the authority of Revelation ("of the prophets"). Rather, if possible, the words of the rabbis or of the Torah should be interpreted "in such a manner that they agree with fully established facts [of science]." He concludes, "It is the duty of every educated and honest man to do so."[53]

The contemporary *Haredi* attribution of divinity to statements contradicted by reality is not made any more authoritative or correct by the fact that other *Gedolim* believed this way. Nor should we accept this assertion on the basis of a general claim of inerrancy on the part of *Gedolim*. Modern Orthodox (or other types of) Jews are not bound by an ideology of *Da'at Torah*, developed in modern times to ward off the persuasive views and claims of modern culture. The claim of infallibility is equally refuted by the facts of Jewish history. Many *Gedolim*, including the Vilna Gaon, disqualified Hasidism as a religious movement. In the end, Hasidism provided the most powerful base for the continuation of Torah Judaism in Europe – up to the *Sho'ah*. Most *Gedolim* opposed Zionism. This disastrous position reduced the growth and size of the modern, pre-state Jewish community (in the Land of Israel); as a result, the State of Israel was much smaller at birth than it could have been.

---

51. Maimonides, *Guide*, II:8, 48.
52. Ibid., III:14, 59.
53. Ibid.

Anti-Zionism also left millions exposed to destruction in the Holocaust, whereas they could have been saved had they gone to Palestine.

IV. HEART TRANSPLANTS: RABBI MOSHE FEINSTEIN AND THE CHIEF RABBINATE OF ISRAEL

Rabbi Moshe Feinstein

Despite his lack of medical training or modern education, Rabbi Moshe Feinstein had a highly sympathetic conduit for scientific information as well as a source of empathy with the needs of medicine in the form of his learned son-in-law, Rabbi Dr. Moshe Tendler, whom he trusted and respected. To his credit, as a result of continual updates on the state of medicine, Rabbi Feinstein changed his rulings in some cases.

Rabbi Feinstein issued four responsa on heart transplants, ranging from rejection of heart transplants and brain death criteria to affirmation of both.[54] Finally, on 1 Kislev 5745 (November 25, 1984), just a few months before his death, he wrote a letter to a Dr. Elliot Bondi. This brief responsum was dictated in Yiddish, typed and translated by a student of Rabbi Feinstein's, and bore a note confirming that he had read it in its entirety before signing it. In this letter, he accepts brain death as established by the Harvard criteria as valid halakhically.[55]

Rabbi Feinstein's first responsum (IM YD 2:174; dated 19 Tammuz 5728/July 15, 1968) prohibited heart transplants, calling them "double murder."[56] This judgment is extremely harsh, especially since donors were tested before harvesting and judged to be dead by EEGs, etc. Furthermore, transplant recipients were generally very close to death, having been offered this option because they had little to lose, so to speak. Both donor and

---

54. See the expanded discussion of each individual responsum in David Shabtai, *Defining the Moment: Understanding Brain Death in Halakhah* (New York: Shoresh Press, 2012), 184–269. For an alternative view (and critique of Shabtai), see Rabbi Daniel Reifman's essay in this collection. See also Rabbi Ariel Picard's essay in the organ donation volume. In addition to his responsa, Rabbi Feinstein had countless conversations on this topic; many were reported.

55. This letter was published posthumously in IM YD 4:54 (1996).

56. Rabbi Binyamin Walfish quotes Rabbi Soloveitchik as saying the same. See the interview with Rabbi Walfish in this volume.

recipient were arguably at least *treifot* (people who will die within twelve months). While *treifot* are not allowed to be murdered in halakha, one who kills a human *treifa* is not judged – or punished – as a murderer.[57]

Moreover, there are strong halakhic views that a *treifa* who is irreversibly close to death may give up his life and grant permission to use his organs in order to save another person. There are likewise strong views that terminating the life of such a *treifa* is not considered murder.[58] Rabbi Feinstein gives no weight – not even as extenuating circumstances – to the fact that the doctors are trying to overcome an otherwise terminal disease and thus heed the call of "*ve-rappo yerappei* – he shall surely heal" (Exod. 21:19). This verse is understood in the Talmud as God's instruction to humans to cure disease and heal injuries, thus validating the practice of medicine in Jewish tradition.[59]

Furthermore, Rabbi Feinstein gives doctors no credit for their ethical guidelines in research.[60] The doctors review with the patient his or her grave medical condition; explain the research treatment whereby they are trying to overcome or cure the illness; and outline the risks and likelihood of success/failure, including the long odds. The patient must then consent before treatment starts. In effect, the initial cardiac transplant recipients knew the chances were abysmal (although compared to inevitable death!) but agreed because their deaths might very well pave the way for saving others in the future. Giving such permission – risking one's life to save another – is recognized by many *posqim* as a legitimate right.

Far from acknowledging the legitimacy of informed consent – not to mention that countless negligence lawyers would pounce on any questionable procedure and sue over a bad outcome – Rabbi Feinstein

---

57. See, for example, the review in Rabbi Judah Dick, "Organ Donation from a Moribund Patient to Save a Person's Life," in *Establishing the Moment*, 224–32 [229–32] [Hebrew].

58. Ibid., 231–32.

59. See b. *Bava Qamma* 85a and Tosafot ad loc., s.v. *she-nitna reshut le-rofei lerappot*. See also *Torah Temima*, Exod. 20:19, para. 145.

60. To be fair, even many doctors criticized the ethical casualness of heart surgeon Christiaan Barnard of Cape Town; as this was before the introduction of immunosuppressants, almost all heart recipients died within weeks or months.

accused physicians of lying and tricking patients into being killed. Understandably, he was deeply troubled by the high death rate and brief survival of the initial transplant recipients.[61] However, he ignored the fact that if the patient wasn't told the truth about the likelihood of survival with and without the treatment, the physician would be violating the requirement of informed consent. Also, it's hard to accept Rabbi Feinstein's statement that donors could have lived on for years if not for the transplants; what patient would agree to a transplant highly likely to soon be fatal if he knew that without it he could live on for years? Only someone misinformed would make such a wild decision. Clearly, Rabbi Feinstein sees the medical profession as consisting of people with no regard for human life and no ethical restraints.

Moreover, Rabbi Feinstein dismisses the fact that the authorities would restrain and punish such malpractice, and he wonders how any country allows doctors to experiment on their patients in this way. These statements are the words of someone who considers most doctors wicked, and the government incompetent and uncaring. These are the words of someone with little or no firsthand contact (and no empathy) with the profession or its regulators.

Rabbi Feinstein's passion is ethically motivated. He is outraged by the very low survival rates of transplant recipients. In a responsum written ten years later (ḤM 2:72; 1 Adar 11 5738/March 10, 1978), he

---

61. Even Rabbi Regensberg ("Heart Transplants," 8), who affirmed transplants and other scientific advances, wrote before immunosuppressants were used, and therefore doubted the ethics of a rabbi advocating heart transplantation:

והלכה למעשה, כיון שטרם ניתוח זה הוכר כמוצלח וטרם קנה לו מהלכים רפואיים בעולם הרפואה והישועה. איני חושב שיש רב בישראל שיקח עליו את האחריות ליעץ לעשות ניתות מסוכן זה למרות שלאדם החולה אין מה להפסיד הרבה שחייו חולניים ואפשר שהם קצרים, אך בכל זאת אין הוא נכנס לספק שמא יצליח בניתוח קשה זה.	Practically speaking, since this surgery [heart transplantation] is not yet considered successful and hasn't yet received wide acceptability in the medical world, I don't think a rabbi should take responsibility for advising people to submit to this dangerous procedure. Though the patient has little to lose, for his life is full of illness and possibly very short, nevertheless, [the rabbi] shouldn't enter into a calculation that maybe this difficult operation will succeed.

reiterates that transplants are "double murder."[62] He refers to the work of Dr. Norman Shumway of Stanford University, an American pioneer in heart transplantation.[63] Shumway's initial results were indeed so poor that they drew a professional rebuke and led to his suspension. Nevertheless, in condemning Shumway (and the profession), Rabbi Feinstein shows little awareness of the process of experimentation and change whereby medicine has made major strides in saving lives. In exploring why transplants failed, Shumway himself developed cyclosporine, a drug that suppresses the body's immune system which eventually attacks all transplants as "foreign bodies." This breakthrough dramatically boosted survival rates in all transplants. But the achievement is no thanks to the decisors who would have stopped his practice and labeled it murder long before he discovered how to overcome the body's rejection of transplants.

According to the United States Department of Health and Human Services, as of July 2011 survival rates for cardiac transplants at one- three- and five-year intervals are at 88%, 79%, and 73%, respectively. This triumph of medicine saves thousands of lives annually, limited only by the shortage of donor hearts. I regret to say that these lives are being saved only because many doctors – Jewish and non-Jewish – defied or ignored the prohibitions applied by *posqim*. This supreme religious achievement – *piqu'aḥ nefesh* – goes on in the face of continuing opposition by many (most?) traditional *posqim*.

Unlike many other *posqim*, Rabbi Feinstein at least learned of the improved survival rates (from Rabbi Tendler) and changed his ruling. Rabbi Tendler also persuaded Rabbi Feinstein that the EEG and other medical tests – especially the radionuclide scan – that attest to the

---

62. According to Rabbi Moshe Tendler, this "double murder" comment in the later responsum applies only to patients in a persistent vegetative state (PVS), not to those considered dead by the Harvard criteria. Otherwise, Rabbi Feinstein would appear to reject brain death two years after reversing himself and accepting the Harvard criteria in his responsum written to Rabbi Tendler (IM YD 3:132, May 5, 1976). For a discussion of the problematics of Tendler's suggestion, see Shabtai, *Defining the Moment*, 249.

63. See *Responsa of Rav Moshe Feinstein*, vol. 1, *Care of the Critically Ill* (trans. Moshe Dovid Tendler; Hoboken: KTAV, 1985), 38, cited in Shabtai, *Defining the Moment*, 246.

cessation of all brain activity (including the brainstem) are reliable indicators of death; that although the patient's breathing is maintained by a ventilator, spontaneous respiration has irreversibly ceased. This is the state of death, although this definition goes against the fundamentalist reading of the Talmud that there must be no breathing before declaring the patient dead.[64]

Apparently Rabbi Tendler made his case more convincing halakhically by stating that the breathing criteria were still valid and would be applied to define most deaths – while suggesting that the new criteria suited the talmudic category of death by decapitation; Tendler described brain death as the *equivalent* of "physiological decapitation."[65] The Mishna in *Oholot* (1:6) states that in the case of decapitation, even if the body continues to move agitatedly (*pirkus*), these reflexive spasms don't change the fact that the person who has been decapitated is dead.

Rabbi Feinstein points to the injection of dye as part of the nuclide scan, one of the tests used to establish death by the Harvard criteria.[66] In brain dead patients, the injected radioisotope doesn't display in the brain, suggesting that the dye doesn't circulate there. Thus, the brain is "cut off" from the body – as in decapitation. (Rabbi Tendler also convinced Rabbi Feinstein that the tests were so benign that they didn't violate the Talmud's ban on hastening the death of a goses.) Based on this evidence, Rabbi Feinstein deemed a cardiac transplant halakhically legitimate and even a mitzva, for it is likely to save a life. As a corollary, he states that patients on a ventilator might continue

---

64. According to Rabbi Binyamin Walfish, Rabbi Joseph B. Soloveitchik went through a similar process of changing his views. At first he agreed with Rabbi Moshe Feinstein that heart transplants should be forbidden. However, with the advent of the apnea test and the introduction of immunosuppressants, he concluded that a declaration of brain death would suffice, and that the heart operation was viable enough for the patient to take the risk. For more details, see the interview with Rabbi Binyamin Walfish in this volume.

65. Moshe David Tendler, "Halakhic Death Means Brain Death," *Jewish Review* 3, no. 3 (January 1990 /Kislev 5750): 6, http://thejewishreview.org/articles/?filename=tendler3_3&route=fromsearch.

66. For a description of this test and other confirmatory exams, see Dr. Zelik Frischer's essay in this volume.

breathing even though they're already dead; such breathing is no sign of life (IM YD 3:132).

Despite Rabbi Feinstein's acceptance of brainstem death, more traditional *posqim* continue to reject it. Some have tried to neutralize this late responsum – by claiming it doesn't reflect Rabbi Feinstein's true views, or by directly disagreeing with him.[67] Some deny that Rabbi Feinstein wrote the responsum or upheld its validity. Some have claimed that he upheld his earlier views instead – or that the letter to Dr. Bondi is fraudulent. The Feinstein/Tendler families have tired of contradicting these baseless reports.[68]

Rabbi Shlomo Goren, Rabbi Shaul Yisraeli, and the Decision of the Chief Rabbinate

In Israel, on the other hand, things took a different turn, at least in the Religious Zionist community. In the early 1980s, two important religious leaders began to express strong support for brain death, arguing that this definition was actually the best fit for halakha.

Rabbi Shlomo Goren, already an outspoken supporter of organ donation, wrote an article in 1980 that touched upon brain death:

---

67. See, for example, the essays by Rabbi Dr. Mordechai Halperin, Dr. Israel Lewinstein, and Rabbis Shlomo Zalman Auerbach, Eliezer Waldenburg, Shmuel ha-Levi Wosner, and Shaul Yisraeli in *Establishing the Moment*, 65–72, 73–74, 78–80, 84–96, 97–99, 101–111. See also the letter to the editor from Dr. Rafael Tzvi Shulman and Prof. Yaakov Fleishman in the same work, 233–34. And see Shabtai, *Defining the Moment*, 217–43, and his various treatments of the views that disagree with Rabbi Feinstein, 309–338.

68. Some of their efforts are found in *Establishing the Moment*, 65–72, and in Rabbi Dovid Feinstein's essay in that volume, 75. Shabtai also deals with the denials or attempts to undermine the authenticity of Rabbi Feinstein's final rulings. Rabbi Feinstein wasn't a pioneer in *pesaq* on brain death, as evident in the next section. However, I have focused on his views because (a) he became the "establishment" *poseq* in American Orthodoxy in recent decades; (b) when rendering its permissive ruling, the Chief Rabbinate leaned heavily on his views and on his switch from prohibiting to permitting heart transplants; (c) his writings show that access to important new medical information can change *pesaq* (unfortunately, most *posqim* – especially in Israel, where Ḥaredi *posqim* dominate – lack (or ignore) access to changing medical data); (d) the ongoing attempt to overturn and/or deny his *pesaq* proves that the claim of *Da'at Torah* is invoked – and respected – only when it suits the Ḥaredi leadership.

והנה מבחינה רפואית הפסקת
הנשימה פירושה מות המוח,
דהיינו שהנזק בו בלתי-הפיך,
כי מרכז הנשימה הוא במוח.
ולכן ברור שלא מות קליני קובע
את המות לפי ההלכה, כי אם
מות המוח המתבטא מבחינת
ההלכה בהפסקת הנשימה.

Medically speaking, cessation of [auton-omous] respiration means the brain has died, i.e., the damage is irreversible, since the breathing center is in the brain. Therefore, it is clear that clinical death does not determine death according to halakha, but rather brain death [does], which is expressed in halakha as cessation of respiration.

אלא שקיימת אפשרות סבירה
לחייב הוספת הזמן הקריטי
אחרי הפסקת הנשימה, כי
לאחרונה אירעו מקרים בהם
הודגם במכשיר החשמלי
לבדיקת הפעילות של המוח
(EEG) רישום חשמלי שטוח
שפירושו אפס פעילות, ובכל זאת
חזרו החולים לחיים ולהכרה.
אלא שהדבר תלוי במשך הזמן
הקריטי שעובר אחרי הפסקת
הפעילות של המוח. כי רק לאחר
הזמן הקריטי, ללא פעילות,
נמצא המוח במצב של נזק
בלתי-הפיך על כל הפונקציות
שבו. שיטה זו המקובלת כעת
בעולם הרפואי כולו, תואמת את
ההלכה.

However, one could make the reasonable argument that a certain amount of time after cessation of respiration should be required, for recently there were cases where the machine that tests for electrical activity in the brain (EEG) showed a flat line, meaning no activity, but nevertheless the patients returned to life and consciousness. Rather, the matter is dependent upon a critical amount of time that must pass after the cessation of brain activity. Only after this critical time has elapsed without brain activity does the brain find itself in an irreversible situation regarding all its functions. This position, which is accepted nowadays throughout the medical establishment, fits well with halakha.[69]

Around the same time Rabbi Goren wrote these words, Rabbi Shaul Yisraeli, then one of the most respected *dayanim* in Israel, made a similar argument. He took the line that the views of the sages dovetailed

69. Shlomo Goren, "Discontinuing Life Support for a Terminal Patient," in Goren, *Torat ha-Refu'a* (ed. Yisrael Tamari; Jerusalem: Ha-Idra Rabba, 2001), 57–78 [63], originally published in *Me'orot* 2 (1980) [Hebrew].

with contemporary medical science and that when they speak of cessation of breathing as the definitive sign of death, they mean the end of involuntary breathing due to – and coincident with – damage to the brainstem. Rabbi Yisraeli felt more comfortable suggesting that Ḥazal, through holy spirit, had intuited the ultimate scientific truth:

ודברי חז"ל, וכפי שהבינם החת"ס, הם תואמים בדיוק את מסקנות המדע הרפואי, כפי שהם ידועים כיום. והוא שכל הפעולות הנעשות בגוף האדם שלא מכוח הכוונתו המודעת, וזה כולל את הנשימה, דהיינו הפעלת הריאות לשאיפה ונשיפה, הן נעשות ע"י גזע המוח, ורק על ידה ועל כן הפסקת הנשימה (להוציא מקרים שע"י סיבה חיצונית) הנה ללא תקנה כשבאה ע"י פגיעה בגזע המוח.

The words of the sages, as understood by the Ḥatam Sofer, fit perfectly with the conclusions of medical science as understood today, meaning that all bodily functions that don't stem from the person's conscious control – including respiration, i.e., breathing in and out – are controlled by the brainstem, and only by it. Therefore, cessation of respiration – ignoring cases where in which it occurs due to an outside stimulus – is irreversible if accompanied by damage to the brainstem.

ואילו הלב יש לו גם מנגנון פעולה עצמית (אלא שגזע המוח מווסת אותה). ועל כן, עם ביטול פעולת גזע המוח ע"י שנפגע, פעולת הריאות היא בלתי אפשרית. אכן, אין זה מחייב ביטול מידי של פעולת הלב, שכן כאמור, יש לו מנגנון עצמי, שיכול עוד להמשיך לפעול זמן מועט. אולם גם הלב יפסיק פעולתו, כיון שהריאות הממציאות לו את הדם המנוקה כדי שיעבירם לכל אברי הגוף, כולל המוח על כל חלקיו, הפסיק פעולתו, ממילא גם הלב יפסיק מלפעול. אולם זהו רק אחר עבור זמן מה.

Now the heart has its own independent controls, even if the brainstem helps pace it. Therefore, once brainstem function ceases, due to injury, lung function is no longer possible. However, this doesn't mean the heart must stop beating, for, as stated, it has its own independent controls that can continue running for a short time. In truth, the heart will stop functioning [soon afterward]: Since the lungs – which supply it with cleansed [= oxygenated] blood to pump to all the organs of the body (including the brain with all its parts) – have ceased to function, by necessity the heart will stop functioning as well. But this will happen only after a short time has passed.

ואם חבר יחוברו הריאות למכונת
הנשמה, ימשיך הוא להזרים הדם
בכוח פעולת המכונה, והלב יוכל
להמשיך לפעול בדרך זו. אולם
כיון שגזע המוח נהרס, הזרמת
הדם שוב לא תוכל להחיותו,
ולהפעיל שוב כל הקשור בו.
על כן נקבעה ההלכה כדעת
אותו מ"ד, שהכל תלוי בנשימה,
וכל שהדבר מתברר שהפסקת
הנשימה נובעת מהרס גזע המוח,
אין פעימת הלב אלא בחינת
"זנב הלטאה המפרכסת" (לשון
המשנה פ"א דאהלות) ודינו מת
לכל דבר. ומכאן הסבר ההלכה
שבפיקוח הגל משהגיעו לחוטמו
ונתברר שאין נשמה באפיו,
אעפ"י שמאד יתכן שהלב עדיין
פועם, אין משגיחים בזה....

Now if the lungs are connected to a respirator, such that it will continue to [cleanse][70] the blood due to the function of the machine, the heart can continue to function. However, since the brainstem is destroyed, the pumping of the blood cannot continue to support life. Therefore, the halakha was decided according to the opinion that everything depends on respiration. Therefore, whenever it becomes clear that the cessation of respiration stems from the destruction of the brainstem, heartbeat cannot be considered anything but the convulsions of a lizard's tail (as per the Mishna in *Oholot*, ch. 1), and the person is dead in every way. Hence the reason for the halakha that in clearing away rubble [on Shabbat or Yom Tov], once one arrives at the trapped person's nose, and it's clear he isn't breathing, though it's very possible his heart is still beating, we don't concern ourselves with this....

ומפליא הדבר, שחז"ל למרות
העדר המכשירים שהרופאים
משתמשים בהם בזמננו, כיוונו
ברוח קדשם ע"י עיון בכתובים
ללמוד מהם את מסתרי פליאות
הבורא במבנה הגוף של החי
והאדם!

It's amazing that the sages, even without the medical equipment doctors use nowadays, still zeroed in – with their holy spirit and through careful reading of biblical texts – on the marvelous secrets of the Creator in the structure of the body of animals and humans.

---

70. The Hebrew says, "to pump," but this seems to be a typo.

...החלטת הרבנות הראשית   ... The decision of the Chief Rabbinate
היא איפוא עפ"י יסודות ההלכה,   is therefore in line with the foundations
ודברי המערערים אין להם יסוד   of halakha, and the words of those who
בהלכה.   argue have no basis in halakha.[71]

The work of these important Israeli *posqim* led to the crucial decision of the Chief Rabbinate a few years later.[72] On 1 Marḥeshvan 5747/November 3, 1986, the Chief Rabbinate ruled that brain death was a valid measure of death for halakhic purposes and that heart transplants would be permitted at Hadassah Medical Center in Jerusalem.[73] Ashkenazic chief rabbi Avraham Shapira and his Sephardic counterpart, Mordechai Eliyahu, wrote their own briefs defending this decision.

Rabbi Eliyahu makes the most reasonable and commonsense suggestion that the religious authorities leave the determination of death to the medical authorities – just as Rambam writes regarding the determination that a person is a *ṭreifa*. Rabbi Eliyahu makes this statement in the context of the irony that the medical and halakhic communities require resuscitation, though the Talmud says someone who isn't breathing is dead, and yet many *posqim* seem to have trouble accepting that sometimes resuscitation is pointless, since the person is actually dead. Rabbi Eliyahu doesn't understand why physicians should be trusted in the first instance but not the second. With this contradiction in mind, he writes in his summation:

71. Shaul Yisraeli, "On the Permissibility of Heart Transplants Today," *Assia* 42–43 (5747/1986–87): 95–104 [Hebrew], http://98.131.138.124/articles/ASSIA/ASSIA7/R007167.asp. (The text quoted above appears at the beginning of the article's conclusion.)

72. Rabbi Yisraeli himself was on the committee that drafted the decision and is considered by many to have been its driving force, intellectually and spiritually. For more on Rabbi Yisraeli's position and its relationship to the Chief Rabbinate's decision, see the essay by one of Rabbi Yisraeli's main students, Rabbi Yosef Carmel, in this volume.

73. *Barkai* 4 (5747): 18–31; reprinted in Halperin, *Establishing the Moment*, 29–44; for extensive discussion, see the essays by Rabbi Prof. Daniel Sinclair and Rabbi Yoel Bin Nun in this volume and by Rabbi Ariel Picard in the organ donation volume.

...לִיתֵר דיוק - דור דור ודורשיו, דור דור ורופאיו, אם הם אומרים שחוסר נשימה אין זה עדיין הוכחה למוות כי אפשר להחיותו על ידי מכשירים, אולם, אם אומרים הרופאים שחוסר נשימה במקום זה הוא מוחלט ואי אפשר להחזירו, מפני שגזע המו[ח][74] נתקלקל והדבר נבדק כמה וכמה פעמים, אם כן הם אמרו והם אמרו. הם אומרים שלפעמים מחזירה מכונת הנשימה חיים, ואם הם אומרים שכעת אי אפשר להחזיר את הנשימה והוי מת....

...to be more precise – every generation and its interpreters, every generation and its physicians. If they say [in a particular case] that lack of breathing is not yet proof of death, since one can still be resuscitated by machinery, but the physicians say that lack of breath in a different case is a definite sign [of death] and resuscitation is impossible, since the brainstem is damaged, and this has been checked numerous times – if so, "they said and they said" [i.e., if we believe them in the first case, we should believe them in the second]. They say that sometimes a ventilator can restore life, and they say that sometimes this is impossible and the person is dead....

ואם הדבר נבדק על ידי מכשירים אף על פי שהמכשירים הללו לא היו פעם, כשם שהם אמינים לענין להחיותו כך הם נאמנים לענין שאין בו חיות.

If the matter is tested by machinery, though this machinery didn't exist in the past, [nevertheless,] just as [physicians] are trusted to resuscitate a person, they should be trusted that the person is no longer alive.

Rabbi Eliyahu expresses here a deep trust in the medical establishment, but his is almost a lone view in a prodigious literature written largely by people with very limited understanding of medicine and scientific method.[75]

The Chief Rabbinate's statement overruled earlier prohibitions on the grounds that (a) the survival rate [by this time] had reached 80% for

---

74. The original has המות, but this is clearly a typo.
75. This acceptance of doctors' definition of death is backed by Rabbi Nachum Rabinovitch in his "What Is the Halakha for Organ Transplants?" *Tradition* 9, no. 4 (spring 1968): 23–24. See the RCA Vaad's quarrel with this approach in Bush et al., *Halachic Issues*, 80–82.

one year and 70% for five years; (b) irreversible cessation of spontaneous respiration (ICSR) is defined as death (congruent with the talmudic reference to testing breathing in order to establish death); (c) ICSR can be established by definitive and reliable tests (= brain tests); and (d) Rabbi Moshe Feinstein, late in life, had permitted heart transplants in the United States. The Chief Rabbinate also required confirmatory tests (as recommended by the President's Commission in the United States).

The Chief Rabbinate conditioned its approval on certain demands, such as (a) participation by a representative of the Chief Rabbinate on the medical committee that reviews and declares the patient/donor to be brain dead; (b) written approval in advance from the family and/or donor; and (c) a joint committee of the Ministry of Health and the Chief Rabbinate to review all heart transplants done in Israel.

In truth, these demands were mostly unaccepted.[76] Nevertheless, heart transplantation continues in Israel, saving thousands of lives annually. Unfortunately, much of this lifesaving takes place with limited halakhic support, or only because doctors defy or ignore the rulings of important *posqim*. Nonetheless, the permission of the Chief Rabbinate continues to be invoked, though its stipulations were never fully met.

Summary Observations and Hope for the Future

Thus, in the case of heart transplants, again the halakha/halakhists were dragged kicking and screaming into the twentieth and twenty-first centuries. (In the case of Rabbi Feinstein, he was lifted gently and lovingly into the late twentieth by his son-in-law.)[77] This validation of brain

---

76. See the aforementioned essays by Bin Nun, Sinclair, and Picard.

77. Although Rabbi Feinstein told Rabbi Tendler that he was proud of having never had to go back on any of his greatest *pesaqim*, this statement (which I would guess reflected the general Ḥaredi emphasis on no change in halakha) doesn't constitute repudiation of his changed position on brain death. Nevertheless, the statement was used by opponents of brain death to challenge the view that Rabbi Feinstein really changed his mind.

As I see it, Rabbi Feinstein's comment to Rabbi Tendler was general and meant to confirm his judicious temperament and *siyata di-Shemaya*. In fact, Rabbi Feinstein did not reverse himself frequently. So I understand this comment as a slightly hyperbolic but overall fair assessment of his career as a *poseq*, but not a statement to be taken so literally. In a handful of cases, Rabbi Feinstein did reverse certain *pesaqim*, and this

death – however grudging and conflicted – gives me hope that again the halakha will end up where it should be: on the side of life.

Despite the halakhic opposition to neurological criteria and the ongoing attempts to roll back permission for heart transplants, I believe the pro-life position will win out. In Israel, this is likely because of the physicians' political and communal power and the fact that the Chief Rabbinate is too caught up in the governmental system to back off its permission (or get doctors to abide by its conditions).

In response to the Chief Rabbinate's endorsement of heart transplantation and brain death criteria, and in light of the political clout of the *Ḥaredi* and *Dati-Le'umi* sectors, the Knesset eventually passed the "Schneller law" (spearheaded by Knesset member Otniel Schneller), which granted the rabbinate's longtime request that one of its representatives sit on any committee that declares a prospective donor to be brain dead. The law also required appropriate testing. Unfortunately, however, the process has created extensive disagreements between the doctors and the Chief Rabbinate, leading to charges of disruptive approach by both sides. The implied cooperation has hardly taken place.

Furthermore, the *Ḥaredi* community has members who've been saved by heart transplants and others who want to be saved when the time comes. This is another factor in the pressure to maintain the present uneasy status quo in which transplants are taking place. Amid this

example is the most famous one, as he went from prohibiting heart transplantation as double murder to affirming its halakhic legitimacy, once he came to believe that the neurological criteria for declaration of death were demonstrably correct. If I could bring Rabbi Feinstein back to life and ask him to explain the claim that he never reversed himself, he might well say that he does not consider his change regarding heart transplants to be a reversal. Rather, the scientific facts changed, and a procedure that killed a high percentage of patients (and led to a shortening of donors' lives) had been upgraded. Hearts were removed from people definitely proven to be dead, were successfully transplanted into people in need of new hearts, and saved countless lives. In effect, he was ruling on a different procedure. That, too, may explain why he allowed himself to say he never reversed a great *pesaq*. For more on this approach to explaining Rabbi Feinstein's *pesaq*, see Rabbi Daniel Reifman's essay in this volume. Either way, to seize on this general statement as a way of undoing what Rabbi Feinstein wrote and said about brain death on several occasions, including in a letter written during the last year of his life, is to take it out of context and way too literally. This claim falsifies Rabbi Feinstein's actual *pesaq* and, if accepted, would cut off many chances to save lives.

Ḥaredi grassroots pressure, even traditional *posqim* who forbid heart transplants have permitted Ḥaredi patients to travel to America and/ or receive transplants from gentile donors – though this procedure is, according to these authorities, murder.[78]

I find such a ruling morally offensive in that it appears to give less weight to the life of a gentile. To ignore and even profit from such a donor's "murder" is a violation of the dignity of *tzelem Elokim*. The fact that this decision exploits existing categories of traditional *pesaq* doesn't diminish the offense. I consider this ruling akin to a contemporary *pesaq* not to save a non-Jew's life on Shabbat. In the generation after the *Sho'ah* – where Jewish lives and bodies were treated instrumentally, their intrinsic sanctity denied – Jews should be especially sensitive (and opposed) to any attempt to use any human body in this manner. Of course, the heart is being used to save a life. Still, to allow a gentile's heart to be "illicitly" acquired and used by a Jew smacks of a devaluation of non-Jewish life and limb. I also believe that such rulings, if articulated and disseminated, would cause a massive *ḥillul Hashem*.

Addendum: Rabbi Shlomo Goren and Kidney Transplants

Since I spent the lion's share of this section describing *posqim* who either couldn't be moved or were dragged into the modern world, I would like to offer a glimpse of a *poseq* who took a very different approach. Already in the sixties and seventies, kidney donation from ventilated (brain dead) patients was in full swing. In Israel, then as now, doctors were having myriad difficulties obtaining consent from the families of these patients.

Dr. Zelik Frischer, elsewhere in this volume, recalls asking Rabbi Shlomo Goren in 1975[79] to mobilize rabbis to assist doctors in obtaining consent. According to Frischer, Rabbi Goren was so successful that Israel was briefly an international model of kidney donation.

This testimony can be buttressed by an official letter from Rabbi Goren's office, written in 1978 in reaction to a refusal to donate:[80]

---

78. See *Nishmat Avraham* YD 339:2, cited in Bush et al., *Halachic Issues*, 68.

79. Rabbi Goren was chief rabbi from 1973 to 1983.

80. Shlomo Goren, "The Text of the Public Statement on the Topic of Kidney Transplants," 28 Tammuz 5738/August 2, 1978, in Goren, *Torat ha-Refu'a* 149.

לאור הפרסום של מקרה סרוב
מצד משפחת נפטר דתית
להרשות נטילת כליה מהנפטר
לצורך השתלה בחולה נזקק,
פרסם היום הרב הראשי
לישראל הרב שלמה גורן פסק
הלכה מחייב שבמקרה של
חולה הממתין להשתלת כליה
שחייו תלויים בכך, ומזדמן נפטר
שכליתו מתאימה להשתלה,
מצוה וחובה על משפחת הנפטר
לאפשר הוצאת הכליה להצלת
חייו של החולה. יש בזה משום
פקוח נפש ומשום "לא תעמוד
על דם רעך". וכל המקיים נפש
אחת כאילו קיים עולם מלא.

In light of the publicity surrounding the case of a religious family's refusing to allow the kidney of a loved one to be harvested for transplantation into a patient in need, the chief rabbi of Israel, Rabbi Shlomo Goren, published a *pesaq halakha* today that when a sick person awaits a kidney transplant on which his life depends, and a recently deceased person happens to have a matching kidney, it is a mitzva and an obligation upon the family to allow the removal of the kidney to save the patient's life. There is an element of *piqu'aḥ nefesh* in this, as well as [observance of the prohibition of] "Do not stand idly by the blood of your fellow" (Lev. 19:16). And "Anyone who saves one life is as if he has saved an entire world" (b. *Sanhedrin* 37a).

Rabbi Goren uses very strong language here. He is not just cajoling or sermonizing on the importance of saving lives or donating organs. Instead, he makes a binding halakhic statement: Donating organs to a patient in need is a halakhic obligation, and not doing so violates a biblical prohibition. To me, Rabbi Goren's proactive stance on kidney donation is a model of *pesaq* that understands the Torah to be a halakha of life.[81]

V. HALAKHA AND MODERN MEDICINE: REFLECTIONS ON THE BRAIN DEATH CRITERIA

As a religious Jew, looking back on the interface between the halakhic tradition of *kevod ha-meit* and the medical use of dead bodies to save

---

81. Without being proactive, Rabbi Soloveitchik also seems to have permitted kidney donation. See the testimonies of Rabbis Maurice Lamm and Binyamin Walfish in this volume.

lives, I'm deeply saddened. Doctors have literally performed miracles, saving millions of lives. These miracles include identifying infectious agents (bacteria and viruses) and vectors of transmission; developing antibiotics and other drugs that reduce or eliminate pathological processes; and, when all else fails, replacing diseased organs with body parts from both living and dead.

In each of these activities, human beings have exercised their image of God – in the words of Rabbi Soloveitchik, "man's inner charismatic endowment as a creative being." This capacity and the call to use it were God's blessing to Adam.[82] Moreover, the Lord gave humans "immeasurable resources" with which to master nature, "the most outstanding of which is the intelligence, the human mind." God gave humanity these capacities because strengthening life is God's "mandate" to humankind. As the Rav sees it, Psalms 8:6 defines the human as a being "with glory and honor (dignity)"; therefore, "to be human means to live with dignity."[83] To do this, humans had to develop great medicine:

> Dignity of man expressing itself in the awareness of being responsible ... cannot be realized as long as he has not gained mastery over his environment.... Man of old who could not fight disease and succumbed in multitudes to yellow fever or any other plague with degrading helplessness could not lay claim to dignity. Only the man who builds hospitals, discovers therapeutic techniques, and saves lives is blessed with dignity.[84]

In doing all this, the human being is "a creative agent of God."[85]

In his posthumous *Out of the Whirlwind* collection, the Rav broadens the significance of this activity:

---

82. See Gen. 1:28.
83. Soloveitchik, "Lonely Man," 11–12, 13.
84. Ibid., 12.
85. Ibid., 13.

> Man, on one hand, must struggle with death and try to defeat
> it.... In course of time, Judaism believes, man will succeed in
> taming the death monstrosity, in limiting its power.... How
> can man redeem himself from death...? First... [through] an
> organized scientific-medical effort to limit its power as much
> as possible.... [86]

True, dignity must go hand in hand with responsibility, says
the Rav. While the human must take control over the environment and extend the power of life over death (= medicine), this
power must be exercised responsibly. After all, one is account-
able to God and responsible for the environment. Acting in this
spirit, the *posqim* could argue for limits on medicine. They could
stand guard to assure that proper tests are done and that patients'
lives aren't snuffed out prematurely. But this limiting role can be
played only by someone supportive of the method, who seeks to
keep it on track – not someone unsympathetic and opposed to the
process.

Most *posqim* have been too suspicious or opposed, so they
haven't been able to play a constructive role. Were they responsible,
they would encourage families to permit transplants while pushing
for family rights to approve the donation. This is far more respectful of families than allowing doctors to seize organs for donation.
But the *posqim* have by and large not encouraged families to donate.
They have inflamed opposition and played to the culturally inherited, often superstitious opposition to organ donation. Therefore,
doctors have resisted giving them or the family input in the decision to donate.

More important, where were the halakhists and *posqim* when
humanity (especially scientists and doctors) was carrying out the
sacred mission of lifesaving so brilliantly? Were the *posqim* encouraging or leading them? One could argue that the doctors engaged in

---

86. Joseph B. Soloveitchik, *Out of the Whirlwind* (ed. David Shatz, Joel B. Wolowel-
sky, and Reuven Ziegler; New York: Toras Harav Foundation and KTAV, 2002),
47–48.

bringing the *Mashiaḥ* insofar as the messianic world will be marked by either a major extension of life or a complete triumph of life over death.[87] Were the *posqim* or their students likely to join the work and become doctors, as did Rambam and a host of Torah scholars over the centuries?

The ideology currently dominating the world of Torah learning opposes participation in general culture, dismissing any activity other than Torah study as a waste of time. Have Torah scholars encouraged families to permit autopsies that could advance the state of medicine? On the contrary, they've fought these medical procedures tooth and nail. Have the teachers of halakha taught their congregations that it's a mitzva to donate organs and save life? The model of *kevod ha-meit* (which prohibits the use of a dead body) is so ingrained in Jewish culture that Jews in Israel – even secular Jews – have one of the lowest rates of organ donations; devout Jews have the lowest of all. By and large, the more traditional *posqim* have fed and appealed to this entrenched opposition rather than trying to soften or change it.[88]

Nor has the extraordinary rise in successful transplants and survival rates halted opposition to brain death and heart transplantation. Not even Rabbi Moshe Feinstein's acceptance of both has stilled the debate. Thanks to the initial impact of Rabbi Feinstein's ruling and the leadership of Rabbi Moshe Tendler, the Rabbinical Council of America (RCA) Executive Committee accepted the brain death criteria (and the heart transplantations they make possible) for the RCA health care proxy. Ever since, there have been ongoing attempts to repeal and reject this standard.

The most recent attempt came in a report by the Vaad Halacha: *Halachic Issues in the Determination of Death and in Organ Transplantation*:

---

87. "He will destroy death forever" (Is. 25:8); "He who dies at one hundred years shall be considered a youth" (Is. 65:20).

88. Yet the Halakhic Organ Donation Society (HODS) has recruited an impressive number of rabbis and *posqim* (mostly from the Modern Orthodox and *Dati-Le'umi* constituencies) to promote and participate in organ donation.

Including an Evaluation of the Neurological "Brain Death" Standard (2010).[89]

The report could have acknowledged that there is a vigorous debate over brain death criteria; that many Orthodox Jews have given or received organs made available on the basis of a finding of brain death; and that rulings by Rabbis Moshe Feinstein, Chaim David Regensberg, Shlomo Goren, and Shaul Yisraeli, the Chief Rabbinate, and others support such a decision. The document could then have expressed its reservations and the opposing views.

But such a treatment would have given some legitimacy and dignity to this positive approach to heart transplants and the brain death criterion – something this study was determined not to do. The report rejects the brain death criteria, tries to remove Rabbi Feinstein's support for them, impugns doctors' methods and motives, and upholds only the "classic," inherited definition of death (as if medicine has learned nothing in the interim).

The report opposes medical advances in the usual ways. It cites all of Rabbi Feinstein's views – pro and con – as if they were equally weighty.[90] It dismisses his permission on the grounds that he assumed a state of "fully rotted brain," a desiccation level generally not found in donor patients. Therefore, it argues, the permissive opinion cannot be attributed to Rabbi Feinstein.[91] The study also questions the authenticity of the Bondi letter and – just in case – tries to explain away its reasoning.[92]

The report examines at length the views of six other leading *posqim* who oppose the brain death criteria (some, like Rabbis Eliezer Waldenburg, Yitzchak Yaakov Weiss, and Shmuel ha-Levi Wosner, oppose other transplants as well). It includes a section on "Responses of Leading American *Poskim* to Questions Posed by the Vaad Halacha."[93]

89. The study aroused much opposition, and the title page insisted: "This Study Is Designed to Assist Members of the RCA in the Process of *Psak Halacha* and Is Itself Not Intended as a Formal Ruling."
90. Bush et al., *Halachic Issues*, 48–62.
91. Ibid., 42.
92. Ibid., 55.
93. Ibid., 43ff.

There, Rabbis J. David Bleich and Mordechai Willig state that it is definitely prohibited to use brain death as a criterion for death.[94] (This position would make the use of this criterion for transplant an act of murder.) Rabbis Aharon Lichtenstein, Michael Rosensweig, and Hershel Schachter reject the criteria out of doubt.[95]

The report makes clear that as the brain death criteria have no sources in the Talmud, the burden of proof is on the proponents of this method. Despite extensive and respectful citations of medical evidence and issues, the study privileges halakhic definitions based on the state of science in the talmudic era (which lag far behind the contemporary standard); simply because they are "inherited," they're sacred.[96] The report also questions the medical validity of the brain death criteria, despite their overwhelming acceptance and use in medicine.[97]

A Tale of Two *Posqim*: Rabbis J. David Bleich and Shlomo Goren

Although *posqim* often work with the same facts, their approach to them should generally be seen in the context of their overall leanings. In the case of brain death and heart transplantation, trust or suspicion regarding the medical establishment is one important factor; another is creativity or conservatism in halakhic analysis.

To illustrate, it's worth taking a quick look at how two *posqim* approach the continuation of heartbeat in halakha. Advocates of defining brain death as halakhic death argue that the beating of the heart after brain death is nothing more than the convulsions of a lizard's severed tail. This was the argument put forward by Rabbi

---

94. Rabbi Willig was the principal author of a 1991 responsum issued by a majority of the Vaad Halacha rejecting brain death. Rabbi Bleich and Rabbi Hershel Schachter concurred in that ruling.

95. The report cites Rabbi Schachter's view that reports of brain activity after brain death may remove much of the doubt and indeed render the harvesting of organs outright murder. Bush et al., *Halachic Issues*, 44.

96. Ibid., 31 n. 44.

97. Regarding the medical issues of brain death, see the essays by Drs. Zelik Frischer, Noam Stadlan, and Howard Doyle in this volume. See also Rabbi Prof. Avraham Steinberg's description here of a scientific experiment designed to disprove a talmudic medical axiom (or at least force a reinterpretation.)

Nachum Rabinovitch in 1968.[98] However, to the objective observer, it would seem to be quite a stretch. Assuming a person is hooked up to a ventilator, the heart can continue beating regularly for quite a while. Thus, in the RCA paper, Rabbi Asher Bush critique's Rabbi Rabinovitch's position:

> There is an additional and perhaps far broader-reaching question, which also needs to be addressed regarding the very comparison of the case of the severed lizard's tail to brain death. The spasmodic movements that the Mishna dismisses as signs of life are typically of a short-term nature, while the extended life of a brain dead patient can often continue for days, weeks, even months, and, in rare cases, years.[99]

Rabbi J. David Bleich takes this problem and runs with it. He argues that as long as the heart continues circulating blood, the person remains alive:

> The essential and intrinsic criterion of life is motion that is vital in nature; cardiac activity, which, as will be shown, is the primary indicator of life, is simply one form, and indeed the primary example, of vital motion.[100]

Using his God-given creativity, Rabbi Bleich has invented a new concept in halakha, that of vital motion. He uses this notion to declare a person, even one with a dead brain, to be alive as long as blood circulates through the body.

On the other hand, Rabbi Shlomo Goren, noting the same problem of persistent heartbeat in ventilated patients (cadavers), took the opposite approach:

---

98. Rabinovitch, "Halakha for Organ Transplants": 20–27.

99. Bush et al., *Halachic Issues*, 33.

100. J. David Bleich, *Contemporary Halakhic Problems* 4 (New York: KTAV and Yeshiva University Press, 1995), 319 n. 4.

באשר ללב, עלינו להבחין
בין שני סוגי הפעילות שלו.
פעילות פונקציונלית ופעילות
פיסיו-ביולוגית. כי מבחינה
פונקציונלית, מהווה הפסקת
פעילות המוח, כאשר אינו מקבל
את הדם המחומצן מהלב, כמות
פונקציונלי של הלב. מאחר
שהלב נחשב ללב רק כאשר הוא
מתפקד כלב, דהיינו שמזרים דם
מחומצן לכל האברים של הגוף
כולל המוח. כי זהו התפקיד
הפונקציונלי של הלב להעביר
דם לא מחומצן לריאות, ולשאוב
דם מחומצן מהריאות ולהעבירו
למוח ולאברים אחרים. אבל
כאשר הלב מפסיק לתפקד
מבחינה פונקציונלית בגוף, גם
אם הוא עדיין פועם לכשעצמו,
אינו נחשב מכאן ואילך כלב, כי
אם כאבר בודד. ולכן המות של
המוח הוא גם המות של הלב
הפונקציונלי. גם אם הלב ממשיך
לפעום בכח עצמו או על ידי
מיכשור, אין זה הופך אותו ללב.

With regard to the heart, we need to distinguish between two types of activity – functional activity and physio-biological activity. From the perspective of function, once the brain has ceased any activity, when it no longer receives any oxygenated blood from the heart, the heart has died functionally as well. For the heart is considered a heart only when it functions as a heart, meaning it pumps oxygenated blood to all limbs of the body, including the brain. For that is the functional purpose of the heart, to send deoxygenated blood to the lungs and take oxygenated blood from the lungs and send it to the brain and other organs. But when the heart ceases to perform its function in the body, even if still beating on its own, it cannot be considered a "heart" from that point on, but [rather it's] just an individual organ. Therefore, the death of the brain is also the functional death of the heart. Even if the heart continues beating on its own or via a pump, this doesn't turn the organ into a heart.[101]

Rabbi Goren, using the same God-given creative skill as Rabbi Bleich, takes the same facts and pushes in the opposite direction. He argues that, although the heart is pumping blood, no blood is getting to the brain (as determined by confirmatory tests.) If the heart isn't pumping oxygenated blood to perfuse the brain, it's not really functioning, and therefore this "heartbeat" lacks the status of a pulse in halakha.[102]

---

101. Goren, "Discontinuing Life Support," 57–78 [63].

102. For a similar interpretation of Rabbi Feinstein's discussion of a heart functioning as a heart by giving life to all limbs (including the brain), see Rabbi Daniel Reifman's

Although both Rabbi Bleich and Rabbi Goren have invented halakhic concepts, based on traditional sources and scientific facts, they've
done so with very different goals in mind. Rabbi Bleich fears the violation
of halakha and the overturning of tried-and-true norms if Jewish patients
begin accepting brain death as death and donating their organs. Rabbi
Goren, on the other hand, wishes to save the lives of patients in need of
organs and trusts the medical establishment's understanding of death
enough to assist in medicine's quest by formulating a halakhic argument
in support of neurological criteria and against the older, clinical definition.

A Halakha of Death?

Why have most halakhic rulings been cool, if not antagonistic, to the
march of science?

Opponents of brain death maintain that with all due respect to
medical advances, murder, i.e., ending the life of one person (the donor)
in order to save another (the recipient), is unacceptable in halakhic
tradition.[103] Even preferring a vital young life over a dying, older one
(by shortening the latter) is forbidden. This is as it should be. If life is
of infinite value, then the bearer of a few hours or days of life should be
treated with the same respect as someone expected to live a long time.[104]

---

essay in this volume. Also see Noam Stadlan's "Death by Neurological Criteria: A
Critique of the RCA Paper and the Circulation Criteria," in which he discusses a
related concept, "inadequate blood flow":

> The testing for blood flow reveals no flow, although there can be some mini-
> mal flow that is below the sensitivity of the study.... However, the amount
> of blood flow, if present, is not adequate to sustain the function of the brain.
> This blood flow can be termed inadequate flow, which we will define as blood
> flow that is not adequate to sustain the function of the tissue to which it flows.
> As noted above, tissue requires oxygen and glucose. If the blood flow is not
> adequate to supply oxygen and glucose, the tissue ceases to function. (Noam
> Stadlan, "Death by Neurological Criteria," http://torahmusings.com/2010/12/
> death-by-neurological-criteria/)

In other words, circulation is not circulation if it doesn't meet the basic functional
requirement of perfusing the tissue with oxygen and glucose.

103. See b. *Sanhedrin* 74a.

104. This consideration appears in Rabbi Feinstein's responsum opposing brain death
and is repeatedly cited by Rabbi Bleich as part of his opposition.

However, what makes the process of brain-death-based organ donation murder is the interpretation of a halakhic source and the privileging of a definition of death because it is inherited from a talmudic source. In the name of fealty to tradition, a tradition based on very limited and primitive science is upheld against a procedure that has saved thousands of lives. In the name of the sanctity of life, an act of lifesaving is labeled "murder." What purports to be a protection of the weak turns out to be a decree of death for thousands of others, were it to be accepted and followed by doctors. In effect, the sanctity of a tradition, even one based on circumstances that have drastically changed, is worth more than thousands of lives – although life is the most sacred value in Judaism.

This approach defies the spirit of the Talmud's unequivocal statement that saving a life overrides all but three commandments of the Torah.[105] It also clashes with Rambam's insistence that the supremacy of saving lives is proof that

אין משפטי התורה נקמה...	...the laws of the Torah are not [a source
בעולם אלא רחמים וחסד ושלום	of] vengeance in the world but [a source
בעולם.	of] compassion, loving-kindness, and peace in the world.[106]

It reminds us of Rambam's warning regarding those who oppose lifesaving in the name of upholding the commandments (in his case, Shabbat):

...עליהן הכתוב אומר 'וגם אני	...of them Scripture says: "I [God]
נתתי להם חוקים לא טובים	gave them decrees that weren't good
ומשפטים לא יחיו בהם'.	and laws by which they couldn't live" (Ezek. 20:24).[107]

---

105. B. *Sanhedrin* 74a. Admittedly, murder is one of these three commandments (prohibitions), but this procedure is murder only because it's treated as a matter of talmudic interpretation as against an actual case in which life is at stake.

106. Rambam, MT Laws of Shabbat 2:3.

107. Ibid.

That is, while trying to be pious, they turn the Torah's laws into rules that mete out death.

Why Halakhists Have Lagged Behind

We have to look beyond the charge of murder in the case of heart transplants to grasp the broader cultural factors that have made the halakhists bystanders – and often antagonists – to one of the great explosions of lifesaving and life expansion in human history.

First, there is the dominant notion, even in Modern Orthodoxy, that Orthodoxy allows no change in halakha. This is quite simply false. There have been massive changes in halakha from the biblical period through the rabbinic era down to today, as Jews have pursued the covenantal way toward replenishing the deficiency in creation (*tiqqun olam*). Elsewhere,[108] I have argued that the correct understanding of Orthodoxy is not that there is no change, but that we bring the entire tradition with us. Even when we don't actually practice it anymore – such as the laws of the wayward son (בן סורר ומורה) or the rebellious town (עיר הנדחת) – we honor the halakha by learning from it (דרוש וקבל שכר).[109] We no longer practice slavery or sell our daughters into marriage.[110] The rabbis cancelled or made inoperative – and thus neutralized – almost all the death penalties listed in the Torah.[111] Nonetheless, unlike liberal and secular Jews, we don't reject or dismiss these laws as irrelevant or outdated. Once revealed, their sacredness remains forever. We study them as sacred Torah, learning how to guide our lives. They are part of the revelation and part of the record of our journey toward establishing the kingdom of heaven. However, we have developed the halakha and brought it closer to its ideal goals in many areas – such as women's rights in marriage,

---

108. In a book on the development of the covenant in Judaism, tentatively titled *Partners for Life: Tikkun Olam When Humans Come of Age in the Covenant* (forthcoming). See especially ch. 1, "Covenantal Actions," and ch. 3, "The Second Stage of the Covenant: Rabbinic Judaism."

109. See b. *Sanhedrin* 70a–71b.

110. Exod. 21:1–11; see Greenberg, *Partners*, ch. 3.

111. If there was an execution once in seventy years, the presiding Sanhedrin was known as "violent" (m. *Makkot* 1:10).

workers' rights, or new holidays to commemorate the unfolding events of Jewish history.[112]

The idea of no change in halakha arose as a defense against modernity and the erosion of observance. This ideology suits the Haredi community, which has tried to stay outside of modern culture and resist engagement in this civilization, but it doesn't describe the reality of Modern Orthodoxy. The "no change" approach has crippled halakha's capacity to respond to the new realities of Jewish sovereignty and the economy of the State of Israel. It hamstrings our ability to move toward greater recognition of women's dignity and leadership in Israel and the Diaspora alike. Where sources are found to justify women's greater participation and leadership, the last resort of resistance is to claim that this hasn't been done and is therefore unacceptable.

This ideology has even led to resistance to science and medicine and the new practices they bring into our lives. The climax of traditionalism is the insistence that inherited *medical prescriptions* (or definitions of death!) are sacred and not subject to change – because new approaches didn't appear in talmudic (or medieval) sources. This attitude estranges halakhists from medical methods (which have been remarkably innovative and lifesaving) and leads them to treat many medical procedures with suspicion and hostility.

The second factor distorting the attitude of halakhists is their vision of halakha as an intellectual or legal system unto itself rather than as a Torah of living, creating, and guiding society. As a code, the primary emphasis is on adhering to precedents and upholding traditions. There is no obligation to provide for reality and ensure that the halakha actually works in real life.[113]

---

112. In my book *The Jewish Way: Living the Holidays* (New York: Touchstone Books, 1993), I apply this to Yom Ha-Sho'ah and Yom Ha-Atzma'ut as well as Purim, Hanukka, and Tisha B'Av.

113. Take the *heter mekhira*, the temporary sale of Israeli land to gentiles, which enables Israeli farmers to continue working in agriculture during the Sabbatical year. Without the *heter mekhira*, Israeli agriculture wouldn't be economically viable. Until the 1960s, the whole economy would have crumbled had agriculture been destroyed. Yet this *heter* has increasingly been opposed or undermined by halakhists. The alternatives, imports and reliance on Arab farmers, are expensive and insufficient for the majority.

This *Haredi* approach, viz. upholding precedent rather than societal viability, is feasible only for a minority, which – at the great expense of the majority – is subsidized to live this way. Judaism thus becomes a private club for small groups, while the rest of society must violate the law (or ignore it) in order to live.[114] This failure to take responsibility for society and the consequences of their rulings encourages halakhists to rule against medical advances, decreeing death for many patients.

Again, under cover of the reigning ideology (of law without responsibility), unworkable rulings allow society to go on operating – because the majority ignores or violates them. Frequently, the self-righteous minority benefits from the "sins" of the majority. Ironically, were all doctors fully observant and the system bound by halakha, bad rulings would evoke serious backlash and pressure to change. However, most physicians aren't guided by halakha, and the insular approach of the *posqim* only drives them further from tradition, while the halakhists face no consequences, because the medical system goes on without them. Meanwhile, respect for the Torah and its leadership suffers.

The third cultural factor is the triumph of what Abraham Joshua Heschel called in *God in Search of Man* "pan-halakhism." This approach emphasizes behavior and obedience to legal details while denying any overarching values or goals that the halakha seeks to advance (and that would guide *pesaq*). Pan-halakhism makes absolute the talmudic dictum that the words "Timna, concubine of Esau" in the Torah are just as sacred as "love your neighbor as yourself" or "Hear, O Israel, the Lord Our God, the Lord is One."[115] Certainly, there is a minor truth in the equation of all verses in the Torah; after all, the entire Torah is holy.

---

114. The same failure to take responsibility for a living system shows up in the failure to correct such injustices as *iggun*. The *posqim* pledge allegiance to precedents, though these lead to continuing extortion and injustice to married women. The rabbis assert that they lack the authority to make systemic changes. Thus, the majority is doomed either to live non-halakhically or to suffer through obeying halakhic precedents (as against less established alternatives). In the name of legalism, the rabbis cling to precedent in an insulated world, failing to imitate God or do what He wants: "Do justice for the poor [oppressed] and the orphan; deal righteously with the afflicted and the exploited. Rescue the poor and the needy; save them from the hand of the wicked" (Ps. 82:3–4).

115. See b. *Sanhedrin* 99b.

However, taken to an extreme, this understanding gravely distorts Jewish tradition.

The Torah has priorities, goals, and meta-values; to homogenize everything as of equal weight falsifies the Torah's message. If there are no meta-halakhot, no higher values, then there's no way of resolving the conflict of values when two good principles clash. I find this new approach especially shocking among important students of Rabbi Soloveitchik, because it flagrantly contradicts his teaching that "the ultimate goal of Judaism" and "the telos of the halakha in all its multifold aspects and manifestations" is "the creation of [perfected] worlds"; it is the attainment of "the Jewish people's eschatological vision."[116]

The inability to see a higher purpose, a meta-halakha (but rather to insist that the Torah is just a code of behaviors to be observed out of obedience to God without regard to higher values), distinguished the halakha of the Dead Sea Scrolls sect from that of the rabbis. When human life was at stake (as when a person was drowning), the *Damascus Document* of Qumran deemed it prohibited to save the person, because this act would involve the desecration of Shabbat.[117]

By contrast, the rabbis (acting on the axiom that the Torah's highest value is life) declared it a mitzva to override Shabbat and save human life. By implication, God's ultimate value in giving us the mitzvot was not to gain our obedience (in which case dying for the sake Shabbat observance would be correct), but rather to guide us toward a life of upgrading the world, of respecting and preserving the human image of God. Therefore, saving life is the way we obey God and honor His Torah. The Torah was given to us to live by, not die by (b. *Yoma* 85a–b). Conditioned by a system that valorizes inherited actions over the advancement of life, the *posqim* have been unable to give the proper halakhic weight to medicine and its potential for healing the world.

The saddest aspect – and the greatest missed opportunity – is the near absence of halakhic leadership in the movement of advancing

116. Soloveitchik, *Halakhic Man*, 9.
117. *Damascus Document* 11:16–17.

life.[118] When "the modern scientist... in his full resplendent glory as a creative agent of God"[119] improves the world and extends human lives, the halakhic exemplars are nowhere to be seen. Rabbi Soloveitchik celebrates the scientific, industrial, and technological enhancement of the world as an attempt "to carry out the mandate entrusted to [Adam] by his Maker, who... summoned him to 'fill the earth and subdue it.'"[120] When the human being reaches into space, overcomes illnesses, or extends life, "acting in harmony with his [human] nature, which was created, willed, and directed by his Maker," these actions are "a manifestation of obedience to rather than rebellion against God."[121] The silence, lack of involvement, suspicion, and opposition of Torah scholars to all this is stunning. In the name of protecting life, they are blocking lifesaving on a major scale. In the name of protecting the Torah, they are making it irrelevant (or oppositional) to some of the greatest exercises of the capacities of the image of God of all time.

CONCLUSION: A LIFE OF HALAKHA
VS. A HALAKHA OF LIFE

In the end, it comes down to this. For many traditionalists, the highest obligation and greatest expression of loyalty is to live a life of halakha. They define halakhic observance as honoring precedents above all, shirking responsibility for improving the world or building the State of Israel or protecting its citizens. Their rulings define halakha as a traditionalism that stands aside, looks down at, and often opposes human culture, science, creativity, or any other secular activity. Instead of contributing to civilization, they accept many of its benefits parasitically.

The alternative vision, that of Rabbi Soloveitchik, is to live a halakha of life – a halakha that enhances, extends, and heals life. The Jew who observes a halakha of life joins with God in "meting out justice for the oppressed, providing food to the hungry, freeing the imprisoned/enslaved, opening the eyes of the blind [through transplants?]"

---

118. There are noted exceptions, such as Rabbis Regensberg, Goren, Yisraeli, and Tendler, Rabbi Prof. Avraham Steinberg, etc.
119. Soloveitchik, "Lonely Man," 15.
120. Ibid., 16.
121. Ibid

(Ps. 146:7–8). A halakha of life cooperates with doctors and enables them to research and pioneer.[122]

It's not that halakhists must approve everything secularists do. Opposition, regulation, and the curbing of excesses are all very important. Limits – covenantal limits – are essential to keeping human behavior on the side of life. But limits are helpful only when imposed by someone who participates in the system, affirming its goals and seeking to keep human activity within the bounds of morality and accountability to God. Much of a halakha of life would be exercised in secular activity – in business, medicine, and culture – but it would be inspired, guided, and kept healthy by halakhic guidelines and models. Such a halakha would move Jews and humanity to choose life every day and in every act. Such choices would put a halakha of life at the center of contemporary civilization and at the heart of the struggle to keep it on the side of life and justice and *tiqqun olam*. Then people would know that whatever they accomplish – or fail to – is not in vain. For they side with life – the side God has promised will win – and they are partners with God in making the promise come true.

PERSONAL POSTSCRIPT

Here I will allow myself one personal note; I will speak as a parent – one of two parents who honored what they believed their child would want when he was dying, and who donated his usable organs to others.[123] His liver saved the life of an Arab father of six who was hours away from death; his two kidneys saved two people when dialysis had started to fail them; his two corneas restored sight to a doctor and a budding young artist. The heart was too bruised to be used.

When one is overwhelmed by a catastrophic loss of an infinitely valuable, unique loved one, there is no consolation in saving others. There is no replacement for a child torn violently away, never to return.

---

122. Although my thinking on the religious importance of saving lives through science is drawn primarily from the writings of Rabbi Joseph B. Soloveitchik, and he is my model for a theology of halakha dedicated to life, I acknowledge the gap between his theological forward thrust and his *pesaq*. The Rav, in general, was less involved in actual *pesaq*. His views on heart transplants, while moderate, generally followed the crowd rather than leading it.

123. See the essay by my wife, Blu Greenberg, in the organ donation volume.

One lives with the curse that one's son or daughter has been snatched away, and "your eyes see it and you look longingly [for him/her] every day/all day, but there is nothing you can do" (Deut. 28:32).

Still, if you understand religious life as being a member of the covenantal community in a battle of life against death, there follows a deep realization inside, under the layers of numbness and pain. Thanks to the God-given mind and talent of some doctors, the final word goes not to death but to life. First you undergo Job's shock of recognition that "the world goes on its way (עוֹלם כמנהגו נוהג),"[124] that creation is vastly larger than you.[125] Then comes the bitter pill that Hashem won't shift those laws for your benefit at this moment – no matter that you grasped at straws and prayed for miracles. Those whose relationship to God is not conditioned on rewards and punishments, but is rooted in solidarity (*imo anokhi ve-tzara*)[126] and love, won't be driven off by this blow. They'll renew their commitment to the covenant of *tiqqun olam* and work harder that the next accident be prevented or the death effect be reversed.

According to the laws instilled in this universe by its Creator, a teenager driving with a learner's permit but unaccompanied by an adult can run a red light, and when he strikes someone on a bike, whether this person is a *tzaddik* or a *rasha* is immaterial. The blow will cause fatal brain damage, which contemporary medicine cannot yet prevent or reverse. Still, you recognize that at some awful and irreconcilable cost, thanks to your flesh and blood's donation and the doctors' covenantal medicine, the balance shifts, however slightly, from death to life. Until the resurrection comes – for which I pray three times a day – that's as close as we'll get to partnering with God in the divine mission to destroy death forever. "My Lord God will wipe away the tears from all faces" (Is. 25:8).[127]

---

124. B. *Avoda Zara* 54b; Maimonides, *Guide*, II:29, 139, states that this means there can be no permanent miracles that override the laws of nature (although there can be temporary overrides).
125. This, I believe, is the message of the book of Job.
126. Ps. 91:15.
127. I thank Rabbi Zev Farber for his editorial judgment, which shaped and upgraded this essay. I'm particularly grateful for his suggestion to incorporate the pro-life, science-affirming views of Rabbis Regensberg and Goren, and for supplying their sources. As a result, the piece is more balanced and hopeful.

Chapter 17

Death and Halakha
in the Modern Age:
A Philosopher's Perspective

Jeremy Rosenbaum Simon

INTRODUCTION

I have been invited to participate in this colloquium as a philosopher, and perhaps this invitation requires a bit of explanation. Other contributors to this volume have a clear place in the discussion. Rabbis need no explanation. Doctors are needed to elucidate the facts on which the halakha is based. Even medical ethicists can clearly contribute, to the extent that our sense of right and wrong may be independent of but inform halakhic judgments. But what place does a philosopher have in a discussion seeking to determine or understand halakha?

Philosophers are trained to analyze questions and discussions in order to reveal their presuppositions and contradictions, and to provide conditions for satisfactorily resolving the issues at hand. Furthermore, philosophers have been exploring the nature and determination of death for as long as the debate has been active. Therefore, I'd like to raise four issues that, philosophically, have not been adequately considered in many discussions surrounding the determination of death in halakha: (1) the distinction between a sign and a definition of death, (2) the nature of life, (3) the modern nature of the problem of accepting or rejecting brain death, and (4) the conceptual problems raised by *both* sides of this debate. These four issues are essentially separate (though the first and second have some connection), and there is no correct response to any. However, some response is necessary, because without a position on these matters – or at least an understanding of them – it is impossible to coherently discuss the determination of death.

Terminology

Before we proceed, a brief note on terminology. The term "brain death" is standard in these discussions, although it can refer to different events. Most commonly, it means a loss of higher-brain (cortical) functions, or of all brain functions. The former may also be known as "cortical brain death" or "higher-brain death," and the latter as "whole-brain death." Because loss of brainstem function is the most salient addition that whole-brain death makes to cortical brain death, whole-brain death is also sometimes called "brainstem death," though loss of brainstem functions alone is generally not considered adequate to declare a person dead. In what follows, I use the generic term "brain death," but, with one exception, I mean by it "whole-brain death," as this is the version of brain death that's relevant to the halakhic debate.[1]

Although the term "brain death" always occurs in discussions such as these, there is less agreement as to what to call the position opposed to it. It is variously referred to as "cardiac death," "cardiorespiratory death," and "circulatory death." These terms refer to the position that death can be declared only when one or more of the following are missing – heartbeat, breathing, or circulation. Different authors, at different times, use different combinations of these criteria. All are apparent from a general inspection of a body; that is, they are clinically evident. Hence these criteria are also often known as "clinical

---

1. The one exception is in part 4 below, where we'll make no assumptions about what part of the brain must be lost to declare brain death.

death." The exact details of what biological functions must be lost for death to occur according to those who reject brain death do not matter for us here. Therefore, I will use the term "clinical death" throughout, as it avoids unnecessary commitments to a particular version of the position.[2]

I. SIGN VS. DEFINITION OF DEATH

One distinction that's been largely overlooked, at least in public discussions to which I've been privy, is that between a sign (or criterion) of death and a definition of death. A sign of death tells us how, practically, to identify dead people. A definition of death tells us, fundamentally, what it is to be dead. A less controversial example may clarify this distinction.

The definition of a licensed physician is one who has been granted legal permission by the state to practice medicine. This is what it means to be a licensed physician. This is, however, not a fact to which most people have easy access. We therefore have certain signs of licensure; in particular, a certificate that the doctor can hang on his or her wall. Possession of this certificate is not what makes one a licensed physician, but it is connected to licensure in such a way – it cannot be readily counterfeited and is issued only to licensed physicians – that its possession is a clear sign of a licensed physician.

In the case of death, the question of sign or definition presents itself particularly regarding heartbeat and spontaneous respiration. Is lacking either of these the definition of death – by virtue of which a person can no longer be considered living? Or is it merely closely tied to some other fact; for example, the absence of brain function or a spirit (*neshama*),[3] which itself provides the definition of death? In other words, is one dead because one cannot breathe (and/or has no heartbeat), or is it simply that no living person could fail to breathe?

The importance of distinguishing a sign of death from a definition can be seen if we consider a talmudic passage in b. *Yoma* 85a,

---

2. Again, in part 4 there will be some deviation.
3. By *neshama*, I don't mean to invoke any particular account of what the *neshama* is, or to contrast it, say, with *nefesh* or *ru'aḥ*. I refer only to the Jewish concept of an animating soul, as mentioned in m. *Oholot* 1:6 (or 1:7, depending on the edition).

often cited as the primary source in discussions of death in halakha.[4] The Talmud there tells us, at least according to most explanations, that if we examine a body at the nose and find no breathing, the person is dead. But why? If it's because, according to halakha, absence of breathing constitutes death, then there is little more to discuss, even in modern times.

If we accept the Talmud's statement here as halakhically determinative, then if one can still breathe, one is alive, and if one cannot, one is dead. However, if breathing was, for the rabbis of the Talmud, simply a sign of some deeper fact, then we may ask whether we have other signs of this deeper fact nowadays, such as electroencephalograms, which directly detect brain activity, or echocardiograms, which show cardiac motion even when that motion is not strong enough to produce a pulse. We can even ask whether breathing is still connected to that underlying fact in the same way that it was in the time of the Talmud, or whether technology has severed the direct connection between breathing and death. Unless we know whether a source – in this case, the Talmud – is giving a sign or a definition, we won't know how to apply it when medical understanding has changed.

II. WHAT IS LIFE?

To determine whether a given physical observation *signifies* death or *defines* it, one must have a clear account of what it is to be dead. Otherwise, there is no way to evaluate the relationship of the observation in question (say, lack of breathing) and death.

An account of death is further necessary, given one sign of death, to identify others. This too we cannot accomplish unless we know what these signs are supposed to indicate. Since dying is (almost) always understood to be the loss of that which makes us alive, another way of saying one must have an account of death is to say that one must have an account of what it is to be alive.

---

4. Although the mishna in *Oholot* (referenced in the previous note) is often cited as well, the *Yoma* passage seems to be the primary source cited in this regard. My points apply equally to the mishna and the Talmud. However, for simplicity's sake, I will discuss only one source.

An account of what it is to be alive, therefore, is necessary to establish halakhic criteria for determining death. However, such an account may not be sufficient. For example, one plausible Jewish answer to the question of what makes us alive is the *neshama*, and when it leaves the body, one is dead.[5] While such an understanding of life and death would make it clear that cessation of breathing doesn't define death, it in no way allows us to determine whether other physical signs indicate the end of life – the loss of the *neshama* – at least as reliably as cessation of breathing. To determine other physical signs of death according to this model, we would need a more elaborate account of the relationship between the *neshama* and human physiology.

Even if the account of what it is to be alive is insufficient to establish halakhic criteria for death – as, for example, might well be the case if a *neshama* is what makes one alive in halakha – it's important to understand the role that an account of life plays in our ability to build on earlier criteria for declaring death. For if we understand it, we'll also understand that if we don't know the physiology (broadly construed) underlying the Talmud's discussion of death, we won't be able to extend it, and we'll be left applying only the criteria the Talmud directly endorses (whatever one takes those to be), with no possible interpretation or expansion.

A clear understanding of what halakha considers to be the nature of life is thus essential for knowing (1) whether the criteria halakha provides for identifying death are signs or definitions, and (2) how, or even if, we can expand on these criteria.

III. THE MODERN NATURE OF THIS PROBLEM

The question of whether brain death constitutes actual death is a modern problem not only in that no one asked the question until recently, but in that it could not have been asked until recently, for several reasons.

First, until the past few centuries, the role of the brain in both physiology and consciousness was poorly understood, if at all. Even the brain's control of respiration has been understood only for around two

---

5. That is, when it leaves the body permanently. The *Modeh Ani* prayer references the return of the soul after sleep, but this doesn't mean sleeping people are dead.

hundred years. This lack of knowledge made it impossible to identify the brain as even a candidate for being the essential, defining organ of life. One would hardly think of the brain thus if one didn't know how it controls our physical and mental functioning. Consequently, even if death truly is the loss of brain function, we could not have appreciated this until recently, as we didn't know what that function was.

Furthermore, even if one somehow thought, in the absence of such knowledge, that brain death was the relevant event, our lack of a thorough understanding of the brain's various functions would have made it impossible to evaluate a person for it. We can directly sense heartbeat, circulation, and breathing. But we can identify brain activity only indirectly, either through technological means (such as an electro-encephalogram) or by understanding the brain's control of other parts of the body and observing the behavior of those parts. Clinical death is directly evident in a way brain death is not.

Another modern development that has been essential to our ability to even consider brain death as marking death was the invention in the last century of the ventilator, the machine that provides oxygen to those who cannot breathe. Until we could perform this essential function for patients who cannot breathe on their own, there were, for all intents and purposes, no patients who were brain dead but not also dead by more traditional criteria, and vice versa. When the brainstem stopped functioning, breathing would immediately and irreversibly cease, and the heart would stop beating within minutes.

Likewise, anyone who stopped breathing (because of a fractured neck) or whose heart spontaneously stopped beating would lose all brain function within seconds to minutes. There was thus no reason or even opportunity to try to tease apart these various events and attribute death to one or the other. For all practical purposes, they occurred simultaneously. Only when the ventilator allowed us to supply oxygen to patients who couldn't breathe on their own did we gain the ability to separate brain death (the cause of the patients' inability to breathe) from other candidates for the marker of death, in particular, the loss of cardiac activity.

Not only did the ventilator make it possible to distinguish between brain death and clinical death, it also made that distinction relevant. If anyone *had* thought about the distinction before ventilators entered clinical use, it would have been essentially a theoretical exercise – any brain dead person would be dead by all criteria before one could make anything of the distinction.[6] However, once we could maintain patients (for lack of a neutral term) on ventilators beyond the point of brain death, the question of whether such patients were in fact alive became important.

Most famous, of course, is the question of whether organs might be removed from these patients. More relevant, however, because it applies to every such patient and not just to potential organ donors, is the question of how long to maintain patients on ventilators. There are a limited number of ventilators and intensive care unit (ICU) beds in any hospital, and while they are generally not taken away from one patient to be given to another, there is certainly a desire not to waste this valuable resource on patients who are, in fact, dead. If brain dead patients are dead, it is unnecessary, even inappropriate, to keep them on ventilators in an ICU.

The modern nature of the question of distinguishing brain death from other criteria explains why this question was not addressed in halakhic literature prior to the twentieth century. More important, it also explains why one cannot draw any conclusions from this silence. It is impossible to know whether halakhic discussions that don't refer to brain death fail to do so because the rabbis would not have referred to it even if they had had access to the concept, or because the formulation that they in fact used (e.g., the absence of respiration) was the best they could do using the concepts and knowledge available at the time, but, had they been aware of and understood brain death, they would have accepted it as a better account of death than the one they used. Thus, while brain death is clearly a new idea, there is an important sense in which clinical death is as well. When clinical death is understood as

---

6. Nonetheless, this distinction could have had halakhic relevance, if, for example, one asked whether to continue unburying a victim of a building collapse on Shabbat once the person was known to be brain dead, or to exhibit neither pulse nor breathing. However, to the best of my knowledge, this question was never asked, and given the medical and philosophical inattention to brain death at that stage in history, this is hardly surprising.

specifically excluding brain death, it is being understood in a way it never was before the twentieth century. This, of course, doesn't mean that pre-twentieth-century halakhic literature isn't directly relevant to halakhic standards for death in the twenty-first century. However, it does mean that the relationship between these precedents and the current debate must be treated with care.

IV. ALL ACCOUNTS OF DEATH HAVE CONCEPTUAL PROBLEMS

Discussions about halakhic criteria for death often fail to acknowledge that clinical death and brain death both have significant conceptual problems that must be resolved before either can be coherently adopted as an account of death. Without reviewing the entire philosophical literature on this issue, I do want to raise a few salient points.

I will start with clinical death, focusing for the moment on clinical death as loss of heartbeat or circulation. Whereas, as we saw above, the invention of the ventilator was essential for our ability to recognize brain death, the development of cardiac resuscitation techniques – in particular defibrillation (electrically "jump-starting" a stopped heart) – played a role in questioning the validity of clinical death. Until we had defibrillators, a heart that had stopped beating would almost without exception never beat again. Thus, someone whose heart had stopped was unquestionably dead by clinical criteria. However, once we could restart a heart that had suffered what would formerly have been irreversible insult, it became unclear how we could say that one was dead simply because one's heart had stopped. If it was restarted, had this person risen from the dead? And what of patients whose hearts are stopped while they undergo coronary bypass surgery?

To respond to this concern, the idea of "permanent cessation" of cardiac activity is often introduced.[7] A person is dead only if his heart has permanently and irreversibly stopped beating. This concept resolves some issues but raises others. First, the connection between heartbeat and life has now been attenuated. Before, a person was dead simply by virtue of his heart having stopped beating. Now, however, one can be

---

7. For a discussion of how this idea evolved, see Rabbi Alan Brill's essay in this volume.

alive without a beating heart. Something further is needed before death occurs.

Even if we accept that a shift from loss of heartbeat to irreversible loss of heartbeat entails a somewhat new understanding of life and death, problems remain. With current technology, patients can now be kept alive (by any naïve definition of that term) after their hearts have permanently stopped beating. The most obvious example is via heart transplant. Once the diseased heart is removed, and certainly within a few minutes, it has permanently and irreversibly stopped beating. The patient then spends some time on bypass before the new heart is connected, all this time without a beating heart. But there are other ways to maintain life without a heartbeat. In principle, at least, extracorporeal membrane oxygenation (ECMO), a technology somewhat analogous to bypass, can keep a person alive for some time even with a totally nonfunctioning heart by circulating and oxygenating blood via an external circuit. More permanently, we will almost certainly soon have mechanical, implantable hearts with which patients can live independently for some time, possibly years, with no functioning heart of their own. Are all these people dead?

The recognition that some people must certainly be considered alive even without a heartbeat has led some to shift the focus from heartbeat to circulation. All the patients mentioned in the last paragraph have or would have circulating blood. So if we use that as our criterion for life, we will solve those problems. This focus on circulation, however, creates new problems. Although ECMO can keep people alive without a heartbeat in such a way that they are clearly alive according to any reasonable understanding of that term, it can also circulate blood indefinitely through bodies that are *not* alive according to any reasonable understanding of that term. One could take a body that has had no cardiac, respiratory, circulatory, or brain activity for over one hour, hook it up to ECMO, and circulate blood through it. This body is clearly not alive, but why not? What criterion separates this body from a living one?

Let us now turn to problems with brain death. Although brain death is often presented as a way around the ambiguities raised by clinical death, it is, in fact, subject to its own difficulties. It is clear that neither the loss of cortical functioning (essentially, consciousness) nor the loss of brainstem functioning is alone sufficient to call a person dead. If only the brainstem stops functioning, we have a locked-in patient, who is conscious but unable to move anything except his or her eyes. (Locked-in patients retain brainstem reflexes, but in extreme cases, even these may be lost.) That these people are conscious was amply demonstrated by Jean-Dominique Bauby, who wrote the book *The Diving Bell and the Butterfly* while locked in, by blinking. Certainly someone who writes a book is not dead.

Loss of cortical functions alone is likewise insufficient to consider someone dead. With proper nutrition and hydration, the bodies of such patients can function more or less indefinitely, as the case of Terri Schiavo proved.[8] Just as one who can write a book cannot easily be considered dead, one whose body continues to breathe, circulate blood, metabolize nutrients, and resist decay for years cannot either. An understanding of death that would allow us to consider such people dead is a far cry from the way we understand death now.

Combining the loss of both cortical and brainstem function doesn't entirely solve the problem either (even if we add in loss of *all* brain functions). We're still left with a body that, with the assistance of a ventilator and artificial nourishment (both of which locked-in patients need as well), can persist without deterioration for at least several days. If a body that can maintain itself is not dead, then brain dead patients aren't either. The fact that they need help by way of ventilators and nutrition is irrelevant, as other patients who are incontrovertibly alive need this help as well. Indeed, we need not have these patients rely on external help. Although it would be technically difficult, it is easy to imagine developing an artificial, implantable brainstem to take over at least some functions lost in brain death. In particular, it could regulate breathing, serving as a sort of pacemaker for the lungs. With such an implant, a patient's body could function for many days with no intervention, until

---

8. Terri Schiavo was kept alive in a persistent vegetative state, that is, without cortical function, for fifteen years simply with a feeding tube. This nutritional support was the focus of a long-running and ultimately highly politicized legal battle. After the courts finally ruled in favor of her husband, who wanted to remove the feeding tube in accordance with what he believed her wishes to be, the feeding tube was removed and Schiavo died after two weeks.

dehydration (usually) led to a breakdown of the homeostatic systems that had been maintaining the body until then. Does our understanding of death allow us to bury a body that is still maintaining itself?

Although the problems raised in the last few paragraphs are meant only as examples, in light of the distinction raised above between signs and definitions of death I should point out that these difficulties apply regardless of how we understand brain death and clinical death. If we understand them as presenting *definitions* of death, then the questions raised above show that under these proposed definitions we would have to call "dead" someone who was clearly alive, e.g., someone with a heart transplant. If, on the other hand, these accounts are taken to be *signs* of death, then the cases above show that they are not reliable. Taking the heart transplant patient as an example again, although such a person has clearly not died, he demonstrates the signs of clinical death, showing that those signs are not in fact reliable. Either way, there would be conceptual barriers to adopting either account.

Given that all potential accounts of death currently available suffer from conceptual problems, one response might be that halakha should ignore such problems in deciding what the halakhic account of death is, and work only with the halakhic evidence. This approach would be a mistake. For while all accounts have similar problems, their implications are not the same.

For instance, if declaring a patient on ECMO dead is unacceptable, then a circulatory account of death is highly problematic, regardless of its (internal) halakhic merits. On the other hand, if we accept as dead a body that has not even begun to decay – such as a body with the hypothetical lung pacemaker described above – then accepting a brain death standard may be more acceptable. All this is another way of saying that sensitivity to the conceptual issues presented by the accounts of death currently proposed by science is necessary to decide whether any given proposal should even be considered a candidate for giving an account of what we mean by death.

CONCLUSION

I hope two things have become clear by now. First, the considerations raised here are neutral as to whether brain death, clinical death, or

some other criterion should be recognized by halakha. Neither side
has the clearly "right" answers to these questions, though the consensus
responses to them may favor one account of death or another. Second,
one standard way, if not the only way, the debate about determining
death in halakha has been conducted is untenable. It is highly problematic to understand authors from previous generations – most specifically the Talmud, but also *posqim* such as Rambam and Rabbi Moshe
Sofer – as referring to either brain death or clinical death, and decide
the halakha accordingly.

Too much has changed in the last fifty years, and too much was
left unsaid and unconsidered before then, for this approach to work. The
entire topic must be analyzed from its fundamentals.[9] Only then will it
be possible to follow that standard halakhic practice of answering current questions in light of past decisions.

---

9. As it isn't my area of expertise, I haven't even mentioned issues raised by the history
   of medicine. A parallel essay written by a historian, however, could add another
   equally necessary dimension to the analysis here. In addition to clarifying whether
   the sages in *Yoma* were proposing a sign of death or a definition of death, and perhaps
   even as a prerequisite to answering this question, for example, we must know what
   they understood this sign/definition to be. How did they understand the role of
   breathing (and perhaps heartbeat) in human physiology? Certainly not the way we
   understand it now, and perhaps not the way their Greco-Roman contemporaries did
   either. Nevertheless, until we understand what they thought, it will be impossible to
   know why they ruled as they did and what to do with these rulings.

Chapter 18

Immanuel Jakobovits and the Birth of Jewish Medical Ethics

Alan Brill

INTRODUCTION

Modern medicine began in the second half of the twentieth century, flowering into unheard-of lifesaving procedures in the last quarter of that century. Prior to wonder drugs and new surgical methods, medicine was closer to the home health care of healing herbs, dressing wounds, diet, and bed rest. As late as 1925, it was still an even wager whether a doctor's care would improve your chances of survival. In the Middle Ages, medicine was a non-standardized field in which ideas were credited to their authors. When reading about a technique, one asked: Whose remedy is it? Whose suggestion? Generally, the words "medicine" and "doctor" as understood by medievals are not analogous to their pre-twentieth-century counterparts. Any analogy to premodern medicine requires a leap, with many chasms to be jumped.[1]

---

1. *Medicine and Society in France: Selections from the Annales Economies, Sociétés, Civilisations*, vol. 6 (ed. Robert Forster and Orest Ranum; Baltimore: John Hopkins University Press, 1980).

In a prior era, many halakhic authorities limited the Torah's mandate to heal to external wounds and assumed that internal medicine was forbidden.[2] For most, sickness served as a chance to repent or demonstrate one's faith in God.[3] When modern medicine became widespread in the United States and England, however, Jews were among its most aggressive users.[4] Then we witnessed the rapid rise of miracle surgeries, organ transplants, mechanical internal organs, and the creation of the intensive care units. Rabbi Immanuel Jakobovits was the first Jewish author to seriously confront these changes by creating the field of Jewish medical ethics.

Immanuel Jakobovits: Background

Rabbi Lord Immanuel Jakobovits[5] began his studies at the Etz Chaim Yeshiva in England and obtained ministerial training at Jews' College. In the late 1940s, Jakobovits started writing and lecturing on medical ethics. In 1947, he became rabbi of the Great Synagogue in London, and two years later moved to Dublin to become chief rabbi of Ireland. He subsequently relocated to New York to become rabbi of the Fifth Avenue Synagogue and finally returned to England to serve as chief rabbi of the British Commonwealth. In this last capacity, Jakobovits became a friend and confidant of Prime Minister Margaret Thatcher. He was knighted in 1981 and raised to the peerage as Lord Jakobovits in 1987. In 1991, Rabbi Jakobovits was the first Jewish recipient of the Templeton Foundation's Award for Progress in Religion, often referred to as the "Nobel Prize in Religion."[6]

Rabbi Jakobovits largely founded Jewish medical ethics, now an established academic field. The phrase first appeared in Jakobovits' doctoral thesis, *Jewish Medical Ethics: A Comparative and Historical Study*

---

2. Avraham Borenstein, *Avnei Nezer* ḤM 193.
3. For example, see Ḥaim Volozhiner, *Nefesh ha-Ḥaim* 11:11.
4. Paul Starr, *The Social Transformation of American Medicine* (New York: Basic Books, 1982); David Mechanic, "Religion, Religiosity, and Illness Behavior: The Special Case of the Jews," *Human Organization* 22, no. 3 (1963): 202–208.
5. B. Koenigsberg, Germany, 1921; d. London, 1999.
6. Fred Rosner, "Lord Immanuel Jakobovits: Grandfather of Jewish Medical Ethics," *Israel Medical Association Journal* 3 (2001): 305.

of the Jewish Religious Attitude to Medicine and Its Practice, submitted to London University in 1955 and published by New York's Philosophical Library in 1959.[7] This monograph was a landmark publication, not merely because the term/concept was unknown, but because the subject itself had never been explored and thus had no literary or scholarly expression in any Western language.

This essay will address from a historical perspective some of Jakobovits' statements about method in medical ethics, organ transplant, and passive euthanasia. These pronouncements will help elucidate the foundations on which later discussions of respiratory and brain death are built. Since medical ethics was a new field, many of its foundations were ambiguous or involved deviations from prior literature. Some authors continued Rabbi Jakobovits' premises, while other thinkers refuted and negated them. A full study of Lord Jakobovits' writings is a desideratum.

METHOD

Jakobovits built medical ethics as a form of ethics, not as a legal concern. The ability to create moral principles from prior cases is based on the abstraction of values. "Medical ethics" is not, therefore, used here in the technical, myopic sense of professional propriety, but rather as it is understood in Roman Catholic moral philosophy. In contrast to the founders of medical halakha, Rabbis Shlomo Zalman Auerbach, Moshe Feinstein, and Eliezer Waldenburg, Rabbi Jakobovits focused on moral problems raised by medicine and medical practice as opposed to those raised by Jewish law.

> Judaism considers that the great moral principles are profoundly enough rooted in the religious conscience of the nation to make it possible to tolerate exceptional cases.... It acts thus in conformity with its general spirit, which is to be strict in its principles, but human and clement in its application as it concerns the individual person.... [I]t is the human factor of the ethical code which will complete the lacunae of the law. (*JME*, xxvii–xxviii)

---

7. All subsequent citations of Jakobovits' thesis in this essay refer to a later edition (New York: Block Publishing Company, 1975; hereafter *JME*).

Jakobovits admits that there are gaps in the law, but he doesn't turn to casuistry or a priori principles. Rather, he draws on the broad, humanizing values of Jewish textual tradition. Acknowledging gaps, as Jakobovits does, is diametrically opposed to the legal positivist's approach to halakha.

Jakobovits confronts the medical changes of his time by arguing that Judaism's ethics have been unchanging:

> The Jewish people have been studying, writing about, and practicing Jewish medical ethics for thousands of years.[8]

Jakobovits considers the ethical focus to be on human life and saving it, rather than on patient autonomy or compassion. He lists the core principles of Jewish lifesaving ethics, including the following:

1. Human life is sacrosanct, and of supreme and infinite worth.
2. Any chance to save a life, however remote, must be pursued at all costs.
3. The obligation to save a person from any hazard to his life or health devolves on anyone able to do so.
4. Every life is equally valuable and inviolable, including that of criminals, prisoners, and defectives.
5. One must not sacrifice one life to save another or even any number of others.
6. No one has the right to volunteer his life.[9]

Rabbi Jakobovits believes modern medicine to be dehumanizing. The goal of Jewish and general medical ethics, in his view, is to humanize the process:

> Jewish thought will be particularly concerned to preserve man's spirituality and humanity against the encroachments of mechanization in which human love will be replaced by syringes and test tubes in the generation of life, and the designs of Providence

---

8. Rosner, "Lord Jakobovits," 304.
9. Ibid., 306.

by the arbitrary manipulation of genes and lethal agents in the determination of life and death, or in which human beings will be constructed to specified orders.[10]

To modernize the discourse around medical ethics, Jakobovits took several "nontraditional" stances, including the dismissal of talmudic medicine, the rejection of Eastern European wariness of medicine, and the continuous use of Jewish folk medicine. Following the regnant trends of Western European Jewish thinkers, Jakobovits rejects talmudic medicine by quoting the *Geonim*:

> Sherira's views paved the way for even more radical opinions by later Jewish teachers. Accordingly, it was not only unnecessary or unwise, but positively wrong to rely on the medical prescriptions in the Talmud. (*jme*, 6)

On the other hand:

> Several sources mention that it was, in fact, forbidden to put the application of talmudic remedies and medicines to the test, since their failure might be attributed, not to changed conditions of time and place, but (possibly without justification) to the limited or erroneous knowledge of the talmudic sages. (Ibid., 19)

Anti-medicine as a trend within Judaism is moderated or outright denied by Jakobovits, who speculates:

> Rabbi Nachman's bitterness, his cynical hatred of physicians, may have been due to the unhappy personal experiences which led to his death from tuberculosis in 1811. (Ibid., 6)

---

10. Immanuel Jakobovits, "Future Trends and Currents in Jewish Medical Ethics," in Fred Rosner, ed., *Pioneers in Jewish Medical Ethics* (Northvale, NJ: Jason Aronson, 1997), 231–34, cited in Rosner, "Lord Jakobovits," 310. Jakobovits focuses largely on preventing the encroachment of the medical profession on the dying, emphasizing the importance of allowing people to preserve their dignity. Nevertheless, as shown below, he states explicitly that his goal is not to determine the moment of death.

But what of the healing powers of the Hasidic saints and the visits to tombs? Jakobovits concludes that "The belief in the curative powers of religious shrines and saintly relics is unknown among the Jews" (ibid., 19). He is willing to confront the textual evidence and acknowledge that "Jewish sources, and more especially the Talmud, abound with references to the occult virtues in both legend and law" (ibid., 29). However, he denies any value or authority in these irrational accretions and concludes that they are to be ignored along with "the great influx of demonological and magical ideas," which entered into Jewish writings "mainly in the thirteenth century" (ibid.).

Like most graduates of Jews' College, Jakobovits was mildly historical in his orientation toward Jewish texts and held a broad view of the authoritative Jewish sources:

> Judaism's religious and moral directives in medical practice represent [the] accumulated wisdom and intellectual labors of millennia.[11]

He rejects the notion that "Halakha has ceased to develop since the suspension of the Sanhedrin two thousand years ago, or since the completion of the *Shulḥan Arukh* four hundred years ago."[12] The change needs to come through "an organic process which cannot be hastened artificially, or through popular agitation and lobbying."[13] The canon includes halakha, aggada, philosophy, ritual and all other aspects of the Jewish textual tradition. Jakobovits refuses to limit Judaism to halakha and claims that "to talk of 'halakhic Judaism' is … a distortion of Judaism." "Aggadic Judaism," "ritual Judaism," or "philosophical Judaism" are all variations on a theme. Authentic Judaism combines all these.[14]

The question ultimately in creating a Jewish medical ethic is, do we listen to the medical expertise of doctors, or do the talmudic texts have enough upon which to base modern discussions? Jakobovits notes

---

11. Immanuel Jakobovits, "Halakhah in Modern Jewish Life," *Judaism* 29, no. 1 (1980): 5.
12. Ibid., 5.
13. Ibid., 7.
14. Ibid.

that "Moses Schreiber [the Ḥatam Sofer]...would accept the general facts established by medical research but not necessarily an individual diagnosis made by a doctor," thereby reserving the understanding of the facts for the rabbis. "Another rabbi subscribed to almost the reverse view," in which the rabbi establishes the facts and the doctor determines the situation. "A third authority admitted the reliability of medical evidence only in respect of cures and medicines, but not in regard to the cause of pathological symptoms" (*JME*, 236).

According to Jakobovits, underlying the growing hesitation to acknowledge medical findings as absolute was the belief that the standards of medical science had declined since the time of the Talmud (ibid.). Jakobovits dismisses these views and accepts the revolutionary progress of medical knowledge. He notes that the eighteenth-century Rabbi Isaac Lampronti already cites the writings of Hippocrates and engages in his own experimental study of nature (ibid., 237). Even the sages sought doctors' advice and didn't think the Torah contained medical knowledge. "Even in regard to the interpretation of biblical laws, the rabbis often relied on the counsel of medical experts," and in later rabbinical literature "the rabbinical authors sought and accepted technical guidance on medico-religious questions from physicians, midwives and even...the medical faculties of various universities" (ibid.).

Jakobovits sharply distinguished between Jewish law as applying ethics based on prior law and "secular medical ethics," which seeks "to turn ethical guidelines or rules of conscience into law" (ibid., 7). Compared to the secular approach, "Jewish medical ethics does the reverse," in that "We determine law or legislation, distill it, and then come to the conclusion that it includes certain ethical guidelines." Thus, according to Jakobovits, "Jewish medical ethics...does not lead to legislation... as rulings of law that have been given, i.e., halakha, which means law or legislation." Rather, medical ethics' goal is to "extrapolate ethical rules from the legislation" (ibid.).

Jakobovits goes further: "Neither the Bible nor the Talmud nor other ancient works of Jewish law could foresee some of the ethical issues facing people today." For example, he writes of "an ongoing debate" within Jewish philosophy about when abortion should be allowed. "There is a degree of flexibility here.... [T]he halakha continues to be in formation" (ibid., 7). He doesn't discuss absolutes or definitions; rather, the law is in flux.

In a 1983 article, Jakobovits is closer to reflective equilibrium, a widespread method in modern bioethics. Reflective equilibrium involves

> ... working back and forth between our moral intuitions about particular cases.... According to the important philosopher John Rawls, there is a constant back-and-forth between our intuitive or considered judgments and theoretical ethical principles until a morally accepted conclusion is reached.[15]

Jakobovits exemplifies this flexibility in his treatment of autopsies, toggling between the prior halakhic ban on these procedures and his ethical stance, which seeks to permit them. In these cases, Jakobovits moved from the Catholic approach to that of reflective equilibrium:

> . As a consensus gradually emerges from the many often conflicting judgments given, this consensus is recognized as a valid precedent and embodied in the accepted corpus of rabbinic law.[16]

In a 2011 article, Alan Jotkowitz argues against this aspect of Jakobovits' thinking. Instead, Jotkowitz maintains that Jewish medical ethics relies heavily on casuistry and that the material incorporated into the Talmud serves as the source material for much of the modern discussion. "Decisions are usually reached by a careful analysis of the relevant cases and an extrapolation to modern dilemmas." For Jotkowitz, this method "works well when there are relevant cases comparable to modern dilemmas."[17] He asks, "How does one define 'dying' in an age of mechanical ventilation, left ventricular assist devices and dialysis?"[18]

---

15. Alan Jotkowitz, "Chimeras and the Limits of Casuistry in Jewish Bioethics," *Ḥakirah: The Flatbush Journal of Jewish Law and Thought* 11 (2011): 149–58 [153].

16. Immanuel Jakobovits, "Jewish Medical Ethics – A Brief Overview," *Journal of Medical Ethics* 9 (1983): 109–112 [112].

17. Jotkowitz, "Chimeras," 150.

18. Ibid., 151; Baruch Brody has already commented on these gaps, especially on the difficulty in distinguishing, in the contemporary medical setting, between removing

He claims that "Jewish ethicists must therefore rely on their intuitive judgments and ethical principles in rendering a decision."[19] Jotkowitz in 2011 returns us to Jakobovits in 1983, who acknowledged the paucity and ambiguity of prior material applicable to contemporary cases.

LOSS OF DEATHBED RITUALS

From a historian's perspective, analyzing Jakobovits' thinking offers a good vantage point for viewing the dismissal of centuries of deathbed rituals from Judaism, including preparations for a good death and easy passage to the afterlife. In the 1960s, the value of preserving human life in the ICU displaced asking about repentance and the angel of death. The biological concerns of preserving life took precedence over the psychological, spiritual, and metaphysical.

Philippe Ariès, a French historian, spent twenty years investigating the changing attitudes toward death in Western civilization. In the Middle Ages, the "art of dying" (*ars moriendi*) came to primacy as people came to terms with their ultimate demise. What was then important was how the dying faced death. In the mid-twentieth century, advances in medical technology (particularly the development of the respirator) meant that death could now be delayed, occurring in hospitals following a "great war against death." A death in the ICU is a weakness of medicine rather than a good death. Death is now culturally invisible. The entire process of fighting death shows more belief in and focus on medicine than in/on religion and the afterlife. No religious service culminates with the kiss of death.[20]

Social historian Elliott Horowitz describes an Italian controversy from 1556 in which a Jewish man died suddenly without confessing as part of his Jewish "last rites" and was thus refused burial. Those on the side of the deceased claimed that the movements of the man's lips

---

impediments to death and hastening it. Baruch A. Brody, "A Historical Introduction to Jewish Casuistry on Suicide and Euthanasia," in *Suicide and Euthanasia: Historical and Contemporary Themes* (ed. Baruch A. Brody; Dordrecht, the Netherlands: Kluwer Academic Publishers, 1989), 39–75.

19. Jotkowitz, "Chimeras," 153.

20. Philippe Ariès, *Western Attitudes toward Death: From the Middle Ages to the Present* (Baltimore: Johns Hopkins University Press, 1974).

immediately preceding death constituted a confession.[21] Rabbi Yechiel Michel Tucazinsky's *Gesher ha-Ḥaim* records that in Jerusalem in 1947, someone shouted confession every day in the hospital, so that everyone could affirm a confession before dying.[22]

The Talmud (b. *Shabbat* 32a) teaches:

מי שחלה ונטה למות אומרים לו: "התודה, שכן כל המומתין מתודין".

If one falls sick and his life is in danger, he is told: "Make confession, for all who are sentenced to death make confession."

In the *Shulḥan Arukh*'s codification (YD 338:1), based on the language in Tractate *Semaḥot*, Rabbi Joseph Karo rules that the following text should be recited to the terminally ill:

הרבה התודו ולא מתו, והרבה שלא התודו, מתו, ובשכר שאתה מתודה אתה חי, וכל המתודה יש לו חלק לעולם הבא.

Many have confessed but have not died; and many who have not confessed have died.[23] By the merit of your confession, you shall live. And all who confess have a place in the World to Come.

The early modern works on deathbed procedures, such as the *Ma'avar Yabboq* of Rabbi Aharon Berechia, were still essentials for the early twentieth century. These works build on talmudic and medieval conceptions and create full orders and regulations for deathbed rituals.[24] In contrast, Jakobovits states that the "predominantly 'this-worldly' character of Judaism is reflected in the relative sparsity

---

21. Elliott Horowitz, "The Jews of Europe and the Moment of Death in Medieval and Modern Times," *Judaism* 44, no. 3 (1995), 271–81.
22. Yechiel Michel Tucazinsky, *Gesher ha-Ḥaim* (Jerusalem, 1951), 9.
23. The passage in *Semaḥot* ends differently:

והרבה שהיו הולכין השוק ומתודין, שמא בזכות שאתה מתודה אתה חיה.

And many who are walking outside in the marketplace confess. Perhaps by the merit of your confession, you may live. (Tractate *Semaḥot* 1:2)

24. These works are also the source for the activities of the *ḥevra qaddisha* in performing the *ṭahara* on the deceased.

of its regulations on the inevitable passage of man from life to death" (*JME*, 119).

In the Jewish works on the art of dying, the goal, according to social historian Avriel Bar-Levav, was to preserve self-control, unlike our current ICU deaths.[25] Typically, deathbeds required a confession of the dying before a *minyan*. However, if such control is lacking, Rabbi Berechia states that the confession is said on behalf of the person – conscious or not – by an appointed messenger.[26] Originally, there was an unknown moment of death described in deathbed rituals as the "kiss of death," which signified the social moment when the person was believed to have died. The prayer said by those standing around the dying person appears in the standard guide to religious services, *Ha-Madrikh*, and begins with verses calling for God's mercy. It includes the Priestly Benediction and the prayer calling upon God's angels and protective spirit. This prayer is said even if the deathly ill person (*goses*) is incontinent or cannot hear it. According to these authorities, the prayer affects the person's soul as well as those who are praying. Even Rabbi Yekutiel Greenwald's 1951 work, *Kol Bo Aveilut*, assumes these practices, asking questions such as, if only one rabbi arrives at the hospital to perform a last rite, but two people are dying, do we send the rabbi to the sinner or the saint?

In contrast, Jakobovits assumes that only Christian religious literature has devoted much attention to ascertaining the exact moment of death. In Judaism, he believes this problem has little or no significance, since there are no sacramental rites to be accorded to the dying prior to the soul's final departure from the body. From the ritual point of view, the only practical distinction in Jewish law between a live body and a dead one concerns the defilement caused by the latter. Whereas originally there would have been a process of dying that included the soul, in Jakobovits' view we are now limited to the body (*JME*, 126).

---

25. Avriel Bar-Levav, "Jewish Manuals for the Dying in the Early Modern Period," *Sh'ma* 34/603 (September 2003): 11–12; Avriel Bar-Levav, "Ritualisation of Jewish Life and Death in the Early Modern Period," *The Leo Baeck Institute Yearbook* 47 (2002): 69–82.
26. Aharon Berechia, *Ma'avar Yabboq*, ch. 19.

In the full deathbed service, in works such as *Ma'avar Yabboq*, there are important practices to perform for the dying person and for family and friends, signaling the transition between realms. Physical death occurs at the end of this process, and the ritual helps demarcate the living from the dead. Even after physical death, the soul's departure from the body takes the entire seven-day *shiva* period. In modern terms, even after the clinical signs of death, a transitional process remains in which the body is still spiritually alive. Jakobovits does away with this transitional realm and limited the process to the modern clinical realm of the undertaker:

> When the patient dies, his body generally passes from the attention of the physician into the care of the undertaker and the religious officials who attend to its interment. (*JME*, 126)

Jakobovits acknowledges that

> ... the earliest rabbinic sources usually speak of death as the "going out of the soul," they also concede the view that the association between body and soul is not altogether severed until three days after death. (Ibid., 129)

Nevertheless, Jakobovits trusts in modern medicine's designation of biological death and considers doctors able to ascertain death. In contrast, Rabbi Moshe Isserles "altogether denies our competence 'nowadays' to ascertain the exact moment of death" (ibid., 127).

Jakobovits leaves us with an acceptance of the modern clinical definition of death. Now, following Jakobovits, the moment of death is identified entirely with physical death. Gone are discussions of afterlife or how sickness and death are part of the religious cycle of the community. Equally important, gone is any discussion of the social declaration of death, such as how families and communities are to note the transition of a member from life to death.

Death rituals assumed a period between life and death, a process of dying. From the perspective of ordinary end-of-life cases, the issues of futility, refusal, and withdrawal of care are paramount, while the definition of death is a much rarer concern.[27] The new approach of medical death in the ICU, and the halakha created for it, makes all death a failure of medicine. It turns dying into a moment, not a process. We deal with the denial of death by controlling it through medical definition. Philippe Ariès, in his work on death in the Middle Ages, has shown that there were many stages of dying, from becoming sick to maggots on a decaying body. The assumption was that the body as organism felt the pain of the grave and the maggots. Even physical decay was not the end. For many Jewish authorities, the claim of the dying on his or her body continues until the resurrection of the dead. This position was still held in modern times by halakhic luminaries such as Rabbi Eliezer Waldenburg, but was scoffed at as superstition by those with medical models, among whom Immanuel Jakobovits was perhaps the most influential.

It may seem unfair to pin so much on Jakobovits when virtually everything written on death and mourning in English for popular audiences ignores the soul and recasts all the mourning rituals in modern psychological terms. However, Jakobovits' approach has been continued by almost all halakhic/Orthodox rabbis who address medical ethics. Their comments deal almost exclusively with problems of life rather than

---

27. Aristotle designates four souls: mineral, plant, animal, and human. Platonists added a fifth: the spiritual. The plant soul is digestion, the animal soul is reactive, and the human soul is rational or thought processes. Much of the halakhic death debate concerns the vegetable and animal souls, little is said about the human soul, and much of the traditional process of death is now viewed as a legal moment. Rabbi Joseph B. Soloveitchik considers the vegetable soul to be the definition of life. See Joseph B. Soloveitchik, *The Emergence of Ethical Man* (Hoboken: KTAV, 2005), 29. Similarly, the Jewish philosopher Hans Jonas considers nature a stage for the moral, and one that we must respect. See Hans Jonas, "Against the Stream," in Jonas, *Philosophical Essays: From Ancient Creed to Technological Man* (Englewood Cliffs, NJ, 1974), 132–40. In contrast, Rabbi Aharon Lichtenstein claims that we care about *nomos*, not *physis* – law, not the natural order. See Aharon Lichtenstein, "Does Jewish Tradition Recognize an Ethic Independent of Halacha?" in Lichtenstein, *Leaves of Faith*, vol. 2, *The World of Jewish Living* (Jersey City: KTAV, 2004), 33–56. However, the proper place to start the discussion would be Menaḥem Azaria De-Fano, *Asara Ma'amarot* (Venice, 1597), which lists thirty-two "souls," including ones we recognize (such as the nervous system, circulation, and reflexes) and ones we don't (such as auras and astral bodies).

with the subject of death. Sociologist Peter Berger notes that death is an essential feature of the human condition that requires people to develop means of coping with it.[28] To neglect death in the ICU is to ignore one of the few universal parameters in which social and individual life is constructed. Contemporary sociologist Anthony Giddens argues that our era of "late modernity" has seen three changes: The experience of death has become increasingly privatized, there is greater identification of the self with the body, and the scope of the sacred has shrunk.[29]

GOSES AND THE CREATION OF PASSIVE EUTHANASIA

Rabbi Jakobovits asked Rabbi Yitzchak Yaakov Weiss, then of Manchester, about keeping a person on a respirator in order to donate his heart to another person. Weiss replied that one should not keep one person alive for the sake of another.[30] Jakobovits took this to mean:

> The classic definition of death as given in the Talmud and Codes is acceptable today and correct. However, this would be set aside in cases where competent medical opinion deems any prospects of resuscitation, however remote, at all feasible.[31]

For Jakobovits, halakhic respiratory death meant that breathing should be defined as spontaneous breathing, without irrevocable cessation.

Despite rejecting the traditional Jewish deathbed rituals, Jakobovits retains the focus on the alleviation of suffering. For example, he doesn't assume that doctors need to be aggressive in all cases in applying modern medical techniques. Instead, Jakobovits distinguishes between "natural" and "extraordinary" means:

---

28. Peter Berger, *The Sacred Canopy: Elements of a Sociological Theory of Religion* (New York: Anchor Books, 1967), 22.
29. Anthony Giddens, *Modernity and Self-Identity: Self and Society in the Late Modern Age* (Stanford, CA: Stanford University Press, 1991), 49–50, 161–62, 204.
30. Rabbi Yitzchak Yaakov Weiss, *Minḥat Yitzḥaq* 5:7.
31. Immanuel Jakobovits to Fred Rosner, August 1, 1968, http://www.medethics.org.il/articles/JME/JMEB2/JMEB2.28.asp#_ftn28.

The reference to the removal of the pillow, and the reason for this law, is further amplified by Isserles: "it is forbidden to cause the dying to pass away quickly; for instance, if a person is in a dying condition for a long time and he cannot depart, it is prohibited to remove the pillow or the cushion from underneath him following the popular belief that feathers from some birds have this effect [of delaying death]."

All these acts are prohibited because they may hasten the patient's death by moving him; for in the words of the Talmud, "the matter can be compared with a flickering flame; as soon as one touches it, the light is extinguished." Hence, any movement of the dying body must be avoided, even for the purpose of returning a shifted limb to bed or of relieving pain, except in order to save the patient from a fire....

It is clear, then, that, even when the patient is already known to be on his deathbed and close to the end, any form of active euthanasia is strictly prohibited. In fact, it is condemned as plain murder. (*JME*, 122–23)

Jakobovits uses the case of *goses* but expands it into a full acceptance of passive euthanasia.

He concludes his discussion with the following broad statement:

At the same time, Jewish law sanctions, and perhaps even demands, the withdrawal of any factor – whether extraneous to the patient himself or not – which may artificially delay his demise in the final phase. (Ibid., 124)

The widespread acceptance of passive euthanasia in traditional sources was reiterated by Baruch Brody in response to contemporary authors who negate these texts.[32]

---

32. Baruch A. Brody, "Jewish Reflections on Life and Death Decision Making," in *Jewish and Catholic Bioethics* (Washington, DC: Georgetown University Press, 1999), 17–24.

CHRISTIAAN BARNARD AND BRAIN DEATH

An underreported side of the story was Jakobovits' connections to Christiaan Barnard, the South African surgeon who performed the first heart transplant in 1967.[33] The chief rabbi and the surgeon exchanged formal letters on medical ethics and spoke both by phone and in person. These conversations seem to have created a common language even when the two differed. They appeared in public together and presented completely opposite opinions on when to allow passive euthanasia; the doctor would refuse the patient even basics such as food, whereas the rabbi distinguished between basics and extraordinary procedures. Nevertheless, on many issues they seem to frame their discussions in similar terms. Barnard wrote *Good Life Good Death: A Doctor's Case for Euthanasia and Suicide.*[34] In this volume and in several prior articles, the doctor discussed his conversations with the chief rabbi.

Immediately after performing the first heart transplant (December 26, 1967) in South Africa, Barnard wrote to Rabbi Jakobovits asking for his opinion. The rabbi replied, in part:

> An organ may never be removed for transplantation from a donor until death has been eventually established. The prohibition of *nivul ha-meit* would then be suspended by overriding consideration of *piqu'aḥ nefesh*. Hence, I can see no objection in Jewish law to the heart operations recently carried out, provided the donors were definitely deceased at the time the organ was removed from them.[35]

In his book, Barnard offers a vigorous advocacy of passive euthanasia based not on vital signs but on a quality of "being alive."

> And by living I do not mean simply exhibiting one or two vital signs, such as respiration or the registration of heartbeat. I mean rather the whole conglomeration of sensual experiences that the

---

33. This section appeared in somewhat different form as a blog post: http://kavvanah. wordpress.com/2012/11/12/rabbi-immanuel-jakobovits-and-christiaan-barnard/.

34. Christiaan Barnard, *Good Life Good Death: A Doctor's Case for Euthanasia and Suicide* (Englewood Cliffs, NJ: Prentice-Hall, 1980).

35. Rosner, "Lord Jakobovits," 305.

patient calls "being alive" – the experiences that by their very complexity and subtlety are not amendable to measurement or statistical analysis and are usually known only to the patient, his closest associates, and his doctor.... (*Good Life*, viii)

Today's sophisticated medical technology can lead to situations in which few of the rules apply. For example, it is possible to have a heart beating for many hours in a body that is dead, and conversely, a patient can be very much alive even though the heart's beat has stopped for hours. (Ibid., 8)

Barnard sought religious guidance to determine life and death. He found that the modern issues were first broached "in 1957 when, at the international Congress of Anesthesiologists in Rome, Pope Pius XII was asked, 'When does death occur?'" Barnard was satisfied with the pope's reply that "human life continues for as long as its vital functions, distinguished from the simple life of the organs, manifest themselves spontaneously without the help of artificial processes." What is important in this definition is the insertion of the words "spontaneously" and "without ... artificial processes." The pope added: "The task of determining the exact instant of death was that of the physician" (*Good Life*, 30). This definition was given even before the widespread use of heart/lung machines or the ability to perform organ transplants.

Barnard adopted the pope's definition as his own:

A person will be considered medically and legally dead if, in the opinion of a physician based on ordinary standards of medical practice, there is an absence of spontaneous brain function; and if based on ordinary standards of medical practice, during reasonable attempts to either maintain or restore spontaneous circulatory or respiratory function in the absence of aforesaid brain function, it appears that further attempts at resuscitation or supportive maintenance will not succeed, death will have occurred at the time when these conditions coincide. Death is to be pronounced before artificial means of supporting respiratory and circulatory function are terminated and before any vital organ is removed for purpose of transplantation. (*Good Life*, 43)

This definition of spontaneous breathing and irreversible condition was then adopted by Jakobovits and, through him, by later authors. The phrase "spontaneous respiration" originated in 1880s and was used through World War I to refer to resuscitation of a person. It declined in usage between 1915 and 1969. The term resurfaced during the 1970s in connection with acute pulmonary failure. Adjectives such as "irreversible" and "spontaneous" became the assumed terms for respiration in these conditions. Jakobovits appears to be the first authority to bring the term into the halakhic discourse. The Talmud, not accounting for ventilators or CPR, assumes solely that no breath equals no life.[36]

Barnard declares that "most doctors know deep in their hearts that euthanasia is the right form of treatment for some terminally ill patients." He further muses that he "would have expected, for example, that those most opposed to it [passive euthanasia] would be Orthodox Jews." However, when he "conferred with Rabbi Immanuel Jakobovits" and "read his book on medical ethics," he found that "the Orthodox Jewish view accepts the legality of expediting the death of an incurably ill patient in acute agony by withholding such medicaments as would sustain his continued existence by 'unnatural means.'" For Orthodoxy, "there is nothing opposed to passive euthanasia, merely agreement that no special treatment should be used to continue a life that is already at an end." Barnard concludes that he is "struck by the fact…that euthanasia is more in keeping with religious teachings than it is with medical teaching" (*Good Life*, 52, 89–90).

Jakobovits recounts how, on a visit to Cape Town, he had a fascinating discussion with Christiaan Barnard. The two were at loggerheads over the definition of death. Barnard was willing to condone almost any form of euthanasia,[37] to which Jakobovits responded:

---

36. Joan Margaret Ross, Daniel Merlin Pryce, and Charles Frederick Ross, *Post-Mortem Appearances* (New York: Oxford University Press, 1963).

37. Barnard was initially not well received; there was an op-ed against him in the *New York Times* in 1968, and in a famous 1972 trial in Japan, several doctors who imitated him were accused of murder. Barnard emphasized quality of life, not even waiting for respiratory or brain death. A 2006 account of the original surgery based on

The rule remains firmly fixed to the extent that Jewish law cannot accept the concept of "clinical death." So long as any spontaneous life action by the heart or lungs persists, even "irreversible brain damage" or a flat electroencephalogram (EEG) reading does not legally establish death. Any action, even at that stage, which would precipitate the patient's final demise is to be regarded as homicide and strictly condemned.[38]

In principle Jakobovits accepts breathing and heart as the criteria for life, but he opposes artificially prolonging a life, especially amid great pain. For Jakobovits, *goses* means non-spontaneous and irrevocable, so in such cases he allows passive euthanasia, letting nature take its course:

So long as the heart still functions and the blood circulates, death has not yet set in. But this does not mean that a lingering life, especially when experiencing great pain, must be prolonged at all costs and in all circumstances. While one may not actively cause or hasten the onset of death, and no one may therefore ever withhold normal and natural means to sustain life – such as food, drink, blood, or oxygen (or air) – one need not artificially prolong life…by administering antibiotics…to suppress infection. Thus, one may allow nature to take its course by withholding such treatment.[39]

Describing a prior policy decision, he states:

There was, however, limitation of care to allow the heart to stop beating as soon as possible within the limits proposed by Jewish

the testimony of Barnard's brother Marius, reveals that the surgical team debated whether to wait for the donor heart to stop beating (they did not). See Donald McRae, *Every Second Counts: The Race to Transplant the First Human Heart* (New York: G. P. Putnam's Sons, 2006), 191–92.

38. Jakobovits, "Jewish Medical Ethics," 109–112 [112].
39. David Inwald, Immanuel Jakobovits, and Andy Petros, "Brainstem Death: Managing Care When Accepted Medical Guidelines and Religious Beliefs Are in Conflict," *BMJ* 320 (May 6, 2000): 1267.

law. Invasive and non-invasive monitoring were stopped and antibiotic treatment was withdrawn. There was to be no resuscitation in the event of an arrhythmia, no endotracheal suction, and no renal support.

Such patients must be treated as live persons, though one need not apply artificial methods in hopeless cases at the terminal stage. In such cases, it may indeed be wrong to prolong the suffering by artificially maintaining lingering life. If resuscitation fails, the patient is considered as retroactively dead from the time breathing ceased.[40]

Jakobovits leaves us with an ambiguity in that heart transplants are theoretically permitted, if the donor is dead, yet his definition of death would preclude them. Jakobovits was vague enough to be able to combine a reliance on Rabbi Weiss with allowing passive euthanasia.

OBSERVATIONS

Robert Truog, professor of medical ethics at Harvard, argues that brain death is incoherent. It's a legal fiction created in order for doctors not to be considered murderers. Focused on legal culpability, it is neither ethical nor biological.[41] Halakha has been busy following this reductionist category, not mentioned in the Talmud, creating a definition of death that is solely pragmatic.

Before organ transplants, doctors turned off ventilators informally. The Harvard criteria simplified the definition process, which became more complex in the 1980s and 1990s. Now, in the twenty-first century, there is a choice of up to a dozen different medical tests to determine death.

According to anthropologist Sharon Kaufman, there is currently a realm understood as neither life nor death by traditional criteria. How we die has moved from a natural order to a choice of treatment decisions and indecisions; choice has replaced nature.[42] However, the two

---

40. Ibid.
41. Robert D. Truog, "Brain Death – Too Flawed to Endure, Too Ingrained to Abandon," *Journal of Law, Medicine & Ethics* 35, no. 2 (2007): 273–81.
42. Sharon R. Kaufman, *And a Time to Die: How American Hospitals Shape the End of Life* (Chicago: University of Chicago Press, 2005).

processes of recognition of death and definition of death involve different approaches, both of which pose essential questions about the status of an individual. There can be *recognition* of a particular state, such as irrecoverable brainstem function. But the *definition* of a state of brain death can be only a philosophical exercise. "When the clinical criterion to recognize 'brain death' is considered certain," then it is considered a warrant for "intervention in anticipation of fulfillment of actual death."[43] But is it the traditional view of death? We may not have recognizable criteria for our decisions or the courage to make them.

This essay doesn't directly address the question of whether to accept or reject brain death. Instead it tells the backstory of how we came to discuss many of the issues involved in the discourse surrounding this topic. Jakobovits leaves a legacy of a naturalized death process reliant on the medical model and with a legal definition of death. He lived with the tension between the sanctity of life and the quality-of-life argument for passive euthanasia. He argued against dehumanization and the tendency to treat the patient as an object, but he never questioned the medical model itself. He employed a moral model in line with the Catholic model, believed that Jewish law must incorporate history and values, and rejected talmudic science.

Jakobovits naturalized the Jewish understanding of death using medical ideas, but he didn't deal with death process. His legacy has had an enormous effect on the discourse surrounding brain death, which forms the backdrop of the modern debate. Dr. Fred Rosner and Rabbi Dr. Moshe Tendler, for instance, continued Jakobovits' approach when they crafted the halakhic brain death definition, modifying his views in conversation with their own medical and scientific training. Conversely, Rabbi Dr. J. David Bleich, one of the most vociferous opponents of the brain death definition, continues the process of "modernized religion" but explicitly rejects Jakobovits' approach.

Bleich's critique and ultimate rejection of Jakobovits' method includes: disqualifying the Catholic moral model, negating the role of history and values in Jewish law, and accepting talmudic science by

---

43. Peter J. McCullagh, *Brain Dead, Brain Absent, Brain Donors: Human Subjects or Human Objects?* (Chichester, England: Wiley, 1993), 4.

stating that talmudic medicine is directly applicable to the contemporary. Additionally, Bleich rejects the possibility of passive euthanasia, redefines *goses* as only when life cannot be prolonged by artificial means, and argues for the sanctity of life. More important, he sees halakha not as a human process dealing with lacunae, but as an a priori legal world.[44]

The contrasts between these two positions – that of Jakobovits and his followers and that of Bleich – should have been set out and debated in the early 1980s. Having a clear sense of the possible underpinnings of Jewish medical ethics would be of tremendous use in navigating the constant flow of new medical developments and the possibilities they create. Instead, more than a half century later, we still have no major study of the various premises formed to create Jewish medical ethics. In my opinion, most of the issues around the moment of death are more likely to be clarified by broad, basic discussions of nature, science, and death in Judaism than by debating any particular and derivative question of medical ethics, such as that of the status of brain death in halakha.

44.J. David Bleich, *Ethical Dilemmas* (Hoboken: KTAV, 1986).

Chapter 19

Torah U-Madda and the Brain Death Debate

Charles Sheer

INTRODUCTION: DEFINING THE ISSUE

Over the past three decades, the Rabbinical Council of America (RCA) has struggled to define its position on brain death. A few years after the Uniform Determination of Death Act (UDDA) was passed in 1981,[1] defining both cardiopulmonary and neurological failure as death (see below), the RCA Executive Committee articulated its position in a brochure, "A Torah Perspective Regarding the Health Care Proxy":

> In accord with the ruling of Ha-Rav ha-Gaon Moshe Feinstein, z"tl, and of the Chief Rabbinate of Israel, brainstem death, together with other accepted neurological criteria, fully meets the standards of halakha for determining death.

---

1. See http://uniformlaws.org/ActSummary.aspx?title=Determination%20of%20 Death%20Act. This act was drafted by the National Conference of Commissioners on Uniform State Laws and was "approved and recommended for enactment in all the states" by the American Medical Association and American Bar Association. Over the years, most states in the US have adopted this act as law.

This clear and simple pronouncement accorded with the UDDA, which stated (section 1):

> An individual who has sustained either (1) irreversible cessation of circulatory and respiratory functions, or (2) irreversible cessation of all functions of the entire brain, including the brainstem, is dead. A determination of death must be made in accordance with accepted medical standards.

The RCA brochure concealed a major rift between its Executive Committee and its Vaad Halacha.[2] After the committee's declaration, the Vaad Halacha issued a responsum (1991) challenging brain death. The internal debate continued for twenty years, until December 2010, when the RCA released a 110-page study titled *Halachic Issues in the Determination of Death and in Organ Transplantation: Including an Evaluation of the Neurological "Brain Death" Standard* (dated June 2010).[3]

The purpose of the study was "to assist members of the RCA in the process of *psak halacha* and is itself not intended as a formal ruling." The motivation for the project was spelled out:

> This paper is not being one-sided...it merely recognizes that, as a "*ḥiddush*," the neurological standard must stand up to close scrutiny. This paper analyzes forty years of accumulated halachic opinion and the concurrent progress in medical knowledge, to ask whether a determination of death based upon the neurological "brain death" standard is warranted beyond reasonable doubt.[4]

Despite its claim of evenhandedness, the study patently seeks to challenge brain death as a determinant of death, and the information

---

2. For more on this decision and the process that led to it, see the interviews with Rabbis Marc Angel and Binyamin Walfish in the Organ Donation volume (forthcoming).
3. Authored by Asher Bush et al., *Halachic Issues* comments with laudatory candor: "In the wake of these two documents [the RCA brochure and the responsum of the Vaad Halacha], much confusion and even ill-will have surrounded this issue" (p. 10).
4. Bush et al., *Halachic Issues*, 7.

and analysis provided reflect this orientation.[5] According to one neuro-surgeon:

> The medical section ... is not an unfettered presentation of the truth. Not only does it present only the facts supporting just one side of the debate, but some are not factually correct, and some that are correct are presented in a way that misleads the reader.[6]

Though the Vaad Halacha assumes that brain death still needs to be proven "beyond reasonable doubt," this definition of death has been widely adopted within the medical, legal, religious, and ethics worlds.[7] In January 2012, the "American College of Physicians (ACP) Ethics Manual" stated:

---

5. The study focuses predominantly on those who challenge or reject brain death. It doesn't cite Rabbis Shlomo Goren and Ḥaim David ha-Levi, for example, who offer alternative positions on brain death. Rabbi Goren addressed this topic in many essays in his *Torat ha-Refu'a* (Jerusalem, 2000), esp. 27–39 and 57–78. For Rabbi Ha-Levi's view, see his *Aseh Lekha Rav* 5:29, 198–211, published in English in *Crossroads* (Zomet, 1987), 147–55. On the other hand, the positions of Rabbis Moshe Feinstein and Joseph B. Soloveitchik receive extended treatment. In both cases, the report concludes that their sons, sons-in-law, and students preserve different memories of these positions. According to the study, the legacy of the two major *posqim* of the RCA community is sadly clouded with contradictory testimonies and dubious evidence.

   The most egregious instance of the paper's dismissal of evidence as disputed is a letter signed by Rabbi Moshe Feinstein and printed on his stationery. It was published by his son-in-law, Rabbi Moshe Tendler, in *Responsa of Rav Moshe Feinstein*, vol. 1, *Care of the Critically Ill* (trans. Moshe Dovid Tendler; Hoboken: KTAV, 1996), 35–37, 154. In this letter Rabbi Feinstein states regarding the Harvard criteria that "in my opinion, these criteria are in agreement with the halakha.... When a patient is neurologically unresponsive to all stimuli and, in addition, has lost the ability to breathe on his own, he is unquestionably dead, as I explain in my responsum." Regarding this historic and clearly pivotal expression of Rabbi Feinstein's position, the study states: "It is widely acknowledged that this is not the work of Rav Moshe" (p. 55).

6. Dr. Noam Stadlan, http://torahmusings.com/2010/12/death-by-neurological-criteria/. See also Dr. Stadlan's essay in this volume.

7. See Avraham Steinberg, M.D., *Encyclopedia of Jewish Medical Ethics* (trans. Fred Rosner; Jerusalem: Feldheim Publishers, 2003), s.v. "moment of death," 695–706. Dr. Steinberg states:

   > At the end of the 1960s, various national and international organizations accepted brain death as death. These include the World Health Organization, the

Medicine, law, and social values are not static. Reexamining the ethical tenets of medicine and their application in new circumstances is a necessary exercise…. The irreversible cessation of all functions of the entire brain is an accepted legal standard for determining death when the use of life support precludes reliance on traditional cardiopulmonary criteria. After a patient has been declared dead by brain death criteria, medical support should ordinarily be discontinued. In some circumstances, such as the need to preserve organs for transplantation or to counsel or accommodate family beliefs or needs, physicians may temporarily support bodily functions after death has been determined.[8]

On December 6, 2011, the New York State Department of Health released new "Guidelines for Determining Brain Death."[9] Although these guidelines – like the ACP manual – appeared after the RCA study,

---

World Medical Association and many other European and American groups…. Since then there has been nearly universal acceptance of the concept of brain death in the West…. Most countries in the world and most physicians and philosophers accept brain death as death, both socially and legally.

One strong supporter of brain death is the Catholic Church, whose position was presented by Pope John Paul II at the Eighteenth International Congress of the Transplantation Society (August 29, 2000) as follows (www. vatican.va/holy_father/john_paul_ii/speeches/2000/jul_sep/documents/ hf_jp_ii_spe_20000829_transplants_en.html):

With regard to the parameters used today for ascertaining death – whether the "encephalic" signs or the more traditional cardiorespiratory signs – the Church does not make technical decisions. She limits herself to the Gospel duty of comparing the data offered by medical science with the Christian understanding of the unity of the person, bringing out the similarities and the possible conflicts capable of endangering respect for human dignity. Here it can be said that the criterion adopted in more recent times for ascertaining the fact of death, namely the complete and irreversible cessation of all brain activity, if rigorously applied, does not seem to conflict with the essential elements of a sound anthropology.

This approach, that religion should accept and work with science, seems to me a useful model.

8. "American College of Physicians (ACP) Ethics Manual," *Annals of Internal Medicine* 156, no. 1 (2012): 73–104 [84].
9. See http://www.health.ny.gov/professionals/hospital_administrator/letters/2011/ brain_death_guidelines.htm.

the acceptance of brain death in the medical community and by all health agencies over the past decades is evident from its citations and references. In accordance with the UDDA, brain death has been codified as law throughout the United States and in much of the Western world. Hospital policies, mandated by law and regulatory agencies, include brain death within their definition of death.[10]

The study correctly notes that some physicians critique the current variation in standards by which hospitals evaluate the status of suspected brain dead patients.[11] The implication of this critique – according to the Vaad Halacha – is that these neurologists are unsure about brain death altogether and that the "range of standards" is "disturbing," because it could entail ending the life of someone still alive. The study misunderstands the neurologists' position, however, and the call for standards review. Leading neurologists are revising their protocols – how many clinical examinations are needed and how such procedures are to be done, etc. In the medical world, all procedures and protocols are regularly evaluated, and many are modified in response to new research, data, or understandings. But the discussion within the field and changes in protocols don't imply rejection of brain death. It has become the norm because convincing studies have confirmed its reliability: This condition is irreversible, and no proper brain death determination – despite the current variation in protocol – has been withdrawn subsequent to a declaration of death.[12]

The medical section of the paper concludes with a high-profile case of a potential donor who, about to be transplanted, was found to be

10. I surveyed six hospitals in the New York City area that treat large Jewish and, in particular, Orthodox and Hasidic patients. All accepted brain death as their protocol.
11. "A recent review of fifty leading medical centers revealed a significant and disturbing range of standards and practices regarding the determination of 'brain death'" (Bush et al., *Halachic Issues*, 20).
12. The recent New York State "Guidelines" provide a full review of these studies. Some medical professionals do express reservations about the brain death standard, however. See, for example, D. Alan Shewmon, "Brain Death: Can It Be Resuscitated?" *Hastings Center Report* 39, no. 2 (2009): 18–24; Robert D. Truog, "Brain Death – Too Flawed to Endure, Too Ingrained to Abandon," *Journal of Law, Medicine & Ethics* 35, no. 2 (2007): 273–81; and Franklin G. Miller and Robert D. Truog, "The Dead Donor Rule and Organ Transplantation," *NEJM* 359, no. 7 (2008): 674–75. See also Dr. Howard Doyle's essay in this volume.

alive. The study declares that this case, although unique and probably the result of hospital error, "casts a giant shadow over this entire discussion."[13]

This unfortunate finale to the medical introduction reflects a lack of understanding of hospital events. It misrepresents this error as evidence that a brain death declaration is unreliable. Sadly, errors can and do occur in hospitals. However, one would not conclude that a "giant shadow has been cast" over surgery if a patient's right leg were operated upon instead of his or her left. The episode reflects a hospital error; it doesn't "cast a giant shadow" on the legitimacy of brain death.

In hospitals today, patients who have been declared neurologically dead are considered dead. The family is so advised. The respirator is removed, meds are terminated, and the patient is moved from the ICU to allow the valuable facility to be available for those in need. If the family won't accept the determination of death for religious or moral reasons, hospitals in New York State are mandated by law to extend "reasonable accommodation."[14] The hospital generally ends up absorbing the cost of continued care, since insurance won't reimburse for hospital/medical expenses extended to a cadaver. When the family rejects a brain death declaration, the hospital and its staff are sorely challenged.

Death is such a painful moment. If family members espouse differing or unclear definitions of death, they often turn to their rabbi for guidance. The lack of a unified rabbinic position on brain death can foster confusion in our community when rabbinic guidance is needed most.

Consider a family whose loved one was hospitalized due to a traumatic car accident. After hovering beneath the shadow of the angel of death for a few days, the patient is declared by the physician to be deceased on neurological grounds. But family members differ on brain death. Some accept the hospital's determination. They don't wish to delay burial and, in accordance with Jewish law, start calling the *ḥevra qaddisha* and organizing the funeral. Other members, sustained by the RCA study, demur, "Mom's not dead; it's not time to say goodbye."

---

13. Bush et al., *Halachic Issues*, 22.
14. What this means varies from hospital to hospital. Some will allow the brain dead patient to remain on a ventilator. I know of no hospital in which a physician will order new medications, or the staff will initiate medical intervention – CPR, etc.

In many arenas of Jewish law, divergent positions are the norm, and the lack of uniformity may bring some discomfort. But in most contexts, accommodation is possible and the hardship is minimal. In this area of life and death, however, where a family's loss is so encumbered by pain and sadness, the last thing rabbis should do is increase that pain and abet dissention and discord. Unintentionally, the study might become a source of confusion and heartache for the Orthodox community when it turns to its rabbinic leadership for guidance and solace amid tragedy.

The report could also lead to a *ḥillul Hashem* in terms of organ donation. Once someone has been declared deceased by the usual cardiopulmonary standards, it's too late to harvest his or her organs. When a patient is declared brain dead, however, organ donation is still possible. Yet a person who rejects brain death will not allow his or her organs to be harvested to save the life of another. Nevertheless, many *posqim* rule that this same person may accept an organ from another.[15] Although the logic is coherent, the implication in practice is clearly discriminatory. The denial of brain death casts aspersions upon members of our community who receive the gift of life from others but won't reciprocate.[16]

Despite its claim to the contrary, the study doesn't merely review the brain death issue from medical and halakhic perspectives. It reverses RCA policy in deference to the Vaad Halacha, which opposed the decision of the Executive Committee over twenty years ago. Hence the fact that the RCA's Health Care Proxy, which overtly accepted brain death, was withdrawn from the RCA website shortly after the paper was promulgated.

In summation, the study places the Orthodox world in opposition to the medical establishment regarding brain death. If Orthodox Jews reject a neurological declaration of death, our community will require substantial accommodation by institutions whose protocols conflict with our religious norms. Families could be divided in their treatment of brain dead loved ones due to differing rabbinic views. And the image

---

15. See, for example, Abraham S. Abraham, *Nishmat Avraham*, YD 339:3 and 339:9.

16. For more on the issue of taking but not giving organs, see the essays by Rabbi Yitz Greenberg, Dr. Noam Zohar, and Rabbi Yosef Carmel in this volume as well as those by Rabbi Dr. Eugene Korn, Rabbi Joseph Telushkin, and Rabbi Yuval Cherlow in the organ donation volume. For a somewhat different perspective, see the essay by Rabbi Yaakov Love in this volume.

of Orthodox Jews will be tarnished due to our reluctance to participate in organ donation as equal partners in this lifesaving endeavor.

I. FRAMING THE HALAKHA-AND-SCIENCE QUESTION

Many articles about brain death, including the RCA study, approach this topic using the standard method: What do the sources say, how might we apply them, and which authority do we follow? Of course, these questions are vital. The bedrock of Orthodoxy is our textual heritage, and we naturally turn to our rich resources – biblical and rabbinic – to guide us through difficult waters.[17] Some issues, however, seem beyond the easy reach of rabbinic decisors. This is especially so when the matter in question hasn't been treated in our literature, since it didn't exist in previous generations, or its understanding has changed due to new discoveries or perspectives.

Additionally, determining a position on brain death is so challenging to the Orthodox community because it's not merely a question of deciding the halakha regarding a specific case. It involves the much

---

17. Rabbi Dr. Abraham S. Abraham devotes almost thirty pages in his *Nishmat Avraham* to brain death (vol. 2, 451-89; expanded second edition, Jerusalem, 2007). Most of this entry deals with the writings and decisions of Rabbis Shlomo Zalman Auerbach and Yosef Shalom Elyashiv, who contend that a victim of neurological death is *safeq goses*, meaning such a patient is at end stage but not considered deceased; they therefore oppose the removal of an organ from this person, as that would entail an act of homicide. Rabbi Auerbach opined: "...since there is no definition like this [i.e., brain death] in the Talmud, we cannot create any such definition in our day" (ibid., 458).

Dr. Abraham presents the permissive position of the Israeli Chief Rabbinate in one quarter of a page. He examines various responsa of Rabbi Moshe Feinstein on this topic but concludes that, even if Rabbi Feinstein accepted the Harvard criteria of death – meaning he ruled permissively regarding brain death – he did so only to permit the removal of a ventilator. "...it seems to me that he in no way intended to rely upon [these] medical determinations [which affirmed brain death] in order to perform an active intervention, to actually extract organs [for transplantation]" (ibid., 478).

Dr. Abraham concludes with a résumé of the opinions he has cited, including major *posqim* in Israel and elsewhere, and reflects that although some maintain that "it is permissible or imperative to take an organ from a Jew who has died according to a brain death declaration, nonetheless, this case remains a *safeq de-oraita* (a question of Torah law). Since this matter might entail the death of the donor, we must be stringent [and not allow such an action]" (ibid., 489).

broader question of the relationship and roles of Torah and *madda*. How do we regard the teachings of our halakhic authorities on scientific issues? This question is especially urgent when classical Jewish texts conflict with modern science. Do we follow our traditional teachings nonetheless and endure the resulting intellectual dissonance as the price of our faith? Or may we consider our sources a reflection of the popular or scholarly wisdom of their time?

These factors complicate the brain death debate. As I will argue, the principal obstacle to the resolution of this issue is the fact that classical Jewish texts – from the Bible through the talmudic/midrashic sources – do not define death itself. How do Jewish law and Jewish thought understand the nature of death? What aspects of a human being, when they no longer function or exist, define him or her as "deceased"? Without a basic definition of death, how can we ascertain if brain death fulfills normative criteria?

II. YOMA

The principal talmudic source cited in discussions of brain death is b. *Yoma* 85a. The eighth chapter of *Yoma* contains many pericopae dealing with the mitzva of saving lives (*piqu'aḥ nefesh*). The Mishna presents a case of a building collapse. If someone might be buried alive under the rubble, the Mishna mandates that a passerby undertake a rescue operation even on Yom Kippur. Although some aspects of this mission might desecrate the holy day, the mitzva of saving lives takes precedence. The discussion presents various opinions that, at first glance, seem to address the definition of death.

The *Baraita*

The Talmud introduces the following *baraita*:

תנו רבנן: עד היכן הוא בודק?	Our rabbis taught: Up to where [on the
עד חוטמו, ויש אומרים: עד לבו	body] do we check [for signs of life]? Up
[ס"א: טיבורו].	to his nostrils. Some say: Up to his heart. (Some texts read: his navel.)[18]

---

18. This is also the text of the Jerusalem Talmud.

Section IV – Historical and Ethical Considerations

Rashi comments:

עד חוטמו – ואם אין חיות   Up to his nostrils – If there is no life
בחוטמו, שאינו מוציא רוח, ודאי   presence (*hayut*) in his nostrils, meaning
מת, ויניחוהו.   he doesn't exhale, he has surely died, and
they leave him.

Thus, according to Rashi, the first opinion in the *baraita* is that breathing observed at the nostrils indicates *hayut*, life presence. Rashi's interpretation reflects the simple meaning of this passage, that an examination of the nostrils of a buried party would entail a search for respiration. This understanding is uncontested.

The examination at the heart or navel, however, tolerates several interpretations. Although ancient societies were unaware of the physiological meaning of the various bodily systems – and, as I shall suggest later, it is anachronistic to apply modern concepts to our talmudic/ medieval sources – the debate in the *baraita* seems to reflect different opinions regarding what physical signs are reliable indicators of life.

Although the nature of circulation was not understood until William Harvey (d. 1657), the heart examination could still have been a search for a heartbeat. The presence of an enduring beat would have indicated that the person was still alive. The examination also could have sought to access movement of the diaphragm. Since the objective of the search was to exclude the possibility of death, any sufficient demonstration of life would have allowed the rescue to continue.

Regarding the heart examination, Rashi states:

...מר אמר: בלבו יש להבחין, אם   ...one said to check his heart, to look for
יש בו חיות, שנשמתו דופקת   signs of life (*hayut*), since his spirit/breath
שם, ומר אמר: עד חוטמו,   (*nishmato/neshimato*) beats there, and the
דזימנין דאין חיות ניכר בלבו,   other said until his nose, since sometimes
וניכר בחוטמו.   no life (*hayut*) is detectable in his heart,
but it is detectable in his nostrils.

The word *nishmato* is problematic. It can't mean "his soul," because the verb, *dofeqet* (beats), would make no sense in this context.

The cleanest interpretation is to understand the word as *neshimato*, from the word *neshima*, breath. Thus, according to Rashi's understanding of this talmudic passage – and his view of human anatomy (see below) – the heart examination shared a similar objective with the nostril exam: to ascertain that the buried party was still breathing. The debate in the *baraita* regards the preferred or necessary locus for the breathing test.

Rabbi Dr. Edward Reichman proves that Rashi presumed "that the heart is a respiratory organ and that…the inspired air ultimately reached the heart, ideas widely held throughout antiquity and the Middle Ages."[19] The air inhaled through the nostrils passed to the heart, where it cooled this organ so its innate heat would be contained. Rashi's understanding of the human body – like that of the sages – was largely shaped by the teachings of Galen (d. ca. 200 C.E.) and other Greco-Roman scholars. Galen's vision of human physiology dominated from the ancient period until the Renaissance. His conceptions, of course, have been long superseded by other perspectives.

The Jerusalem Talmud

The Jerusalem Talmud's presentation of this case (j. *Yoma* 8:5) is difficult to understand on terminological as well as interpretive grounds.[20] Its assumptions – especially the connection between physiology and embryology – are problematic, and everything is complicated by different versions of the text. Given these challenges, this passage cannot convincingly serve as a halakhic source.

Interestingly, the principal commentator on the Jerusalem Talmud, Rabbi Moshe Margalit (d. 1781), in his commentary, *Pnei Moshe*, interprets this case in a fashion that sustains the above analysis of the

---

19. Edward Reichman, "The Halakhic Definition of Death in Light of Medical History," *Torah U-Madda Journal* 4 (1993), 148–74 (esp. 152–55).

20. The Jerusalem Talmud's case is discussed in Bush et al., *Halachic Issues*, 24–29. See also Reichman, "Halakhic Definition," 152–55. Regarding the textual variants of *Yoma* in the Babylonian and Jerusalem Talmuds, see Alexander Tal, "Nostrils, Navel or Heart? Significant Textual Talmudic Variations Concerning Signs of Life," http://www.hods.org/pdf/Nostrils,%20Navel%20or%20Heart%281%29.pdf. This issue is discussed elsewhere in this collection as well.

Babylonian Talmud's passage.[21] Following Rabbi Margalit's text, the Jerusalem Talmud reads:

עד איכן? תרין אמורין: חד אמ]ר[: עד חוטמו, וחורנה אמר: עד טיבורו.

Up to where [must one check]? Two opinions are recorded. One says: Up to his nose. The other says: Up to his navel.

מאן דאמר עד חוטמו – בהוא דהוה קיים. ומאן דאמ]ר[עד טיבורו – בהוא דהוה רכין.

According to the one who says, "Up to his nose" – the reason is that it remains firm. According to the person who says, "Up to his navel" – the reason is that it is soft.

Rabbi Margalit explains:

מ"ד עד חוטמו וכו'. כלומר ולא פליגי דמ"ד עד חוטמו מיירי בהוא דהוה קיים כלומר שחזק וקשה הוא ונרגש בבדיקת חוטמו אם יש בו איזה חיות ומ"ד עד טיבורו בהוא דהוה רכין שהוא רך כשממשמשין בו ואינו נרגש בחוטמו ובודקין אותו עד טיבורו שאפשר שעוד ירגישו בו חיות.

According to the one who says, "Up to his nose," etc. – meaning they aren't really arguing. The person who says "Up to his nose" is discussing a case where *it* [unclear antecedent] is *qayam*, meaning firm and hard; it can be detected by checking his nose [to see] whether he has any life force (*ḥayut*). The person who says "Up to his navel" refers to when *it* [unclear antecedent] is *rakin*, meaning he/it feels soft to the touch; one cannot detect [life force] by checking his nose, so he is checked up to his navel, since perhaps some life force can still be detected there.

Like the Babylonian Talmud, the Jerusalem Talmud offers two options; however, Rabbi Margalit explains that the two opinions don't

---

21. There are other interpretations of this passage, but this is not the place for a survey.

disagree. Both are describing optimal ways of determining ḥayut, and it is clear from his interpretation of the first position that he understands ḥayut to mean the "life force" demonstrated by respiration at the nostrils. Possibly this opinion held that the firm cartilage of the nose would allow for a proper examination even under the rubble.

The second opinion recommends the navel, possibly because, under a collapse, the nose could be crushed, precluding examination of the nostrils. The soft midsection, however, might not be compressed by the debris. Rabbi Margalit believes that it may still be possible to detect breathing in the navel. Either way, according to Rabbi Margalit, both opinions in the Jerusalem Talmud provide a location on the body of the buried party where *breathing* can be located; neither is interested in any other vital sign.

Rav Pappa's Position
The discussion in the Babylonian Talmud concludes with a statement by Rav Pappa, who also argues that the two parties in the *baraita* do not disagree in certain situations.

אמר רב פפא: מחלוקת ממטה למעלה, אבל ממעלה למטה, כיון דבדק ליה עד חוטמו שוב אינו צריך, דכתיב: "כל אשר נשמת רוח חיים באפיו".	Rav Pappa said: The dispute is when [uncovering the person] from bottom to top, but from top to bottom once one checks the person's nose [for signs of breath], one need check no further, as it says: "All in whose nostrils was the breath of life" (Gen. 7:22).

The nostrils/heart debate, Rav Pappa maintains, is only when the rescuer uncovers the person from the direction of his or her feet. In such a situation, the first location where a test for respiration might be made is the midsection. At this locus, some hold that an examination can indeed be made. The first opinion in the *baraita* disagrees. This view considers the heart an unacceptable location for a respiratory examination. One must uncover the body until the nostrils are revealed.

According to Rav Pappa, however, both opinions agree that if the rescue proceeds from the head of the buried party, and no breathing is observed at the nostrils, no further examination is necessary. He cites Genesis 7:22 to support his position regarding the sufficiency of a breathing test.

This passage occurs at the conclusion of the description of the flood. After forty days of rain, Genesis (7:21–22) states:

וַיִּגְוַע כָּל בָּשָׂר הָרֹמֵשׂ עַל הָאָרֶץ בָּעוֹף וּבַבְּהֵמָה וּבַחַיָּה וּבְכָל הַשֶּׁרֶץ הַשֹּׁרֵץ עַל הָאָרֶץ וְכֹל הָאָדָם. כֹּל אֲשֶׁר נִשְׁמַת רוּחַ חַיִּים בְּאַפָּיו מִכֹּל אֲשֶׁר בֶּחָרָבָה מֵתוּ.	And all flesh that stirred on earth perished – birds, cattle, beasts, and all the things that swarmed upon the earth, and all mankind. All in whose nostrils was the breath of life, all that was on dry land, died.

The verse is interpreted to mean that all creatures died since their nostrils were covered by the all-encompassing waters. More significantly, it is further understood to imply that the "breath of life" is located in the nostrils.

This reading of Genesis 7:22 appears twice in b. *Yoma* 85a. It is first presented anonymously a few lines before Rav Pappa's statement, within the Talmud's analysis of a teaching by Abba Shaul. The Talmud doesn't use this verse to *derive* a respiratory definition of death. Rather, it sees Genesis 7:22 as reflecting the commonsense association between breathing and being alive.[22] The Bible contains hundreds of references to death and numerous narratives concerning the death of an individual; none of these defines death.[23]

---

22. Thus, in his responsum regarding the definition of death (which will be examined in the next section of this essay), Rabbi Moshe Sofer understood this reading as a homily. He identifies Genesis 7:22 as a "support" for the respiratory definition, not a proof.

23. The root of the standard Hebrew word for "death," מות, is used in most of these passages. It appears 780 times in the Hebrew Bible in verb forms, and 161 times in noun forms. The synonymous root גוע appears twenty-four times. See A. Even-Shoshan, *New Concordance of the Bible* (Jerusalem, 1983) [Hebrew]. Neither root conveys specific actions or behaviors.

Since the Talmud records no objection to Rav Pappa's statement, both opinions must agree that breathing observed at the nostrils indicates *ḥayut*.[24]

The simplest reading of the text in both Talmuds is that the purpose of the examination is to assess that the party is not deceased. All agree that breathing is a universally accepted demonstration of life, which is necessary to allow the restrictions of Yom Kippur to be suspended in the context of a lifesaving rescue. The pericope deals with the exceptional case of a threatened life, seeking to clarify the context for a continued rescue. Nothing broader – such as a definition of death – is intended. The RCA study similarly states: "…the entire purpose of this *sugya* in *Yoma* is to offer practical direction to those involved in a rescue from a collapsed building, and not to address the deeper issue of what actually marks the end of life" (p. 26).[25] The *Yoma* pericope *does not* shed light on the definition of death.

In this regard, *Yoma* resembles all the other talmudic discussions of death. As Rabbi Prof. Avraham Steinberg has noted:

> There are numerous references to death in the Bible, but there is *no definition* of the *moment* of death [Steinberg's emphasis]. Many rabbinic and talmudic references to death relate to the laws of the Sabbath, the laws of ritual defilement…the beheaded heifer… deserted wife…terminally ill (*goses*). All these are exceptional circumstances. *There is no clear definition, however, of death for normal and routine death* [my emphasis].[26]

Neither biblical nor talmudic sources provide a clinical definition of death.

---

24. See also Tal, "Nostrils," 9: "In both cases at issue is detection of breath, revealed either directly in the nostrils or indirectly in the rise and fall of the trunk, be it the chest or the abdomen."

25. Also, "…it is highly debatable whether any conclusion regarding the validity of the 'brain death' standard for death can be gleaned from [b. *Yoma* 85a]" (Bush et al., *Halachic Issues*, p. 24).

26. Steinberg, *Encyclopedia*, 799.

III. ḤATAM SOFER

In a responsum included in his collection *Ḥatam Sofer* (YD 338), Rabbi Moshe Sofer (d. 1839) discusses, among other things, how to determine when death has occurred. Understandably, his text became a standard feature within discussions about the halakhic definition of death. In the RCA study, it is analyzed as a principal source, cited in subsequent halakhic writings and by contemporary authorities.

Rabbi Sofer is responding to the suggestion of Rabbi Tzvi Hirsch Chajes that a *kohen* who's also a doctor should be permitted to declare whether a patient is or is not deceased. Since the patient has not yet been declared dead – and, indeed, the *kohen*-physician might find that the patient is not deceased, and medical treatment might be recommended – Chajes argued that this *kohen* could attend to the patient. As a precedent, Rabbi Chajes cites Rabbi Moses Mendelssohn, who stated – regarding the delaying of burial – that non-experts can verify death only by waiting for the decomposition of the body. Rabbi Sofer vehemently rejects this assertion and prohibits the *kohen*-physician from examining the moribund patient.[27]

Rabbi Sofer's first and most significant point is that determining death is less "complicated" than Rabbis Chajes and Mendelssohn imply. In fact, in Rabbi Sofer's opinion, the halakha is clear:

...when his breathing stops, we no longer violate the Sabbath [to save him]. This is a general principle relative to all [examinations of] the dead, for this is *the definition that has been accepted as our tradition* [my emphasis] ever since the assembly of God became a holy nation. All the forces (*ruḥot*) in the world…cannot move us from the position of our holy Torah.

...כשפסקה נשמתו שוב אין
מחללין שבת וע״כ כלל הוא
לכל המתים שזהו שיעור
המקובל בידינו מאז היתה
עדת ה׳ לגוי קדוש וכל הרוחות
שבעולם...לא יזיזונו ממקום
תורתינו הקדושה.

---

27. For an overview of these and other important debates relevant to the modern controversy, see Eytan Shtull-Leber, "Rethinking the Brain Death Controversy: A History of Scientific Advancement and the Redefinition of Death in Jewish Law" (BA honors thesis, University of Michigan, 2010), esp. 39–55, http://deepblue.lib. umich.edu/bitstream/2027.42/77671/1/eytansht.pdf.

Later in his responsum, Rabbi Sofer states that experts perceive the situation differently from the uninitiated:

אלא האמת יורה דרכו כי כמה שעות או אפי' יום ויומים קודם החלט מיתתו עפ"י בקיאי' המבינים סי' מיתה כמו אנשי החברא המתעסקים עם מתים בזמנינו קודם לזה כבר בטלו חושיותיו והרגשותו ומוטל כאבן דומם בעילוף הסמוך למיתה והמתעסקים עומדים עליו ומצפים רגע יציאת הנפש עפ"י קבלתם שבידם והוא הרגש כ"ש בנשימה ודפיקה ידועה אבל לכל ההמוני' אין הפרש בין צורתו ושכבו קודם יציאת הנשמה ובין כמה שעות אח"כ עד התחלת ס' עיכול וא"כ משעת עילוף ההוא עד סי' עיכול שהוא לפעמים יום ויומים אין שום היכר לההמונים אעפ"י שבינו לבינו הבינו המבינים שיצאה נשמתו בביטול נשימה קלה ההיא.

But the truth will show its way, for a few hours or even a day or two before a person's death is declared by experts who understand death – such as the members of the *ḥevra* [*qaddisha*], who deal with the dead nowadays – his senses and feelings have already ceased, and he lies still as a stone in the unconscious state (*iluf*) that precedes death. Those involved stand before him and watch for the moment of death, based on traditions they have inherited. This entails looking for any sign of breathing or detectable pulse. However, to the average person, there is no difference between how he appears lying down before his soul departs and a few hours later, until he begins to decompose. If so, from the time of this unconscious state until decomposition begins – which is sometimes a day or two – the average person has no way of knowing, though among themselves the experts know that the soul has departed once any breathing has ceased.

Elsewhere in the responsum, Rabbi Sofer again declares that there must have been some known definition of death, since the Torah commands prompt burial upon death and prohibits any delay. Given these positive and negative biblical commandments regarding burial, some definition of death must have been transmitted.[28] But what was its source? Rabbi Sofer suggests three.

אולי הי' אז מסורת מבעלי
טבעיים הראשונים אעפ"י
שנשכח מרופאי זמנינו
ועליהם סמכו חז"ל בהרבה
ענינים מעניני התורה,
כמבואר פר"ע פ"ה ע"א
וסמכו אקרא לא תסיג גבול
ריעך אשר גבלו ראשונים.

Perhaps there was a tradition from the early naturalists (*ba'alei ṭivi'im ha-rishonim*) – though it was lost to our contemporary physicians – and the sages relied upon them regarding many Torah matters, as explained in b. *Shabbat* 85a, where they relied upon the verse "You shall not move your countryman's landmarks, set up by previous generations" (Deut. 19:14).

או אם לא היה להם מסורת
מהטבעיים ע"כ קבל מרע"ה
השיעור מהלכה למשה מסיני.

Or, if there was no such tradition among the naturalists, Moses our teacher must have received it as a *halakha le-Moshe mi-Sinai*.

או שסמכו עצמן אקרא כל
אשר רוח חיים באפו דהכל
תלוי בנשימת האף וכמבואר
ביומא פ"ה ע"א ופסקו
רמב"ם וטוש"ע.

Or they [the sages] supported [this position] with the verse "All in whose nostrils was the breath of life," implying that everything depends on respiration, as explained in b. *Yoma* 85a and codified by Rambam and *Ṭur Shulḥan Arukh*.

The First Proposed Source

Rabbi Sofer's first proposed source for defining death as cessation of breathing is derived from what he calls the *ba'alei ṭivi'im ha-rishonim* – literally, early naturalists. This unusual term is found in only a handful

---

28. In Rabbi Sofer's words:

הנה בלי ספק כשאמרה התורה
כי יהי' באיש חטא משפט מות
והומת וכו' לא תלין וכו' כי קבור
תקברנו והעובר על זה בשום מת
עובר על עשה ול"ת ע"כ אז נמסר
לנו שיעור מיתה.

Undoubtedly, when the Torah stated: "when a man commits a capital crime and is executed ... do not let his body hang [until morning]; rather, be sure to bury him" (Deut. 21:22–23), [such that] one who violates this regarding any deceased person violates a positive commandment and a prohibition, clearly, the time [it takes to] die was communicated [as a part of this mitzva].

of Hebrew texts.[29] It refers to ancient figures who, due to scholarship or experience, possess knowledge or expertise regarding the natural world. This ancient wisdom has a unique standing as accepted, established, and common knowledge.

Rabbi Sofer cites b. *Shabbat* 85a as a talmudic context in which such knowledge serves as the basis for rabbinic law and normative Jewish behavior. *Shabbat* 84b–85a discusses how different types of seeds may be sown within a given field without violating the prohibition of *kilayim*, improper mixtures of planting.

[ומנלן] דקים להו לרבנן מילתא היא? דא״ר חייא בר אבא א״ר יוחנן: לא תשיג גבול רעך אשר גבלו ראשונים - גבו[ל] שגבלו ראשונים לא תשיג.	[How do we know] that the [agricultural guidelines] upon which the rabbis relied are correct? Rabbi Ḥiyya said in the name of Rabbi Yoḥanan: What is the meaning of the verse "You shall not move your countryman's landmarks, set up by previous generations" (Deut. 19:14)? A landmark set up by previous generations should not be moved.

According to Rabbi Yoḥanan, the verse in Deuteronomy teaches that we may not ignore the boundary markers of the ancients. By this he means that certain planting ratios must have been accepted as common knowledge by prior generations. In the next section of the passage, Rabbi Yonatan and others argue that the original settlers of the land, Hurrians as well as Hivites, had special expertise in its agricultural norms: "They would say, 'Mark this spot for a vineyard, mark this spot for fig trees.'" Their knowledge of agricultural practices – derived either from their own experience or, possibly, from preceding generations – became the standard. When the people of Israel entered the land, they followed these principles.

---

29. I thank Dr. Gabriel Birnbaum of the Academy of the Hebrew Language, Jerusalem, who assisted me by searching for other instances where this phrase appears in Hebrew texts. *Ba'alei ṭivi'im* appears in Maharsha, *Ḥiddushei Aggadot*, b. *Ta'anit* 9b; *ṭivi'im* is found in a few philosophical works, where its usage is the same as or similar to Rabbi Sofer's usage here.

Rabbi Sofer doesn't identify who these ancient naturalists were. However, given the similarity between the sages' understanding of natural phenomena, the human body, etc., and the wisdom transmitted by Greco-Roman scholars such as Galen – as noted above – the latter are quite likely the ones who transmitted the respiratory definition of death, especially since their teachings were regnant for over fifteen hundred years. Although Rabbi Sofer doesn't identify the source of this definition, he correctly reflects that this concept had become part of the heritage of Western civilization.

The Second and Third Proposed Sources

Rabbi Sofer's second and third proposals revert to standard Jewish methods of proof. The second proposal alleges that the respiratory definition of death was one of those teachings deemed *halakha le-Moshe mi-Sinai*. This terminology appears throughout talmudic literature, starting with the Mishna (*Yadayim* 4:3).[30] The application of this term to the rabbinic discussion of death, however, cannot be traced to a source prior to Rabbi Sofer; its usage in this context is unique to him.

Rabbi Sofer was surely aware that the Talmud cites no *halakha le-Moshe mi-Sinai* identifying death as cessation of respiratory function. Instead, he seems to use this term in the sense of an established and normative precept.[31] His usage reflects his desire to moor the respiratory definition in ancient, immutable law.

Rabbi Sofer's third proof turns to the biblical verse cited in the Babylonian Talmud: "All in whose nostrils was the breath of life." As noted, he identifies this citation as a "support" for respiratory function. Respiratory death is not *derived* from this passage either by a literal

---

30. Rabbi Yair Chaim Bacharach (1638–1702) devoted an entire responsum to a study of sixty-six talmudic texts where this term appears (*Havvot Ya'ir* 192). Its range of meanings as noted by Rabbi Bacharach is beyond the scope of this essay.

31. Thus, when m. *Yadayim* 4:3 uses this term to describe a particular law, one standard medieval Mishna commentator, Rabbi Samson ben Abraham of Sens (ca. 1150–ca. 1230), remarks: "Not exactly [at Sinai], since this [law] is not [written] in the Torah. Rather, it is like 'a law [revealed] to Moses at Mount Sinai.'" (See also Rabbeinu Asher, Laws of *Miqva'ot* 1, who cites an interpretation of the term to mean "a clear matter, like a law revealed.")

reading or by exegetical means. Rather, one could read the verse homiletically to provide support for this idea, which is extraneous to the text. Creative word play allows a reader to associate this concept with this passage, but it remains a "support," not a source.

Thus, despite three attempts, Rabbi Sofer doesn't provide a convincing source for the definition of death as cessation of respiratory function.[32]

Conflicting Definitions of Death in *Ḥatam Sofer*

These passages demonstrate how strongly Rabbi Sofer wished to sustain respiration as his definition of death. Yet other lines in his responsum seem to present a different set of indicators:

כל שאחר שמוטל כאבן דומם ואין בו שום דפיקה ואם אח"כ בטל הנשימה אין לנו אלא דברי תורתינו הקדושה שהוא מת.	Anyone lying still as a stone, with no heartbeat, and whose breathing then terminates – all we have are the words of our holy Torah that he has died.
...כבר בטלו חושיותיו והרגשותו ומוטל כאבן דומם בעילוף הסמוך למיתה.	...his senses and feelings have already ceased, and he lies still as a stone in the unconscious state (*iluf*) that precedes death.

What do these passages mean? How are we to understand the sudden appearance of heartbeat (*defiqa*) in Rabbi Sofer's list? Is he suggesting that cardiac function is a factor? If so, on what textual basis? Rabbi Dr. Reichman notes that "nowhere in the Talmud, to the best of my

---

32. Rabbi Dr. J. David Bleich discusses Rabbi Sofer's responsum in his article "Spontaneous Generation and Halakhic Inerrancy," *Tradition* 44, no. 4 (winter 2011): 55–75. He claims that Rabbi Sofer's definition of death derived from "the natural scientists of [his] age," and that "*Ḥatam Sofer* spells out in a clear and concise manner the criteria of death as culled from much earlier halakhic sources" (p. 72). He further states, "Most fundamentally, the authority for such provisions of halakha is derived directly from revelation at Sinai rather than from communal acceptance of the corpus of halakha" (p. 73). The above discussion undermines Rabbi Bleich's use of Rabbi Sofer's responsum to argue for the Sinaitic origin of this law.

knowledge, is there a mention of the taking of the pulse."[33] Furthermore, what are the patient's "senses (*hushiyotav*) and feelings (*hargashoto*)"? To understand Rabbi Sofer's position, we must convert his descriptions into medical terms. It's hard to do so convincingly, since we don't know his understanding of various medical concepts.

Is Rabbi Sofer suggesting a sequence of events that depicts the stages of death: a traumatic episode, which induces a comalike state, followed by cardiac and respiratory failure? If so, what is the relative strength of each stage, and does he believe every death follows this order? How precisely are we to interpret his sequence of indicators? Finally – and most important – what is the relationship of this set of indicators to Rabbi Sofer's earlier respiratory definition?

There are various resolutions and interpretations of his position, and many are cited in the RCA study.[34] Given Rabbi Sofer's halakhic authority, and since his responsum is one of the earliest attempts to define death, it is understandable that his words reverberate in the literature on this topic. However, his responsum presents many interpretive challenges.

Lack of Scientific or Empirical Support

None of Rabbi Sofer's three proposals regarding the source of the respiratory definition is based upon science. He lacked scientific data with which to refute the physicians of his era who questioned any declaration of death prior to bodily decomposition.[35] The objective of his responsum, however, was to defend the Jewish practice of a speedy burial and to prohibit a *kohen* from functioning as a coroner. While the secular authorities declared that contemporary physicians could not ascertain irrevocable death, Rabbi Sofer sought to demonstrate that Jewish tradition had long-established principles that were known by the *hevra qaddisha*.

---

33. Reichman, "Halakhic Definition,"152.

34. See also the many resolutions cited in Steinberg, *Encyclopedia*, 700–702, as well as in the discussions of Rabbi Yoel Bin Nun (this volume) and of Rabbi Ariel Picard and Dina Najman (next volume).

35. See, however, Rabbi Sofer's well-known responsum (*Hatam Sofer* YD 167) in which he discusses Rashi and Tosafot's disagreement with Rambam regarding the nature of the female anatomy. After reviewing their opinions, Rabbi Sofer declares:

Its "experts" *could* reliably determine that death had taken place. His aim was not to argue the scientific validity of Jewish law but to defend the autonomy of the Jewish community in matters pertaining to death.

Evaluating Rabbi Sofer's Position

Given the historic context and objective of Rabbi Sofer's responsum, it cannot be used as a definitive source for a halakhic definition of death. Although his words can be appropriated as an argument for a respiratory definition, the thrust of his responsum was not to define death as a religio-medical concept but to demonstrate that immediate burial was the long-standing Jewish practice, and that the *hevra qaddisha* had sufficient indicators to determine when a person was dead.

Rabbi Sofer wasn't championing any *definition* of death. He was simply addressing Rabbi Chajes' query about whether a *kohen* could serve as the doctor who would declare patients dead, since before the official declaration no one really knows whether a person is dead or not. To this, Rabbi Sofer responded forcefully that we do know, and that the halakha forbidding a *kohen* to enter a room containing a dead body is

---

אבל באמת כל זה כתבו תוס' לפי הבנתם...הכל לפי שכלם אבל אחר בקשת המחילה מרבותינו הקדושים לא צדקו דבריהם בזה כי האמת עם הרמב"ם כאשר יעיד הניסיון עפ"י חכמי וספרי הניתוח אשר לפנינו מספרי בני ישראל.... ויש לפני עוד ספרים מדויקים מרופאים מומחים אשר לא מבני ישראל המה.... כולם יעידון ויגידון כהרמב"ם ז"ל ומיני' לא ניזוע גם שאלתי רופאים וכך אמרו לי.

In truth, Tosafot wrote all this in accordance with their understanding...everything according to their logic. However, after requesting forgiveness from our holy teachers, [I must say that] their words were incorrect in this regard. Rather, the truth accords with Rambam, as examination/experience will demonstrate, in accordance with surgeons and texts about anatomy that we have before us, written by Jews.... I also have other accurate books [written by] physicians who are experts, although not Jewish.... All of them support Rambam, and we shouldn't veer from his position. Additionally, I've asked physicians, and they've confirmed it for me.

Rabbi Sofer accepted the position of Rambam over that of Rashi and Tosafot on the basis of scholarly consensus, medical textbooks, and physical examination. The teachings of Rashi and Tosafot weren't based in observable fact. Rabbi Sofer rejected their opinions in favor of one sustained by actual observation and accepted medical knowledge.

in full force. Rabbi Sofer could very well have written the same forceful defense for immediate burial if, for example, he accepted neurological death, given today's knowledge of the human organism. To appropriate his staunch defense of respiratory death as an unequivocal rejection of brain death is to take his words out of context.

IV. PREMODERN SCIENCE

I have contended that neither b. *Yoma* 85a nor the responsum of Rabbi Sofer provides a halakhic definition of death. In addition, a broader question presents itself about the appropriateness of using our classical texts dealing with scientific matters: What is the standing of such texts, which, of necessity, reflect the wisdom of antiquity or the Middle Ages?

I cannot imagine a physician today turning to a seventeenth- or eighteenth-century medical work to diagnose a medical problem or determine treatment. Clearly, the moral responsibility of a physician to provide optimal medical care mandates that he or she rely upon the most advanced understanding of the human body. Rabbi Sofer himself did so in other cases. Should we not follow that model when it comes to ascertaining such issues as the definition of death, and our position on brain death?

Judaism, like other religious systems, is on familiar turf when it considers the philosophical or moral *implications* of death. How can mortals understand the end of life? How might our perception of death influence how we live our lives? Does the character of one's death reflect divine judgment upon an individual, community, or nation? What happens after death? Can we justify the frequent travail that accompanies this final journey, and is it indeed final?

Jewish texts from all periods and schools of thought discuss human mortality and the meaning of death as an event in our individual and communal lives.[36] These varied responses illustrate how vital this

---

36. To cite just a few from various periods, see m. *Avot* 2:10 ("Rabbi Eliezer used to say: 'Repent a day before you die'") and Rabbi Yisrael Salanter, *Or Yisrael*, ch. 3 ("Our entire existence is due to the compassion of Heaven, and by a miracle do we endure … and not for one moment does [the possibility of] death not stand before our eyes").

topic has been since the origin of collective memory. The *meaning* of death has been an abiding theme of all cultures.

But discussions in our sources about the meaning of death do not define the term. This lacuna is understandable; our literature reflects the state of medicine and science in the premodern world. Until the mid-twentieth century, it was impossible to sustain an individual artificially after his or her cardiopulmonary system had failed. Such failure was usually coterminous with death; it served as the indicator of death and its definition, both in the medical world and in the popular mind. Modern technological advances allow us to tease out the various components of human existence, however, and call for a more precise definition of death.

Contemporary ethicists struggle to define the term. Stuart J. Youngner, M.D., proposed:

> A formulation of death must have three components: a concept or *definition* of what it means to die, operational *criteria* for determining that death has occurred, and specific medical *tests* showing whether or not the criteria have been fulfilled.[37]

Youngner maintains that a conceptual framework is needed to explain "What quality is so essentially significant to a living entity that its loss constitutes the death of that entity?"[38]

The search for a definition of death is exceedingly complex, since it entails scientific phenomena as well as values drawn from fields such as religion, ethics, and philosophy. Ideology plays a vital role.

The texts and authorities cited in the RCA study do not endeavor to define death. Rather, they focus on Youngner's second and third components: the clinical phenomena that demonstrate death has occurred, and the tests that verify these indicators. The study discusses which

---

In contrast to the finality of death as expressed in Ecclesiastes 3:18–21, see virtually any page in *Ma'avar Yabboq* by Aharon Berechia (Italy; d. 1639), where the *neshama* and its afterlife are a constant and vital concern.

37. Stuart J. Youngner, "Defining Death: A Superficial and Fragile Consensus," *Archives of Neurology* 49 (1992): 570–72. See also the comments by Vladimir Hachinski, M.D., ibid., 572. I thank Dr. Noam Stadlan for referring me to this source.

38. Youngner, "Consensus," 570.

physical changes in the human being indicate that life has concluded. If cellular activity is still detected in the brain, does that mean the patient is alive? And what about a functioning hypothalamus? Is that organ considered part of the brain? What is the standing of medical tests such as the EEG, nuclide scan, Transcranial Doppler, etc.? Does the information derived from these tests allow *posqim* to declare an individual alive or dead, despite no clear halakhic precedent? The RCA study doesn't seek to develop a conceptual definition of death. It concentrates on clinical indicators and medical protocols. In other words, it discusses issues relative to *madda* rather than Torah.

These issues are challenging grist for the halakhic mill. Our authorities sorely strain to find reliable precedents for modern medical procedures. The RCA study contains many forced interpretations of earlier sources. We can, with homiletic license, impose all sorts of meanings upon our revered texts. However, such anachronistic interpretations are not very convincing. The study makes this observation at various points. After offering an interpretation based on "our medical knowledge," it notes that "the possible difficulty of this approach is that it is perhaps projecting knowledge into the world of *Hazal* which may not have been available yet."[39] As a result of these challenges to our halakhic process and decisors, there are numerous conflicting positions on brain death.

If *posqim* could develop a widely accepted position on brain death, the Orthodox community would be beholden to follow it. The brain death debate would be over. Given the many diverse opinions recorded in the study and in Rabbi Prof. Steinberg's *Encyclopedia of Jewish Medical Ethics*, however, it is clear that no convincing consensus exists. That is what prompted the RCA study and the organization's recent shift regarding its position on brain death.

As I've shown, this shift comes at great cost. I therefore wish to propose another approach to this question, drawn from the writings of Rambam (ca. 1136–1204). Reviewing how he sought to integrate *madda* within the halakhic system, I will argue that his conceptual and halakhic approach can benefit the brain death debate.

---

39. Bush et al., *Halachic Issues*, 25 n. 33; see also ibid., 26 and (intermittently) throughout.

V. RAMBAM'S POSITION ON SCIENCE

A. Judges Must Be Knowledgeable About Scientific Issues

Rambam held that judges of Jewish law had to be versed in many disciplines. In his *Mishneh Torah* (Laws of Courts 2:1), he writes:

אין מעמידין בסנהדרין בין בגדולה בין בקטנה אלא אנשים חכמים ונבונים, מופלגין בחכמת התורה בעלי דיעה מרובה, יודעים קצת משאר חכמות כגון רפואות וחשבון ותקופות ומזלות ואיצטגנינות ודרכי המעוננים והקוסמים והמכשפים והבלי ע[בודה] ז[רה] וכיוצא באלו כדי שיהיו יודעים לדון אותם.	Members of the Sanhedrin – whether the supreme court or lower courts – may be appointed only if they are men of wisdom and discernment, great in Torah wisdom and possessing much knowledge. They should know a little about other classes of wisdom, such as medicine, mathematics, astronomy, constellations, astrology, and the ways of horoscope readers, diviners, sorcerers, foolish idolatrous practices, and the like, that they might know how to judge them.

It seems that this last justification – "that they might know how to judge them" – was inserted regarding the last fields in this list, the various forms of prognostication and idolatrous divination. To try such cases, a judge must be familiar with these prohibited systems of belief and worship. But what was Rambam's rationale for requiring knowledge of medicine, mathematics, and astronomy?

The earliest critic of *Mishneh Torah*, Rabbi Moshe ha-Kohen of Lunel (twelfth century), was dismayed by Rambam's judicial requirements.

לא ידעתי מאין הוציא זה, ותימה הוא מה צורך לדיינין שידעו רפואות וחשבונות וחכמת המזלות? וצריך עיון.	I do not know whence he derived this! It is a wonder: What need is there for judges to know medicine, mathematics, and astronomy? This matter requires further study.

Rabbi David ibn Abi Zimra (Radbaz; 1479–1573) suggested practical reasons.

רפואות מה צורך לסנהדרין?
וי"ל לדעת הדברים המרפאים
בטבע שנתנה השבת לדחות
בשבילם אבל לא בדברים
המרפאים בסגולה ולדעת
מי שהשקה את חבירו סם מן
הסמים ומת אם ראוי אותו הסם
להמית או לא וכיוצא בזה.

Why is knowledge of medicine necessary for members of the Sanhedrin? One can suggest that they need to know what things are natural remedies, such that Shabbat may be overridden for them but not for things that heal with powers (*segula*); and to know if a person gave his fellow some sort of drug and that person died, if that drug was lethal or not; and other such things.

Radbaz argues that proper juridical decision-making demands that judges be conversant with many aspects of human knowledge. Although this suggestion is plausible, I sense that Rambam's unique requirements also reflect his worldview, which is reflected throughout his oeuvre (see below).

Rambam's standards of judicial competence are based on ideology, not merely practical necessity. His personal life and writings amply illustrate his understanding of the nature of true scholarship. In the introduction to his *Guide of the Perplexed*, for example, he reviews the broad education – starting with astronomy and mathematics – that he provided to the student to whom he dedicated this philosophical treatise. For Rambam, a true scholar must master many fields of wisdom. What Rambam considered to be a self-evident requirement – for any Torah scholar as well as a judge – was anathema to other rabbinic authorities.

B. Acceptance of External Sources of Knowledge

In the *Mishneh Torah* (Laws of Sanctifying the Month 17:24), Rambam discusses the astronomical information and skills needed to calculate the lunar cycles in order to determine the Jewish calendar. He explains that Jewish works regarding such matters were composed during the prophetic period and subsequently lost.[40] In the absence of a reliable Jewish tradition, however, he notes that many Greek astronomy texts are available.

---

40. Rambam's account of lost scientific knowledge recalls Rabbi Sofer's reference to the forgotten tradition of the "early naturalists."

וטעם כל אלו החשבונות...היא
חכמת התקופות והגימטריות
שחברו בה חכמי יון ספרים
הרבה והם הנמצאים עכשיו
ביד החכמים, אבל הספרים
שחברו חכמי ישראל שהיו
בימי הנביאים מבני יששכר
לא הגיעו אלינו.

The reason behind all these calculations... is part of the science of astronomy and math, which was formulated by Greek scholars, and [they wrote] many books, and these are now in the hands of scholars. But the works written by Israelite scholars in the times of the prophets – [these scholars being] members of the tribe of Issachar – didn't survive to our day.

ומאחר שכל אלו הדברים
בראיות ברורות הם שאין בהם
דופי ואי אפשר לאדם להדהר
אחריהם, אין חוששין למחבר
בין שחברו אותו נביאים בין
שחברו אותם גוים, שכל דבר
שנתגלה טעמו ונודעה אמתתו
בראיות שאין בהם דופי אין
סומכין על זה האיש שאמרו
או שלמדו אלא על הראייה
שנתגלתה והטעם שנודע.

Since all these matters are [based upon] clear and incontrovertible evidence, it is impossible to question their [veracity]. We are not concerned whether the author who composed [these texts] was a prophet or a gentile, for in every matter whose reason is known and whose truth is affirmed by incontrovertible evidence, we don't depend upon the person who stated or discovered it, but upon the proof that has been presented and the reasoning that is known.

Although Rambam used Greek wisdom to determine Jewish holidays, he taught that when it comes to scientific knowledge derived by scholarly research and rational inquiry, we follow the experts. Their expertise provides the perspective or data that can and should underpin Jewish law.

C. When Science Conflicts with Torah

What if Jewish tradition regarding the nature of the world clashes with the understanding of non-Jewish experts? How did Rambam negotiate a conflict which might arise between Jewish ideas and other systems of knowledge?

Here too, he consistently argues that reason and accuracy determine the truth. In his *Guide of the Perplexed*, he refers to various theories regarding the "very fearful and mighty sounds" produced by the motion of the heavenly spheres. The sages of Israel (b. *Yoma* 20b) concurred with the Pythagoreans that a great noise was emitted but unheard. Rambam remarks:

> Aristotle ... does not accept this and makes it clear that the heavenly bodies produce no sound.... You should not find it blameworthy that the opinion of Aristotle disagrees with that of the sages.... In these astronomical matters they [the sages] preferred the opinion of *the sages of the nations of the world* to their own. For they explicitly say: *The sages of the nations of the world have vanquished.* And this is correct. For everyone who argues in speculative matters does so according to the conclusions to which he was led by his speculation. Hence the conclusion whose demonstration is correct is believed.[41]

Rambam based his opinion regarding speculative matters upon the example set by the sages themselves. Alluding to a talmudic discussion that is unidentified in the *Guide*, Rambam states that the rabbis "explicitly" preferred the wisdom of the gentile sages over their own, and that their preference was due to the speculative nature of this matter, which was verified by objective criteria.[42] Once a convincing proof was given, the idea was accepted even against traditional Jewish texts or teachers.

Elsewhere in his *Guide*, Rambam discusses talmudic teachings about astronomical matters not sustained by scientific knowledge:

> I have always heard from all those who had some smattering of the science of astronomy that what the sages, may their memory be blessed, have said regarding [astronomical] distances was exaggerated.... Do not ask of me to show that everything they have said concerning astronomical matters conforms to the way things really are. For at that time mathematics were imperfect. They did not speak about this as transmitters of dicta of the prophets, but rather because in those times they were men of knowledge in these

---

41. Moses Maimonides, *The Guide of the Perplexed* (trans. Shlomo Pines; Chicago: University of Chicago Press, 1963), II: 8, 267.
42. Both English translations of the *Guide* (by Pines and Friedlander) understand Rambam to mean that his proof emerged from a specific talmudic source.

fields or because they had heard these dicta from the men of knowledge who lived in those times. Because of this I will not say with regard to dicta of theirs...that they are incorrect or have been said fortuitous[ly]. For whenever it is possible to interpret the words of an individual in such a manner that they conform to a being whose existence has been demonstrated, this is the conduct that is most fitting and most suitable for an equitable man of excellent nature.[43]

In a famous correspondence during the last decade of his life, Rambam applied this understanding of *Torah u-Madda* to resolve a major question he received from scholars of Montpellier. A group of Talmud scholars in Lunel were perplexed by contradictory sources regarding the acceptability of astrology in Jewish thought.[44] They cited various talmudic and midrashic passages indicating that astrological factors (*mazal*) could determine the destinies of individuals and nations. A well-known pericope in the Babylonian Talmud (b. *Shabbat* 156a–b) debates whether ethical deeds or the observance of a commandment could overcome astrological forces that had predetermined the character or fate of an individual. At issue is the effectiveness of these merits to impede the impact of the *mazal*, not whether such forces could determine human affairs. Clearly, some rabbis in the Talmud affirm astrology. Yet other classical sources seemed to dispute or repudiate it.

The French scholars beseeched Rambam to declare the authoritative Jewish view.

"Those scholars [who accept astrology] have destroyed the foundations of faith..." they lamented, "for why should one give

---

43. Maimonides, *Guide*, III:15, 458–59.
44. Alexander Marx published this letter (from a unique manuscript in the library of the Jewish Theological Seminary) together with an introduction as well as Rambam's responsum. See Alexander Marx, "The Correspondence Between the Rabbis of Southern France and Maimonides About Astrology," *Hebrew Union College Annual* 3 (1927): 311–58. Y. Sheilat published Rambam's responsum based upon various editions, some of them unavailable to Marx. See Rambam, *Iggerot ha-Rambam* (ed. Y. Sheilat; Ma'aleh Adumim: Ma'aliyot, 1988–89), II, 478–90. See also Sheilat's introduction to the letter, ibid., 474–77. Rambam's letter was translated by Ralph Lerner in *Medieval Political Philosophy: A Sourcebook* (ed. R. Lerner and M. Mahdi; 1963), 227–36. Quotations in this paper are based on his translation with some adjustments.

charity or pray for one whose life was in jeopardy" if all depended upon the stars?[45]

In his responsum Rambam first confirmed his own expertise in astrology:

כמדמה לי שלא נשאר חבור בעולם בענין זה בלשון ערבי, שהעתיקו אותן משאר לשונות, עד שקראתי אותו והבנתי עניניו, וירדתי לסוף דעתו.	It seems to me there does not remain in the world a composition on this subject, having been translated into Arabic from other languages, but that I have read it and have understood its subject matter and have plumbed the depth of its thought.[46]

Based on this mastery of the field, Rambam declares:

כל אותן הדברים אינן דברי חכמה כלל, וטפשות הן, וראיות ברורות יש לי שאין בהם דפי לבטל כל עיקרי אותן הדברים....	All those assertions are far from being scientific; they are stupidity, and I have incontrovertible proof to undo the entire basis of these matters....
חכמים יון הפילוסופים, שחברו בחכמות ונתעסקו בכל מיני מדע מהתלין ושוחקין ומלעיבין באלו... ועורכין ראיות ברורות לבטל כל דבריהן שרש וענף... ולא ידבק באותן הדברים אלא פתי שיאמין לכל דבר או מי שרוצה לרמות אחרים.	The wise men of Greece – and they are the philosophers who wrote on wisdom matters and busied themselves with all the species of science – mock and scorn and ridicule the [proponents of these matters] ... and compose clear evidence to overturn their words root and branch.... Only fools who accept everything take part in these matters, or else those who wish to fool others....
דעו שכל חכמי העולם, והם הפילוסופים הגדולים בעלי השכל והמדע, הסכימו כלן שיש לעולם מנהיג.	Know that all the wise men of the gentile nations – and they are the great philosophers, men of intellect and science – were all in accord that the world has a Governor.[47]

45. See Marx, "Correspondence," 344 (lines 30–33).
46. Lerner, *Medieval Political Philosophy*, 229.
47. Ibid., 229–31.

In this section of his responsum, Rambam buttresses his repudiation of astrology with the fact that the great scholars of Greece rejected it and never wrote on the subject. He invokes "the wise men of the gentile nations…the great philosophers, men of intellect and science," as the ultimate verification of his opinion. In his rejoinder to the scholars of Lunel, Rambam upholds the values that guided his intellectual and halakhic life. Rationality, verifiable truths, accepted scholarship – these were the fundamentals of his worldview.

In their letter, the Lunel scholars cite a talmudic passage in which many rabbis affirm astrology. How did Rambam deal with texts that openly conflicted with his principles? He wrote:

ואני יודע שאפשר שתחפשו ותמצאו דברי יחידים מן החכמים בתלמוד ובמדרשות שדבריהם מראין שבשעת תולדתו של אדם יגרמו לו הכוכבים כך וכך. אל יקשה זה בעיניכם.... אין ראוי לאדם להניח דברים של דעת, ושכבר נתאמתו בראיות, וינער כפיו מהן, ויתלה בדברי יחדי מן החכמים, שאפשר שנתעלם ממנו דבר, או שיש באותן הדברים רמז, או אמרן לפי שעה ומעשה שהיו לפניו....

I know that you may search and find sayings of some individual sages in the Talmud and "Midrashot" whose words appear to maintain that at the moment of a man's birth, the stars will cause such and such to happen to him. Do not regard this as a difficulty.... It is improper to abandon matters of reason that have already been verified by proofs, shake loose of them, and depend on the words of a single one of the sages, from whom possibly the matter was hidden. Or there may be an allusion in those words; or they may have been said with a view to the times and the business before him....

ולעולם אל ישליך אדם דעתו אחריו, שהעינים לפנים הן ולא אחור.

A man should never cast his reason behind him, for the eyes are set in front, not in back.[48]

Rambam's position couldn't be clearer. His decisive and unequivocal dependence upon science and the integration of wisdom within his

---

48. Ibid., 234–35.

religious life were essential to his view of astrology. He was beholden to follow rational thought, because "eyes are set in front, not in back." He adopted this stance even when it entailed a rejection of the teachings of the venerable scholars in the Talmud.

The pericope in Tractate *Shabbat* cited by the scholars of Montpellier was no obscure passage known only to the advanced. It was a popularly known section at the conclusion of the tractate, requiring no special "search" to locate. Rambam's reply – that one might "find sayings of *some individual sages* [my emphasis] in the Talmud" – was a bit disingenuous: The teachers referenced in this pericope were some of the greatest of the *Tanna'im* and *Amora'im*, such as Rabbi Ḥanina, Rabbi Yoḥanan, Rav, Shmuel, Rabbi Akiva, and Rav Naḥman bar Yitzḥaq. This was no group of minor players in the development of Jewish law and thought. Rambam therefore offered other interpretations of this pericope to justify their espousal of a worldview he opposed. Clearly, his final remark was what motivated him: "A man should never cast his reason behind him."

Rambam is explicit: Judaism cannot interpret the world based upon false wisdom. Although some ancients affirmed astrology – including certain giants of our tradition, as recorded in numerous talmudic passages – he had to reject any system that was irrational, inaccurate, and unverifiable by logical proofs.

D. A New Law of *Ṭreifot* Based upon Science

In another responsum, Rambam replies to another group of Lunel scholars who object to his position that a missing upper jaw renders an animal a *treifa*.[49] They point out that whereas the Mishna states that an animal missing its lower jaw is not a *treifa*, the texts are silent regarding an upper jaw.

ואנחנו בעניותנו לא שמענו עד	We, in all humility, have never heard of
היום הזה ולא מצאנו כתו[ב] כן	this [decision] until now, nor have we
בשום חבור הנעשה בשום לשון	seen this [law] written in any code in any
והיה בעינינו דבר זה פלא.	language, and it seems to us a surprise.

---

49. Rambam, MT Laws of Ritual Slaughter 8:16, 23; 10:9.52.

Rambam first confirms that the Talmud indeed discusses only the lower jaw. He continues with a mini-course in bovine anatomy.

לחי העליון קבוע הוא והחוטם הקבוע בו הוא עיקר נשמת רוח חיים הנכנסת ללב דרך הריאה עם הנשימה שתכנס מן הפה ואותו הלחי העליון כמו גג הוא לכסות הקנה כדי שלא תכנס נשמת הרוח והיא קרה לריאה וימות החי.... ואין לך מי שאין כמוה חיה יותר מזו....

The upper jaw is fixed, and the nose that's a part of it is the main means of inhaling the life-sustaining air that enters the heart through the lungs with the breath that enters the mouth. The upper jaw forms a ceiling to cover the windpipe so that cold air not enter the lungs and the live animal die....[50] There is no better example of "a defect with which an animal cannot survive"[51] than this [missing upper jaw]....

וזה שאמרתם שלא שמעתם ולא ראיתם בחיבור מי שמנה טרפה זו הרבה דברים לא יזכירו אותם המפרשים מפני שלא שמו דעתם להם וכשיבין אדם באותם הדברים יראו.

Regarding what you stated, that you have never learned or read in any code an opinion that counted such a *treifa* – there are many things that the commentaries don't mention because they didn't put their minds to such issues. If they understood such things, they would see [that I'm right].[52]

Rambam defends his position on the basis of his knowledge of anatomy, which he's willing to apply to determining Jewish law, even without talmudic or rabbinic precedent.[53] He declares that if scholars ignorant of science would study this body of knowledge, they would concur.[54]

---

50. According to ancient medicine, the heart is the source of the body's heat, and if cold air cooled off the heart, the person or animal would die.

51. M. Ḥullin 2:1.

52. *Responsa of Rambam* 315.

53. Isadore Twersky points out that Rabbi Saadia Gaon preceded Rambam in pronouncing such an animal a *treifa*. Rambam didn't cite him and, apparently, was unaware of this precedent. See Isadore Twersky, *Introduction to the Code of Maimonides* (Yale University Press, 1980), 56.

54. Rambam's position regarding the upper mandible is problematic. Although it illustrates his willingness to include external, scientific information in his determination of halakha – and therefore, I have cited it in this paper – it's inconsistent with his

Section IV – Historical and Ethical Considerations

Rabbi Yitzḥaq bar Sheshet (1326–1408), known by the acronym Rivash, disagreed forcefully with Rambam on this point:

ידעת האדון נ"ר שאין לנו, לדון בדיני תורתנו ומצותיה, על פי חכמי הטבע והרפואה. שאם נאמין לדבריהם, אין תורה מן השמים, חלילה, כי כן הניחו הם, במופתיהם הכוזבים. ואם תדין בדיני הטרפות, על פי חכמי הרפואה; שכר הרבה תטול מן הקצבים, כי באמת, יהפכו רובם: ממות לחיים, ומחיים למות....	You understand that we do not determine laws of our Torah and its commandments according to the scholars of science and medicine, for if we would affirm [our laws] in accordance with their opinions, the Torah would not be "from Heaven," Heaven forbid, since this is what they determined with their fake proofs. If we determined matters regarding *treifot* in accordance with medical scholars, we would receive much reward from the butchers, for in truth most of [the animals] would turn from dead to alive and from alive to dead….

remarks in this section of *Mishneh Torah*. Many have noted that his inclusion of a missing upper jaw within his list of seventy types of *treifot* (Laws of Ritual Slaughter 8:23 and 10:9.52) seems to contradict his declared principle that "one is not allowed to add to these *treifot* at all," since they were "calculated by the scholars of the early generations, and the courts of Israel agreed upon them." He also states there that "even if it becomes known to us through the medium of healing [sciences] that the animal will not ultimately expire," we don't alter the traditional list, but follow "what the scholars calculated" (ibid., end ch. 10).

Rashba (*Torat ha-Bayit*, quoted in Rabbi Joseph Karo, *Kesef Mishneh*, Laws of Ritual Slaughter 8:23) was impressed with Rambam's decision regarding the upper jaw but wished to ponder it, since this kind of *treifa* had not been included in the Mishna or Talmud. Rabbi Karo wrote that Rashba's objection was resolved by Rambam's explanation in his responsum to Lunel that this abnormality was included within the mishnaic concept that any defect that doesn't allow the animal to survive renders it a *treifa*. Thus, it is not a new kind of *treifa*.

Herbert Davidson, in his *Moses Maimonides: The Man and His Works* (Oxford: Oxford University Press, 2005), 222 n. 141, cites J. Levinger's conclusion (in his *Maimonides' Techniques of Codification* [Jerusalem: Magnes Press, 1965] [Hebrew]) that "Maimonides can never be seen to set a norm in open opposition to the classic rabbinic sources." But Levinger himself (ibid., 140) states that Rambam's conclusion was a "commentary" on the talmudic sources based upon his knowledge of animal anatomy, and he also notes Rambam's remarks that *treifot* are not to be derived from medical science. Davidson cites I. H. Weiss as well, who considered Rambam's position regarding the upper jaw to be an instance when he did define Jewish law based upon science.

384

והרמב"ם ז"ל כששנה מעט...
לא הודו לו!...ואעפ"י שהיה
הרב ז"ל חכם בחכמת
הרפואה, והטבע, ובקי
בנתוח; כי לא מפי הטבע
והרפואה, אנו חיין! ואנחנו
על חכמינו ז"ל, נסמוך. אפילו
יאמרו לנו על ימין: שהוא
שמאל. שהם קבלו האמת,
ופירושי המצוה; איש מפי
איש, עד משה רבינו, ע"ה.
לא נאמין אל חכמי היונים,
והישמעאלים; שלא דברו רק
מסברתם, ועל פי אי זה נסיון,
מבלי שישגיחו: על כמה
ספקות יפלו בנסיון ההוא....
ובכמה ענינים, בסוד היצירה,
הם חולקים על דברי רז"ל.

Moreover, when Rambam, of blessed memory, offered a different ruling,[55] they [i.e., the Lunel scholars] didn't agree with him…even though the rabbi, of blessed memory, was a scholar of medicine and science and an expert in surgery. For we do not base ourselves upon science and medicine. Rather, we rely upon our sages, even if they tell us right is left, for they received the truth and the explanation of the mitzvot, person after person, all the way back to Moses our teacher. We do not trust Greek or Arab scholars, who established their positions on the basis of speculation (*sevara*) and upon whatever experience, without being attentive to various doubts/problems pertaining to that experience…. In a number of matters regarding the secrets of the natural world, [the gentile authorities] disagree with the rabbis.[56]

Rivash held Rambam in the highest esteem, listing him with Rabbi Yitzḥaq Alfasi as worthy of utmost consideration by all rabbinic scholars, since both were "authorities acclaimed by the [entire] Jewish world, and pillars of the Torah."[57] Nonetheless, Rivash couldn't countenance Rambam's distinctive integration of scientific wisdom into rabbinic jurisprudence.[58] These different attitudes of Rambam and Rivash regarding *Torah u-Madda* are the same ones underlying the brain death debate.

Prof. Isadore Twersky captured Rambam's position on Torah and science:

55. Rambam, MT Laws of Ritual Slaughter 8:16, 23; 10:9.52.

56. *Responsa of Rivash* 447.

57. Ibid. 337. Although he harbored reservations about following the *Mishneh Torah* blindly without prior mastery of the relevant talmudic and rabbinic sources (ibid. 44), Rivash cited Rambam most frequently of all the Spanish authorities. See Abraham Moses Hershman, *Rabbi Isaac ben Sheshet Perfet and His Times* (New York: Jewish Theological Seminary, 1943), 78.

58. See also *Responsa of Rivash* 251: "The Torah contradicted these doctors."

The natural integration, without any trace of self-consciousness or tinge of defensiveness, of Talmud with other sciences, which will remain a pivot of his life and his achievement, is clearly noted. Ḥokhma (wisdom, science) is pervasive and indispensable....[59]

Special mention should be made of Maimonides' use in the Code of non-Jewish sources: medical literature, works on astronomy, mathematics, and geometry, and the whole range of classical philosophy.... This use is striking but not at all problematic for Maimonides, inasmuch as the harmony of faith and reason...is a commonplace of the medieval religious philosophy and epistemology which guided Maimonides.[60]

E. Rambam's Interpretation of a Medical Treatment in the Talmud

The Talmud (b. *Sanhedrin* 101a) quotes a *baraita* that refers to an incantation to be recited on behalf of one bitten by a snake or scorpion:

לוחשין לחישת נחשים ועקרבים בשבת.   One may recite incantations to cure snake and scorpion [bites] on Shabbat.[61]

Rambam (MT Laws of Idolatry 11:11) codifies this rule with his own explanation:

מי שנשכו עקרב או נחש מותר ללחוש על מקום הנשיכה ואפילו בשבת כדי ליישב דעתו ולחזק לבו, אף על פי שאין הדבר מועיל כלום הואיל ומסוכן הוא התירו לו כדי שלא תטרף דעתו עליו.   He who has been bitten by a scorpion or a snake is permitted to recite an incantation over the place of the bite, even on Shabbat, in order to calm his spirit and strengthen his resolve. Though this practice accomplishes nothing, since his life is in danger [the rabbis] permitted him [to do this] so that he not lose his mind.

---

59. Twersky, *Introduction*, 9–10.
60. Ibid., 59–60.
61. This translation follows Rambam, with the point being that the recitation of incantations doesn't violate the prohibition of healing on Shabbat. Rashi, in contrast, assumes that the incantations ward off snakes and scorpions, and that the point of the *baraita* is that reciting these incantations doesn't violate the Sabbath prohibition of hunting.

In other words, Rambam presumes that the Talmud allowed this incantation due to its placebo effect on the victim. He openly declares the talmudic remedy of no medical value.

Rabbi Joseph Karo incorporates Rambam's statement verbatim in his own code (*Shulḥan Arukh* YD 179:6). However, Rambam's explanation elicited a severe critique from Rabbi Eliyahu Kramer, better known as the Vilna Gaon:

וכ"כ בפי' המשנה לפ"ד דעבודת כוכבים אבל כל הבאים אחריו חלקו עליו שהרי הרבה לחשים נאמרו בגמרא.

This is in accordance with [Rambam's] Mishna commentary (*Avoda Zara*, ch. 4), but all who came after him disagreed with him, for many incantations are recorded in the Talmud.

והוא נמשך אחר הפלוסופיא [הארורה] ולכן כ' שכשפים ושמות ולחשים ושדים וקמיעות הכל הוא שקר. אבל כבר הכו אותן על קדקדו שהרי מצינו הרבה מעשיות בגמ' ע"פ שמות וכשפים.... והתורה העידה ויהיו תנינים.

He was drawn to that [cursed][62] philosophy, so he wrote that magic, recitation of mystical names, incantations, demons, and charms are all false. But [his opponents] already refuted him forcefully,[63] for we find many cases in the Talmud of mystical names, magic, etc.... Even the Torah testifies [regarding the efficacy of such actions, commenting about the Egyptian magicians], "[their rods] turned to serpents" (Exod. 7:22).

והפלסופיא הטתו ברוב לקחה לפרש הגמרא הכל בדרך הלציי ולעקור אותם מפשטן.

It was philosophy that led him astray, causing him to interpret the Talmud metaphorically and uproot its plain meaning.

---

62. This word was removed by censors and doesn't appear in most versions of the *Shulḥan Arukh*.
63. Literally, "beat him on his head."

Rabbi Kramer was certainly correct that Rambam's commitment to rational analysis and contemporary wisdom engendered a distinctive attitude toward the natural world. Incantations – even those with a talmudic pedigree – were rejected on principle. Rambam couldn't accept ideas and practices that defied logic or accepted scholarship.

Rambam's son, Rabbi Avraham, also addresses the standing of rabbinic pronouncements about medicine and other aspects of science. Early in his "Statement Regarding the Homilies of the Sages," he discusses how to verify a non-Torah matter treated in a talmudic passage. Rabbi Avraham insists that the values of Judaism and the dictates of logic both mandate an unflinching commitment to objective truth.

...כל מי שירצה להעמיד דעת	... anyone who wishes to sustain a partic-
ידועה, ולישא פני אומרה,	ular point of view, to favor the individual
ולקבל דעתו בלי עיון והבנה	who stated it, and to accept his opinion
לעניין אותו דעת אם אמת אתה	without carefully examining whether
אם לא, שזה מן הדעות הרעות,	that opinion is true or not – this is a per-
והוא נאסר מדרך התורה וגם	nicious perspective. It violates the way of
מדרך השכל.	both Torah and logic.[64]

Rabbi Avraham understands from the biblical prohibitions of favoritism – such as "do not favor the poor or defer to the rich" (Lev. 19:15) – that in matters such as medicine and natural science, one mustn't rely upon the talmudic rabbis due merely to their expertise and standing as interpreters of Torah law. Justice mandates that, in areas beyond their jurisdiction, we apply logic to their teachings and opinions. Rabbi Avraham clearly follows his father on this subject.

Neither Rambam nor Rabbi Avraham bases this position on a prior authority. Note, however, a responsum by Rabbi Sherira Gaon (ca. 906–1006), who was asked about remedies cited in b. *Giṭṭin* 68b:

---

64. The essay can be found in *Milḥamot Hashem* (ed. Rabbi Reuven Margoliot; Jerusalem: Mossad Harav Kook).

צדיכין אנן למימר לכון דרבנן
לוא אסותא אינון ומילין בעלמא
דחזונין בזמניהון.... ולאו דברי
מצוה אינון. הלכך, לא תסמכון על
אלין אסותא וליכא דעביד מינהון
מידעם אלא בתר דמבדיק וידע
בודאי מחמת רופאים בקיאים
דההוא מילהא לא מעיקא לה
וליכא דליתי נפשיה לידי סכנה.
והכין אגמרו יתנא ואמרו לנא
אבות וסבי דילנא.

We need to declare that the rabbis [in the Talmud] are not physicians, and they stated the opinions of their age.... These statements are not binding. Therefore you shouldn't rely upon these treatments or use them for anything until medical experts determine that they aren't harmful or dangerous. Thus our fathers and ancestors [or "elders," i.e., scholars] taught us.[65]

Rambam's approach concurs with Rabbi Sherira Gaon's and may reflect that tradition. Whereas the Vilna Gaon afforded the sages and their teachings a decisive role in every area of life, Rambam, Rabbi Avraham, and Rabbi Sherira Gaon all distinguished between Jewish law/thought and non-Torah matters.[66]

---

65. Benjamin M. Lewin, *Otzar ha-Geonim* 10 – *Gittin* (Jerusalem, 1941), responsum 152.
66. When this essay was largely concluded, I discovered Rabbi Bleich's article "Spontaneous Generation and Halakhic Inerrancy," in which he discusses the sages' apparent acceptance of spontaneous generation of a species of piscatorial parasites. He presents various understandings of their position, especially that of Rabbi Avraham Yeshaya Karelitz (the *Hazon Ish*), who maintained that "everything stated in the Gemara [related to halakhic matters]...are matters revealed to us by means of prophetic power" (Bleich, "Spontaneous," 62). Bleich also cites Rivash (responsum 447), who wrote that Deuteronomy 17:11 ("you shall not turn aside from that which they teach you") "demands abnegation of personal conviction in favor of the teachings of the sages, because their veracity has been divinely declared" (ibid., 66). Bleich briefly mentions Rabbis Avraham ben ha-Rambam and Sherira Gaon as well: "[Both]... did not accept all dicta of *Hazal* regarding medical care, natural science, and astronomy as factually correct" (ibid., 62). Yet he prefers the *Hazon Ish*, who "certainly espoused a much broader concept of inerrancy." In summation, Bleich writes: "With the exception of *Pahad Yitzhak*, I am hard-pressed to identify any *Rishon* or *Aharon* who believes that, *properly understood*, *Hazal* were fallible in their specific halakhic pronouncements" (ibid., 63). This appears to be overstating the case. Most important, Rabbi Bleich doesn't cite the rich legacy of Rambam presented in this essay, which offers a different approach to the integration of Torah and *madda*, and to the status of talmudic teachings on scientific phenomena.

CONCLUSION

During the waning centuries of the Middle Ages, controversy surrounded Rambam's philosophical writings and his integration of *hokhma* within Jewish thought and law.

In the late thirteenth and early fourteenth centuries, for example, a dispute raged regarding the study of philosophy. In 1305, Rashba, the great sage of Barcelona, declared that students under age twenty-five should be prohibited from such study. Although Rashba didn't ban philosophy, many Jews in Provence inferred a broader restriction on the integration of *hokhma* into Jewish thought and life.

In a respectful but firm appeal to Rashba, the poet and philosopher Rabbi Yedaya ben Avraham ha-Penini (Beziers, ca. 1270–1340) invoked many ideas presented in this essay. The numerous Jewish communities of southern France were deeply devoted to Torah study and observance, he wrote, and equally committed to *hokhma*, especially Rambam's. In Provence, for instance:

כי לא יסוב לבב העם מאחרי אהבת החכמה וספרי' כל עוד יסוד בפניהם ונשמה בגופותיהם.... ואלו אמרה יהושע בן נון מפומיה זאת לעולם לא יאבו שמוע. כי על כל כבוד הרב הגדול וספריו הם חושבים להלחם ועל קדושת תורתו ימסרו ממונות ותולדות ונפשותם עוד נשמת רוח חיים באפם. וכן יצוו את בניהם אחריהם לדורותם.	The people will never turn away from their love of *hokhma* and its literature as long as they live…. And even if Joshua son of Nun declared [it prohibited], they wouldn't listen. For they do battle for the honor of the grand rabbi [Rambam] and his writings, and for his holy teachings they'll sacrifice their fortune, their children, and their souls, so long as "the breath of life is in their nostrils" (Gen. 7:22).[67] And thus will they charge their children and the generations after them.[68]

---

67. Remarkably, Rabbi Yedaya adapts the same verse – Genesis 7:22 – quoted by Rav Pappa (b. *Yoma* 85a) to support the primacy of the breath exam in the case of someone crushed in a collapse.

68. Rabbi Yedaya ben Avraham ha-Penini, "Letter of Apology," in *Responsa of Rashba* 1:418 [Hebrew].

Rabbi Yedaya's words are quite strong, and some might object to his gushing affirmation of *madda*. However, his argument to Rashba was that rational wisdom occupied a natural place within Provençal Judaism and could not be severed from intellectual and communal life. Furthermore, Rabbi Yedaya argues, these Jews saw no reason to repudiate their ideology, since it derived from the grand master, Rambam.

This historic controversy was driven by the same issues that underlie the debate over brain death. Rabbi Yedaya's words can be appropriated to argue against any attempt to restrict the integration of scientific knowledge into contemporary halakhic decisions. Whether we realize it or not, science is seamlessly integrated into our lives, and it surely plays a determining role in our medical care.

If an Orthodox Jew visited a doctor today because of an injury – say, a snake or scorpion bite – he or she wouldn't agree to recite an incantation, even if derived from the Talmud. With all due respect to the great Vilna Gaon, that debate has ended. Similarly, we would balk if our physician turned to the Talmud instead of a medical book to diagnose our illness and present a cure.

Rambam's integration of *madda* within Torah provides a model with which to approach brain death. Whereas the RCA study places the Orthodox community apart from the world of contemporary science and medical practice, Rambam's emphasis on rational inquiry and evidence allows for a positive encounter with modernity. May we have the wisdom and courage to emulate him.[69]

---

69. This essay is a tribute to my wife, Judy Adler Sheer. She has been a true *ḥavruta* to me in our life together as well as in our love and learning of Torah. We discussed the ideas presented here, and the entire essay was enhanced by her strong editorial skills. My life and learning have been enriched by her. I also thank the following who read my paper and offered helpful comments: Drs. Kenneth Prager, Noam Stadlan, Baruch J. Schwartz, and Gabriel Birnbaum, and Rev. Susan Lunning.

Chapter 20

Is Our Public Policy on Brain Death Ethical?

Noam Zohar

The issue of brain death and public policy is both intricate and emotionally charged. In this essay I approach the issue from a dual perspective, as a bioethicist in Israel and as one who studies the philosophy of halakha.

I. THE PHILOSOPHY OF HALAKHA AND
THE BRAIN DEATH DEBATE

Halakha as Indeterminate

To my mind, the main contribution of the philosophy of halakha to this vexing issue is the clear understanding that for a question with truly unprecedented elements, like the determination of death by neurological criteria, no halakhic answer can be derived by pure deduction.

I don't mean that halakhic sources are irrelevant. The Torah is eternal, and our faith in it implies that it surely can instruct us in such novel and grievous situations. But any unbiased observation of how halakha has operated in its recorded history of nearly two thousand years shows that in matters of even minimal complexity, its rulings are produced not by deduction but by interpretation – sometimes straightforward, sometimes creative. Moreover, those issuing the ruling must, in true covenantal spirit, select among alternative interpretations (or alternative arguments from various sources), and their choice is properly guided by the inherent values and guidelines of Torah.[1]

The intense debate over "brain death" is a case in point. The very fact that eminent scholars and broadly recognized *posqim* continue to disagree indicates that each side has mustered meaningful sources, plausible interpretations, and valid arguments. Any aspiration to incontrovertible proof of one's own position, or to complete refutation of the opposing view, is entirely misguided.[2]

Thus, adopting one stance over the other is not simply a matter of discerning the "halakhic truth"; it's also a question of values and policy. I certainly don't mean that a *poseq* should adopt a false teaching for the sake of a desirable outcome. On the contrary: According to the rabbinic doctrine of *elu ve-elu*, both positions are valid, equally encompassed within the truth of Torah.[3] For practical purposes, of course, a decision is needed, but that ruling can't possibly be based merely on "halakhic truth," excluding values and policy. Such considerations are part and parcel of the essential halakhic tradition and discourse.

Weighing Positions on Brain Death and Halakha

Consequently, if Torah sources can legitimately be interpreted both in defense of brain death and in opposition, what halakhic values might determine the appropriate ruling? The answer is quite simple: the

---

1. See Moshe Halbertal, *Interpretative Revolutions in the Making: Values as Interpretative Considerations in Midrashei Halakha* (Jerusalem: Magnes Press, 1997) [Hebrew].
2. Cf. Nahmanides' introduction to his *Milḥamot Hashem*, where he emphasizes: "There are no absolute proofs in this science [of talmudic-halakhic interpretation], as there are in algebra or astronomy."
3. See Michael Walzer et al., *The Jewish Political Tradition*, vol. 1, *Authority* (New Haven: Yale University Press, 2000), ch. 7, "Controversy and Dissent," 307–378.

overriding Torah value of saving life.[4] It is no accident that the Israeli donor card cites Rambam (MT Laws of Courts 12:3):

כל המקיים נפש אחת בעולם   Anyone who saves a single life in the
מעלין עליו כאילו קיים עולם   world is as if he has saved the entire
מלא.   world.

The direct contribution of cadaver organ transplantation to the saving of lives is undeniable.

One might counter that it is morally and halakhically forbidden to kill one person in order to save others, and thus organ retrieval cannot be permitted unless the donor is dead beyond doubt. But defining "beyond doubt" as complete certainty – as though a clinical/legal definition of "death" ought to be established as an absolute biological "fact" or by a foolproof halakhic deduction – both begs the question and deviates from traditional halakhic practice and reflection.

II. CADAVER ORGAN TRANSPLANTATION: BIOETHICS AND RELIGION

I would not go so far as to claim, in light of the above, that a halakhic ruling disallowing cadaver transplantation of vital organs – based on non-recognition of "brain death" – is absolutely unjustifiable. But it does require a lot of explaining. The supremacy of lifesaving in halakha, and the concomitant severity of letting people die needlessly, yield a strong presumption in favor of such transplantations. Against this, it is not enough to point to some sources that appear to support a prohibition, while explaining away countervailing ones. One must also account for why this set of interpretations is preferable to the lifesaving alternative.[5]

---

4. Cf. Rashi, b. *Sanhedrin* 71a, s.v. *ḥarashin*.
5. In contrast to this, see the one-sided exposition by Joshua Kunin, "Brain Death: Revisiting the Rabbinic Opinions in Light of Current Medical Knowledge," *Tradition* 38, no. 4 (winter 2004): 48–62. Note the response by Edward Reichman in the same issue, "Don't Pull the Plug on Brain Death Just Yet," 63–39; Reichman observes: "Dr. Kunin focuses entirely on one peripheral dimension of the basis of halakhic acceptance of brain death criteria" (65) [and] "cites extensively from rabbinic authorities who have always rejected the brain death criteria" (67).

This responsibility carries over to Jewish laypersons. With regard to saving lives, it is expressly forbidden to wait upon the word of halakhic authorities. As the Jerusalem Talmud (*Yoma* 8:5) states:

תני: הזריז משובח והנשאל
מגונה והשואל הרי זה שופך
דמים.

It was taught: Whoever is quick to act is praiseworthy, whoever is asked is disgraced, and whoever [stops to] ask sheds blood!

The indisputable prospects of lifesaving – and the fact that Israel's Chief Rabbinate as well as several venerated *posqim* have endorsed brain death – should compel a layperson to register as an organ donor and to allow retrieval of organs from his or her brain dead relative in the tragic event that this option arises.

In my view, then, failing to allow transplantations is both morally reprehensible and halakhically sinful. Yet I recognize that some people will continue to believe otherwise. My final remarks here will focus on such people and how public policy should deal with them.

III. HALAKHA AND PUBLIC POLICY REGARDING NON-DONORS

Non-Acceptance of Brain Death

First I will address the issue of rabbis who reject brain death and consequently forbid vital organ retrieval from brain dead patients. These rabbis and their adherents deem themselves not guilty of "standing idly by the blood of others" (Lev. 19:16), because they regard organ retrieval as illicit killing of a "donor" who is still alive.

Considering this stance, said rabbis should at the very least forbid anyone to *receive* a vital organ transplant. Moreover, they ought to campaign not only against donor cards but also against receiving a transplant or even being on a waiting list. After all, agreeing to be on the list constitutes complicity in acts of "killing." If there were no queue of people desperately awaiting transplantation, no vital organs would be removed from those declared dead by neurological criteria.

By quietly allowing their followers to be recipients, and by failing to promulgate a stringent prohibition against it, such rabbis are hypocrites; for how can they not take action if they honestly believe that such organ retrieval is killing?[6]

Unprincipled Free-Riding

Others simply do not sign up to donate organs, perhaps for less principled reasons. This group cannot necessarily be accused of hypocrisy. Many such people may see nothing wrong with donation, indeed they might regard it as praiseworthy, yet (for some reason or other) prefer not to contribute.

All these people, however – including the aforementioned rabbis and their adherents – are exposed, of course, to the accusation of exploitative free-riding as long as they seek to receive transplant organs.

Free-Riding and Public Policy

Regarding other socially organized services to which people might claim an entitlement of similar urgency – such as protection against fire or crime, or provision of clean water or air – free-riding is in principle precluded by taxation.

The equivalent here would be routine retrieval of cadaver organs, obviating individual "donation" or family permission. Yet even countries that have adopted such a policy (known, less precisely, as "presumed consent") allow individuals to opt out, evidently due to the sensitivity of the resource under consideration. The disposition of the bodies of deceased humans involves significant emotions, personal beliefs, and religious practices, so the privilege of "registering an objection" – as it is termed in Singapore (a prominent locus of this policy) – seems appropriate.

To eliminate free-riding, those opting out must forgo any claim on the pool of cadaver organs, or at least take a backseat to others who do participate in this form of resource sharing. Thus in Singapore, anyone

---

6. Within the realm of moral discourse – which is the framework for my comments here – this question is surely unanswerable. I do realize (sadly) that persons inclined toward halakhic *pilpul* unconstrained by morality can produce various answers *leṭaher et ha-sheretz*.

who has registered an objection is given lower priority in allocation of cadaver organs should the need arise.[7]

Similarly, Israel's 2008 Organ Transplant Law (which follows the more common opt-in regimen) accords priority to those who hold donor cards as well as to those who have facilitated organ retrieval from their deceased relative.

Religious Discrimination?

Prior to the implementation of the law, some debated whether it is fair not to distinguish between those who *refuse* to sign a donor card and those who simply *cannot* do so because of their faith – i.e., Orthodox (or Ḥaredi) Jews who abide by the halakhic ruling opposed to brain death. Doesn't freedom of religion require that the state (especially a Jewish one) respect this religious commitment?

As stated, I consider this halakhic stance far from inescapable and, in fact, quite hard to justify in terms of Torah values. Nevertheless, I agree that its adherents deserve the respect due to most believers, however peculiar their views.

Nevertheless, the implications of respect here should not be perverted. Respect for religious freedom in this case mandates the unique freedom to withhold vital organs from the common pool. However, this mandate should not be understood as a license for staking exploitative claims against that very pool. Ironically, such a misunderstanding would threaten the very communal solidarity upon which it depends.

---

7. For the current language of Singapore's Human Organ Transplant Act (1987, 2004), see http://statutes.agc.gov.sg/non_version/html/homepage.html.

Afterword

Thinking Ahead and Out Loud

Although the issues seem clear, it is doubtful whether we as a medical society have yet achieved enough emotional and sociologic maturity to handle this question boldly. Nevertheless, to fail to do so verges on the unethical.

DR. HENRY K. BEECHER[1]

Now, embarked on the journey, we cannot go back. Yet we are increasingly troubled by the growing awareness that there is neither a natural nor a rational place to stop. Precedent justifies extension, so does rational calculation: We are in a warm bath that warms up so imperceptibly that we don't know when to scream.

DR. LEON KASS[2]

---

1. Henry K. Beecher, "After the 'Definition of Irreversible Coma,'" *NEJM* 281, no. 19 (1969): 1070–1071 [1071].
2. Leon Kass, "Organs for Sale? Propriety, Property, and the Price of Progress," *Public Interest* 107 (April 1992): 65–86 [85–86].

INTRODUCTION

The essays in this book have approached the question of brain death from a variety of perspectives: medical, ethical, halakhic, personal, historical, etc. In this piece I wish to share with the reader my own thoughts on the subject of brain death in general, with an eye to future challenges. This essay is *not* an attempt to summarize this book or express a consensus on behalf of the contributors; it is meant *only* as an expression of my own thoughts, having spent the last few years thinking deeply about this topic.

I. RESPIRATION AND "BRAINSTEM FUNCTION" AS DEFINING LIFE

When all is said and done, does halakha have a definition of death? In my opinion, no such definition appears in rabbinic literature. Nevertheless, many authors in this work refer to the talmudic text in b. *Yoma*, which concludes that in order to determine whether a person has died one must check the person's breathing. Others refer to the passage in m. *Oholot*, which describes a beheaded animal as dead. It has been pointed out that, fortuitously, both of these passages correlate well with the concept of brainstem death. The brainstem regulates breathing, and the ability to breathe is the sign of life. Therefore, if the brainstem is dead or detached from the body, the patient cannot breathe and is not alive.

Anatomical Aside 1: The Brainstem

Before analyzing the cogency of this argument, some terminological clarity on the medical side is necessary.[3] Throughout this book, as in

---

3. To make my points as clearly and accurately as possible, I've included two "anatomical asides" to explain in detail some of the facts upon which I build my arguments. These may seem a bit tedious, but they offer windows into biological and scientific realities that are both fascinating and little known. Most important, I believe it is vital to keep up with scientific developments in order to ensure that legal, halakhic, and philosophical argument remains current. Since I am neither a neuroscientist nor a neurologist, I consulted a number of people and read a number of books and articles (popular as well as scholarly) in order to get a better sense of the biological realities. I thank Dr. Noam Stadlan (neurosurgeon), Dr. Howard Doyle (emergency medicine), and Dr. Mayim Bialik (neuroscientist) for reading over early drafts of this essay and giving me detailed feedback. I also thank Dr. Lisa Aziz-Zadeh and my brother-in-law Dr. Samuel Neymotin (both neuroscientists) for sending me sources and suggested

most works on brain death, the term "brainstem death" has been used, and the claim that the "brainstem" regulates breathing as well as several autonomic reflexes has been taken for granted. This claim is generally true but, I would argue, insufficiently specific. The brainstem, like many other areas of the brain, has a number of sectors, which do different things.

The section toward the bottom of the brainstem, making up most of the medulla oblongata, contains the nuclei (like the vagus nerve and the glossopharyngeal nerve) that control respiration, heart rate, and the various reflexes assessed in the barrage of tests required to determine brain death. It is the destruction of this area of the brain that is generally meant when invoking the concept "brainstem death."

However, there are other sections of the brainstem as well, and they seem to control different aspects of cognitive function. For example, damage to the posterior region of the pons and mesencephalon (the upper tegmentum) correlates with coma or vegetative state.[4] Although this area is part of the brainstem, such patients are not "brainstem dead," since the section of their brainstem that controls respiration and other bodily tasks still functions. Alternatively, damage to the anterior region of the tegmentum leads to the frightening condition known as "locked-in syndrome,"[5] wherein the person is conscious but almost completely paralyzed (some can blink or move their eyes).

Considering the above, I prefer the term "lower-brainstem death," since this is what the more general "brainstem death" means.[6]

---

reading that allowed me to fine-tune and expand my understanding of brain anatomy and its relationship to the mind and consciousness. In the end, despite my limited knowledge of brain anatomy, I wrote this section myself and ask the reader to bear with me if any of my anatomical explanations are not fully accurate or clear. I assume that the point of this piece will emerge regardless, since I am invested in theoretical issues and their impact on ethics and halakha, not in specific biological claims.

4. Many other factors can contribute to a vegetative state, mostly having to do with the destruction of areas in the upper brain. However, detailed discussion of the neurology of PVS (persistent vegetative state) would lead us too far afield, and anything more than basic summary details would take me beyond my own limited knowledge in this area.

5. Technically, it is known as Ventral Pontine Syndrome or De-Efferented State.

6. Although death of the lower brainstem generally correlates with death of the entire brainstem and, often, the entire brain (hence the term "whole-brain death"), this

Objection to the Lower-Brainstem Paradigm

Returning to the above, should lower-brainstem death be defined as death, since with the death of this area of the brain a person has lost the ability to regulate his or her own breathing? In my opinion, both the halakhic and the medical versions of this argument suffer from the same flaw. Breathing is an excellent *indicator* of life, but it doesn't *define* it. Breathing is a mechanism to oxygenate the blood by which the various body parts can be sustained. As such, it is vital, yet it plays only a supporting role in life; it is not coterminous with life. The lower brainstem is the part of the brain that regulates breathing. To argue that a functioning lower brainstem is the definition of life is little different from arguing that breathing defines life; the lower brainstem merely regulates the body's respiratory system. Granted, the lower brainstem keeps the body alive, but is a living human body the same as a living human being?

Thought Experiment 1: Breathing Without Lungs

Imagine the following scenario:[7] A person's lungs have been destroyed, and he or she cannot breathe. The body is quickly losing oxygen, the heart will stop beating shortly, and the brain will die. The doctors quickly attach the patient to an "oxygenating machine," which oxygenates the blood and removes the excess carbon dioxide, etc.[8] The patient stabilizes, and the doctors eventually install a miniature blood oxygenator in the person's chest, so he or she can go home and live a normal life. Since the lower brainstem wasn't designed to control this machine, a computer chip is installed to regulate this artificial breathing.

---

need not be the case. In certain forms of quadriplegia, the lower brainstem ceases to function while other parts of the brain (including those that contribute to consciousness) remain functional.

7. Due to the complexities of this issue, I make recourse to several thought experiments. Some are my own, and some are taken from other writers on this subject. Many are borrowed from science fiction, since it is fast becoming science. Some of these scenarios were designed during my many discussions on this subject with Rabbi Michael Broyde.

8. This stage of the thought experiment is hardly science fiction. Mechanically oxygenating the blood is one of the main functions of ECMO (extracorporeal membrane oxygenation), aka the heart-lung machine.

This person has no lungs and doesn't breathe. Even if the lower brainstem is still alive, it is useless as a breathing regulator. However, this person's blood is oxygenated, and he or she can do almost everything any normal person can do. Is this person alive? Of course. Why? Because of his or her oxygenated blood? Maybe, but then lower-brainstem death isn't coterminous with death; after all, a patient who has been declared dead based on neurological criteria but is maintained by mechanical ventilation has oxygenated blood.

Regulation vs. Function

In essence, the claim that the person is dead because he or she cannot regulate his or her own breathing confuses the maintenance or self-regulation of a certain function (respiration) with the existence of that function. In their 2012 monograph, *Death, Dying, and Organ Transplantation,* Franklin Miller and Robert Truog point out the fallacy of this argument, responding to the idea that a patient declared dead based on neurological criteria is dead because the person/organism as a whole has ceased to function.

> This mistakenly presumes that the conceptually important aspect of integration of the organism as a whole is the natural source of the functions rather than the functions themselves.... For example, individuals with the permanent cessation of renal function have lost integrative functioning, and will soon die unless that function is replaced by artificial dialysis. Similarly, an individual who suffers the acute onset of complete heart block...has lost integrative functioning and will soon die unless treated with an artificial pacemaker. Even a patient with severe hyperthyroidism has lost integrative functioning and will soon die unless treated with artificial thyroid hormone. Nor is there anything special about breathing. Patients with high-level cervical quadriplegia are unable to breathe without mechanical ventilation. Assuredly, all of these individuals are alive, and they retain integrative functioning because the necessary functions persist with artificial support. In other words, the fact that integrative functions are supplied or supported

artificially is irrelevant to the determination of whether individuals are alive.[9] ˙

In short, it is illogical to define the death of a person by the death of his or her lower brainstem.

II. AN ALTERNATIVE PARADIGM: DEATH OF
THE CONSCIOUS MIND

> *Consciousness is a fascinating but elusive*
> *phenomenon; it is impossible to specify what it*
> *is, what it does, or why it evolved. Nothing worth*
> *reading has been written about it.*
>
> DR. STUART SUTHERLAND[10]

> *Consciousness is a state of mind in which there is*
> *knowledge of one's own existence and the existence*
> *of surroundings.*
>
> DR. ANTONIO DAMASIO[11]

Intuitively, most people accept that a conscious person is alive no matter what other parts of the body no longer function. The reverse situation is more difficult to categorize. Can a person be alive if he or she has irreversibly lost his or her conscious self? There has been an attempt in the medical literature to move to a more consciousness-based definition. Some have called it "higher-brain death" or "neocortical death."[12] The logic of this position is that when the conscious

---

9. Franklin G. Miller and Robert D. Truog, *Death, Dying, and Organ Transplantation: Reconstructing Medical Ethics at the End of Life* (Oxford: Oxford University Press, 2012), 66.

10. Stuart Sutherland, *International Dictionary of Psychology* (2nd ed.; New York: Continuum, 1996).

11. Antonio Damasio, *Self Comes to Mind: Constructing the Conscious Brain* (New York: Vintage Books, 2010), 167.

12. Robert Veatch has been one of the more vociferous defenders of this position. See Robert M. Veatch, "The Whole-Brain-Oriented Concept of Death: An Outmoded

mind is destroyed, although the body may live on, the human being as such is gone. In religious/Jewish terms, one could suggest that the person's soul has left his or her body, leaving only a shell – in this case, a living shell.

Anatomical Aside 2: Mind and Consciousness

I use the term "conscious mind" because, although "consciousness" and "mind" are sometimes interchangeable in common parlance, neuro-scientists distinguish between them.[13] Antonio Damasio describes the mind as the consequence of a brain's ability to map.

> A spectacular consequence of the brain's incessant and dynamic mapping is the mind. The mapped patterns con-stitute what we, conscious creatures, have come to know as sights, sounds, touches, smells, tastes, pains, pleasures, and the like – in brief, images. The images in our minds are the brain's momentary maps of everything and of anything, actual or previously recorded in memory.... The process of mind is a continuous flow of such images, some of which correspond to actual, ongoing business outside the brain, while some are being reconstituted from memory in the process of recall. Minds are a subtle, flowing combination of actual images, recalled images, in ever-changing proportions.... Minds can

---

Philosophical Formulation," *Journal of Thanatology* 3 (1975): 13–30. See also the exchange between Veatch and Koppelman: Elysa R. Koppelman, "The Dead Donor Rule and the Concept of Death: Severing the Ties That Bind Them," *American Journal of Bioethics* 3, no. 1 (2003), 1–9; Robert M. Veatch, "The Dead Donor Rule: True by Definition," ibid., 10–11. For a more extreme take on the subject, discussing long-term usage of the bodies of the neocortically dead for organs and scientific study, see David R. Smith, "Legal Issues Leading to the Notion of Neocortical Death," in *Death: Beyond Whole-Brain Criteria* (ed. Richard M. Zaner; Dordrecht, the Netherlands: Kluwer Academic Publishers, 1988), 111–44.

13. Neuroscientists differ somewhat in defining/describing "mind" and "consciousness." I follow the definitions of Damasio in his most recent (non-specialist) work, *Self Comes to Mind*. When appropriate, I will supplement or contrast Damasio's thinking with that of Christof Koch in his most recent (non-specialist) work: *Consciousness: Confessions of a Romantic Reductionist* (Cambridge: MIT Press, 2012).

be either non-conscious or conscious. Images continue to be formed, perceptually and in recall, even when we are not conscious of them.[14]

Consciousness, on the other hand, is what occurs "when self comes to mind," in Damasio's words. "[T]he brain constructs consciousness by generating a self process in an awake mind."[15] A conscious mind is something very different than a non-conscious mind:

> Minded behavior became very complex in numerous nonhuman species, but it is arguable that the flexibility and creativity that hallmark human performance could not have emerged from a generic mind alone. The mind had to be protagonized, had to be enriched by a self process arising in its midst.[16]

Even consciousness, Damasio explains, is not all of a piece. He argues that there are three levels:

> The simplest stage emerges from the part of the brain that stands for the organism (the *protoself*) and consists of a gathering of images that describe relatively stable aspects of the body and generate spontaneous feelings of the living body (primordial feelings). The second stage results from establishing a relationship between the *organism* (as represented by the protoself) and any part of the brain that represents an *object-to-be-known*. The result is the *core self*. The third stage allows multiple objects, previously recorded as lived experience or as anticipated future, to interact with the protoself and produce an abundance of core self pulses. The result is the *autobiographical self*. All three stages are constructed in separate but coordinated brain workspaces.[17]

---

14. Damasio, *Self Comes to Mind*, 74–76.
15. Ibid., 191.
16. Ibid., 304.
17. Ibid., 191–92.

To put it in simpler terms, Damasio believes that consciousness begins with some form of self-awareness (*protoself*). This develops into awareness of one's surroundings as they relate to oneself (*core self*), and finally into the autobiographical self-awareness we experience (*autobiographical self*).

Christof Koch conceptualizes consciousness somewhat differently. He uses a mathematical model, based on Guilio Tononi's theory of "integrated information."[18]

> [Guilio] posits that the *quantity of conscious experience* generated by any physical system in a particular state is equal to the amount of integrated information generated by the system in that state above and beyond the information generated by its parts. The system must discriminate among a large repertoire of states (differentiation), and it must do so as part of a unified whole, one that can't be decomposed into a collection of causally independent parts (integration).... Integrated information theory introduces a precise measure capturing the extent of consciousness called φ.[19]

In other words, because the various parts of the mind are integrated, it can differentiate pieces of information (like a computer) and also produce greater understanding. The greater the integration (as long as

---

18. Koch also has a rather radical understanding of the phenomenology of consciousness. He writes:

> I believe that consciousness is a fundamental, an elementary, property of living matter. It can't be derived from anything else; it is simple substance, in Leibniz's words.... Consciousness comes with organized chunks of matter. It is immanent in the organization of the system. It is a property of complex entities and cannot be reduced to the action of elementary properties. We've arrived at the ground floor of reductionism.... You and I find ourselves in a cosmos in which any and all systems of interacting parts possess some measure of sentience. The larger and more highly networked the system, the greater the degree of consciousness. (Koch, *Consciousness*, 119–20)

This idea, that everything is conscious at some level, is very difficult to digest.

19. Ibid., 126–27. "Expressed in bits, φ quantifies the reduction of uncertainty that occurs in a system, above and beyond the information generated independently by its parts, when that system enters a particular state" (ibid., 127).

the information remains differentiated and does not become a blur of noise, such as occurs in an epileptic seizure), the more consciousness is experienced.[20] The amount of consciousness can even be quantified.

The Upper Brainstem and Consciousness

The importance of the above discussion of mind and consciousness, for the purposes of this essay, is that neuroscience is beginning to isolate the parts of the brain that contribute to the creation of the conscious mind. Koch focuses mostly on the corticothalamic complex as the source of consciousness. Damasio agrees that the thalamus and cerebral cortex are crucial for consciousness, but he adds a third region.[21] Damasio argues

---

20. Koch even describes experimental methods of testing how much conscious experience a patient may be having. Additionally, following his idea that consciousness is a property of matter, Koch argues that each conscious experience is unique, like a crystal.

> Each conscious experience is fully and completely described by its associated crystal, and each state feels different because each crystal is utterly unique.... The crystal is not the same as the underlying network of mechanistic, causal interactions, for the former is phenomenal experience whereas the latter is a material thing. The theory postulates two sorts of properties in the universe that can't be reduced to each other – the mental and the physical. They are linked by way of a simple yet sophisticated law, the mathematics of integrated information. (Koch, *Consciousness*, 130)

Although I have trouble wrapping my head around these rather esoteric and even mystical views, there seems to be an uncanny connection with certain qabbalistic ideas of creation, divine emanations (*sefirot*), and even the Lurianic idea of the shattering of the vessels (*shevirat ha-keilim*). This would be interesting to explore further; sadly, I lack the expertise.

21. In this section I am limiting myself to discussing the areas of the brain that create consciousness, not those involved in the mind. An interesting question is how to relate to parts of the mind that make up a conscious person's core identity. For instance, a person's memories are stored/created in the hippocampus, part of the limbic system. Koch (*Consciousness*, 65) quotes the work of Itzhak Fried, which has demonstrated that individual neurons in this area – the technical term is "concept neurons" – are coded to "recognize" one image or idea apiece. The death of these neurons – each concept neuron gone is the loss of a particular memory or idea – is a standard feature of Alzheimer's disease, which tragically destroys a person but not his or her consciousness. Another interesting question is how to relate to the parts of the brain that create emotion, like the amygdala. Koch lumps both these areas and

that the key area where consciousness begins – his "protoself" – is in the upper brainstem, specifically in the nucleus tractus solitarius and the parabrachial nucleus.[22] Although Koch doesn't include this area, he admits that when it is impaired, "consciousness is dramatically reduced and may be absent altogether."

This point is critical since, as pointed out above, the standard usage of the term "brainstem death" masks the fact that this area of the brainstem seems closely related to consciousness and, if Damasio is correct, might actually be the seat of the most basic form of the conscious mind. Hence our language must become more precise, and terms like "higher-brain death" and "brainstem death" should be replaced with "death of the conscious mind" and "lower-brainstem death," respectively. These terms can also be fine-tuned as neurologists and neuroscientists uncover more details of brain function.

I propose that defining death as the death of the conscious self instead of lower-brainstem death would be a preferable way to approach brain death, even in halakha.

III. CRITIQUE OF THE CONSCIOUSNESS MODEL AND RESPONSE

> *A habitual misperception is that science first*
> *rigorously defines the phenomena it studies,*
> *then uncovers the principles that govern them.*
> *Historically, progress in science is made without*

---

more (basal ganglia and claustrum) in his corticothalamic complex. This approach seems reasonable, although what remains of a person whose conscious mind is dead but whose concept neurons or emotional dispositions remain alive is unclear.

22. Damasio, *Self Comes to Mind*, 81. Damasio cites several studies as proof. One such deals with hydranencephalic babies, i.e., babies with fluid where the cortex should be. These babies are far from vegetative, and their behavioral functions demonstrate basic conscious awareness (ibid., 85–88). Regarding this study, Dr. Howard Doyle (in his notes on a draft of this essay) questions the use of hydranencephalic babies to make this argument, since these areas may not function the same way in those with normal brains. The brain has plasticity, and if one area fails to develop, others can take up some functions of the missing parts. What is the case in hydranencephaly cannot necessarily be generalized.

> *precise, axiomatic formulations. Scientists work*
> *with malleable, ad hoc definitions that they*
> *adapt as better knowledge becomes available.*
> *Such working definitions guide discussion and*
> *experimentation and permit different research*
> *communities to interact, enabling progress.*
>
> DR. CHRISTOF KOCH[23]

Some argue that an observant, tradition-minded Jew cannot regard death of the conscious mind as a definition of death. After all, the halakhic sources consider breathing to be the determining sign of life. At most cessation of breathing could be correlated with lower-brainstem death, but there is no way to jump from breathing to death of the conscious mind. Breathing is the only halakhic barometer referenced in the Talmud (unless one wants to include heartbeat.) This argument, however, contains two significant fallacies.

Response 1: Determination vs. Definition

First, as stated, the halakhic sources discuss the method of *determining* death, not the *definition* of death. According to the Talmud, when a person is no longer breathing, that person is dead. Given the realities of the time, that was no doubt true. Nevertheless, with the development of cardiopulmonary resuscitation (CPR), many halakhists subtly adjusted the method of determining death from "cessation of respiration" to "*irreversible* cessation of respiration." Somewhat later, with the advent of respirators, authorities modified the definition further, specifying that death could be determined only upon the "irreversible cessation of *spontaneous* respiration."[24] The motivation for this tinkering is clear. If a person could be revived, then he or she wasn't really dead. If the person could not breathe on his or her own at all, then he or she could not really be alive.

---

23. Koch, *Consciousness*, 33.
24. For an analysis of Rabbi Immanuel Jakobovits' part in these incremental revisions of the description of determining death by respiratory failure, see Rabbi Alan Brill's essay in this volume.

It is evident in these revisions that breathing *indicates* the presence of life whereas lack of breathing indicates absence of life, the tacit assumption being that breathing or lack thereof does not *define* life. Since breathing is only an indicator, it is subject to context and various forms of counterevidence. Therefore, if the lack of respiration is reversible, this means only that the person's ability to breathe has been interrupted. If he or she isn't resuscitated immediately, the ability will cease and the person will be dead; however, at this point, even without breathing, the person is alive and must be saved. Contrariwise, if the patient cannot initiate a breath at all, and fails the apnea test, even though a machine is pumping the lungs and the person is "breathing," the fact that he or she cannot initiate a breath on his or her own proves that the person is dead.[25] The above confirms that checking for breath functions as a method of determining whether a person is dead. This doesn't mean that no other method can override it.

This point was intuited in the responsa of Rabbis Moshe Sofer and Shalom Mordechai Schwadron referenced in some of the essays in this book.[26] Rabbi Schwadron (*Responsa of Maharsham* 6:124) addressed a case where a noise was heard coming from the "deceased," who was then checked for signs of life. Although this *poseq* defends the decision to bury the deceased man immediately, he agrees that those who stopped to check behaved properly. Rabbi Schwadron believes that even if a person shows no signs of breathing, if he or she demonstrates other signs of life, such making a noise, that could potentially override the respiratory test.

The famous and oft-quoted responsum of Rabbi Sofer (*Ḥatam Sofer* 338), I believe, makes a similar point. The key line reads:

כל שאחר שמוטל כאבן דומם	Anyone lying still as a stone, with no
ואין בו שום דפיקה ואם אח"כ	heartbeat, and whose breathing then
בטל הנשימה אין לנו אלא דברי	terminates – all we have are the words of
תורתינו הקדושה שהוא מת.	our holy Torah that he has died.

---

25. This section illustrates how halakhic thinking has approached this topic. My own view with regard to both these innovations will be set out later.
26. A similar understanding of these sources can be found in Rabbi Yoel Bin Nun's essay in this volume.

Many have understood Rabbi Sofer as offering a definition or at least a set of criteria without which the declaration of death would be prohibited. To my understanding, such interpretations derive from reading this responsum through the modern lens of patients on respirators.

Rabbi Sofer was tackling the question of whether a *kohen* should be allowed to function as the coroner or physician who declares a person dead. In the days before people died in hospitals, a coroner or physician would come to a person's house to make the official declaration so that legal burial could be prepared. Since a *kohen* is forbidden to enter a room with a dead body, in theory he should not be allowed to function as the coroner. Rabbi Tzvi Hirsch Chajes suggested allowing the *kohen* to serve as coroner, arguing that we don't really know if the person is dead, and if he or she may still be alive, it would be a mitzva for the *kohen* (presumably a licensed physician) to treat this patient. If, upon examination, the patient was declared dead, that would only be an unavoidable part of the *kohen's* job as a doctor. To support this contention, Rabbi Chajes quoted Rabbi Moses Mendelssohn's permission to wait three days (when decomposition sets in) before burying a person to make sure he or she is really dead.

Rabbi Sofer rejects the claim that we do not know a person is dead until his or her body begins to decompose. As I understand it, his point is simply that once a person fulfills the halakhic criterion of cessation of breath,[27] and there is *no reason* to think the person is alive – since the body exhibits no movement or pulse – what else can one possibly be worried about? Rabbi Sofer invokes a *commonsense* argument here; he is not attempting to define death. There is, in my opinion, no way of teasing out of this responsum what Rabbi Sofer would have said if faced with a brain dead patient whose body was being maintained by machinery.

---

27. Rabbi Sofer refers to the "holy Torah's" criterion of cessation of respiration, since it is learned from the biblical verse about the breath of life being in the nostrils (Gen. 7:22). Presumably, the Talmud and even Rabbi Sofer would admit that if the blood were oxygenated in some way other than breathing through the nose, and the body – including the brain – were successfully maintained, such a person would be considered alive according to the Torah. As argued above, no rabbi in the world would argue that a person maintained on an ECMO (a heart-lung machine) is dead because he or she isn't breathing.

In short, the first fallacy of applying the traditional halakhic construct to the modern situation is that assuming sources in halakha define life and death. The sources only provide commonsense methods of determining whether a person is alive or dead. These methods involve situations like a person dying of a stroke (*Ḥatam Sofer*) or being crushed by fallen debris (*Yoma*) or beheaded (*Oholot*). These thinkers could not possibly have envisioned brain dead individuals attached to respirators. Therefore, the status of such individuals cannot possibly be derived from the classic halakhic literature.[28]

Response 2: Medieval Science

The second fallacy concerns the relationship of science and Torah, as noted in several essays in this volume.[29] Unless one adopts the fundamentalist stance that the rabbis had a *mesora* (divine tradition) regarding human biology, one must assume that even if they were attempting to make definitive statements about when a person should be considered dead, they were doing so based on their limited – and now outdated – knowledge.

For instance, as I discussed in my essay, the sages reference the head, liver, and heart as vital body parts. Nevertheless, it seems clear that the rabbis didn't actually know how any of these parts functioned. Until a few hundred years ago, the science and biology of Galen (ca. 130–200 CE) reigned supreme.[30] According to this system, the brain, heart, and liver each control or house a different aspect of the soul, or pneuma,[31] and perform a biological function.

Air enters the body through the lungs and is converted into *pneuma zoticon* (vital force) by the heart. "Pumping" arterial blood, the heart

---

28. The argument that one cannot deduce what the ancient halakhists would say about the current situation, considering how unprecedented and unimaginable our reality would seem to them, has been put forward by Rabbi Dov Linzer and Dr. Jeremy Rosenbaum Simon in this volume, the former from a halakhic perspective and the latter from a philosophical one.

29. See especially the essays by Rabbi Dr. Donniel Hartman and Rabbi Dr. Avraham Walfish in the organ donation volume and by Rabbi Charles Sheer in this volume.

30. For a description of Galen's system, see Donald Fleming, "Galen on the Motions of the Blood in the Heart and Lungs," *Isis* 46, no. 1 (1955): 14–21.

31. The "three-soul" system of the pneuma originates with Aristotle.

infuses the *pneuma zoticon* into the arterial bloodstream.[32] The blood in the veins is produced by the liver,[33] which transforms digested food into venal blood. The liver further transforms the air into *pneuma physicon* (natural force) and sends it to the body's organs through the veins. Finally, the brain turns air into *pneuma psychicon* (psychic force), which is responsible for a person's consciousness and intellectual awareness.

All of the above is quite intricate and fascinating and explains why the head, liver, and heart should be considered vital. Nevertheless, it is incorrect and irrelevant to medical or scientific reality. The same is true for other theories the sages may have had. For example, Erasistratos (304–250 BCE) believed the arteries were filled with air, which the heart pumped through the body. This seems to be Rashi's position as well.[34]

Furthermore, most ancient medical systems maintained that the purpose of air was to cool the body's "innate heat." This concept was popular among the sages as well, and appears in halakhic literature all the way to Rabbi Tzvi Ashkenazi's famous "chicken without a heart" responsa about why the heart is so essential to life (*Ḥakham Tzvi 74, 77*).[35] Certainly, before the discoveries of Andreas Vesalius (1514–1564) and William Harvey (1578–1657), the rabbis could not have known that the heart's function is to circulate the blood through the body, since circulation had not yet been discovered.

Considering the sages' (understandable) lack of knowledge about modern medicine, it would be entirely unreasonable for us to uphold their rulings about which body parts are essential to maintain life or what makes a person dead or alive. Personally, I consider it a form of sacrilege to follow

---

32. Technically, Galen didn't believe the heart actively pumped the blood; rather, the heart sucked blood in during diastole. The blood was then pumped by the pulsation of the arteries themselves.

33. According to Galen, the arteries and veins are two separate blood systems. Arterial blood is created by venous blood passing from the left ventricle to the right through "pores" in the interventricular septum.

34. See Edward Reichman, "The Halakhic Definition of Death in Light of Medical History," *Torah U-Madda Journal* 4 (1993): 148–74; Edward Reichman, "The Incorporation of Early Scientific Theories into Rabbinic Literature," ibid. 8 (1998–99): 181–99.

35. See Edward Reichman, "The Incorporation of Pre-Modern Scientific Theories into Biblical Literature: The Case of Innate Heat," *Jewish Bible Quarterly* 32, no. 2 (2004): 73–83.

the ancient medical pronouncements of the sages in matters as serious as life and death. In effect, one takes the best efforts of the great rabbis of old and turns them inside-out. Whereas these scholars were attempting to incorporate the latest scientific knowledge of their time and to use it to save lives, modern rabbis condemn people to die by forbidding organ transplantation based on antiquated medical notions that the sages had no opportunity to update. In effect, this approach transforms our great sages of the past from beacons of hope and life into prophets of darkness and death. I can think of no greater insult to their memories.

Summary

In short, although we must follow the pronouncements of the sages when based upon halakhic traditions, we must update their verdicts in the area of medicine, so their overall purpose remains in consonance with the medical realities of today. Since the sages' grasp of the human body was based upon antiquated medical thinking, and no halakhic sources define life and death, one must attempt to understand death *medically*, and place this understanding in conversation with the Torah values expressed in traditional sources. In so doing, one must keep in mind that the problem of dead brains within live bodies is completely new ground and reflects a reality that the sages of old could never have even dreamed possible.

IV. LOSS OF THE PERSON VS. DEATH OF THE ORGANISM

> *Brain dead but otherwise alive human bodies are warm to the touch and are respiring, albeit with mechanical assistance. They appear to be alive because they are in fact alive. It is because human biological life continues unabated that transplant surgeons are interested in such bodies as an ideal source for harvesting organs.*
>
> DR. H. TRISTRAM ENGELHARDT[36]

---

36. H. Tristram Engelhardt, *The Foundations of Bioethics* (New York: Oxford University Press, 1986), 246.

Using purely medical facts and logical argumentation about what defines death leads to a quandary. Medical specialists and bioethicists debate whether brain death is equivalent to death. The debate takes place in this volume as well, with Drs. Noam Stadlan and Howard Doyle offering two different approaches to the question. Although each of these essays is a fresh, up-to-date articulation of its respective side, the debate itself is hardly new; it has been raging in medical journals for decades.

The public is unaware of this debate for two reasons. First, in many (most?) countries, brain death is legally death. In the United States, the UDDA (Uniform Determination of Death Act) made neurological criteria one way to determine death, and this legislation was adopted in all fifty states. Nevertheless, law is one thing and science another. Second, many of the doctors and bioethicists maintaining that brain death does *not* equal death also have no ethical problem with removing organs from a person declared dead by neurological criteria, provided it is done with consent (whether the patient's, when possible, or the family's). As Dr. Doyle put it in his essay, these patients are "dead enough," or "beyond harm."

This argument was recently put forward at length by Drs. Miller and Truog, in *Death, Dying, and Organ Transplantation*. They contend that the dead donor rule, which states that one may not take organs from a living person, is not absolute:

> The requirement of valid consents for stopping treatment and donating organs means that the patient-donors are not wronged, despite the fact that they are not dead prior to procuring vital organs.... Insofar as it is justifiable to cause the patient's death by withdrawing LST [= life-sustaining treatment], based on a valid refusal of continued life support, it is also thereby justifiable to extract vital organs prior to stopping LST when doing so is validly authorized.[37]

Miller and Truog parry the question of whether it is absolutely wrong to end a person's life with the response that doctors end lives all the time. Every time LST is removed from a patient who requires it, the doctor is essentially killing the patient. Only because society finds this

---

37. Miller and Truog, *Death, Dying, and Organ Transplantation*, 117.

unpalatable – whether morally or for fear of abuse – has there been a push to distinguish between removing LST and active euthanasia.[38] Miller and Truog assert that this same repugnance causes physicians and bioethicists to equate brain death and death; it's a kind of denial that the bodies from which they're harvesting organs are alive.

The debate hinges on whether a person whose brain has irreversibly ceased to function is dead, even if that person's body can be maintained by machinery. There have been two basic approaches to defending a neurological definition of death. First, the brain keeps the body functioning. Second, the brain is what makes a human being human.

In essence, the first argument states that the brain is the chief regulator of the body and without it, the body will die. There are three problems with this claim. First, it conflates prognosis with diagnosis; saying that the body will die without a brain is not the same as saying that the body without a brain is already dead.

Second, recall my argument against the halakhic position that death is determined by the irreversible loss of lower-brainstem function. What this really means is that the functions controlled by the brain are what make a person alive. In that sense, it is really the living body that defines a person, not the brain – it's just that we cannot "imagine" at this stage how a body could go on living without the brain. Valuing the body above the brain seems to me incorrect.

Third, as pointed out by Doyle (in this volume) and Miller and Truog (in their monograph), with current medical technology, the body can be maintained without a functioning brain. In the short term, this fact was demonstrated by the sheep experiment Rabbi Prof. Avraham Steinberg described in his essay. In this experiment, a pregnant sheep's brain was removed, yet researchers kept the animal alive for thirty minutes and then extracted a live fetus from its womb through cesarean

---

38. I am oversimplifying a bit. There is one important difference: Since a patient has the right to refuse treatment, a doctor must comply with a request to remove LST, assuming the patient is in his right mind. However, in very few cases would a doctor, based on the professional requirement to assist in alleviating pain, be ethically "required" to perform active euthanasia, considering the highly sophisticated palliative care currently available. Miller and Truog (*Death, Dying, and Organ Transplantation*, 31) use the example of a military field doctor who has run out of painkillers and is treating a dying patient in agony.

section. In the long term, it was demonstrated most dramatically by the case of a four-year-old boy who contracted meningitis and became brain dead. As the researchers who did the autopsy recount:

> Our pathologic findings at autopsy confirmed that his brain had been destroyed by the events associated with the episode of H influenzae type b meningitis, whereas his body remained alive (brain death with living body) for an additional two decades, a duration of survival following brain death that far exceeds that of any other reports.[39]

The child's body continued living for twenty years after his brain had died. Furthermore, according to the report, there was no brain what-soever left at autopsy – yet the body could still be maintained by machinery. Clearly, the body can maintain homeostasis without the brain.

In a series of articles, D. Alan Shewmon surmises why physicians believed the body couldn't maintain itself without a brain, even with mechanical assistance. This belief stemmed from a phenomenon called spinal shock, a form of hemodynamic instability. When the brain is disconnected from the body, whether by brain death or by cervical cord transection, the loss of modulatory input to the brain is initially so disruptive that it overwhelms the body and causes death. This, at least, was the case before the perfection of ICU technology. The modern ICU supports the patient during this process such that ICU care can be understood as a "surrogate brainstem." Once this acute reaction is under control, the body eventually stabilizes and develops the capacity to self-regulate if not indefinitely, then for a very long time.[40]

39. Susan Repertinger et al., "Long Survival Following Bacterial Meningitis-Associated Brain Destruction," *Journal of Child Neurology* 21, no. 7 (2006): 591–95 [594]. The case was referenced in an earlier study as well: D. Alan Shewmon, "Chronic 'Brain Death': Meta-Analysis and Conceptual Consequences," *Neurology* 51, no. 6 (1998): 1538–45.
40. See D. Alan Shewmon, "Spinal Shock and Brain Death: Somatic Pathophysiology Equivalence and Implications for the Integrative-Unity Rationale," *Spinal Cord* 37, no. 5 (1999): 313–24; D. Alan Shewmon, "The Brain and Somatic Integration: Insights into the Standard Biological Rationale for Equating 'Brain Death' with Death," *Journal of Medicine and Philosophy* 26, no. 5 (2001): 457–58; D. Alan Shewmon, "The 'Critical Organ' for the Organism as a Whole: Lessons from the Lowly Spinal Cord," *Advances in Experimental Medicine and Biology* 550 (2004): 23–41. See also Miller and Truog, *Death, Dying, and Organ Transplantation*, 65.

For all these reasons, the argument that equates the death of the brain with the death of the person because the brain controls the body must be rejected. This leaves the second explanation, i.e., that the brain is what makes a human being human. Although this assertion seems intuitively correct, Miller and Truog put forth a vigorous challenge, arguing that the claim is tautological, or "question-begging." Saying that the brain is what makes humans alive, and therefore those without a brain are not alive even if their bodies function, is just an assertion. In fact, the authors point out, this assertion requires one to do violence to language.[41] Why else are patients still called "brain dead" and not just "dead"? In any other scenario, we would not use the word "dead" to describe a being whose body still mostly functioned.

> Plants and lower animals are not persons, nor is the human fetus before the development of the neural capacity for consciousness. But these beings are certainly alive. Why should death be something essentially different on the human level than in the rest of the biological realm?[42]

Miller and Truog make a strong case for the argument that brain death is not coterminous with death, which is one reason they push for reexamining the dead donor rule. However, I believe they leave a different avenue unexplored. To clarify, I would like to offer my own version of the division scenario.

Thought Experiment 2: The Division Scenario Revisited

In this scenario, suggested by D. Alan Shewmon, a person is beheaded and his or her head and body are kept alive separately on machinery.[43]

---

41. This point is explored in depth in Fred Feldman, *Confrontations with the Reaper: A Philosophical Study of the Nature and Value of Death* (New York: Oxford University Press, 1992), 19.

42. Miller and Truog, *Death, Dying, and Organ Transplantation*, 89.

43. D. Alan Shewmon, "The Metaphysics of Brain Death, Persistent Vegetative State, and Dementia," *The Thomist* 49 (1985): 24–80; also see D. Alan Shewmon, "Caution in the Definition and Diagnosis of Infant Brain Death," in *Medical Ethics: A Guide for Health Professionals* (ed. John E. Monagle and David C. Thomasma;

Shewmon argues that since we would clearly consider the brain to be the living person and the body to be no more than amputated limbs, brain function must be the sole criterion for determining life. Shewmon revisits this scenario in later publications as well, struggling with how to define the "living body." He fluctuates between what he calls a reductionist viewpoint, which would see the body as a "humanoid organism," and a religious/theological position, where he agonizes over whether this body could have a soul.[44]

In a later article, George Khushf uses this scenario slightly differently. He argues that since the body and the head can't be the same person, one must choose which is the real person, and the answer is obviously the head.

> The moral/existential death concept simply blocks the absurdity... that two individual organisms might arise by dividing one, and if one arbitrarily "turns off" just one of the two, then the original organism has not died. When considering the division scenario in the context of the determination of human death, either one part is an individual continuous with the previous individual or no part is. To determine our answer, we can independently turn off the mechanical devices that are used to perfuse the two parts. First, we can disconnect the body and ask: does the loss of the body imply the death of the individual? If, after doing this, the head says, "Too bad, I liked that body," it would be very strange to say the individual is dead. Alternatively, let the head say, "Please don't turn me off," and despite protestations, we turn it off. We now ask: is the "individual" or "organism" still alive? I think nearly everyone would say, "No, the individual died when the animated

<hr>

Rockville, MD: Aspen Publishers, 1988), 38–57; Shewmon, "Brain and Somatic Integration," 474 n. 6. For a critique of Shewmon's proof, see James Bernat, "A Defense of the Whole-Brain Concept of Death," *Hastings Center Report* 28, no. 2 (1998): 14–23 [19].

44. See D. Alan Shewmon, "Mental Disconnect: 'Physiological Decapitation' as a Heuristic for Understanding 'Brain Death,'" *Working Group on the Signs of Death 11–12 September 2006* (ed. H. E. Msgr. Marcelo Sanchez Sorondo; Vatican City: Pontifica Academia Scientiarum, 2007), 292–333 [316–22]. See Dr. Noam Stadlan's discussion of this thought experiment and Shewmon's analysis in this volume.

head was no longer perfused." This scenario makes clear that a body without a brain is in the same category as a kidney without a body.[45]

Miller and Truog critique Khushf's argument:

> We agree that the person John now inhabits the severed head in the thought experiment above; whereas John's headless, and personless, body remains alive as a separate being. We see no absurdity in this. When John's life support is stopped, John dies – the person or individual named John ceases to exist. But John's separated body continues to live, albeit in a brainless, vegetative state. Of course, normally a living person and a living person's body are continuous, which makes this account of the division scenario bizarre, but not absurd.[46]

I believe this critique is correct, but it contains the seed of an altogether different theory of brain death. To clarify, Miller and Truog argue that people declared dead by neurological criteria are alive. However, they admit that in the division scenario, the head is the person, even though the body is alive. I agree with both of these assertions: The head is the living person (or at least a conscious being continuous with that person) and the body is a living body. What is our moral responsibility to these two entities?

To follow Khushf's description, the head says, "Please don't turn me off." Is it ethical to turn the head off? I would argue that doing so is a form of murder. What about the body? Assuming there is no way of reattaching the person's head (or any other head), may the body be turned off, or is *that* murder? I would argue that even though this course of action kills a human body, we bear no moral responsibility to mindless bodies, only to beings with functioning human minds. In other words,

---

45. George Khushf, "A Matter of Respect: A Defense of the Dead Donor Rule and of a 'Whole-Brain' Criterion for Determination of Death," *Journal of Medicine and Philosophy* 35, no. 3 (2010): 330–64 [353].

46. Miller and Truog, *Death, Dying, and Organ Transplantation*, 85.

perhaps it is "killing," but so is hunting or picking carrots and we don't call either of these activities "murder."

We must distinguish between the killing of a human and killing in general; part of making this distinction means defining what makes a life human. Bioethicist John Lizza (who uses the division scenario to argue for the humanity of the head over against the living – but not human – integrated organism, i.e., the body) states the moral and philosophical point very well:

> Because human death has always signified a transformation from our being a human being into the remains of one, to ignore how our psychological, moral and cultural nature defines the kind of being that we are and to focus exclusively on our biological nature to define our coming into being and passing away distorts our nature and the ordinary meaning of human life and death. At bottom, to think defining death for human beings is a strictly biological matter commits the familiar error in bioethics of thinking that what is fundamentally a philosophical issue can be resolved by medicine or biology.[47]

I agree. The ethics surrounding proper treatment of humans can hardly be argued biologically but they stem from beliefs that humans have about the significance of human life.

To clarify, I am not claiming that no moral relationship with a live human body remains once the brain no longer functions. Rather, our relationship with such entities is comparable to our relationship with corpses. As Rabbi Nehemia Polen argues (in his essay in the organ donation volume), dead bodies – and even more so brain dead or brainless living bodies – retain a certain relational persistence. Although they themselves are dead, they retain their relationships with the living, and we our relationships with them. A related concept, *kevod ha-meit*, requires that we treat bodies with respect in honor of the person they once were (or had the potential to be). In this sense, although we have

---

47. John P. Lizza, "Where's Waldo? The 'Decapitation Gambit' and the Definition of Death," *Journal of Medical Ethics* 37 (2011): 743–46 [746].

no requirement to maintain the life of the decapitated body, as it is not a person, we still relate to the body with respect (including whatever disposal-of-body customs the deceased person or his family would want).

In short, murder, the wrongful killing of a *person*, applies only to people with functioning brains (I would say conscious minds). Although killing a brain dead patient means killing a live body, this action poses no moral problems, as the living body without the mind is not a person.

Caveat: PVS and Anencephaly

Two matters that remain lightning rods for medical ethics debates nowadays demonstrate the need for caution until brain function is more clearly understood and the nature of what contributes to the conscious mind is more carefully considered. The first is the case of patients in a persistent vegetative state (PVS), and the second is anencephalic babies.

Regarding PVS, Adrian Owen et al. write:

> The vegetative state is one of the least understood and most ethically troublesome conditions in modern medicine. The term describes a unique disorder in which patients who emerge from coma appear to be awake but show no signs of awareness.[48]

In other words, although PVS patients maintain lower-brainstem functions, and many have sleep-wake cycles, they apparently lack conscious awareness. I say "apparently," because recent studies have shown that PVS patients are not all woven of one cloth.

For example, in Owen's well-known and very disturbing study, a PVS patient was attached to an fMRI and asked to envision playing tennis and walking through her home. The study concludes, "Her neural responses[49] were indistinguishable from those observed in healthy volunteers performing the same imagery tasks in the scanner." This strongly implies that the patient heard what the examiners said and followed their

---

48. Adrian M. Owen et al., "Detecting Awareness in the Vegetative State," *Science* 313, no. 5792 (September 8, 2006): 1402.

49. Activation of the supplementary motor area for the former, activation of the parahippocampal gyrus, the posterior parietal cortex, and the lateral premotor cortex for the latter.

instructions. What level of consciousness this demonstrates, if any, is difficult to say, but it certainly demonstrates that the mind of such a person may still be active and that some awareness of surroundings persists.[50]

Although most PVS patients do not appear to have rudimentary awareness of their environment, this test reveals that certain ones do. Furthermore, some patients in PVS-like states seem to show sporadic signs of conscious behavior. This finding has led some experts to devise the term "minimally conscious," or "minimally responsive." Regrettably, without sophisticated (and expensive) procedures like the fMRI or very complex reflex tests, these patients are all but indistinguishable from those lacking awareness.[51] As Christof Koch writes:

> Unfortunately, distinguishing between a patient in a persistent vegetative state, who has regular sleep-wake transitions, and somebody in a minimally conscious state, who can sporadically communicate with people around them [sic], is often difficult.[52]

Dealing with this problem, James Bernat writes:

> Systematic examinations are necessary to distinguish purely reflex responses to stimuli from responses that require awareness. Confidence in this important distinction is not always possible. Careful and repeated assessment is particularly important given the alarmingly high rate of error in diagnosing vegetative state.[53]

---

50. This is Damasio's interpretation (*Self Comes to Mind*, 171–73).
51. Alan Shewmon suggests disturbingly that patients apparently lacking awareness may actually be "super-locked-in." See D. Alan Shewmon, "Recovery from 'Brain Death': A Neurologist's Apologia," *Linacre Quarterly* 64, no. 1 (1997): 30–96 [60]. Hopefully, tests like fMRI and other brain imaging techniques will be able to clarify whether this is the case.
52. Koch, *Consciousness*, ch. 5.
53. See James L. Bernat, "Chronic Disorders of Consciousness," *Lancet* 367, no. 9517 (2006): 1181–92 [1183]. See also the discussion in Miller and Truog, *Death, Dying, and Organ Transplantation*, 91–95; and Koch, *Consciousness*, ch. 5.

Although Koch describes state-of-the-art methods devised by neuro-scientists to distinguish the minimally conscious from the unconscious, these are new, expensive, and not (yet) readily available.

Even more frightening than the possibility of misdiagnosing a minimally responsive patient as a PVS patient is that of mistaking a locked-in patient for a PVS patient. Patients with locked-in syndrome are totally conscious, completely aware of their surroundings, and feel whatever healthy patients feel – they just can't respond or communicate. Although it is "easy" – in Bernat's words[54] – to distinguish locked-in patients from PVS ones based on pupil size and voluntary eye move-ment, mistaking a locked-in patient for a PVS patient occurs as well.[55]

In short, before one can discuss whether a patient with a func-tioning lower brainstem but no capacity for consciousness or mental functions should be considered a "personless" live body, a number of advances are necessary. First, the exact places in the brain that control consciousness and other mental activities must be isolated. Second, there should be a clearer differentiation between types of PVS and minimally conscious states, to make sure discussion relates only to patients whose conscious minds have been irreversibly destroyed. Third, diagnosis of PVS must reach a level of refinement such that the misdiagnosis of a con-scious patient as nonconscious can occur only because of negligence or improper procedure, not because diagnosis is tricky or requires training or machinery not readily available to the average clinician.[56]

The moral questions surrounding anencephalic babies are similar. In anencephaly, a baby is born without any upper brain. Without aggressive treatment, the baby generally cannot survive for more than a few hours, although cases like that of Nickolas Coke, who survived more than three

---

54. Bernat, "Chronic Disorders," 1184.

55. See Keith Andrews et al., "Misdiagnosis of the Vegetative State: Retrospective Study in a Rehabilitation Unit," *BMJ* 313 (July 6, 1996): 13–16. See also the discussion in Margaret Lock, *Twice Dead: Organ Transplants and the Reinvention of Death* (Berkeley: University of California Press, 2001), 349–53.

56. I am *not* discussing here the question of whether PVS patients with minimal con-sciousness have an "acceptable" quality of life and whether there should be aggressive treatment to maintain them. This would take the discussion far afield into questions of discontinuing life-sustaining treatment and euthanasia.

years, problematize this statistic. Several medical ethicists have argued that anencephalic babies are not "alive," or at least not live humans, and that use of their organs for transplant should be permitted. To avoid frightening the public, circumlocutions like "anencephalic monster" have been used.

> Terms that mark the anencephalic as human – *baby, infant, newborn* – are conspicuously absent from the literature in support of the procurement of their organs.[57]

As with PVS patients, it appears to me (as a non-specialist) that there must first be clarity about exactly what parts of the brain are missing from anencephalic babies. For example, these infants are born with a brainstem (otherwise they could not breathe), but this brings up the possibility raised by Damasio that humans with a functioning upper brainstem have some capacity for consciousness. As in PVS, there may be a range or continuum of conditions covered by the term "anencephaly," with some babies capable of rudimentary consciousness and others not. In my opinion, before any question of organ donation can be applied to anencephalic babies, we need to know that clinical testing can determine which babies have only a functioning lower brainstem and no capacity for consciousness whatsoever.[58]

V. PROBLEMATIZING IRREVERSIBILITY AND RETHINKING NHBD

> *Man: Hello... Can we have your liver? ...*
> *Mr. Brown: ... I can't give it to you now.*
> *It [= the organ donor card] says, "In the*
> *event of death"....*
> *Man: No one who has ever had their liver taken*
> *out by us has survived.*
>
> MONTY PYTHON, *THE MEANING OF LIFE*

---

57. Lock, *Twice Dead*, 354.

58. See discussion in ibid., 353–355. Lock also brings up the frightening reality of misdiagnosis of anencephaly, even referencing cases where a healthy baby was mistakenly sent for organ procurement instead of an anencephalic one. As horrific

Although I understand why the older "cessation of respiration" was replaced with "irreversible cessation of spontaneous respiration," I don't consider this a reasonable criterion for determining death. In part 3 of this essay, I explained why the addition of "spontaneous" seems problematic. First, some who are clearly alive cannot breathe spontaneously – high-level cervical quadriplegics, for example. Second, if the point is to determine whether the person is breathing, it shouldn't matter whether this is controlled by the brain or by a machine, assuming the breathing oxygenates the blood as it is supposed to. However, I want to go further and problematize irreversibility.

As touched upon earlier (and described at greater length in Alan Brill's essay), with the advent of CPR, the term "irreversible" was added to the description of declaring death by cessation of respiration. Otherwise, modern ethicists (Jewish or non-Jewish) would have faced the moral absurdity of not requiring resuscitation since the patient has been declared dead; technically, doctors aren't required to resurrect the dead. Therefore, it was decided that such patients are not yet dead and may not be declared dead until resuscitation proves futile.

Ironically, Miller and Truog, adept at calling out others for question-begging assertions, follow Bernat in offering one on this topic:

> Because no mortal can return from being dead, any resuscitation or recovery must have been from a state of dying but not death.[59]

Why can no mortal return from being dead? Arguably, a resuscitated patient has done just that. The patient was clinically dead, but his or her body remained in sufficiently good condition that it could be restarted. Why not describe this as a case of a dead person being brought back? I would argue that defining such a person as "alive" avoids the moral complexity of a modern-day fact – not every dead person must remain dead.

---

as this sounds, negligent error sadly happens in all types of medicine. The glaring problem of properly diagnosing the PVS patient seems less applicable to anencephaly.

59. James L. Bernat, "Are Organ Donors After Cardiac Death Really Dead?" *Journal of Clinical Ethics* 17, no. 2 (2006): 122–32, quoted in Miller and Truog (*Death, Dying, and Organ Transplantation*, 106) as "correctly observed."

Mostly Dead

In my opinion, the state of such a person is best captured by the sardonic teaching of Miracle Max in *The Princess Bride*: "There's a big difference between mostly dead and all dead." Clinically dead patients, even if they can be resuscitated, are not dying – they are dead, or at least "mostly dead."

Once upon a time, death was irreversible. However, given our current technology, some dead people – the mostly dead/clinically dead, as it were – can be resuscitated. Perhaps in the future, this category will expand and even more of the dead will be resuscitatable. (Consider cryogenically frozen people. Are such people dead or alive? Their bodies aren't functioning, but they retain the capacity to be reanimated.) Ethicists – religious and secular ethicists alike – need to begin discussing the nature of our obligation to resuscitate and how we categorize the "sin" or "crime" of *not* resuscitating, or of blocking resuscitation.

Thought Experiment 3: The Transporter

If this concept seems difficult to accept, let me illustrate with a thought experiment from popular science fiction: *Star Trek*. Imagine Scotty has begun beaming up Sulu from a mission. First Sulu's body is disintegrated, and his internal map (down to the atom) is stored in the transporter's memory. However, before Scotty rematerializes Sulu, a Romulan spy destroys the transporter. Sulu is now gone forever, but who killed him?

The spy? Possibly, but there's a problem. Sulu wasn't alive when the spy destroyed the transporter. How could he have been? He didn't even have a body! All that remained of Sulu before the spy's act of destruction was a map of his configuration in a machine. In essence, every time a person is transported in *Star Trek*, he or she is killed and rebuilt.

I would argue that Scotty killed Sulu, or at least caused his death. Nevertheless, Scotty isn't culpable.[60] Given the technology available on

---

60. As Miller and Truog point out (*Death, Dying, and Organ Transplantation*, 22), causation and culpability are two different things.

the *Enterprise*, being killed and reconstructed was in Sulu's best interests. The Romulan spy didn't kill Sulu; rather, he blocked Scotty's ability to rebuild Sulu with the transporter. However, unlike Scotty, the spy *is* culpable – for making Sulu's death permanent.

Along these lines, I would argue that a person whose heart and lungs are not functioning, but can be restarted, is dead. This person has lost consciousness, and his or her entire body – including the brain – has ceased to function. Nevertheless, our society has clearly decided that such persons have a right to be resuscitated. In fact, it's a moral imperative to resuscitate them, and anyone who blocks this resuscitation makes their death permanent instead of temporary.

Thought Experiment 4: The Man Who Was Drowned and Then Shot

Another illustration of the above point: A drowns B. C pulls B out of the water and is about to begin CPR when D draws a gun and shoots B in the head. Who killed B? I would argue that A killed B by drowning him. Does this mean that D has committed no crime? No. D made B's death permanent. Whether this act is as bad as murder, and what the punishment should be, is far beyond the scope of this essay. However, I believe the matter would be entirely different if the case were as follows: A is drowning B. C dives into the water to fight off A and save B, but before he can get there, D shoots B in the head. Clearly, D killed B, and A is guilty only of attempted murder.

Ethics of NHBD

The above analysis is exceedingly important in dealing with the moral issues underlying NHBD (non-heartbeating donation).[61] As described in Dr. Kenneth Prager's essay, in NHBD, the patient is detached from life support and allowed to die by cardiac arrest in controlled conditions. After the person dies, the doctors wait two minutes and then leave the

---

61. This procedure is also known as DCD (donation after cardiac/cardiocirculatory death); DCDD (donation after circulatory determination of death), the term preferred by Bernat as well as Miller and Truog; and NHBCD (non-heartbeating cadaveric donation). Following the lead of Dr. Kenneth Prager and his essay, this book uses the term NHBD.

room with the family, allowing the transplant team to harvest organs. The waiting period is intended to rule out spontaneous recovery. The argument goes that since there is no known case of autoresuscitation after two minutes, and since the patient (or the patient's proxy) has signed a DNR, after two minutes it is clear that the patient's cardiopulmonary systems have permanently and irreversibly ceased to function, allowing the transplant team to harvest organs from the cadaver.

However, ethicists have detected some sleight of hand in this argument. Dr. Robert Veatch notes that this approach makes the transplantation of such a patient's heart inherently immoral.

> It is impossible to transplant a heart successfully after irreversible stoppage: if a heart is restarted, the person from whom it was taken cannot have been dead according to cardiac criteria. Removing organs from a patient whose heart not only can be restarted, but also has been or will be restarted in another body, is ending a life by organ removal.[62]

This problem is no longer theoretical. Three hearts from infants declared dead by "irreversible" cessation of the cardiocirculatory system were successfully transplanted between May 2004 and May 2007 at the Denver Children's Hospital. The cases were reported in the very same journal issue in which Veatch lobbed his critique.[63] He attempts to deal with this problem in a follow-up article.

> One workaround to this problem – that is, that patients suffering cardiac arrests that can and will be reversed are not dead – would be to further amend the definition of death law to hold that heart irreversibility applies only while the heart is still in the original patient's body. In that case, irreversible circulatory loss combined with cardiac function loss while in the original patient would

---

62. Robert M. Veatch, "Donating Hearts After Cardiac Death – Reversing the Irreversible," *NEJM* 359, no. 7 (2008): 672–73 [673].

63. See Mark M. Boucek et al., "Pediatric Heart Transplantation After Declaration of Cardiocirculatory Death," *NEJM* 359, no. 7 (2008): 709–714. I thank Dr. Howard Doyle for pointing out the significance of this case to me.

count as death even if the heart were later restarted in another patient.

That reformulation would apparently cover the Denver cases (assuming there was an adequately confirmed waiting time to rule out autoresuscitation). However, this seems strangely like gerrymandering our definition. I am sure no original participant in the NHBCD and DCD discussion had exactly this in mind. I would not favor any informal adjustment in our understanding of cardiopulmonary irreversibility on this basis.[64]

Veatch's point, that defining irreversibility as applying only to the original host's body appears like gerrymandering (or what Doyle, in his article, calls the Red Queen running in place), is well taken. The alternative, assuming one insists on retaining "irreversibility" in the definition of death, is allowing hearts to go to waste and patients on waiting lists to die. It is a terrible conundrum.

In a similar critique of the NHBD rules, Miller and Truog contend that claiming the heart has irreversibly stopped beating because doctors won't do CPR is mistaking prognosis for diagnosis.

> Under DCDD protocols it is true that the cessation of circulation following ventilator withdrawal will not be reversed, given the decision not to attempt resuscitation. It therefore is permanent. But the realistic possibility that it could be reversed if resuscitation were attempted means that the cessation of circulation is not known to be irreversible; hence the donor is not known to be dead at the time that vital organs are procured.[65]

In other words, if death is by definition irreversible, then a person who has suffered cardiac failure and whose heart has ceased to function for only two minutes is not dead, or at least not known to be dead, since

---

64. Robert M. Veatch, "Transplanting Hearts After Death Measured by Cardiac Criteria: The Challenge to the Dead Donor Rule," *Journal of Medicine and Philosophy* 35, no. 3 (2010): 313–29 [319].

65. Miller and Truog, *Death, Dying, and Organ Transplantation*, 108.

people in this situation have been resuscitated. The fact that the person will not be resuscitated just means that the prognosis is certain death, not that he or she is already dead. (A person standing in Hiroshima at the exact spot where the atomic bomb was dropped five seconds before impact has zero chance of surviving and will be dead in five seconds without question, but he or she could hardly be called dead.) According to the dead donor rule, however, one may not remove organs from a living person, even if such a person is certain to die (*goses* in halakhic terminology).

Miller and Truog use this logical problem with NHBD to argue for modifying or jettisoning the dead donor rule. However, my solution to the brain death problem works for NHBD as well. When a body has ceased to function, the person is dead; clinical death is death. Generally, there's a moral imperative to resuscitate a clinically dead patient. In the case of NHBD, however, the patient – or his or her proxy – has signed a DNR making it immoral (even illegal) to perform CPR. Therefore, since such a patient is dead and there is no moral imperative to resuscitate him or her, there's no moral problem with harvesting the person's organs.[66]

To put this argument into more halakhic terminology, once a person has ceased to function (clinical death), he or she has died. Generally we have a moral obligation to resuscitate such a person as a logical extension of the mitzva of *piqu'ah nefesh* and the prohibition of "do not stand idly by the blood of your fellow" (Lev. 19:16).[67] However, if no resuscitation will occur (such as when there's a DNR order due to quality-of-life issues), the person may be considered dead either from the moment his or her body has ceased to function or, at most, once autoresuscitation is no longer possible.

---

66. I'm not even sure, given the above analysis, if one must wait to see if the person autoresuscitates, but I'll leave this question for a different venue.
67. An obligation to save the life of a dead person may seem counterintuitive, but as Rabbi Nehemia Polen so eloquently points out in his essay in the organ donation volume, we retain certain obligations to the dead after their passing, and continue to relate to them as humans as much as possible. It therefore seems reasonable to me that if any deceased person is resuscitatable – putting aside quality of life – resuscitation would be obligatory.

VI. PROBLEMS AND FUTURE ISSUES RELATING TO THE "DEATH OF THE CONSCIOUS MIND" PARADIGM

> *Let us... remember that a slower progress in the*
> *conquest of disease would not threaten society,*
> *grievous as it is to those who have to deplore that*
> *their particular disease be not yet conquered, but*
> *that society would indeed be threatened by the*
> *erosion of those moral values whose loss, possibly*
> *caused by too ruthless a pursuit of scientific*
> *progress, would make its dazzling triumphs not*
> *worth having.*
>
> DR. HANS JONAS[68]

At this stage in scientific progress, organ transplantation requires organ donation. Nevertheless, I believe it won't be long – a matter of generations at most – before organs are grown in the laboratory, eliminating the need for cadaveric organs. Then the entire question of organ harvesting from patients with dead brains and live bodies will be a matter for historians of medicine and medical ethics. However, I also believe this breakthrough won't be the end of the brain death question. A much more complex period of medical ethics awaits us.

It is currently possible to transplant almost any organ into a patient in need. Although there is as of yet no way to transplant nerves, the idea of regrowing nerves for spinal injuries has already arisen. More and more, the body is becoming akin to a machine with replaceable parts. What will happen when the brain itself can be moved from one body to another?[69]

---

68. Hans Jonas, "Philosophical Reflections on Experimenting with Human Subjects," *Daedalus* 98, no. 2 (1969): 219–47 [245] (reprinted in *Experimentation with Human Subjects* [ed. Paul A. Freund; New York: George Braziller, 1970], 1–31).

69. Christof Koch raises a more radical, futuristic possibility. He believes that, in theory, consciousness can be copied from a human brain to some other artificial construct:

> Functionalism applied to consciousness means that any system whose internal structure is functionally equivalent to that of the human brain possesses the same mind. If every axon, synapse, and nerve cell in my brain were replaced with wires, transistors, and electronic circuitry performing *exactly* the same

Thought Experiment 5: Brain Transplant

Imagine that A's body is crushed in an accident, but the brain is preserved and eventually transplanted into the body of B, a brain dead patient kept alive on a ventilator. Who is this new person? Is it B coming back from the dead? Is it A in a new body? Is it a new, hybrid individual?[70] As disturbing as this question seems, I think most people intuitively understand that this person is essentially A, although the new body will significantly affect his or her core identity, especially if this body is very different from the original one. The idea that this person could be B reborn seems intuitively incorrect.[71]

This thought experiment also demonstrates why the lower brainstem cannot really define life or identity. If a person were to suffer an injury to the lower brainstem and receive a transplant or stem cell replacement, I believe there would be no question about who he or she was. However, if the person suffered a brain injury and another's brain (with or without the lower brainstem) were placed in his or her skull, the matter would be totally different. The person's spouse, children, or parents would, I believe, rightfully claim that this was not their loved one, but an alien presence in the body of their now deceased relative.[72]

---

function, my mind would remain the same.... It is not the nature of the stuff that the brain is made out of that matters for mind, it is rather the organization of that stuff – the way the parts of the system are hooked up, their causal interactions. A fancier way of stating this is, "Consciousness is substrate-independent." (Koch, *Consciousness*, 120–21)

A fascinating idea. If correct, it will certainly have important implications for discussions of the nature of life and the soul.

70. Ignoring the question of mechanism, the idea of transferring a person's essence into another's body has inspired countless movies and stories (*Freaky Friday, Like Father, Like Son, 18 Again*, and *Heaven Can Wait* – to name a few). In every case I know of, the premise is that the "person" is the inhabiting intelligence.

71. In his essay in this volume, Dr. Noam Stadlan makes a similar point using society's treatment of conjoined twins. As he notes, dicephalic twins (conjoined twins with two heads) are considered two people, but this is not the case for duplication of any other organ, even the heart.

72. I wish to avoid here the more complicated brain switch questions: For instance, if two married men have their brains switched, what relationship, if any, does either man have to either wife? Discussion of this conundrum takes us beyond the scope of this essay.

Thought Experiment 6: The Dybbuk

To me the above seems so obvious that I was stunned to see the following exchange with Rabbi J. David Bleich:[73]

> *Jewish Review*: Philosophers sometimes speculate about the nature of human personality or what we might regard as the essence of an individual, his *nefesh* or his soul. One argument they use to show that the "person" is most closely associated with the brain and consciousness, thoughts and ideas, is the hypothetical situation of one person's brain in another person's body. They argue that if Shimon's brain, for example, were in Reuven's body, we would relate to and regard such an individual as Shimon because he would have Shimon's consciousness, thoughts and memories. Therefore, the argument goes, the essence or "soul" of an individual resides in the brain or in his mental processes, not in his heart or his breath. Could you comment on the validity of this as a philosophical argument?
>
> *Rabbi Bleich*: Let me answer the question with a question. Tell me, if a *dybbuk* (evil spirit) enters Reuven, is Reuven no longer Reuven? Is he now the *dybbuk* or is he still Reuven? The answer, as far as halakha is concerned, is that he is still Reuven, but that Reuven now harbors a *dybbuk* inside his body. In formulating your question you're telling me something very similar: that there is a *dybbuk* called "Shimon" who entered Reuven.

Although I strongly support the use of analogy and imaginary possibilities in order to tease out the philosophical implications of end-of-life decisions, I am more than a little surprised at Rabbi Bleich's choice of analogy. Assuming I understand what Rabbi Bleich is picturing by the *dybbuk* entering Reuven, I assume Reuven's mind and personality are still inside him. Demonic possession is, at least in theory, reversible,

---

through exorcism or the like.[74] In other words, when Reuven is possessed by the *dybbuk*, he still lives and inhabits his body, only he is dormant. Perhaps, in a certain sense, he could be conscious of what occurs if not in control of it. In this sense, the *dybbuk* case is not at all comparable to that of a brain transplant, wherein the person of Reuven, assuming his brain has been removed or destroyed, is gone and the body has no conscious occupant.

Thought Experiment 7: Patching

The complicated nature of determining what defines a person is best illustrated by an absurd exchange in *Sky Island,* a children's book written in 1912 by the master of fairy tales, L. Frank Baum. In this book, child protagonists Button Bright and Trot travel to a magical fairy island in the sky and encounter an evil king, Chief Boolooroo of the Blues. Since his subjects are fairies and therefore immortal, the Boolooroo delights in a cruel punishment called "patching." Button Bright learns of this fate by questioning a man who appears to comprise two different people:

> "What is your name, please?"
>
> "I'm now named Jimfred Jonesjinks, and my partner is called Fredjim Jinksjones…. We've had the misfortune to be patched, you know."
>
> "What is being patched?" asked the boy.
>
> "They cut two of us in halves and mismatch the halves – half of one to half of the other, you know – and then the other two halves are patched together. It destroys our individuality and

---

74. Just to clarify, I believe in *dybbuks* no more than I do in any of the other fictional cases I quote, but I'm trying to respond to the theoretical possibility raised by Rabbi Bleich, i.e., the takeover of a person's mind by another being. The idea of mental takeover by a foreign intelligence has captivated fiction writers for years. In one famous *Star Trek* episode, "Return to Tomorrow," three telepathic beings (Sargon, Henoch, and Thalassa), who've had their brains preserved, attempt to take over the bodies of three crew members. The premise of the show is that wherever the brain/consciousness presides, the person presides, but that since these inhabiting intelligences could be removed, it was a moral imperative to restore the crewmen's control of their brains and bodies.

makes us complex creatures, so it's the worst punishment tha[t] can be inflicted in Sky Island."[75]

The idea of patching is meant to be humorous, partly because of its absurdity as a punishment and the comically grotesque picture of two people attached this way. Nevertheless, the patched man makes a deep point in this dialogue; both he and his "other half" have lost their individuality. Each one's identity is now hybrid ("complex" in Baum's words), and he is no longer himself, as evident from his and his fellow's composite names.

Since this is a children's book, the author doesn't take the point to its logical conclusion, but the story implies that the Boolooroo has killed both men and created two new creatures in their places. Baum seems to have hit upon the one "transplant operation" that would not be a simple replacement of parts, but would destroy the human being who once was.

Since neither secular law nor halakha has even begun to approach the question of partial replacement of the brain, I won't speculate here on the legal or halakhic status of a person with a partially transplanted brain in relationship to his or her past identity. Nevertheless, it seems clear that as long as a person's upper brain remains intact and functional, his or her identity resides in whatever body houses that brain.

VII. TWO FURTHER REFRAMINGS OF THE PROBLEM FROM JEWISH SOURCES

> *Without being careful, it is easy to conflate the issue of whether someone has a humanly significant life with the question of whether the individual is dead.*
>
> DRS. FRANKLIN MILLER AND
> ROBERT TRUOG[76]

---

75. L. Frank Baum, *Sky Island* (Chicago: Reilly and Britton Company, 1912), 76.
76. Miller and Truog, *Death, Dying, and Organ Transplantation*, 90.

Although a consciousness-based definition of human life seems convincing to me, I understand that many will remain skeptical. For this reason I would like to offer further thoughts about the ethics of organ donation from living bodies with dead conscious minds, inspired by some of the essays in this book.

Not All Lives Are Equal

In general, halakha presumes that all lives are equally precious, so one person may not be killed to save another (the famous "who's to say your blood is redder?" question [b. *Yoma* 82b]). However, in his essay in this volume, Rabbi Yaakov Love points to the opinion of Rabbi Yisrael Lifshuetz (*Tiferet Yisrael, Boaz*, end of m. *Yoma*):

<table>
<tr><td>

ונראה לי דאיכא למימר דאף
על גב דקיימא לן דחיישינן
לחיי שעה, היינו באין חיי קיום
כנגדו, אבל ביש חיי קיום כנגדו
ודאי דדם חיי קיום שלו סומק
טפי מדם חיי שעה של חבירו
שאינו סומק כל כך, ואפילו ספק
חיי קיום עדיף מודאי חיי שעה,
ויכול להציל את עצמו בו.

</td><td>

It seems to me that one can argue that even though we are concerned about short-term life, this is only when it is not up against stable life. However, when it is up against stable life, certainly the blood of the person with stable life is "redder" than the blood of the person with short-term prospects – such a person's blood is not all that red. Even [the life of] a person with only a possibility of stable life is preferable to [that of a person] who will survive only a short while, and [the former] may save himself at [the latter's] expense.

</td></tr>
</table>

According to Rabbi Lifshuetz, it's a mistake to say that all life is equal, or that every moment of every person is equally precious.[77] Instead,

---

77. In quite a few rabbinic sources, a person's death is prayed for because his (or her) life is no longer worth living (b. *Bava Metzia* 84a; b. *Ketubbot* 104a; *Midrash Peṭirat Moshe*; *Midrash Tanḥuma*, Buber ed., *Va-Etḥanan* 6, etc.). These are all cases of physical or emotional suffering, since the possibility of life without a conscious brain was unimaginable in the talmudic period. For an academic discussion of the "value of life for the severely compromised" in Jewish sources, see Goedele Baeke, Jean-Pierre Wils,

Rabbi Lifshuetz believes that stable life is more precious than the short-term variety, that the stable person's blood is, in fact, "redder." Following this train of thought, even if one were to disagree with my contentions and argue that live bodies with dead brains (or without conscious minds) should be considered living humans, nevertheless, their lives should be considered "less" than those of conscious patients with strong prognoses that require organs. In other words, Howard Doyle's concept of "dead enough" and Miller and Truog's thesis that it is ethical to remove organs from living patients when they're beyond harm, assuming one has valid consent, would seem to be supported by Rabbi Lifshuetz's halakhic claim.

Miller and Truog express the ethical considerations in such cases best:

> In view of the permanent loss of consciousness, it is reasonable to hold that the person who previously occupied the still-living body has ceased to exist. Absent belief in the value of maintaining merely vegetative human life, the lack of any prospect of recovering mental life precludes the possibility that brain dead patients can be harmed or wronged by extracting vital organs prior to stopping life-sustaining treatment.... To prohibit vital organ donation, because it causes death to the donor, would devalue the lives of potential recipients who will die in the absence of transplantation. Prohibiting harmless commission – the act of procuring vital organs from still-living patients under the justificatory conditions that we have specified – would entail a harmful omission of lifesaving vital organ transplantation.[78]

Although Rabbi Lifshuetz's interpretation is novel and debatable, considering the overriding ethical considerations, it seems a worthy *snif lehaqel* (supporting consideration to be lenient).

---

and Bert Broeckaert, "'There Is a Time to Be Born and a Time to Die' (Ecclesiastes 3:2a): Jewish Perspectives on Euthanasia," *Journal of Religion and Health* 50, no. 4 (2011): 778–95; Goedele Baeke, Jean-Pierre Wils, and Bert Broeckaert, "Orthodox Jewish Perspectives on Withholding and Withdrawing Life-Sustaining Treatment," *Nursing Ethics* 18, no. 6 (2011): 835–46.

78. Miller and Truog, *Death, Dying, and Organ Transplantation*, 124–25.

The Trapped Soul

The Jewish corollary to the concept of "conscious mind" is the soul. A belief in a soul plays an essential role in the meaning-making of religion. A belief that each person has something otherworldly in his or her makeup works in tandem with the belief that there is something important about each of us, something that makes our lives meaningful; that what we think or do in this world is important. This belief is also a key element in the various Jewish iterations of morality. Although there are many philosophically based speculations on the nature of morality, most make some use of the otherworldly nature of the human soul. From a Torah perspective, since humanity was formed in the image of God, a human can be held to a certain moral standard.

Whatever one believes about the connection between the brain and the soul, it seems clear that with the destruction of the part of the brain that allows for consciousness, feeling, and intellect, the soul no longer has any part in whatever remains of the person's life. All that's left is the machinery.[79] For this reason, I have argued that once a person's conscious mind is dead, even if he or she has a functioning lower brainstem, all that remains is a body with an intact "on" switch; the human being – the mind, soul, and personality – is gone forever. However, even if one disagrees with my analysis, keeping this person alive isn't necessarily a value. In fact, within halakha and Jewish thought, it may be that this type of life is not worth living, that it tortures the soul.

In his essay in the organ donation volume, Rabbi Aryeh Klapper points to a halakha in Rabbi Joseph Karo's *Shulḥan Arukh* (YD 370) with an unusual title:

---

79. In sociologist Margaret Lock's fascinating book-length study of American and Japanese reactions to brain death and organ donation, *Twice Dead*, she suggests that part of the difference between the reactions of the two societies to the harvesting of organs from patients declared dead by neurological criteria (Japan has been significantly more negative) derives from these societies' different views of the soul. Western society identifies the soul with the brain, whereas Japanese society sees the soul as permeating the entire body. My own argument is less about where the soul resides and more about the fact that, without the brain, the conscious mind/soul has no access to this world and is gone. However, for a very different take on the relationship between the soul and the body, live or dead, see Rabbi Nehemia Polen's essay in the organ donation volume.

מי הוא החשוב כמת אף על פי   Who Is Considered Dead Though He's
שעודנו חי   Still Alive?

This halakha refers to people who have been beheaded or chopped in half. Klapper connects this statement with the analysis in Rabbi Ahai Gaon's *She'iltot* (*Emor* 103):

והיכא דאיכא איניש דנפל   Where there is a person who fell and his
ונפרקה מפרקתו ורוב בשר   neck broke in two, with most of the flesh
נחתך עמה, אע"ג דלא נפק   cut apart along with it, even though his
נשמתיה - מת הוא, והרזוקי   soul has not yet departed – he is dead,
בעלמא הוא דמהרזקא ביה   and his soul is merely imprisoned within
נשמתיה.   him.

Rabbi Ahai describes such people as having souls trapped in their bodies. Although neither Rabbi Karo nor Rabbi Ahai meant to allude to killing or facilitating the death of people with "trapped souls," the idea found its way into the halakhic literature as part of the discussion about not connecting patients to respirators or turning them off when the process becomes futile.[80] For those uncomfortable saying that a person whose conscious mind is dead has ceased to be a living human, perhaps they would be more comfortable saying that the souls of such people are trapped by mechanical ventilation in a mindless living body and yearn to be freed.[81]

Pastoral Question

Much of the opposition to removing life-sustaining treatment from living bodies with dead brains may stem from the fact that these bodies don't look or feel dead. That's because they're not. The people inside them are

---

80. See, for example, Rabbi Ḥaim David ha-Levi, "Removing a Sick Person with No Chance of Living from the Mechanical Ventilator," *Tchumin* 2 (5741): 297–305 [Hebrew]; Rabbi Eliezer Waldenburg, *Tzitz Eliezer* 13:89, 14:80–81; Rabbi Yitzchak Yaakov Weiss, *Minḥat Yitzḥaq* 5:7–8.

81. Rabbi Klapper also suggests a third defense: It may be ethical/permissible to sacrifice one's own life for someone else's. Nevertheless, this possibility raises a host of halakhic issues and would take us too far afield to explore.

dead, but this type of death – where the body is maintained – is so new that we don't know how to think about them, feel about them, act in their presence, etc. In his essay in the organ donation volume, Ari Schick suggests that rabbis, halakhists, and ethicists begin to think carefully and critically about providing special ritual and spiritual framing to family members in this doubly jarring situation. This may be the most critical next step for Jewish leaders advocating organ donation from bodies declared dead by neurological criteria while maintained on ventilators.

Caveat: Feeding Tubes

Some doctors and ethicists have applied the above "quality of life" argument to PVS patients. As stated, I believe this application is theoretically possible, assuming one has the technology/capacity to certify that the entirety of the person's conscious mind (including the upper brainstem) has irreversibly ceased to function. Disregarding the fact that such certainty is generally unavailable, applying this argument encounters legal problems, namely the dead donor rule. Since PVS patients are not considered legally dead, it would not be legal to kill their bodies – at least in the United States, where active euthanasia is illegal in virtually all states.[82]

For this reason, doctors and judges alike have turned to the expedient of removing feeding tubes, calling this "passive euthanasia." They claim that by not feeding these patients, physicians aren't killing them, but allowing them to die. I cannot accept this analysis on legal, halakhic, or ethical grounds. Doctors are required to feed their patients just as parents are required to feed their infants. It would be absurd, not to mention grotesque, if parents accused of starving their baby to death were to claim they'd merely left the infant in his or her crib indefinitely and "allowed nature to take its course." No judge or jury in the country would accept such a defense.

I understand that this reasoning is applied to PVS patients due to quality-of-life issues or even to an intuitive sense that the person is really dead but the law has not yet caught up with that reality. Nevertheless, I find the argument unacceptable. To quote Koch:

---

82. I will ignore the question of assisted suicide for now, since it's irrelevant in PVS patients.

I understand the historical forces that gave rise to laws prohibiting euthanasia. But allowing a patient, even an unconscious one like Schiavo, to die by withdrawing all liquid or solid sustenance and starving to death seems barbaric to me.[83]

If a PVS patient is really a dead human in a live body – though the lower brainstem is intact and regulating respiration – then the process of starving the body to death is a form of disrespect to the dead. If the body really should be "shut off" so the soul can escape, this can be done quickly and without starvation. On the other hand, if the patient is a live human, this process looks like torture, and probably feels like it to the person's loved ones. Finally, considering the many difficulties of properly diagnosing PVS, and distinguishing total unconsciousness from states of mild consciousness, the possibility that conscious patients may be starved to death in this "passive" process is horrific.

The legal system forbids physicians to euthanize these patients, even at their own request or that of their proxies, but allows doctors to withhold nutrition – guaranteeing a slow death, perhaps even a painful one if sufficient palliative care is not administered and our understanding of PVS is incorrect. In my opinion, this policy forces the medical establishment into an unethical quandary and the families into an untenable position. It bespeaks both ethical and legal cowardice, as lawmakers will neither decide on the status of PVS patients on their own nor leave it up to doctors; instead they employ an irrational legal fiction, despite the moral turpitude of doing so in cases with so much at stake. Needless to say, I find withholding nutrition halakhically and morally indefensible.

CONCLUSION

The most cogent definition of human life relates to consciousness. As long as a person's conscious mind remains alive, and he or she has a vestige of awareness, feelings, personality, intellect, etc., the person is alive. However, if this part of the person is destroyed, but the body remains

---

83. Koch, *Consciousness*, ch. 5. Terri Schiavo was in a persistent vegetative state for years and was being kept alive with a feeding tube. Eventually, her husband had the feeding tube removed and she died two weeks later.

alive – even if the lower brainstem continues to maintain respiration and heart rate – in my opinion, the person should be considered dead.

Unfortunately, the death of the conscious mind is much more complicated to demonstrate than lower-brainstem death, as the latter can be determined by a standard battery of reflex tests and an apnea test, while diagnosis of the former requires blood flow exams, tests for electrical output in the brain, imaging techniques, etc. For this reason, my suggestion may make no difference in what is done nowadays with neurological definitions of death; nevertheless, it seems like a necessary direction to consider for the future.[84]

In simple terms, I believe that with the death of the conscious mind the human being has died, leaving behind a live body. I have argued that although the Talmud uses breathing as the indicator of life, and Rabbi Moshe Sofer refers to pulse and bodily movement as well, these are signs of life, not a definition of life. Furthermore, both the Talmud and Rabbi Sofer based themselves primarily on the science of their times, which is no longer relevant. For some, the Talmud's use of respiration as the definitive sign of life *is* a definition, which they've updated by adopting lower-brainstem death as the modern-day conceptual equivalent, but this approach simply begs the question: Why the regulator of breathing and not breathing itself?

We must modernize the conversation. Though in the past a dead body meant, by definition, a dead human, and a live body a live human, this is no longer true. Bodies can be maintained with machinery after the human has died. Such bodies need not be maintained in the absence of their humanity. Just as it is not forbidden to "kill" a live heart or kidney unattached to a body, it is not forbidden to kill a live body unattached to a person. In other words, the prohibition of murder does not apply to a body unattached to a conscious mind.

---

84. The question of the accuracy of brain death determinations is really one for doctors, not rabbis or academics. Certain aspects of the accuracy of the exams and what they demonstrate are debated in this volume; see the essays by Drs. Noam Stadlan and Howard Doyle. For discussions and critiques of the process of brain death determination, see Stuart J. Youngner, Robert M. Arnold, and Renie Schapiro, eds., *The Definition of Death: Contemporary Controversies* (Baltimore: Johns Hopkins University Press, 1999), 368; Miller and Truog, *Death, Dying, and Organ Transplantation*, chs. 3–5.

In short, considering the lack of clear halakhic criteria for a definition of death, and the conceptual difficulty of identifying the lower brainstem as definitive of life, the discussion surrounding life and death must focus on the conscious mind. This part of the human expresses our individuality, our soul, and without it we have fundamentally ceased to exist.

POSTSCRIPT

Regardless of whether one accepts my analysis, and whether my predictions prove accurate, I hope this essay – and much more important, this volume – will stimulate serious conversation and respectful debate in our community about the fundamental issues surrounding the definition of life and death, and the obligation to save lives and avoid murder. We can only do our very best and pray that the Almighty direct our thoughts and actions in the proper way.

Zev Farber

Contributors

Marc Angel – Rabbi Marc Angel, Ph.D., is the founder and director of the Institute for Jewish Ideas and Ideals (www.jewishideas.org). He is rabbi emeritus of Congregation Shearith Israel, the historic Spanish and Portuguese Synagogue of New York City. Rabbi Angel received his B.A., M.S., Ph.D., Th.D. (*honoris causa*), and rabbinic ordination from Yeshiva University. He also has an M.A. in English literature from the City College of New York. Rabbi Angel is a recipient of the Bernard Revel Award in Religion and Religious Education, a past president of the Rabbinical Council of America, and founding president of the International Rabbinic Fellowship.

Yoel Bin Nun – Rabbi Yoel Bin Nun, Ph.D., is one of the founders of Yeshivat Har Etzion. Rabbi Bin Nun received his rabbinic training at Yeshivat Merkaz HaRav under the tutelage of Rabbi Tzvi Yehuda Kook. He received his Ph.D. from the Hebrew University of Jerusalem. In 1986, he established Herzog College for training Jewish studies teachers, especially in Bible instruction. In 2000–2006 he served as the Rosh Ha-Yeshiva of Yeshivat HaKibbutz HaDati in Ein Tzurim.

Alan Brill – Rabbi Alan Brill, Ph.D., is the Cooperman/Ross Endowed Professor in Honor of Sister Rose Thering at Seton Hall University, where he teaches Jewish studies in the graduate program of Jewish-Christian Studies. Rabbi Brill received his B.A., M.A., and ordination from Yeshiva University and his Ph.D. from the Department of Theology at Fordham University. In 2013–2014, he was awarded a Fulbright-Nehru Senior Scholar Award to research and teach in Varanasi, India, creating a Jewish-Hindu theological encounter.

Yosef Carmel – Rabbi Yosef Gershon Carmel is the Av Beit Din of Gazit, the rabbinical court of the Eretz Hemdah Institute for Advanced Jewish Studies in Jerusalem, which he co-founded in 1987 with Rav Moshe Ehrenreich, and where he serves as the rabbinical dean. He is also a senior lecturer at Michlalah – Jerusalem College for Women. Rabbi Carmel is a graduate of the Nir Kiryat Arba Hesder Yeshiva and was Rosh Metivta there and then Rosh Yeshiva at Machon Meir. Rabbi Carmel heads the Ask the Rabbi program, which provides halakhic answers in English to questioners around the world.

Howard Doyle – Howard R. Doyle, M.D., is an anesthesiologist who practices in surgery, surgical critical care, and critical care medicine at the Montefiore Medical Center, Bronx. He received his medical education at the National University of Columbia, did his residency at the University of Texas Medical Branch Hospitals, and received a fellowship at the University of Pittsburgh School of Medicine.

Zev Farber – Rabbi Zev Farber, Ph.D., is a fellow of Project TABS and the editor of TheTorah.com. He was ordained (*Yoreh Yoreh* and *Yadin Yadin*) by Yeshivat Chovevei Torah Rabbinical School. He holds a B.A. in psychology from Touro College, an M.A. in Jewish history from the Hebrew University of Jerusalem, and a Ph.D. in Jewish studies from Emory University.

Zelik Frischer – Zelik Frischer, M.D., is a urologist at Stony Brook University Hospital and a professor of urology at Stony Brook University's School of Medicine. He earned his medical degree at I. P. Pavlov First Leningrad Medical Institute and trained at Mechnikov University Hospital in Leningrad. He later did his residency at Leningrad Cancer and Research Institute Second Mercy Hospital, and took fellowships at Beilinson Medical Center in Tel Aviv and Beth Israel Hospital in New York. He is a fellow of the American College of Surgeons (FACS).

Irving (Yitz) Greenberg – Rabbi Irving (Yitz) Greenberg, Ph.D., is the founder and former president of Clal, the former president of the Jewish Life Network, and rabbi emeritus of the Riverdale Jewish Center. He was an associate professor of history at Yeshiva University and was a founder and chairman of the Department of Jewish Studies of the City College of New York, where he served as a professor. Rabbi Greenberg was ordained at Yeshiva Beis Yosef. He earned a B.A. from Brooklyn College and an M.A. and Ph.D. from Harvard University.

Maurice Lamm – Rabbi Maurice Lamm is the president of the National Institute for Jewish Hospice and a professor at Yeshiva University's Rabbi Isaac Elchanan Theological Seminary (RIETS), where he holds the chair in professional rabbinics. He received his B.A., M.A., and Ph.D. (*honoris causa*) as well as his rabbinic ordination from Yeshiva University. For years, he served as rabbi of Beth Jacob Congregation, in Beverly Hills, CA.

Joseph Isaac Lifshitz – Rabbi Joseph Isaac Lifshitz, Ph.D., teaches in Shalem College's Interdisciplinary Program in Philosophy and Jewish Thought as well as at Michlalah – Jerusalem College for Women. He received his rabbinical ordination from rabbis Yitzhak Kulitz and David Nesher. He earned his Ph.D. in Jewish thought from Tel Aviv University and holds an M.A. in Jewish history from Touro College.

Dov Linzer – Rabbi Dov Linzer is the Rosh Yeshiva and dean of Yeshivat Chovevei Torah (YCT) Rabbinical School. He received ordination from the Israeli Chief Rabbinate and is a recipient of the Javits Graduate Fellowship. Previously he headed the Boca Raton Kollel. Rabbi Linzer spearheaded the development of the YCT Rabbinical School curriculum.

Asher Lopatin – Rabbi Asher Lopatin is the president of Yeshivat Chovevei Torah Rabbinical School. Previously he was the spiritual leader of Anshe Sholom B'nai Israel Congregation, a Modern Orthodox synagogue in Chicago. Ordained by Rabbi Ahron Soloveichik and Yeshivas Brisk in Chicago, and also by RIETS, Rabbi Lopatin was a Wexner Graduate Fellow. He was both a Rhodes and Truman Scholar. He holds an M.Phil. in medieval Arabic thought from Oxford University, where he also did doctoral work on Islamic fundamentalist attitudes toward Jews.

Yaakov Love – Rabbi Yaakov Love chairs the Department of Halakha at Yeshivat Chovevei Torah. He studied at Yeshivat Netzach Yisrael under Rabbi Yisrael Gustman, and received his *Yoreh Yoreh* and *Yadin Yadin* ordinations from noted rabbis and *dayanim* in Israel. Rabbi Love taught at the David Shappel College of Jewish Studies and the Pardes Institute of Jewish Studies, both in Jerusalem, and at Bruriah High School in New Jersey. He also completed coursework for the M.A./Ph.D. program in Talmud at the Hebrew University of Jerusalem.

Kenneth Prager – Kenneth Prager, M.D., is a pulmonologist. He is professor of clinical medicine, director of clinical ethics, and chairman of the medical ethics committee at the Columbia University Medical Center. Dr. Prager did his medical training at Harvard Medical School, his internship and his residency in internal medicine at Columbia Presbyterian Medical Center, and his chief residency in the University of Chicago's Department of Medicine in Billings Hospital. He also spent two years in the Indian Health Service practicing general medicine on the Cheyenne River Sioux Indian Reservation in South Dakota.

Daniel Reifman – Rabbi Daniel Reifman teaches and serves as *mashgiah ruḥani* at Midreshet AMIT in Jerusalem. He also teaches at Midreshet Lindenbaum. He previously taught Talmud and halakha in the Drisha Scholars Circle and at Yeshivat Chovevei Torah. Rabbi Reifman received ordination from Yeshiva University and holds an M.A. in Bible from its Bernard Revel Graduate School of Jewish Studies. He is currently pursuing a Ph.D. in hermeneutics at Bar-Ilan University.

Charles Sheer – Rabbi Charles Sheer is the director of Cultural Competency Education at Westchester Medical Center, in Valhalla, NY. He is also a faculty member at the Bioethics Institute at New York Medical College. Rabbi Sheer holds a B.A. in history from Yeshiva University, an M.A. in talmudic literature from its Bernard Revel Graduate School of Jewish Studies, and rabbinic ordination from RIETS. He also received a Memorial Fellowship for Advanced Talmudic Research from Yeshiva University. Previously, Rabbi Sheer was the associate rabbi of the Riverdale Jewish Center, the director of the Department of Jewish Studies in Jewish Pastoral Care at HealthCare Chaplaincy, an adjunct professor in the Department of Jewish Studies at CCNY, and the Jewish chaplain and Hillel director at Columbia University/Barnard College.

Jeremy Rosenbaum Simon – Jeremy Rosenbaum Simon, M.D., Ph.D., is assistant professor of clinical medicine in Columbia University's Department of Medicine and a scholar-in-residence at Columbia's center for bioethics. Dr. Rosenbaum Simon received his medical degree from New York University and did his residency in emergency medicine at Bellevue Hospital. He also received his M.A. and Ph.D. in philosophy from New York University. Dr. Rosenbaum Simon is a fellow of the American Colleges of Emergency Physicians (FACEP).

Daniel Sinclair – Rabbi Prof. Daniel Sinclair, LL.B. (Hons) (University of London), LL.M. (Monash University), LL.D. (the Hebrew University of Jerusalem), is the Wolff Fellow in Jewish law and visiting professor of law at Fordham University Law School. He is also professor of Jewish law and comparative biomedical law at the College of Management Academic Studies Law School, Rishon Letzion, and adjunct professor of comparative biomedical law at the Hebrew University. Rabbi Sinclair served as the rabbi of the Edinburgh Hebrew Congregation and the dean of Jews' College, a rabbinical school in London. He also held the medical ethics portfolio in the cabinet of the chief rabbi of England and drew up protocols on the Jewish law aspects of stem cell research, organ donation, and artificial reproductive techniques. Currently, he is a member of the European Union's science ethics committee.

Noam Stadlan – Noam Y. Stadlan, M.D., is a neurosurgeon at Skokie Hospital. He received his medical degree from the University of

Maryland's School of Medicine and did a general surgery internship and neurosurgery residency at St. Louis University Medical Center. Dr. Stadlan is a member of the Chicago Institute of Neurosurgery and Neuroresearch (CINN), a founding member of the CINN Institute for Spine Care, an assistant professor of neurosurgery at Rush Medical College, Rush University Medical Center, Chicago, and associate medical director of the CINN program in the North Shore suburbs.

Avraham Steinberg – Rabbi Prof. Avraham Steinberg, M.D., works as a physician in pediatric neurology at Shaare Zedek Medical Center and directs the Center for Medical Ethics at the Hebrew University Hadassah Medical School, both in Jerusalem. He studied in the Rabbinic Academy of Yeshivat Mercaz HaRav, then studied medicine and completed his internship in the Hebrew University Hadassah Medical School. Prof. Steinberg served as a medical officer in the Israeli Air Force. He was a resident in the Department of Pediatrics, Shaare Zedek, and the Department of Neurology, Albert Einstein College of Medicine and Montefiore Medical Center, Bronx, subsequently becoming a fellow in the latter. Prof. Steinberg is a member of Israel's National Bioethics Council. He chaired the Dying Patient Committee, the Organ Transplantation Committee, the Altruistic Live-Organ Donations Committee, and the Pathological Specimens Committee, and was a member of the Brain-Death Criteria Committee and the Status of the Fetus and Pre-Embryo Committee. A former director of Shaare Zedek's Dr. Falk Schlesinger Institute for Medical-Halachic Research, he has acted as attending physician at Shaare Zedek and at Bikur Cholim Hospital in Jerusalem.

Binyamin Walfish – Rabbi Binyamin Walfish is the president of Otzar Haposkim, the Institute for Responsa Literature, Jerusalem. Rabbi Walfish graduated with honors from the City College of New York and completed his coursework toward a doctorate at Yeshiva University's Bernard Revel Graduate School of Jewish Studies. Ordained by RIETS in 1949, Rabbi Walfish served as the rabbi of congregations in Minneapolis, Quebec City, and Englewood, NJ. He also founded New Jersey's first Sunday school class for developmentally disabled youngsters, and served as executive vice president of the Rabbinical Council of America.

Noam Zohar – Rabbi Noam Zohar, Ph.D., is a senior lecturer in the Department of Philosophy of Bar-Ilan University, where he chairs the graduate program in biotechnology. He is also a senior fellow of the Shalom Hartman Institute in Jerusalem. Rabbi Dr. Zohar received his Ph.D. in philosophy from the Hebrew University of Jerusalem and was a postdoctoral fellow at the Institute for Advanced Study, Princeton. He has been a visiting lecturer at the University of Pennsylvania and Princeton University, and a faculty fellow of the Harvard University Center for Ethics and the Professions. In addition, he has advised Israel's minister of education on religious policy.

The fonts used in this book are from the Arno family

Maggid Books
The best of contemporary Jewish thought from
Koren Publishers Jerusalem Ltd.